Vital Statistics
on American Politics

Vital Statistics
on American Politics

Second Edition

Harold W. Stanley
University of Rochester

Richard G. Niemi
University of Rochester

A Division of Congressional Quarterly Inc.
1414 22nd Street, N.W., Washington, D.C. 20037

Library of Congress Cataloging-in-Publication Data

Stanley, Harold W. (Harold Watkins)
    Vital statistics on American politics.

    Bibliography: p.
    Includes index.
    1. United States—Politics and government—Statistics.
I. Niemi, Richard G.   II. Title.
JK274.S74   1990   320.973′021   89-15823
ISBN 0-87187-537-3
ISBN 0-87187-516-0 (pbk.)

To

Margaret Louise Stanley,
Duncan Gelineau Stanley

and

Andrew David (Niemi) Peckham

Contents

Tables and Figures

Tables and Figures

Tables and Figures

Tables and Figures

Acknowledgments

Producing this volume required the assistance of numerous individuals. Our largest debt, in preparing both the first and second editions, is to Carolyn Whitfield, who made hundreds of searches and phone calls to track down data. Carolyn tirelessly pulled together many of the original tables and figures and then updated, expanded, and extended them, casting a careful eye for the innumerable corrections and changes in data affecting the original tabulations. Without her assistance, even the first edition might still be in the planning stages.

Numerous individuals provided assistance with specific tables or more general advice about entire sets of data. These include Henry Abraham, William Adams, Herbert Alexander, Richard Baker, Larry Bartels, Thad Beyle, John Bolland, Randy Calvert, Kevin Coleman, George Edwards, Stanley Engerman, Sheldon Goldman, Doris Graber, Charles Hadley, David Huckabee, Bruce Jacobs, Andrew Jaffee, Malcolm Jewell, Michael Koenig, Robert Lichter, Jerry Manheim, Leslie McAneny, John Mueller, Richard Noyes, Jerry Ohlsten, Gary Orfield, Margaret Petrella, James Poteat, William Riker, Larry Rothenberg, Tom Smith, Alan Stockman, Jan Vermeer, Gregory Watson, Stephen Wayne, and Michael Wolkoff.

We thank Edward Carmines and David Rohde for their thorough review of the first draft of the manuscript and Burdett Loomis, Paul Quirk, Elliot Slotnick, and David Vogler for their help in the early stages of the project. Shrikant Dash, Annette Steinacker, and Itai Sened were very helpful in combing sources for selected data. Charles Smith helped with permissions, and Christine Montoney with questions and answers for the Instructor's Manual.

Helaine McMenomy organized the efforts of Mary Heinmiller,

Tim Fox, and Dana Loud in providing considerable typing assistance. Joyce Donley, Michael Horn, Sue Robertson, Michael Scott, and Robert Taylor gave needed advice and assistance on calculations, graphics, and word processing.

Reference and government documents librarians Phyllis Andrews, Kim Blood, Connie Fitch, Craig McMaster, Dave Reynolds, Brad Smith, and Kathleen Wilkinson at the University of Rochester and Linda Watson at the University of Alabama were ever-resourceful in responding to our requests.

We would also like to thank the following individuals who, based on their use of the book, made valuable suggestions for improvements in the second edition: Larry Berman, James Fleming, James Gibson, Kenneth Janda, John McGlennon, Steven Puro, William Rust, and Henry Steck.

As they had been during the original production of the book, our families were understanding and supportive during its revision, when nights and weekends became the favored time for work on it.

At CQ Press Joanne Daniels encouraged us and advised us from the beginning. Editing and producing this second edition benefited from the attention and talent of Nancy Lammers, Nancy Kervin, and Tracy Villano. Kathryn Suarez and Ellen Loerke kept us ever-mindful of promotion and advertising.

Introduction

Locating material for the first edition of this book involved a search of several hundred publications, ranging from the traditional to the obscure. For the second edition we have drawn upon an even greater array of sources. Considerable effort has gone into providing the most up-to-date, politically relevant information possible. Some of the material is from volumes that are not generally available. The most recent information is often unpublished. The data from standard sources are often difficult to trace with the historical continuity we have provided, even with extensive library resources, knowledgeable reference librarians, and time to spare. Combined with its broad coverage of subjects, this means that even more than before the book is an invaluable aid for the reader intent on understanding and keeping up with American politics. Along with the Guide to References for Political Statistics (beginning on page 406), it can serve as a fundamental reference volume for those who wish to keep informed about the American political scene.

The volume covers a wide range of topics. In addition to the standard subjects such as elections, Congress, the presidency, and the judiciary, the book provides information on the media, interest groups, foreign, social, and economic policy, and a variety of issues related to state and local government. Coverage is not limited to "hard" data such as votes cast and offices won; rankings of public officials' reputations, content analyses of media coverage, and public opinion data about policy issues are included. The information ranges from simple lists to compilations of outcomes based on implicit analytical concerns. A historical perspective is maintained throughout; depending on available data, the longest possible time periods are covered, even with public opinion data. The sources of material range from the findable to

1

the fugitive: reference volumes, government publications, political science journals, and monographs, among others.

The chapter organization follows introductory American government textbooks. Readers will recognize, of course, that any such organization is somewhat arbitrary and that information relevant to a specific topic may be found in a variety of places. For example, public opinion data about specific policies are found in the policy chapters, while the public opinion chapter is reserved for more general topics such as party identification and liberal-conservative outlooks. The list of tables and figures, along with the index, should make use of the volume straightforward.

The guide provides help for those seeking data beyond that contained here. Literally thousands of tables and figures on the topics covered in this volume and on related topics can be found in the works cited.

The quantity and quality of statistical information have grown enormously in recent years, and this trend has yet to peak. But statistics have a bad image. Even the numerically innocent know that "there're lies, damn lies, and statistics" and that "figures don't lie but liars can figure." But anyone seeking to understand politics—past, present, or future—would be ill-advised to take refuge in such skepticism. Increasingly, both public debates and political analyses contain points couched in or accompanied by statistics. Democracy turns in part on the ability of an informed public to follow such debates and analyses. Now more than ever, understanding politics requires an ability to comprehend numerical data and the assumptions behind them.

Although data are more essential and more readily available, the interpretive skills are all too often lacking. Unless one knows how to read them, tables and figures can be less than useful; they can be intimidating, incomprehensible, and boring. Yet properly understood, tables and figures can be a resource of considerable value.

This volume will not teach statistical methodologies, but it will foster a greater familiarity with the appropriate cautions about reading too much or too little into tables and figures. This introduction, the chapter introductions, the chapter questions, and the guide are all intended to enhance the reader's understanding of how to make better use of tabular information. They are designed to help the reader to extract the maximum amount of information from tables, to understand the level of accuracy in tabular information as well as the various sources of and kinds of inaccuracies, and to find additional information, including up-to-date information that must be found in serial publications rather than books.

Instructors who adopt the book may request a teacher's manual containing the answers to the questions and additional topics for discussion.

Some readers, particularly students who are accustomed to working with numbers as they appear in textbooks, are sometimes frustrated, perhaps even mystified, when confronted with whole tables of numbers. An important point of departure for these readers is to realize that this book is based principally on simple numerical data, not on the results of complicated statistical manipulations. The fanciest statistics presented are averages or medians. Regression coefficients, chi-squares, and the like can be revealing and useful, and increasingly political science has become methodologically sophisticated so that many journal articles are opaque to those without the ability to cope with advanced statistics. But this book fills a more fundamental need for a single volume encompassing a broad range of data about American politics and as such should be useful to the methodologically skilled and unskilled alike.

The figures and tables are easy to read. Many are merely lists, but very useful lists. They are often lengthy because they may cover as many as two hundred years. Long historical stretches mean change, and that creates some complexities, as, for example, when the names of the dominant parties change so that going back in time introduces unfamiliar labels. Footnotes to the tables and figures contain the necessary explanations as well as important qualifications and details; they must be read to understand the table or figure content. Following conventional practice, large numbers are expressed in units of thousands or millions to enhance readability. This, too, can lead to minor problems for readers unaccustomed to reading tabular material, but a bit of practice will overcome any such difficulties. In general, a little care and caution in reading and interpreting numbers is all that is required.

The Accuracy of Published Data

Errors in Data

The material selected for this volume is intended to be the most accurate, up-to-date information possible from the most reputable sources available. But anyone who has used statistical information realizes that it is almost never completely error free. This is inevitably true here as well. Consider, for example, Tables 12-4 and 12-6. Both are taken from the same governmental publication three months apart. The figures reported for public welfare expenditures, which appear in both tables, typically match. For example, the figure $290,080 million for 1975 noted in Table 12-6 appears, correctly rounded, as $290.1 billion in Table 12-4. Similarly, the numbers for 1978-1984 are the same. Yet inexplicably, the figures for 1976 and 1977 do not quite match, differing by $.1 billion and $.3 billion, respectively.

Why do such discrepancies and other kinds of errors (or what appear to be errors) occur? The answer varies.

Rounding. Sometimes what appears to be an error is simply a matter of when rounding is done. For example, 20.2 plus 20.4 equals 41 if one adds and then rounds, but equals 40 if one rounds and then adds. Almost certainly this explains why the 1960 federal and state and local expenditures in Table 12-5 (24,957 and 27,337) do not add up exactly to the total shown (summing to 52,294 rather than 52,293). A similar sort of "error" occurs when percentages sum to 99.8 or 100.2 rather than to 100 plus or minus 1 percent.

Exact Date of Data Collection. Accurate interpretation of data depends on knowing the precise date of collection and the period covered. Sometimes this is obvious. For example, the unemployment rate "at the end of the year" may differ if the phrase means the average of the November and December figures rather than the December figures alone. The time factor can be more subtle—for example, if a U.S. senator-elect dies and someone from the other party is appointed to fill the seat, the number of Democrats and Republicans elected will differ slightly from the number of Democrats and Republicans who actually take office a few months later. Even seemingly similar time spans sometimes conceal important differences. Dollar amounts for given years are likely to differ if one uses calendar years rather than fiscal years.

Handling of "Minor" Categories. "Minor" categories may be uncounted, ignored, or dropped for analytical reasons. Often, for example, votes are given only for the candidates of the two major parties. The small number of votes for the Socialist, Libertarian, and Prohibition candidates, not to mention the stray ballots cast for Mickey Mouse or "none of the above," are unreported or lumped together under "other." Thus a vote may be correctly reported as 42.7 percent (of the total vote) and just as correctly reported as 42.9 percent (of the two-party vote). Occasionally minor categories create more complicated problems. For example, in New York State, the same candidate may be nominated by two parties, such as the Democratic party and the Liberal party. The percentage of Democratic votes then differs from the percentage of votes received by the Democratic candidate.

Changes in Measurement Techniques. Changes in the way measurements are made can produce different figures and can lead to time series that are not fully comparable. A classic example is survey measurements, in which researchers "improve" the questions, only to find that they cannot measure change in public opinion because the new results are not comparable to those of earlier polls. Sometimes, however, changes are forced on reluctant researchers. For example, the "market basket" of items in the Consumer Price Index (Table 13-2) has changed over time. The cost of fountain pens or carbon paper might have been reasonable items in the 1950s but not in the 1980s; VCRs could hardly have been included until recently.

Ad Hoc Problems. All sorts of small discrepancies can occur, with ad hoc explanations for each one. An example that nearly everyone is familiar with involves the counting of presidents. George Bush is usually said to be the forty-first president. But he is only the fortieth individual to hold the office; Grover Cleveland is counted twice because his two terms were separated by four years. So is the correct number forty or forty-one? It depends on precisely what one means. A less obvious problem occurs in counting Supreme Court nominations that failed. In 1987 Douglas Ginsburg was publicly announced as President Reagan's choice, but his name was withdrawn before it was formally submitted to the Senate. Technically, was he nominated? This kind of subtlety is exacerbated when we deal with events of the distant past. It would be easy, for example, to think that the two listings of the nomination of Edward King by President John Tyler are a typographical error. In fact, King was nominated twice, and the nomination was twice withdrawn in a fight between the president and Congress (Table 9-4).

Solutions to Errors in Data

Awareness that data may contain inaccuracies is no reason to ignore the data; nor is it an excuse to ignore the possible inaccuracies.

5

A consideration of some "solutions" to data errors helps illustrate this point. The solutions, like the problems discussed above, are suggestive rather than exhaustive.

Sometimes errors are relatively obvious and can be easily corrected. Misprints occur, for example. One can encounter references to the 535 members of the House of Representatives when obviously the whole Congress is meant. Checking with alternative or more authoritative sources when mistakes are suspected can help remedy such problems.

Outlandish or illogical numbers should also be checked. A classic example of finding and explaining nonsensical results is the case of two researchers who were not willing to believe data from the 1950 Census showing "a surprising number of widowed fourteen-year-old boys and, equally surprising, a decrease in the number of widowed teenage males at older ages." [1] They wrote a "detective story" about how they traced the problem to systematic errors in the way certain data were entered into the census records.

Another method—one that should always be used—is to check footnotes and accompanying text for exceptions and special comments. Recognize that the problem may not really be error, but misreading. Consider the table on U.S. casualties in Vietnam (Table 11-7). For 1973-1986 the bottom row shows there were no U.S. military forces in Vietnam but 1,141 battle deaths—surely an anomaly. But the note reveals that there were troops in Vietnam for nearly a month during this time—the zero indicates the force count as of 31 December 1973, and U.S. forces were withdrawn on 27 January 1973. In addition, forces dying of wounds incurred earlier or those who were missing and later classified as deceased are also considered battle deaths.

Another solution is what is formally called sensitivity analysis. When values are inexact or differ across sources, one needs to ask how sensitive the conclusion is to the precise values used. If the true values differed by some specified amount from the reported values, would the conclusion change? If not, one can be more confident about the conclusion. Similarly, if sources differ, consider the actual values from several sources. If the conclusion to be drawn does not vary with the different values, the discrepancies are only a minor problem. In the welfare expenditures example, almost any conclusion about social welfare would be the same whether 1977 expenditures were $360.6 billion (Table 12-4) or $360.9 billion (Table 12-6), even though the difference represents what in other contexts would be an astonishing three hundred million dollars.

In examining data over time, one way to avoid possible errors is to be sure the data are truly comparable. Again, one must check that the data were collected uniformly or know what the differences are over time and their probable effects. Occasionally guesses about probable error can be confirmed by formal tests. An excellent example is a study in which both old and new survey questions were asked. Differences that had previously been attributed to changes in the electorate over time were shown to be methodological artifacts.[2]

One should also examine data, perhaps especially data over time, for "outliers." If a series of values, say the percentages of votes for the Republican candidate in a given district, are 52, 56, 49, 85, 50, one must check the accuracy of the 85 percent. Is the 85 a transposition of 58? If 85 is the correct number, what is the reason for it? Was the candidate essentially unopposed that year? What conclusion should be drawn if the 85 were omitted?

Finally, after taking all reasonable steps to be sure the data are as good as can be obtained, checking multiple sources, and so on, one should indicate known errors. It is better to point out that there is some question about certain figures than to pretend that they are perfect. If a loftier reason does not come to mind, being straightforward about inaccuracies at least prevents readers from lobbing them back as if the author were too ignorant to even notice the problems.

Obtaining Additional Material

This book provides essential figures and tables, but the coverage is far from exhaustive. Many readers may want data with a slightly different twist or of another sort altogether. The Guide to References for Political Statistics should help orient readers who seek information beyond that contained here. In addition, the sources given for the tables and figures in this book should also be considered in such searches.

Data on current events can be found in newspapers, weekly news magazines, the *Congressional Quarterly Weekly Report*, and the *National Journal*. Indexes for the *Weekly Report*, *National Journal*, and for major newspapers are a valuable guide. The *National Newspaper Index*, *Newsbank*, and the *National Magazine Index* cover many sources.

Readers need to appreciate how useful reference librarians are to those seeking information. Librarians for government documents collections are also invaluable resources. Interlibrary loans can help secure less readily available volumes, although principal reference works and current material seldom circulate in this fashion.

For some material, one may need to contact organizations that compile or disseminate the data. Various directories are available—of party organizations, interest groups, associations, research institutions, and state agencies. At the federal level, Congressional Quarterly's *Washington Information Directory* is a valuable guide to potential sources. The Council of State Governments, with directories such as *State Administrative Officials Classified by Functions* and *State Elective Officials and the Legislatures* provide a similar service at the state level. (See also the references cited in the introduction to Chapter 10.)

For this volume, machine-readable data constituted a valuable source for several tables and figures. Descriptions of available machine-readable data would require another volume. The Inter-University Consortium for Political and Social Research (ICPSR) at the University of Michigan has the largest collection of such data and publishes an annual guide to resources. Most major research universities are members of the consortium. To learn how to obtain data, one should contact the official university representative of the ICPSR.

These hints are merely starting suggestions for those who wish to go beyond this volume to track down particular pieces of information. We hope the reader will find the extensive coverage in this obviously nonexhaustive volume to be convenient and valuable.

Notes

1. Ansley J. Coale and Frederick F. Stephan, "The Case of the Indians and the Teen-Age Widows," *Journal of American Statistical Association* 57 (1962): 338.
2. John L. Sullivan, James E. Piereson, and George E. Marcus, "Ideological Constraint in the Mass Public: A Methodological Critique and Some New Findings," *American Journal of Political Science* 22 (1978): 233-249.

1

The Constitution

Constitutions are documents about rights and authority. At first blush, little about them suggests statistics. However, a great many numbers relate to the fundamental laws that govern the states and the nation. Such numbers, while significant, tend to be straightforward and simple: dates of constitutional revision and amendment, length of gubernatorial terms, requirements for voter registration, and so on. In addition, some important information is found in lists showing, for example, which state constitutions have a certain component, such as the line-item veto.

The image of the U.S. Constitution as a document written on parchment with quill pens is a powerful legacy from the past but a misleading image for understanding the Constitution in the present. The bicentennial year celebrations focused attention on the Constitutional Convention of 1787, but the U.S. Constitution has evolved dramatically over the past two hundred years (Table 1-3). The document, both in content and meaning, has changed as a result of civil war, formal amendments, and Supreme Court rulings. Amendments are not things of the past either; several have been proposed since the 1960s, and a few are still pending (Tables 1-5 and 1-6). Surprisingly, one of the very first amendments proposed, congressional pay, is still pending.

The federal political structure, delineated in the Constitution, has also undergone significant transformations. For instance, the first ten amendments, the Bill of Rights, originally limited only the federal government, but Supreme Court decisions have interpreted almost all of these rights to limit state governments as well (Table 1-4). Other data about federal and state constitutions and their changes (for example, Tables 1-2, 1-7, and 1-8) also reveal the continuing evolution of the basic framework of the U.S. political system.

Because the federal constitution is a brief document that has been changed little during U.S. history, many may think that this is characteristic of all constitutions. State constitutions vary considerably in their length and in their age (Table 1-2). Some also have been amended frequently, and constitutional change has sometimes swept across the entire country, as when Progressives around the turn of the century mounted a major reform effort. Primaries flourish today as one legacy of the Progressive reform movement (Table 4-9). Progressive reformers also pushed the initiative, referenda, and recall; most states have constitutionally adopted at least one of these procedures (Table 1-7).

Constitutions attest to the fundamental values underlying the political order, supposedly capturing and constraining the prevailing political consensus. Although surveys have found public support for civil liberties such as free speech to be less than broadly based (Table 1-9), one of the major contributions of the U.S. Constitution is precisely the protection of minority rights against majority wishes.

Because individuals often fail to agree, even on so-called fundamental issues, and because any change in a constitution may have sweeping effects, constitutions attract controversy. And not surprisingly, data relevant to constitutional issues also reflect controversy. In a number of instances, public opinion reveals clear majority preferences—on school prayer (Table 1-6) and the balanced budget (Table 1-6), for example—and yet legislators have failed to enact these constitutional amendments. This may be understandable, as when the outnumbered opposition is intense or raises legal impediments. The discrepancy between majority opinion and political action serves as a helpful reminder about the distinction between opinion and behavior and raises questions about the meaning, interpretations, and implications of such survey data.

Constitutions reach beyond the words they contain. Vital pieces of the political fabric, such as political parties, are not mentioned in the U.S. Constitution. But much that was unmentioned has increasingly come under the Constitution and the jurisdiction of the federal courts. Voter registration requirements, for example, were originally left to the states, but federal court decisions and the Voting Rights Act have caused greater uniformity among the states since 1965 (Tables 1-15 and 1-17). Similarly, reapportionment of legislative seats, an area the federal courts initially refused to review because it raised "political questions," has changed dramatically since the early 1960s. With its "one person, one vote" ruling, the Supreme Court has imposed strict standards on legislative districts (Table 1-16).

Constitutions are words, not numbers. But it is surprising how many statistics are relevant to the understanding of constitutions.

Table 1-1 The States: Historical Data and Current Populations

State	Population[a]	Date organized as territory	Date admitted to Union	Chronological order of admission to Union
Alabama	3,893,888	March 3, 1817	December 14, 1819	22
Alaska	401,851	August 24, 1912	January 3, 1959	49
Arizona	2,718,215	February 24, 1863	February 14, 1912	48
Arkansas	2,286,435	March 2, 1819	June 15, 1836	25
California	23,667,902	[b]	September 9, 1850	31
Colorado	2,889,964	February 28, 1861	August 1, 1876	38
Connecticut	3,107,576	-	January 9, 1788[c]	5
Delaware	594,338	-	December 7, 1787[c]	1
Florida	9,746,324	March 30, 1822	March 3, 1845	27
Georgia	5,463,105	-	January 2, 1788[c]	4
Hawaii	964,691	June 14, 1900	August 21, 1959	50
Idaho	943,935	March 4, 1863	July 3, 1890	43
Illinois	11,426,518	February 3, 1809	December 3, 1818	21
Indiana	5,490,224	May 7, 1800	December 11, 1816	19
Iowa	2,913,808	June 12, 1838	December 28, 1846	29
Kansas	2,363,679	May 30, 1854	January 29, 1861	34
Kentucky	3,660,777	[b]	June 1, 1792	15
Louisiana	4,205,900	March 26, 1804	April 30, 1812	18
Maine	1,124,660	[b]	March 15, 1820	23
Maryland	4,216,975	-	April 28, 1788[c]	7
Massachusetts	5,737,037	-	February 6, 1788[c]	6
Michigan	9,262,078	January 11, 1805	January 26, 1837	26
Minnesota	4,075,970	March 3, 1849	May 11, 1858	32
Mississippi	2,520,638	April 7, 1798	December 10, 1817	20
Missouri	4,916,686	June 4, 1812	August 10, 1821	24
Montana	786,690	May 26, 1864	November 8, 1889	41
Nebraska	1,569,825	May 30, 1854	March 1, 1867	37
Nevada	800,493	March 2, 1861	October 31, 1864	36
New Hampshire	920,610	-	June 21, 1788[c]	9
New Jersey	7,364,823	-	December 18, 1787[c]	3
New Mexico	1,302,894	September 9, 1850	January 6, 1912	47
New York	17,558,072	-	July 26, 1788[c]	11
North Carolina	5,881,766	-	November 21, 1789[c]	12
North Dakota	652,717	March 2, 1861	November 2, 1889	39
Ohio	10,797,630	May 7, 1800	March 1, 1803	17
Oklahoma	3,025,290	May 2, 1890	November 16, 1907	46
Oregon	2,633,105	August 14, 1848	February 14, 1859	33
Pennsylvania	11,863,895	-	December 12, 1787[c]	2
Rhode Island	947,154	-	May 29, 1790[c]	13
South Carolina	3,121,820	-	May 23, 1788[c]	8
South Dakota	690,768	March 2, 1861	November 2, 1889	40

(Table continues)

Table 1-1 *(Continued)*

State	Population[a]	Date organized as territory	Date admitted to Union	Chronological order of admission to Union
Tennessee	4,591,120	June 8, 1790[d]	June 1, 1796	16
Texas	14,229,191	[b]	December 29, 1845	28
Utah	1,461,037	September 9, 1850	January 4, 1896	45
Vermont	511,456	[b]	March 4, 1791	14
Virginia	5,346,818	-	June 25, 1788[c]	10
Washington	4,132,156	March 2, 1853	November 11, 1889	42
West Virginia	1,949,644	[b]	June 20, 1863	35
Wisconsin	4,705,767	April 20, 1836	May 29, 1848	30
Wyoming	469,557	July 25, 1868	July 10, 1890	44

Note: "-" indicates one of the original thirteen states.
[a] As of 1980.
[b] No territorial status before admission to Union.
[c] Date of ratification of U.S. Constitution.
[d] Date Southwest Territory (identical boundaries as Tennessee's) was created.

Sources: Council of State Governments, *Book of the States, 1988-1989* (Lexington, Ky.: Council of State Governments, 1988), 477-480; population: U.S. Bureau of the Census, "1980 Census of Population, volume 1, Characteristics of the Population, chapter A, Number of Inhabitants, Part 1 United States Summary" (Washington, D.C.: U.S. Government Printing Office, 1983), 1-43.

Table 1-2 State Constitutions

| State | Number of constitutions[a] | Dates of adoption | Present Constitution | | Number of amendments | |
			Effective date	Estimated length (number of words)	Submitted to voters	Adopted
Alabama	6	1819, 1861, 1865, 1868, 1875, 1901	November 28, 1901	174,000	679	471
Alaska	1	1956	January 3, 1959	13,000	30	21
Arizona	1	1911	February 14, 1912	28,876	191	105
Arkansas	5	1836, 1861, 1864, 1868, 1874	October 30, 1874	40,720	160	73
California	2	1847, 1879	July 4, 1879	33,350	768	460
Colorado	1	1876	August 1, 1876	45,679	231	109
Connecticut	4	1818, 1965	December 30, 1965	9,564	26	25
Delaware	4	1776, 1792, 1831, 1897	June 10, 1897	19,000	b	117
Florida	6	1839, 1861, 1865, 1868, 1886, 1968	January 7, 1969	25,100	68	44
Georgia	10	1777, 1789, 1798, 1861, 1865, 1868, 1877, 1945, 1976, 1982	July 1, 1983	25,000	20	18
Hawaii	1	1950	August 21, 1959	17,453	86	78
Idaho	1	1889	July 3, 1890	21,500	186	106
Illinois	4	1818, 1848, 1870, 1970	July 1, 1971	13,200	9	4
Indiana	2	1816, 1851	November 1, 1851	9,377	67	36
Iowa	2	1846, 1857	September 3, 1857	12,500	49	46
Kansas	1	1859	January 29, 1861	11,865	114	86
Kentucky	4	1792, 1799, 1850, 1891	September 28, 1891	23,500	56	27
Louisiana	11	1812, 1845, 1852, 1861, 1864, 1868, 1879, 1898, 1913, 1921, 1974	January 1, 1975	51,488	36	22
Maine	1	1819	March 15, 1820	13,500	184	156
Maryland	4	1776, 1851, 1864, 1867	October 5, 1867	41,349	231	199
Massachusetts	1	1780	October 25, 1780	36,690	143	116
Michigan	4	1835, 1850, 1908, 1963	January 1, 1964	20,000	44	15
Minnesota	1	1857	May 11, 1858	9,500	203	109
Mississippi	4	1817, 1832, 1869, 1890	November 1, 1890	24,000	141	70
Missouri	4	1820, 1865, 1875, 1945	March 30, 1945	42,000	107	68

State	No.	Dates of Adoption	Effective Date	Length (words)	Amendments Proposed	Amendments Adopted
Montana	2	1889, 1972	July 1, 1973	11,866	21	13
Nebraska	2	1866, 1875	October 12, 1875	20,048	278	184
Nevada	1	1864	October 31, 1864	20,770	168	103
New Hampshire	2	1776, 1784	June 2, 1784	9,200	272	141
New Jersey	3	1776, 1844, 1947	January 1, 1948	17,086	49	36
New Mexico	1	1911	January 6, 1912	27,200	224	114
New York	4	1777, 1822, 1846, 1894	January 1, 1895	80,000	272	205
North Carolina	3	1776, 1868, 1970	July 1, 1971	11,000	34	27
North Dakota	1	1889	November 2, 1889	20,564	215	124
Ohio	2	1802, 1851	September 1, 1851	36,900	244	144
Oklahoma	1	1907	November 16, 1907	68,800	264	124
Oregon	1	1857	February 14, 1859	26,090	361	183
Pennsylvania	5	1776, 1790, 1838, 1873, 1968	1968c	21,675	24	19
Rhode Island	2	1842	May 2, 1843	19,026	98	52
South Carolina	7	1776, 1778, 1790, 1861, 1865, 1868, 1895	January 1, 1896	22,500	639	455
South Dakota	1	1889	November 2, 1889	23,300	181	94
Tennessee	3	1796, 1835, 1870	February 23, 1870	15,300	55	32
Texas	5	1845, 1861, 1866, 1869, 1876	February 15, 1876	62,000	459	304
Utah	1	1895	January 4, 1896	11,000	124	75
Vermont	3	1777, 1786, 1793	July 9, 1793	6,600	208	50
Virginia	6	1776, 1830, 1851, 1869, 1902, 1970	July 1, 1971	18,500	23	20
Washington	1	1889	November 11, 1889	29,400	147	80
West Virginia	2	1863, 1872	April 9, 1872	25,600	102	62
Wisconsin	1	1848	May 29, 1848	13,500	167	124
Wyoming	1	1889	July 10, 1890	31,800	96	56

Note: Constitutions as of December 31, 1987. For more details on the constitutions, see source.

a The constitutions include those Civil War documents customarily listed by the individual states. In Connecticut and Rhode Island, colonial charters served as the first constitutions.

b Proposed amendments are not submitted to the voters in Delaware.

c Certain sections of the Constitution were revised in 1967-1968. Amendments proposed and adopted are since 1968.

Source: Book of the States, 1988-1989, 14-15.

Table 1-3 Length of Time between Congressional Approval and Actual Ratification of the Twenty-six Amendments to the U.S. Constitution

Amendment		Time required for ratification	Year ratified
I-X	Bill of Rights	2 years, 2½ months	1791
XI	Lawsuits against states	11 months	1795
XII	Presidential elections	6½ months	1804
XIII	Abolition of slavery	10 months	1865
XIV	Civil rights	2 years, 1 month	1868
XV	Suffrage for all races	11 months	1870
XVI	Income tax	3 years, 6½ months	1913
XVII	Senatorial elections	11 months	1913
XVIII	Prohibition	1 year, 1 month	1919
XIX	Women's suffrage	1 year, 2 months	1920
XX	Terms of office	11 months	1933
XXI	Repeal of prohibition	9½ months	1933
XXII	Limit on presidential terms	3 years, 11 months	1951
XXIII	Washington, D.C., vote	9 months	1961
XXIV	Abolition of poll taxes	1 year, 4 months	1964
XXV	Presidential succession	1 year, 10 months	1967
XXVI	Eighteen-year-old suffrage	3 months	1971

Source: Congressional Research Service, *The Constitution of the United States: Analysis and Interpretation* (Washington, D.C.: U.S. Government Printing Office, 1973), 23-44. 92d Cong., 2d sess., S. Doc. 92-82.

Table 1-4 Incorporation of the Bill of Rights to Apply to State Governments

Year	Issue and amendment	Supreme Court case	Vote
[1868 Fourteenth Amendment to Constitution passed][a]			
1897	Eminent domain (V)	Chicago, Burlington & Quincy RR v. Chicago 166 U.S. 266	9:0
1927	Freedom of speech (I)	Fiske v. Kansas 274 U.S. 380	9:0
1931	Freedom of press (I)	Near v. Minnesota 283 U.S. 697	5:4
1932	Counsel in capital criminal cases (VI)	Powell v. Alabama 287 U.S. 45	7:2
1934	Free exercise of religion (I)	Hamilton v. Regents of the U. of California 293 U.S. 245	9:0
1937	Freedom of assembly and petition (I)	De Jonge v. Oregon 299 U.S. 253	8:0
1947	Separation of church and state (I)	Everson v. Board of Education of Ewing Township 330 U.S. 1	5:4
1948	Public trial (VI)	In re Oliver 33 U.S. 257	7:2
1961	Unreasonable searches and seizures (IV)	Mapp v. Ohio 367 U.S. 643	6:3
1962	Cruel and unusual punishment (VIII)	Robinson v. California 370 U.S. 660	6:2
1963	Counsel in all criminal cases (VI)	Gideon v. Wainwright 372 U.S. 335	9:0
1964	Self-incrimination (V)	Malloy v. Hogan 378 U.S. 1	5:4
		Murphy v. Waterfront Commission 378 U.S. 52	9:0
1965	Right to confront adverse witnesses (VI)	Pointer v. Texas 380 U.S. 400	7:2
1967	Impartial jury (VI)	Parker v. Gladden 385 U.S. 363	8:1
1967	Obtaining and confronting favorable witnesses (VI)	Washington v. Texas 388 U.S. 14	9:0
1967	Speedy trial (VI)	Klopfer v. North Carolina 386 U.S. 213	9:0
1968	Jury trial in non-petty criminal cases (VI)	Duncan v. Louisiana 391 U.S. 145	7:2
1969	Double jeopardy (V)	Benton v. Maryland 395 U.S. 784	7:2

Note: Enumerated rights not incorporated: grand jury indictment, trial by jury in civil cases, excessive fines and bail, right to bear arms, and safeguards on quartering troops in private homes.

[a] The Fourteenth Amendment's due process clause is the basis for applying the Bill of Rights to the states.

Sources: Henry J. Abraham, *The Judiciary: The Supreme Court in the Governmental Process,* 7th ed. (Dubuque, Iowa: William C. Brown, 1988); votes from *U.S. Supreme Court Reports.*

Table 1-5 State Action on Proposed Constitutional Amendments

	Proposed amendment				
State	Congressional pay[a]	Reappor-tionment[b]	Equal rights[c]	Balanced budget[d]	Ban abortion[e]
Alabama	n.a.	yes	n.a.	r	yes
Alaska	n.a.	n.a.	yes	yes	n.a.
Arizona	yes	yes	n.a.	yes	n.a.
Arkansas	yes	yes	n.a.	yes	yes
California	n.a.	n.a.	yes	n.a.[f]	n.a.
Colorado	yes	yes	yes	yes	n.a.
Connecticut	yes	n.a.	yes	n.a.	n.a.
Delaware	yes	n.a.	yes	yes	yes
Florida	n.a.	yes	n.a.	r	n.a.
Georgia	yes	yes	n.a.	yes	n.a.
Hawaii	n.a.	n.a.	yes	n.a.	n.a.
Idaho	n.a.	yes	r	yes	yes
Illinois	n.a.	r[g]	n.a.	n.a.[f]	n.a.
Indiana	yes	yes	yes	yes	yes
Iowa	n.a.	yes	yes	yes	n.a.
Kansas	n.a.	r[g]	yes	yes	n.a.
Kentucky	n.a.	yes	r	n.a.[f]	yes
Louisiana	yes	yes	n.a.	yes	yes
Maine	yes	n.a.	yes	n.a.	n.a.
Maryland	yes	r[g]	yes	yes	n.a.
Massachusetts	n.a.	n.a.	yes	n.a.	yes
Michigan	n.a.	n.a.	yes	n.a.	n.a.
Minnesota	n.a.	yes	yes	n.a.	n.a.
Mississippi	n.a.	yes	n.a.	yes	yes
Missouri	n.a.	yes	n.a.	yes	yes
Montana	yes	yes	yes	n.a.[f]	n.a.
Nebraska	n.a.	yes	r	yes	yes
Nevada	n.a.	yes	n.a.	yes	yes
New Hampshire	yes	yes	yes	yes	n.a.
New Jersey	n.a.	n.a.	yes	n.a.	yes
New Mexico	yes	yes	yes	yes	n.a.
New York	n.a.	n.a.	yes	n.a.	n.a.
North Carolina	yes	r[g]	n.a.	yes	n.a.
North Dakota	n.a.	yes	yes	yes	n.a.
Ohio	yes	n.a.	yes	n.a.	n.a.
Oklahoma	yes	yes	n.a.	yes	yes
Oregon	n.a.	n.a.	yes	yes	n.a.
Pennsylvania	n.a.	n.a.	yes	yes	yes
Rhode Island	n.a.	n.a.	yes	n.a.	yes
South Carolina	yes	yes	n.a.	yes	n.a.
South Dakota	yes	yes	r	yes	yes
Tennessee	yes	yes	r	yes	yes

(Table continues)

Table 1-5 *(Continued)*

	Proposed amendment				
State	Congressional pay[a]	Reappor- tionment[b]	Equal rights[c]	Balanced budget[d]	Ban abortion[e]
Texas	yes	r[g]	yes	yes	n.a.
Utah	yes	yes	n.a.	yes	yes
Vermont	yes	n.a.	yes	n.a.	n.a.
Virginia	yes	yes	n.a.	yes	n.a.
Washington	n.a.	r[g]	yes	n.a.	n.a.
West Virginia	yes	n.a.	yes	n.a.	n.a.
Wisconsin	yes	n.a.	yes	n.a.	n.a.
Wyoming	yes	yes	yes	yes	n.a.

Note: "Yes" indicates state legislature approved the amendment or sent a petition to Congress for a constitutional convention; "n.a." indicates no action was taken or the state legislature rejected the amendment or a proposal to petition for a convention; and "r" indicates previous appeal was rescinded. The equal rights amendment and congressional pay amendment were initiated by Congress and submitted to the states for ratification. The other three proposed amendments were initiated by petition from state legislatures.

[a] Congressional Pay: This amendment as proposed by a resolution of the First Congress of the United States on September 25, 1789, reads: "No law varying the compensation for the services of the Senators and Representatives, shall take effect, until an election of Representatives shall have intervened."

[b] Reapportionment: States acted to petition Congress for a constitutional convention on this issue following two Supreme Court "one person, one vote" decisions concerning how states were apportioned for their state legislatures. As a result, some states called for a convention to consider an amendment that would allow one house of a state legislature to be apportioned on a basis other than population.

[c] Equal Rights: This amendment, as proposed by Congress and voted on by the states, read: "Section 1. Equality of rights under the law shall not be denied or abridged by the United States or by any State on account of sex. Section 2. The Congress shall have the power to enforce, by appropriate legislation, the provisions of this article. Section 3. This amendment shall take effect two years after the date of ratification."

[d] Balanced Budget: This proposed amendment has various forms. In its simplest form, Congress would be required to approve a balanced federal budget each year. In other forms there is a provision that a three-fifths majority of Congress could vote not to balance the budget in any given year.

[e] Abortion: Some states have called for a constitutional convention to consider an amendment that would ban abortions. The most common approach among the various proposed amendments is to apply the constitutional protection of due process against the denial of life and property to unborn children.

[f] The state did not endorse the call for a constitutional convention but petitioned Congress to propose a balanced budget amendment to the states.

[g] Passed by only one house of each of the state legislatures.

Sources: Reapportionment: *Congressional Quarterly Weekly Report* (1969), 1372-1373; equal rights: *Public Opinion* (August/September 1981), 39 (reprinted with permission of the American Enterprise Institute for Public Policy Research); Congressional Research Service, *The Constitution of the United States*, 43; balanced budget: *Congressional Record* citations to state communications relating to constitutional conventions, *The Gallup Report* (September 1985), 11; abortion: *Congressional Record* citations to state communications relating to constitutional conventions; congressional pay: House Joint Resolution No. 6 (71st Legislature of the State of Texas, R.S.).

Table 1-6 Public Opinion on Issues Relating to Proposed
Constitutional Amendments (percent)

Proposed amendment/year	Favor	Oppose	Don't know or no opinion
Abortion			
1974	47	44	9
1981	45	46	9
1983	50	43	7
1986	45	45	10
Reapportionment			
1964	47	30	23
1969	52	23	25
Supreme Court decision			
banning school prayer			
1963	24	70	6
1971	28	67	6
1974	31	66	3
1975	35	62	3
1977	33	64	2
1982	37	60	3
1983	40	57	4
1985	43	54	3
1986	37	61	2
1988	37	59	4
Equal rights[a]			
1975	58	24	18
1976	57	24	19
1978	58	31	11
1980	58	31	11
1981	63	32	5
1982	56	34	10
1984	63	31	6
Balanced budget[a]			
1976	78	13	9
1981 (April)	70	22	8
1981 (September)	73	19	8
1982	74	17	9
1983	71	21	8
1985	49	27	24
1987	53	23	24

Note: Questions: (Abortion) "The U.S. Supreme Court has ruled that a woman may go to a doctor to end her pregnancy at any time during the first three months of pregnancy. Do you favor or oppose this ruling?" (Reapportionment, 1964) "As you know, the U.S. Supreme Court has ruled that the number of representatives of both the lower house and

(Note continues)

Table 1-6 *(Continued)*

---

the Senate in all state legislatures must be in proportion to population. In most states, this means reducing the number of legislators from the rural areas and increasing the number from urban areas. Do you approve or disapprove of this ruling?" (Reapportionment, 1969) "The U.S. Supreme Court has required states to change their legislative districts so that each member of the upper house represents the same number of people. Some people would like to return to the earlier method of electing members of the upper house according to counties or other units regardless of population. Would you favor continuing the present equal districting plan or returning to the earlier plan?" (School prayer) "The U.S. Supreme Court has ruled that no state or local government may require the reading of the Lord's Prayer or Bible verses in public schools. What are your views on this—do you approve or disapprove of the court ruling?" (Equal rights) "Have you heard or read about the Equal Rights Amendment to the U.S. Constitution which would prohibit discrimination on the basis of sex? Do you favor or oppose this amendment?" (Balanced budget) "Have you heard or read about the proposal for a constitutional amendment which would require the federal government to balance the national budget each year? A proposed amendment to the Constitution would require Congress to approve a balanced federal budget each year. Government spending would have to be limited to no more than expected revenues, unless a three-fifths majority of Congress voted to spend more than expected revenues. Would you favor or oppose this amendment to the Constitution?" (Slightly different wording in 1976.)

[a] Of those who were aware of the proposed amendment (except 1984 for equal rights and 1976 and 1987 for balanced budget). Between 88 and 91 percent of those asked were aware of the equal rights amendment. Between 53 and 66 percent of those asked were aware of the proposed balanced budget amendment.

Sources: Abortion: *The Gallup Poll* (Wilmington, Del.: Scholarly Resources, Inc., 1983), 140, *The Gallup Report* (January/February 1986), 17-18; reapportionment: *The Gallup Poll* (New York: Random House, 1972), 1897, 2205-2206; school prayer (1963, 1971): *The Gallup Poll* (1972), 1837; school prayer (1974-1988): General Social Survey, National Opinion Research Center, University of Chicago; equal rights: *The Gallup Poll* (1982), 140, (1984), 242; balanced budget: *The Gallup Poll* (1972), 679, *The Gallup Poll* (1982), 125, 231, (1983), 127, *The Gallup Report* (September 1985), 10-11, and *The Gallup Report* (July 1987), 8.

Table 1-7 State Provisions for Initiative, Referendum, and Recall

State	Initiative[a]	Referendum[b]	Recall[c]
Alabama			all but judiciary
Alaska	direct	petition	all elected officials
Arizona	direct	legislature and petition	
Arkansas	direct	petition	all elected officials
California	direct	petition and constitutional requirement	all elected officials
Colorado	direct	legislature and petition	
Connecticut		legislature	
Delaware			
Florida		constitutional requirement	all elected officials
Georgia		constitutional requirement	
Hawaii			all but judiciary
Idaho	direct	petition	
Illinois		legislature	
Indiana			all but judiciary
Iowa		constitutional requirement	all but judiciary
Kansas		constitutional requirement	
Kentucky		all three	
Louisiana			
Maine	indirect	all three	
Maryland		petition	
Massachusetts	indirect	petition	
Michigan	indirect	all three	all but certain judges
Minnesota			
Mississippi			
Missouri	direct	legislature and petition	all elected or appointed officials
Montana	direct	legislature and petition	
Nebraska	direct	petition	all elected officials
Nevada	indirect	petition	
New Hampshire			

State	Initiative[a]	Referendum[b]	Recall[c]
New Jersey		legislature and constitutional requirement	
New Mexico		constitutional requirement and petition	
New York		constitutional requirement	
North Carolina		constitutional requirement	
North Dakota	direct	petition	all elected officials
Ohio	both	petition and constitutional requirement	
Oklahoma	direct	all three	
Oregon	direct	petition	all elected officials
Pennsylvania		constitutional requirement	
Rhode Island		constitutional requirement	
South Carolina			
South Dakota	indirect	petition	
Tennessee			
Texas			
Utah	both	petition	
Vermont			
Virginia		legislature and constitutional requirement	
Washington	both	all three	all elected but certain judges
West Virginia		legislature and constitutional requirement	
Wisconsin		petition	all elected officials
Wyoming	direct	petition	

[a] Initiative: Allows proposed state laws to be placed on a ballot by citizen petition and enacted or rejected by the electorate. "Direct" means measures may be placed on the ballot with a specific number of signatures and no legislative action; requirements for number of signatures vary. "Indirect" means a measure must be submitted to the legislature for consideration before it can be placed on the ballot.

[b] Referendum: State law passed by the legislature is referred to voters before it goes into effect. Referendum may be held by citizen petition, voluntary submission by the legislature, or, for certain types of decisions, such as tax increases, may be a constitutional requirement.

[c] Recall: Voters are allowed to remove state elective officials in a recall election. Number of signatures needed ranges from 10 to 40 percent; percentage is based on last vote for the office in question or general election. Sometimes percentage is modified by geographical or jurisdictional restrictions.

Source: Book of the States, 1988–1989, 217–220.

Table 1-8 Governors' Terms, Limits, Powers, and Other Statewide Elected Officials

State	Length of term in 1900	Length of term in 1988	Year of change	Maximum number of consecutive terms	Item veto[a]	Other statewide elected officials[b] Number of officials	Other statewide elected officials[b] Number of agencies
Alabama	2	4	1902	2	yes	17	8
Alaska		4		2	yes	1	0
Arizona	c	4	1970	No limit	yes	8	6
Arkansas	2	4	1986	2	yes	6	6
California	4	4		No limit	yes	6	7
Colorado	2	4	1958	No limit	yes	4	16
Connecticut	2	4	1950	No limit	yes	5	5
Delaware	4	4		2[d]	yes	5	5
Florida	4	4		2	yes	6	6
Georgia	2	4	1942	2	yes	12	8
Hawaii	2	4		2	yes	14	2
Idaho	2	4	1946	No limit	yes	6	0
Illinois	4	4		No limit	yes	14	5
Indiana	4	4		2	no	6	6
Iowa	2	4	1974	No limit	yes	6	6
Kansas	2	4	1974	1[d]	yes	15	6
Kentucky	4	4			yes	7	7
Louisiana	4	4		2	yes	21	10
Maine	2	4	1958	2	no	0	0
Maryland	4	4		2	yes	3	3
Massachusetts	1	4	1920, 1966[e]	No limit	yes	5	6
Michigan	2	4	1966	No limit	yes	35	7

State		Year	Limit			
Minnesota	2		No limit	yes	5	5
Mississippi	4		1	yes	13	9
Missouri	4	1962	2^d	yes	5	5
Montana	4		No limit	yes	10	6
Nebraska	2	1966	2	yes	26	8
Nevada	4		2	no	23	7
New Hampshire	2		No limit	no	5	1
New Jersey	3	1949	1^{d,f}	yes	0	0
New Mexico	c	1916, 1970		yes	8	19
New York	2	1938	No limit	g	3	3
North Carolina	4		2^d	yes	9	9
North Dakota	2	1964	No limit	yes	13	11
Ohio	2	1958	2	yes	28	6
Oklahoma	4		2	yes	9	7
Oregon	4		2^f	yes	5	5
Pennsylvania	4		2	yes	4	4
Rhode Island	1	1912	No limit	no	4	4
South Carolina	2	1926	2	yes	8	10
South Dakota	2	1974	2	yes	9	7
Tennessee	1	1954	2	yes	3	1
Texas	2	1974	No limit	yes	29	8
Utah	4		No limit	yes	14	4
Vermont	2		No limit	no	5	4
Virginia	4		1^d	yes	2	5
Washington	4		No limit	yes	8	2
West Virginia	4	1970	2	yes	5	8
Wisconsin	2		No limit	yes	5	5
Wyoming	4		No limit	yes	4	4

(Notes follow)

Table 1-8 (Continued)

[a] Provisions to override vary, requiring as many as two-thirds of the legislators elected. For details, see source.

[b] Popularly elected executive branch officials and the number of agencies involving these officials.

[c] Arizona admitted in 1912, started with two years; New Mexico admitted in 1912 with four years, went to two years in 1916, and back to four years in 1970.

[d] Delaware, Missouri, North Carolina: two terms only, whether or not consecutive. Kentucky, New Mexico, Virginia: one term only, successive terms forbidden.

[e] Massachusetts went from one year to two years in 1920, and from two years to four years in 1966.

[f] New Mexico: two consecutive term limit begins in 1991. Oregon: cannot serve over eight years in any twelve-year period.

[g] Governor has no veto power.

Sources: Book of the States, 1988-1989, 35-36, 39-40; length of term in 1900 and year of change: Congressional Quarterly, *Congressional Quarterly's Guide to U.S. Elections*, 2d ed. (Washington, D.C.: Congressional Quarterly, 1985), 130-131.

Table 1-9 Public Opinion on Civil Liberties (percent)

Issue/year		Allow[a]	Don't forbid[b]
Public speeches against democracy			
1940		25	46
1974		56	72
1976a		55	80
1976b		52	79

Issue/year	Allow to speak	Allow to teach college	Keep book in library
Atheist[c]			
1954	37	12	35
1964[d]	—	—	61
1972	65	40	61
1973a	65	41	61
1973b	62	39	57
1974	62	42	60
1976	64	41	60
1977	62	39	59
1978	63	—	60
1980	66	45	62
1982	64	46	61
1984	68	46	64
1985	65	45	61
1987	69	47	66
1988	70	45	64
Admitted communist[c]			
1954	27	6	27
1972	52	32	53
1973a	60	39	58
1973b	53	30	54
1974	58	42	59
1976	55	41	56
1977	55	39	55
1978	60	—	61
1980	55	41	57
1982	56	43	57
1984	59	46	60
1985	57	44	57
1987	60	46	61
1988	66	48	59
Racist[c]			
1943[e]	17	—	—
1976	61	41	60
1977	59	41	61
1978	62	—	65

(Table continues)

Table 1-9 *(Continued)*

Issue/year	Allow to speak	Allow to teach college	Keep book in library
1980	62	43	64
1982	59	43	60
1984	57	41	63
1985	55	42	60
1987	61	44	64
1988	61	42	62

Note: "−" indicates not available.

[a] Question: "Do you think the United States should allow public speeches against democracy?"

[b] Question: "Do you think the United States should forbid public speeches against democracy?"

[c] Question: "There are always some people whose ideas are considered bad or dangerous by other people. For instance, somebody who (is against all churches and religion/admits he is a communist/believes that blacks are genetically inferior). If such a person wanted to make a speech in your (city/town/community), should he be allowed to speak? Should such a person be allowed to teach in a college or university, or not? If some people in your community suggested that a book he wrote (against churches and religion/[promoting communism]/which said blacks are inferior) should be taken out of your public library, would you favor removing this book?"

[d] In 1964 the question was as follows: "Suppose a man admitted in public that he did not believe in God. Do you think a book he wrote should be removed from a public library?"

[e] In 1943 the question was as follows: "In peacetime, do you think anyone in the United States should be allowed to make speeches against certain races in this country?"

Sources: Public speeches against democracy: Howard Schuman and Stanley Presser, *Questions and Answers in Attitude Surveys* (New York: Academic Press, 1981), 277; 1943, 1964, and 1973b: National Opinion Research Center surveys; 1954: Samuel A. Stouffer, *Communism, Conformity, and Civil Liberties* (Garden City, N.Y.: Doubleday, 1955), 32-34, 40-43; 1973a: Clyde Z. Nunn et al., *Tolerance for Nonconformity* (San Francisco: Jossey-Bass, 1978), 40-43; data for all other years from General Social Survey.

Table 1-10 States with the Death Penalty, Number of Executions (1940-1989), and Number on Death Row (1988)

State	Method	\<center\>Number executed\</center\>					Number awaiting execution[b]
		1940s	1950s	1960s	1970s	1980s[a]	
Alabama	electrocution	50	20	5	0	3	94
Alaska	none	0	0	0	0	0	0
Arizona	gas chamber	9	8	4	0	0	83
Arkansas	lethal injection	38	18	9	0	0	30
California	gas chamber	80	74	30	0	0	238
Colorado	gas chamber or lethal injection	13	3	6	0	0	3
Connecticut	electrocution	10	5	1	0	0	1
Delaware	lethal injection	4	0	0	0	0	7
District of Columbia	none	16	4	0	0	0	0
Florida	electrocution	65	49	12	1	19	296
Georgia	electrocution	130	85	14	0	13	106
Hawaii	none	0	0	0	0	0	0
Idaho	lethal injection or firing squad	0	3	0	0	0	15
Illinois	lethal injection	18	9	2	0	0	119
Indiana	electrocution	7	2	1	0	2	51
Iowa	none	7	1	2	0	0	0
Kansas	none	5	5	5	0	0	0
Kentucky	electrocution	34	16	1	0	0	31
Louisiana	electrocution	47	27	1	0	18	41
Maine	none	0	0	0	0	0	0
Maryland	gas chamber	45	6	1	0	0	18
Massachusetts	none	9	0	0	0	0	0
Michigan	none	0	0	0	0	0	0
Minnesota	none	0	0	0	0	0	0
Mississippi	gas chamber or lethal injection	60	36	10	0	3	47
Missouri	gas chamber or lethal injection	15	7	4	0	1	71
Montana	lethal injection or hanging	1	0	0	0	0	7
Nebraska	electrocution	2	2	0	0	0	13
Nevada	lethal injection	10	9	2	1	1	45
New Hampshire	lethal injection[c]	0	0	0	0	0	0
New Jersey	lethal injection	14	17	3	0	0	25
New Mexico	lethal injection	2	3	1	0	0	2
New York	none	114	52	10	0	0	0
North Carolina	gas chamber or lethal injection	112	19	1	0	3	81

(Table continues)

29

Table 1-10 *(Continued)*

		Number executed					Number awaiting execution[b]
State	*Method*	*1940s*	*1950s*	*1960s*	*1970s*	*1980s[a]*	
North Dakota	none	0	0	0	0	0	0
Ohio	electrocution	51	32	7	0	0	85
Oklahoma	lethal injection	13	7	6	0	0	99
Oregon	lethal injection	12	4	1	0	0	14
Pennsylvania	electrocution	36	31	3	0	0	115
Rhode Island	none	0	0	0	0	0	0
South Carolina	electrocution	61	26	8	0	2	42
South Dakota	lethal injection[c]	1	0	0	0	0	0
Tennessee	electrocution	37	8	1	0	0	70
Texas	lethal injection	74	74	29	0	30	284
Utah	firing squad or lethal injection	4	6	1	1	2	6
Vermont	electrocution[c]	1	2	0	0	0	0
Virginia	electrocution	35	23	6	0	7	39
Washington	lethal injection or hanging	16	6	2	0	0	7
West Virginia	none	11	9	0	0	0	0
Wisconsin	none	0	0	0	0	0	0
Wyoming	lethal injection	2	0	1	0	0	3
U.S. government	[c,d]	13	9	1	0	0	0
U.S. military	lethal injection	[e]	[e]	[e]	[e]	[e]	5
Total[d]		1,284	717	191	3	103	2,182[f]

[a] "1980s" includes through March 31, 1989.
[b] As of December 20, 1988.
[c] Statute but no sentences.
[d] The method of execution for federal offenders is that of the state in which the execution takes place.
[e] One hundred and sixty executions have been carried out under military authority since 1930.
[f] The national total counts multiple death-sentenced inmates once. However, they are included in the state total for each state where they are sentenced to death.

Sources: U.S. Department of Justice, Bureau of Justice Statistics, *Capital Punishment 1987* (Washington, D.C.: U.S. Government Printing Office, July 1988), 1, 5, 6; number executed: U.S. Bureau of the Census, *Statistical Abstract of the U.S., 1988* (Washington, D.C.: U.S. Government Printing Office, 1987), 179; number executed, 1970s-1980s, number awaiting execution: NAACP Legal Defense and Education Fund, *Death Row, U.S.A.,* December 20, 1988 and update "Executions in America Since 1976," January 31, 1989.

Table 1-11 Public Opinion on the Death Penalty, 1936-1988 (percent)

Date	Favor	Oppose	Don't know
April 1936	62	33	5
December 1936	59	38	3
November 1937	61	33	7
October 1953	68[a]	26	6
April 1956	53	34	13
September 1957	47	34	18
March 1960	53	36	11
February 1965	45	43	12
July 1966	42	47	11
June 1967	54	38	8
January 1969	51	40	9
October 1971	48	41	11
February 1972	51	41	8
March 1972	53	39	8
November 1972	60	30	10
March 1973	60	35	5
March 1974	63	32	5
March 1975	60	33	7
March 1976	66	30	5
April 1976	67	27	7
March 1977	67	26	6
March 1978	66	28	6
July 1979	65	27	8
March 1980	67	27	6
March 1981	66	25	9
March 1982	74	21	6
June 1982	71	20	9
March 1983	73	22	5
March 1984	70	24	6
January 1985	72	20	8
March 1985	76	19	5
November 1985	75	17	8
January 1986	70	22	8
March 1986	71	23	5
March 1987	70	24	6
March 1988	71	22	7

Note: Questions: (1936-1937) "Are you in favor of the death penalty for murder?" (1953-February 1972, November 1972, April 1976, January 1981, January, November 1985) "Are you in favor of the death penalty for persons convicted of murder?" (all others) "Do you favor or oppose the death penalty for persons convicted of murder?"
[a] Includes qualified yes or qualified no.

Sources: 1936 through February 1972, November 1972, April 1976, January 1981, January 1985, and November 1985: Gallup surveys; others from General Social Survey.

Table 1-12 Frequency of Legal Abortions, 1973-1985

Year	Total		White		Nonwhite	
	Number of abortions (thousands)	Percentage of pregnancies terminated by abortion	Number of abortions (thousands)	Percentage of pregnancies terminated by abortion	Number of abortions (thousands)	Percentage of pregnancies terminated by abortion
1973	774.6	19.3	548.8	17.4	195.8	25.9
1974	898.6	22.0	629.3	19.6	269.3	31.6
1975	1,034.2	24.9	701.2	21.5	333.0	35.9
1976	1,179.3	26.5	784.9	23.0	394.4	38.9
1977	1,316.7	28.6	888.8	25.0	427.9	40.4
1978	1,409.6	29.2	969.4	26.1	440.2	39.6
1979	1,497.7	29.6	1,062.4	27.1	435.3	38.2
1980	1,553.9	30.0	1,093.6	27.4	460.3	39.2
1981	1,577.3	30.0	1,107.8	27.4	469.6	39.2
1982	1,573.9	30.0	1,095.3	27.1	478.7	39.2
1983	1,575.0	30.4	1,084.4	27.4	490.6	40.1
1984	1,577.2	29.7	—	—	—	—
1985	1,588.6	29.8	—	—	—	—

Note: "—" indicates not available. Although the total number of abortions performed in 1986 and 1987 is not yet known, an Alan Guttmacher Institute survey of 9,480 women who obtained abortions in 1987 at 103 clinics, hospitals, and doctors' offices in all parts of the country revealed that whites, who composed 83 percent of all women aged 15 to 44, made up 69 percent of all abortion patients. For nonwhites, corresponding percentages were 17 and 31. Stanley K. Henshaw and Jane Silverman, "The Characteristics and Prior Contraceptive Use of U.S. Abortion Patients," *Family Planning Perpectives*, 20(4) (1988): 158, 162.

Sources: 1973-1981: Stanley K. Henshaw and Ellen Blaine, *Abortion Services in the United States, Each State, and Metropolitan Area, 1981-1982* (New York: Alan Guttmacher Institute, 1985), 64; 1982-1983: Stanley K. Henshaw, "Characteristics of U.S. Women Having Abortions, 1982-1983," *Family Planning Perspectives*, 19(1) (1987): 6-7; 1984-1985: Stanley K. Henshaw, Jacqueline Darroch Forrest, and Jennifer Van Vort, "Abortion Services in the United States, 1984 and 1985," *Family Planning Perspectives*, 19(2) (1987): 64 (reprinted with permission).

Table 1-13 Public Opinion on Abortion, 1962-1988 (percent)

	Abortion should be legal under these circumstances						
Year	Mother's health	Rape	Birth defect	Low income	Single mother	As form of birth control	Any reason
1962	77	—	55	15	—	—	—
1965	70	56	55	21	17	15	—
1969	80	—	63	23	—	—	—
1972	83	75	75	46	41	38	—
1973	91	81	82	52	47	46	—
1974	90	83	83	52	48	45	—
1975	88	80	80	51	46	44	—
1976	89	81	82	51	48	45	—
1977	89	81	83	52	48	45	37
1978	88	81	80	46	40	39	32
1980	88	80	80	50	46	45	39
1982	90	83	81	50	47	46	39
1983	87	80	76	42	38	38	33
1984	88	77	78	45	43	41	37
1985	87	78	76	42	40	39	36
1987	86	78	77	44	40	40	38
1988	86	77	76	40	38	39	35

Note: "—" indicates not available. Question: "Please tell me whether or not you think it should be possible for a pregnant woman to obtain a legal abortion [in the order asked in the survey] if there is a strong chance of serious defect in the baby? If she is married and does not want any more children? If the woman's own health is seriously endangered by the pregnancy? If the family has a very low income and cannot afford any more children? If she became pregnant as a result of rape? If she is not married and does not want to marry the man? The woman wants it for any reason?"

Sources: 1962 and 1969: Gallup surveys; 1965: National Opinion Research Center surveys; 1972-1988: General Social Survey.

Table 1-14 Public Opinion on Gun Control, 1959-1988 (percent)

Date	Favor	Oppose	Don't know
July 1959	75	21	4
December 1963	79	17	4
January 1965	73	23	4
September 1965	70	25	5
August 1966	67	29	3
August 1967	73	24	4
October 1971	72	24	4
March 1972	70	27	3
May 1972	72	24	4
March 1973	74	25	2
March 1974	75	23	1
February 1975	71	28	1
March 1975	74	24	3
February 1976	73	24	4
March 1976	72	27	1
March 1977	72	27	2
March 1980	69	29	2
March 1982	72	26	2
March 1984	70	27	3
March 1985	72	27	1
March 1987	70	28	2
March 1988	74	24	3

Note: Question: "Would you favor or oppose a law which would require a person to obtain a police permit before he or she could buy a gun?"

Sources: 1959-1971: Gallup surveys; February 1975, February 1976: Survey Research Center, University of Michigan; others: General Social Survey.

Table 1-15 Voter Registration and Type of Political Primary

State	Type of primary[a]	Mail registration allowed for all voters	Minimum state resident requirement (days)	Closing date for registration before general election (days)	Automatic cancellation of registration for failure to vote after —
Alabama	C/P	no	1	10	[b]
Alaska	B	yes	30	30	2 years
Arizona	C	no	50	50	1 general election
Arkansas	C/P	no	[c]	20	4 years
California	C	yes	29	29	[b]
Colorado	C	no	32	25	2 general elections
Connecticut	C/N	yes	[c]	21	[b]
Delaware	C	yes	[c]	Third Saturday in October	2 general elections
District of Columbia	C	yes	[c]	30	4 years
Florida	C	no	[c]	30	2 years
Georgia	C/P	no	30	30	3 years
Hawaii	O	yes	[c]	30	2 years
Idaho	O	no	30	17/10[d]	4 years
Illinois	C/P	no	30	28	4 years
Indiana	C/P	no	30	29	2 years
Iowa	C/P	yes	[c]	10	4 years
Kansas	C/N	yes	1	20	2 general elections
Kentucky	C	yes	30	30	4 years
Louisiana	B	no	[c]	24	4 years
Maine	C/N	yes	[c]	Election Day	[b]
Maryland	C	yes	30	29	5 years
Massachusetts	C/N	no	[c]	28	1 year
Michigan	O	no	30	30	10 years

(Table continues)

35

Table 1-15 *(Continued)*

State	Type of primary[a]	Mail registration allowed for all voters	Minimum state resident requirement (days)	Closing date for registration before general election (days)	Automatic cancellation of registration for failure to vote after —
Minnesota	O	yes	20	Election Day	4 years
Mississippi	C/P	no	30	30	4 years [b]
Missouri	C/P	no	c	28	1 presidential election [b]
Montana	O	yes	30	30	
Nebraska	C	yes	c	Second Friday before Election Day	
Nevada	C	no	30	30	1 general election
New Hampshire	C	no	10	10	10 years
New Jersey	C/N	yes	30	29	4 years
New Mexico	C	no	c	28	1 general election
New York	C	yes	30	30	4 years
North Carolina	C	no [f]	30	21[e]	2 presidential elections
North Dakota	O		30	[f]	[f]
Ohio	C/P	yes	30	30	4 years
Oklahoma	C/N	no	c	10	8 years
Oregon	C	yes	20	21	2 years
Pennsylvania	C	yes	30	30	2 years
Rhode Island	C/N	no	30	30	5 years
South Carolina	C/P	yes	c	30	2 general elections
South Dakota	C	yes	15	15	4 years
Tennessee	C/P	yes	20	29	4 years [b]
Texas	C/P	yes	30	30	
Utah	O	yes	30	5	4 years
Vermont	O	no	c	17	4 years

Virginia	C/P	no	c	31	4 years
Washington	B	no	30	30	2 years
West Virginia	C	yes	30	30	2 general elections
Wisconsin	O	yes	10	Election Day	2 general elections
Wyoming	C/P	no	c	30	1 general election

[a] First letter indicates what ballot a voter receives at the polls: "C" (closed primary), voters receive only the ballot of their party choice; "O" (open primary), voters receive ballots of all parties and select the party of their choice in the voting booth; "B" (blanket primary), voters can choose among the candidates from all parties. The second letter indicates when voters select their party affiliation for primary voting: no indication means voters must declare or change their affiliation prior to election day; "P" means voters select party on election day; "N" means new or unaffiliated voters may declare party at the polls.

[b] No entry under cancellation column indicates no automatic purging of registration lists. See sources for further details.

[c] No residence requirement.

[d] With precinct registrar, seventeen days before the general election; with county clerk, ten days.

[e] Business days.

[f] No voter registration.

Sources: Vote! The First Steps (Washington, D.C.: League of Women Voters Education Fund, 1988); type of primary and residence requirements: *Book of the States, 1988-1989*, 186-187, 211.

Table 1-16 Legislative Reapportionment Deviations from Equality in Size of Congressional and State Legislative Districts, 1960s and 1980s (percent)

	Congressional districts			State legislative districts					
	1960s		1980s	Senate			House		
				1960s		1980s	1960s		1980s
State	Positive	Negative	total	Positive	Negative	total	Positive	Negative	total
Alabama	21.4	17.2	2.45	582	83.4	8.50	239	78.7	9.80
Alaska	AL	AL	AL	408	59.3	9.77	36	39.6	9.99
Arizona	52.9	54.3	0.08	613	91.7	8.40	87	64.4	8.40
Arkansas	28.8	25.4	0.73	59	29.4	9.15	78	72.9	9.15
California[a]	424.4	27.0	0.08	1,432	96.4	4.60	55	63.9	3.60
Colorado	49.1	55.4	0.002	51	66.6	3.98	37	70.6	4.94
Connecticut	63.2	24.5	0.46	138	62.6	3.92	840	97.8	8.35
Delaware	AL	AL	AL	167	84.0	9.78	357	87.3	25.10[b]
Florida	60.3	42.5	0.13	618	92.7	1.05	498	94.5	0.46
Georgia	108.9	31.0	—	664	82.1	9.99	864	90.9	9.94
Hawaii	AL	AL	<0.01	151	66.3	18.60	92	59.5	8.60
Idaho	22.9	22.9	0.04	517	94.0	5.35[c]	48	91.2	5.35[c]
Illinois	31.6	33.6	0.03	226	69.2	1.75	181	39.7	2.80
Indiana	64.6	31.4	2.96	76	54.9	4.04[c]	96	66.2	4.45[c]
Iowa	12.3	10.4	0.05	373	46.2	0.71	421	69.7	1.78
Kansas	23.9	14.3	0.34	529	70.5	6.50	293	88.8	9.90
Kentucky	40.8	19.2	1.39	165	43.6	7.52	123	62.9	13.47
Louisiana	31.6	35.2	0.42[c]	197	62.6	8.40	287	77.2	9.69

State								
Maine	4.3	4.3	0.001	60	54.0	10.18	105	62.8	10.94
Maryland	86.3	37.3	0.35	360	83.5	9.80	181	77.0	15.70
Massachusetts	11.6	12.3	1.09	55	33.6	—	130	83.9	—
Michigan	85.3	71.4	<0.01	234	72.1	16.24	90	52.4	16.34
Minnesota	13.2	12.0	0.01	95	48.0	4.61	281	67.6	3.93
Mississippi	39.9	32.3	—	184	67.9	4.61[c]	282	77.8	4.90[c]
Missouri	17.3	12.4	0.18	22	24.1	6.10	99	85.8	9.30
Montana	18.7	18.7	AL	556	92.6	—	74	87.6	—
Nebraska	12.8	14.0	0.23	57	42.5	9.43	d	d	d
Nevada	AL	AL	0.60	658	96.6	8.20	639	91.9	9.70
New Hampshire	9.3	9.3	0.24	64	37.3	7.60	284	99.7	13.74
New Jersey	44.8	36.9	0.69[a]	222	83.2	7.70	42	51.2	7.70
New Mexico	AL	AL	0.87[c]	783	93.7	9.83[c]	103	86.7	9.87[c]
New York	15.1	14.4	1.64	48	33.6	5.29	34	86.6	8.17
North Carolina	18.7	36.9	1.76[c]	199	50.6	9.46	116	88.7	9.66
North Dakota	5.4	5.4	AL	225	63.6	9.93	52	51.7	9.93
Ohio	79.5	41.6	0.68	52	20.8	8.88	37	85.6	9.67
Oklahoma	42.5	41.3	0.58	554	75.2	5.60	216	77.9	10.98
Oregon	18.2	40.0	0.15	25	49.3	3.73	34	35.7	5.34
Pennsylvania	31.9	27.7	0.24	145	77.1	1.93[c]	158	91.8	2.82[c]
Rhode Island	7.0	7.0	0.02	151	97.9	—	121	94.4	10.47[b]
South Carolina	33.9	31.4	0.28[a]	317	83.6	—	53	55.1	9.88
South Dakota	46.3	46.3	AL	122	48.9	12.90	84	61.2	12.40
Tennessee	58.2	43.6	2.40	120	63.2	10.22	121	90.8	1.66
Texas	118.5	48.5	0.28	303	52.8	1.82[a]	65	46.9	9.95[a]
Utah	28.6	28.6	0.43	81	73.9	7.80	133	91.4	5.41
Vermont	AL	AL	AL	43	77.3	16.18	1,991	97.4	19.33[c]

(Table continues)

39

Table 1-16 (Continued)

	Congressional districts			State legislative districts								
				Senate			House					
	1960s		1980s	1960s		1980s	1960s		1980s			
State	Positive	Negative	total	Positive	Negative	total	Positive	Negative	total			
Virginia	36.0	21.1	1.81	188	47.9	10.65	259	49.8	5.11[a]			
Washington	25.2	16.0	0.06	152	65.5	5.40	102	56.4	5.70			
West Virginia	13.4	18.6	0.50	336	36.4	8.96	112	76.9	9.94			
Wisconsin	40.1	34.2	0.14	73	37.7	1.23	121	50.7	1.74			
Wyoming	AL	AL	AL	147	74.4	63.70	70	50.6	89.40			

Note: "AL" indicates at large district (only one congressional representative). 1960s figures represent the maximum percentage deviation (positive and negative) from the average district population. 1980s figures are total deviations from the average (the sum of the largest deviations above and below the average); positive and negative deviations were not available. 1960s data are from 1962; 1980s data are as of April 1983. "—" indicates not available.
[a] New plan needed.
[b] Plan contains inadvertant errors which increase total deviation, but which were not yet corrected by technical amendments.
[c] Subject to court review.
[d] Nebraska's state legislature is unicameral.

Sources: 1960s: Robert G. Dixon, Jr., *Democratic Representation: Reapportionment in Law and Politics* (New York: Oxford University Press, 1968) Appendices A-B (copyright © 1968, Oxford University Press, Inc., reprinted by permission); 1980s: Bernard N. Grofman, "Criteria for Districting," *UCLA Law Review* 33 (1985): 175-176 (copyright © 1985, Regents of the University of California, all rights reserved).

Table 1-17 Jurisdictions Subject to Federal Preclearance of Election Law Changes and to Minority Language Provisions of the Voting Rights Act

Coverage limited to preclearance provisions	Coverage limited to minority language provisions	Combined coverage under preclearance and minority language provisions
Alabama	California (35)	Alaska
Connecticut (3)	Colorado (33)	Arizona
Georgia	Connecticut (1)	California (4)
Idaho (1)	Florida (2)	Colorado (1)
Louisiana	Hawaii (3)	Florida (5)
Massachusetts (9) [a]	Idaho (2)	Hawaii (1)
Mississippi	Kansas (3)	Louisiana (1)
New Hampshire (10) [a]	Maine (1)	Michigan (2)
North Carolina (37)	Michigan (7)	Mississippi (1)
South Carolina	Minnesota (2)	New York (3)
Virginia	Montana (7)	North Carolina (3)
Wyoming (1)	Nebraska (2)	South Dakota (2)
	Nevada (4)	Texas
	New Mexico (32)	Virginia (1)
	North Carolina (1)	
	North Dakota (5)	
	Oklahoma (25)	
	Oregon (2)	
	South Dakota (6)	
	Utah (4)	
	Washington (5)	
	Wisconsin (4) [a]	
	Wyoming (5)	

Note: "Preclearance" means that changes in election laws must be approved by the U.S. Justice Department. Numbers in parentheses indicate the number of counties in the state affected by the provisions. If there are no parentheses, coverage is statewide.
[a] Number of towns or townships.

Source: United States Commission on Civil Rights, *The Voting Rights Act: Unfulfilled Goals* (Washington, D.C.: U.S. Government Printing Office, 1981), 97-100.

Questions

1. Aside from Hawaii and Alaska, what were the last five states to be admitted to the United States—in order beginning with the last one admitted (Table 1-1)?

2. The U.S. Constitution has fewer than five thousand words. What is the median length of U.S. state constitutions (Table 1-2)? The U.S. Constitution has been amended twenty-six times. Of the states adopting constitutions before the twentieth century, what is the minimum number of amendments adopted by a state, and which state was that?

3. Of the sixteen amendments to the U.S. Constitution since passage of the Bill of Rights, ten have dealt with federal elections, terms of office of those elected, or succession if those elected are unable to serve. Which ten amendments are these (Table 1-3)? The main motivation of three of these ten was to ensure women and minorities the right to vote; Amendments Fifteen and Nineteen were obviously two of them. What was the other amendment that ensured racial minorities the right to vote and why was it necessary?

4. More than half of the rights incorporated to the states (Table 1-4) were done so under one chief justice (Table 9-5). Who was that?

5. Amendments proposed by Congress must be approved by three-fourths of the states. For the states to require Congress to call a constitutional convention, two-thirds of the states must approve. How close is the congressional pay amendment (proposed by Congress) to adoption? The balanced budget and abortion amendments are also considered "live" possibilities. How close are these state-initiated petitions to requiring Congress to call for a convention (Table 1-5)?

6. For which of the five proposed amendments shown in Table 1-6 has public opinion been very closely divided, with a plurality sometimes on one side and sometimes on the other? For the remaining four issues, has a majority of those with opinions favored or opposed the sense of the proposed amendment? (A prayer amendment, which some have proposed, would permit some kinds of prayers in public schools.)

7. How many states have no provisions at all for initiatives, referenda, or recall (Table 1-7)? How many have no such provisions and
   in addition have no limit on the number of consecutive terms a
   governor can serve (Tables 1-7 and 1-8)? Which states are they?

8. Since 1960, how many states have changed from two-year to
   four-year terms for governor (Table 1-8)? How many presently
   have two-year terms?

9. What important insight about public opinion surveys can one gain
   from the "forbid-allow" comparison in the top panel of Table 1-9?

10. The climate for dissenting opinions has changed dramatically since
    the early 1950s (Table 1-9). In what way? Suppose another question
    were asked: "Should (an atheist, Communist, racist) be allowed to
    teach in high school?" What would be the result? (Exact percent-
    ages are not needed, but how would the results compare with the
    percentages in Table 1-9 and why?)

11. Including the states with a statute but no recent sentences, how
    many states have the death penalty (Table 1-10)? Which two states
    have more than two hundred inmates awaiting execution and have
    already executed ten or more people in the 1980s?

12. What has been the trend in public opinion about the death penalty
    since 1970 (Table 1-11)? Has the same trend characterized public
    opinion on gun control (Table 1-14)?

13. What proportion of pregnancies among whites ended in abortion
    in 1983 (Table 1-12)? Among nonwhites in the same year? What has
    happened to the rates since 1973?

14. In what period did public opinion on abortion change dramatically
    (Table 1-13)? What has happened to public opinion since 1980?

15. Note the results for surveys taken one month apart—in February
    and March of 1975 and again in February and March of 1976 (Table
    1-14). There are at least two possible explanations for differences in
    surveys conducted at different points in time. What are these
    explanations? Which do you think is the most likely to be correct
    and why?

16. Combining all types of open primaries (counting "blanket" primaries as open) and all types of closed primaries, are there more of the former or of the latter (Table 1-15)? If one wished to promote party loyalty (voters generally voting in the same party's primary from one election to the next), which type of primary would one favor most? Why?

17. Registration is required fifty days ahead of the general elections in Arizona, and residence requirements are fifty days in Arizona (Table 1-15). At the other extreme, some states have election day registration (North Dakota has no registration at all) or have no residency requirement. How might shorter residency requirements and easier registration requirements affect voter turnout in a state?

18. In the 1960s—prior to the Supreme Court's one person, one vote rulings, how many states had a total deviation (positive plus negative deviations) of greater than 50 percent for congressional districts (Table 1-16)? Of greater than 2 percent in the 1980s? Of greater than 100 percent in state senates in the 1960s? Of greater than 10 percent in the 1980s?

19. Based on the number of whole states that are under preclearance provisions, at which region was the Voting Rights Act originally aimed (Table 1-17)? Is there any region that is completely free of the preclearance requirement? Nearly free?

2

The Mass Media

The mass media thrive on numbers. Nearly every American adult has heard of audience ratings games—serious games with millions and millions of dollars and many individual careers at stake—played by television, newspapers, radio, and magazines. Will the top-ranked television show remain first in the ratings, and how much will it help the show that follows it? Can a "national newspaper," such as *USA Today*, be profitable? Will a radio station increase its audience ratings—and what kind of audience will it attract—by playing more hard rock? How many extra copies and how much more advertising will a weekly news magazine sell with excerpts of soon-to-be-published political memoirs—and how much can the publisher afford to pay for those excerpts? So much money is at stake that media organizations annually spend millions of dollars to find the answers to such questions.

Politics, as it relates to the media, also involves numbers. Some questions simply involve market share and audience, much like the questions noted above: How many and what kinds of individuals pay attention to political news stories, candidate advertisements, campaign debates, and so on? Of course, these matters, while very important, are relatively straightforward. More complicated and controversial are other matters that involve numbers. Some critics charge, for example, that television emphasizes only the "horse race" aspect of political campaigns (who is ahead and by how much) to the exclusion of issues (Table 2-6) and that both print and electronic media give too much emphasis to the very early presidential primaries and caucuses (Table 2-5).

Despite these concerns about numbers as they apply to politics and the media, data are not as publicly available as one might think or hope. General information on how many people watch, read, and listen to the media is readily obtainable (Tables 2-1 through 2-3), but specific information about political material is not. Some material is proprietary—for example, a candidate's private surveys—and therefore mostly unavailable to researchers or to students. (One interesting exception is Table 2-11.) But there are other reasons for the unavailability. One is that television is relatively new (serious coverage of presidential campaigns began only in 1952, and extended coverage only in the 1960s) and is still changing (televised House proceedings began in 1979 and Senate proceedings in 1986). This means that researchers have not yet settled on exactly what data are most relevant and therefore most in need of continued collection. This is especially true of data that go beyond sheer numbers of viewers. Note, for example, that some interesting information about television coverage has been tabulated for only a single election cycle (Tables 2-6 through 2-10).

Fortunately, data collection and publication have expanded and improved, and researchers are beginning to see longer time series of significant information about politics and the media (for example, Tables 2-4 and 2-12 through 2-14 and Figure 2-2). Moreover, the media themselves are increasingly well preserved. Magazines are saved and are relatively well indexed. Major newspapers are widely available and well indexed, and small newspapers—though often kept only locally— combine to give widespread coverage of politics as practiced and perceived throughout the country. CBS News has published transcripts and indexes of its news programs since 1975 to facilitate research. Network television news programs since 1968 have been stored at Vanderbilt University; the archives are indexed and available to researchers. These efforts at preservation mean that studies can be made of the past as well as of contemporary events. Indeed, some of the most interesting studies of politics and the media are yet to come because they will be able to cover long expanses of time.

As in all areas of research, data about the media are rarely self-interpreting. One specific problem here is that the media both shape the news and reflect it. The shift in emphasis from parties to candidates (reflected in Tables 4-7 and 4-8, for instance) is a case in point. To some degree this shift simply reflects the weakening hold of political parties over American voters, a process that began as long ago as the turn of the century, that is, well before the advent of television. On the other hand, the power of television to bring individual candidates directly into one's living room has accelerated the declining influence of party organizations in particular and of party affiliation more generally.

Problems of interpretation—especially whether the media cause or simply reflect events—thus make inferences about media influence difficult. The usual response to such problems of inference is to bring additional data to bear on the subject. With more and more data now becoming available, researchers can safely anticipate better answers to questions about media audiences, coverage, emphasis, and influence as they relate to the political process.

Table 2-1 Growth and Reach of Selected Media, 1950-1989

	Percentage of households with					Average TV viewing per day (hours)[e]	Daily newspaper circulation[f]	
Year	Telephone service[a]	Radio sets[b]	Television sets[c]	Cable TV[d]	VCRs[d]		Number (millions)	Per capita
1950	—	92.6	9	—	—	4.6	53.8	.353
1960	78.5	96.3	87	—	—	5.1	58.9	.326
1970	87.0	98.6	95	—	—	5.9	62.1	.303
1975	—	98.6	97	—	—	6.1	60.7	.281
1980	93.0	99.0	98	19.8	1.1	6.6	62.2	.273
1981	—	99.0	98	25.3	1.8	6.8	61.4	.267
1982	—	99.0	98	29.0	3.1	6.8	62.5	.269
1983	—	99.0	98	37.2	5.5	7.0	62.6	.267
1984	91.8	99.0	98	41.2	10.6	7.1	63.3	.267
1985	91.8	99.0	98	44.6	20.8	7.1	62.8	.262
1986	92.2	99.0	98	46.8	36.0	7.1	62.5	.259
1987	92.5	99.0	98	48.7	48.7	7.0	62.8	.259
1988	92.9	99.0	98	51.1	58.1	7.3	—	—
1989	—	—	98	54.8	64.6	—	—	—

Note: "—" indicates not available.
[a] For occupied housing units. 1950 through 1980, as of April 1; thereafter, as of March.
[b] As of December 31.
[c] 1970-1975, as of September of prior year; all other years as of January of year shown.
[d] As of February. VCR figures exclude Alaska and Hawaii.
[e] Calendar year data.
[f] As of September 30, except 1950 and 1960 as of October 1.

Sources: Telephone service and VCR (1980-1983): U.S. Bureau of the Census, *Statistical Abstract of the U.S., 1989* (Washington, D.C.: U.S. Government Printing Office, 1989), 544; radios: *Radio Facts* (New York: Radio Advertising Bureau); television, 1950-1965: National Broadcasting Company; television, 1970-1989, cable, VCR (1984-1989): *Nielsen Report on Television* and *Nielsen Station Index Diary Projected In-tab Households* (Northbrook, Ill.: A. C. Nielsen) and Nielsen Media Research; newspapers: *Editor & Publisher International Yearbook* (New York: Editor & Publisher).

Table 2-2 Use of Television, Radio, and Newspapers, 1988

| | Total population (thousands) | Television watchers | | | | | | Radio listeners | | Newspaper readers | |
| | | Prime[a] | | Cable | Pay | Early[b] news | Late[c] news | Week-day | Week-end | Daily | Sunday |
		Sports	Documentary/information								
Age											
18-24	27,102	31.3%	14.9%	47.9%	31.1%	10.5%	3.0%	88.7%	79.9%	48.4%	55.3%
25-34	42,405	33.4	18.2	50.2	31.9	11.8	3.0	87.3	72.9	53.8	61.3
35-44	32,452	33.4	20.7	53.3	35.1	13.3	4.5	85.8	65.2	62.0	65.5
45-54	22,858	29.7	25.7	49.2	31.0	17.0	5.7	81.0	63.0	65.6	68.2
55-64	22,564	28.4	28.5	49.6	22.7	19.3	5.7	70.1	59.5	67.6	67.7
65 and older	27,519	25.5	30.6	39.7	9.4	17.7	3.7	58.6	50.9	65.4	61.7
Sex											
Male	83,367	39.3	22.4	50.8	29.6	14.6	4.0	82.0	67.0	61.5	63.7
Female	91,533	22.8	22.4	46.5	25.6	14.3	4.2	77.6	65.2	57.9	62.2
Race/ethnicity											
White	151,131	31.8	22.7	51.3	28.8	14.7	3.8	80.1	65.1	61.3	64.5
Black	19,269	23.7	21.1	30.3	19.0	14.0	6.4	76.5	72.3	51.5	55.8
Spanish-speaking	8,000	27.3	19.7	41.5	26.9	10.0	4.7	80.7	72.2	50.5	51.3
Other	4,490	24.5	18.5	34.4	22.2	9.6	4.3	80.0	71.0	39.8	39.5
Education											
College graduate	30,471	37.7	23.9	55.1	30.5	15.2	4.0	85.1	63.5	71.6	77.0
Attended college	31,585	35.7	23.3	56.9	33.3	14.1	3.9	85.2	69.7	63.0	70.9
High school graduate	68,438	29.8	21.5	48.0	29.2	14.2	4.4	81.5	67.8	59.4	63.6
Not high school graduate	44,406	23.7	22.1	39.0	18.8	14.6	3.7	69.3	62.6	49.4	46.6

(Table continues)

Table 2-2 (Continued)

	Total population (thousands)	Television watchers Prime[a] Sports	Prime[a] Documentary/ information	Cable	Pay	Early[b] news	Late[c] news	Radio listeners Week-day	Week-end	Newspaper readers Daily	Sunday
Employment											
Full-time	98,617	33.7%	20.7%	51.8%	33.5%	13.5%	3.8%	86.3%	69.1%	60.9%	65.7%
Part-time	11,089	27.9	20.9	55.4	29.1	11.8	3.7	83.6	70.6	62.1	68.0
Not employed	65,194	26.6	25.3	42.5	18.2	16.4	4.6	69.1	60.7	57.3	57.8
Income											
Under $10,000	18,647	19.0	20.3	30.8	10.5	12.5	3.5	63.4	58.7	43.5	40.6
$10,000-19,999	31,056	25.6	23.4	40.1	18.4	13.9	3.8	73.4	63.8	50.9	52.4
$20,000-29,999	33,219	30.8	20.8	46.7	25.0	15.5	4.2	79.8	69.2	58.3	61.7
$30,000-34,999	16,195	31.0	22.7	53.4	27.7	13.8	4.9	82.4	67.8	63.4	68.0
$35,000-39,999	14,891	35.9	20.9	53.7	34.7	15.5	4.1	82.8	65.0	63.7	67.2
$40,000-49,999	24,289	35.2	23.7	53.7	32.1	15.4	4.1	84.3	66.0	63.2	71.2
$50,000-59,999	15,122	36.5	22.7	58.4	39.1	14.1	4.8	86.9	68.5	65.2	70.5
$60,000 or more	21,481	35.0	24.5	59.3	41.0	14.3	3.4	88.2	68.7	74.6	78.0
Total	174,900	30.7	22.4	48.6	27.5	14.5	4.1	79.7	66.1	59.6	62.9

Note: Television: average percentage viewing the program type within the most recent frequency period (based on interviews in March and August 1987). Cable and pay TV: the percentage of people living in households that have cable TV and pay TV, respectively. Radio: the percentage of people listening to the radio at any time on a weekday or weekend. Newspapers: read one or more daily newspapers, one or more Sunday newspapers. Based on sample and subject to sampling error; see sources.

[a] Sports includes ABC Monday Night Baseball and Football; Documentary/information includes "60 Minutes" and "20/20."

[b] Early evening network news, weekdays.

[c] Includes "ABC News Nightline" and "Nightwatch," weekdays.

Sources: Multimedia Audiences Report (New York: Mediamark Research, Inc., Spring 1988), 1-47; *Television Audiences Report* (New York: Mediamark Research, Inc., Spring 1988), 1-51.

Table 2-3 Newspaper Circulation, 1850-1987

	Daily papers		
Year	Number[a]	Circulation (thousands)[b]	Circulation as a percentage of population
1850	254[c]	758[c]	3.3
1860	387[c]	1,478[c]	4.7
1870	574[c]	2,602[c]	6.5
1880	971[c]	3,566[c]	7.1
1890	1,610[c]	8,387[c]	13.3
1900	2,226[c]	15,102[c]	19.8
1904	2,452	19,633	23.4
1909	2,600	24,212	26.2
1914	2,580	28,777	28.6
1919	2,441	33,029	31.0
1921	2,334	33,742	31.7
1923	2,271	35,471	30.6
1925	2,116	37,407	32.3
1927	2,091	41,368	35.7
1929	2,086	42,015	34.1
1931	2,044	41,294	33.6
1933	1,903	37,630	29.6
1935	2,037	40,871	32.1
1937	2,065	43,345	34.1
1939	2,040	42,966	32.4
1947	1,854	53,287	37.0
1950	1,772	53,800	35.3
1954	1,820	56,410	34.6
1958	1,778	58,713	33.6
1960	1,763	58,900	32.6
1963	1,766	63,831	33.7
1965	1,751	60,400	31.1
1967	—	66,527	33.5
1970	1,748	62,100	30.3
1975	1,756	60,700	28.1
1978	1,756	62,000	27.9
1979	1,763	62,200	27.6
1980	1,745	62,200	27.3
1981	1,730	61,400	26.7
1982	1,711	62,500	26.9
1983	1,701	62,600	26.7
1984	1,688	63,300	26.7
1985	1,676	62,800	26.2
1986	1,657	62,500	25.9
1987	1,645	62,826	25.9

Note: "—" indicates not available.

[a] Figures since 1970 are for February of the following year.

[b] As of September 30.

[c] Includes a small number of periodicals.

Sources: Daily papers, 1850-1967: U.S. Bureau of the Census, *Historical Statistics of the U.S.* (Washington, D.C.: U.S. Government Printing Office, 1975), 810; 1970-1987: *Editor & Publisher International Yearbook*; population: *Statistical Abstract of the U.S., 1977,* 5, *1988,* 7.

Figure 2-1 Growth of Washington Press Corps, 1864-1987

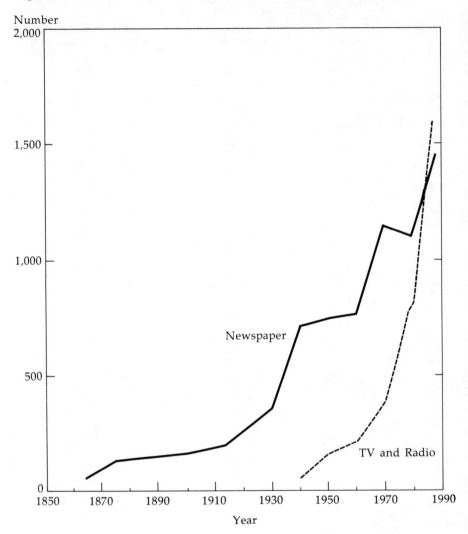

Sources: Samuel Kernell, *Going Public: New Strategies of Presidential Leadership* (Washington, D.C.: CQ Press, 1986), 57; updated by the editors from successive volumes of U.S. Congress, Joint Committee on Printing, *Official Congressional Directory* (Washington, D.C.: U.S. Government Printing Office).

Table 2-4 Presidential News Conferences with White House Correspondents, 1929-1989

President	Average number of press conferences per month	Total press conferences
Hoover (1929-1933)	5.6	268
Roosevelt (1933-1945)	6.9	998
Truman (1945-1953)	3.4	334
Eisenhower (1953-1961)	2.0	193
Kennedy (1961-1963)	1.9	64
Johnson (1963-1969)	2.2	135
Nixon (1969-1974)	0.5	37
Ford (1974-1977)	1.3	39
Carter (1977-1981)	1.2	59
Reagan (1981-1988)	0.5	47
Bush (1989)[a]	1.9	8

[a] As of May 31.

Sources: Kernell, *Going Public*, 69; *National Journal* (May 2, 1987), 1068, updated by the editors from *Congressional Quarterly Weekly Report*.

Table 2-5 Media Coverage of Presidential Nomination and General Election Contests by State, 1980-1988 Elections

State	1980 presidential nomination — Percent of total news coverage		1984 presidential nomination		1988 presidential nomination			1988 General election	
	CBS	UPI	Percent of total news coverage	Percent of total TV news	Percent of total TV news	Percent of total convention delegates — Democrats	Republicans	Percent of total TV news	Percent of electoral vote
Alabama	1	0	3	0	0	2	2	0	2
Alaska	0	0	0	0	0	0	1	0	1
Arizona	0	1	1	0	0	1	1	1	1
Arkansas	0	0	0	0	0	1	1	1	1
California	6	4	7	3	3	9	8	20	9
Colorado	0	0	0	1	1	1	2	1	1
Connecticut	2	2	2	2	2	2	2	1	1
District of Columbia	1	2	0	1	1	1	1	1	1
Delaware	0	0	0	0	0	0	1	0	1
Florida	3	2	1	2	2	4	4	2	4
Georgia	0	0	4	1	1	2	2	0	2
Hawaii	0	0	0	0	0	1	1	0	1
Idaho	0	0	0	0	0	1	1	0	1
Illinois	10	7	4	5	5	5	4	7	4
Indiana	1	1	2	1	1	2	2	0	2
Iowa	14	13	13	23	23	1	2	0	1
Kansas	0	1	0	0	0	1	1	0	1
Kentucky	0	1	0	1	1	2	2	1	2
Louisiana	0	0	1	0	0	2	2	0	2
Maine	4	3	2	1	1	1	1	0	1
Maryland	0	2	1	0	0	2	2	0	2
Massachusetts	7	3	3	0	0	3	2	2	2
Michigan	1	7	1	5	5	4	3	6	4

State								
Minnesota	1	0	0	3	2	1	1	2
Mississippi	0	0	0	0	1	1	0	1
Missouri	0	0	1	0	2	2	2	2
Montana	0	1	0	0	1	1	0	1
Nebraska	0	1	1	0	1	1	0	1
Nevada	0	0	0	0	1	1	0	1
New Hampshire	14	15	19	17	3	3	5	1
New Jersey	1	0	5	1	1	1	1	3
New Mexico	0	0	1	0	0	0	4	1
New York	7	6	11	7	7	6	1	7
North Carolina	0	1	1	1	2	2	0	2
North Dakota	0	0	0	0	1	1	0	1
Ohio	4	2	2	2	4	4	9	4
Oklahoma	0	1	0	0	1	2	0	1
Oregon	1	1	0	0	1	1	1	1
Pennsylvania	9	7	6	4	5	4	5	5
Puerto Rico	1	2	0	0	1	1	0	0
Rhode Island	0	0	0	0	1	1	0	1
South Carolina	2	3	0	3	0	2	1	1
South Dakota	0	0	1	3	2	1	0	2
Tennessee	0	0	4	0	5	2	2	5
Texas	2	2	0	2	1	5	20	1
Utah	0	0	2	0	0	1	0	1
Vermont	1	1	1	1	2	1	1	2
Virginia	0	0	1	0	2	2	0	2
Washington	0	0	1	0	1	2	2	1
West Virginia	0	0	1	0	2	1	0	2
Wisconsin	6	5	1	4	0	2	1	1
Wyoming	0	0	1	1	0	1	0	1

(Notes follow)

Table 2-5 *(Continued)*

Note: "—" indicates not available. Media coverage in a given state is the proportion of seconds of TV coverage or of column inches of print coverage of primary, caucus, or general election contests that mention the state. For 1984, media coverage of multistate stories is calculated by proportionately allocating coverage. For 1988, media coverage of the nomination tabulates state contests mentioned—one story may mention several state contests. Media coverage of the general election includes only those stories discussing the presidential contest in a state. Delegate shares by state for 1980 and 1984 are similar to those shown for 1988.

Sources: 1980 news coverage: Michael J. Robinson and Margaret A. Sheehan, *Over the Wire and on TV: CBS and UPI in Campaign 1980* (New York: Russell Sage Foundation, 1983), 176, 177 (copyright © Russell Sage Foundation, used with permission); percentages calculated by the editors; 1984 news coverage: William C. Adams, personal communication, content analysis of *New York Times* and of ABC, CBS, and NBC evening news summarized in *Television News Index and Abstracts* (Nashville, Tenn.: Vanderbilt Television News Archives, Vanderbilt University); 1988 delegates: *Congressional Quarterly Weekly Report* (1988), 1871-1892, 2155-2174; 1988 news coverage: Center for Media and Public Affairs content analysis of the ABC, CBS, and NBC evening news from February 8, 1987, through November 7, 1988. For a discussion of data on television news coverage of the 1988 nominations, see S. Robert Lichter, Daniel Amundson, and Richard Noyes, *The Video Campaign: Network Coverage of the 1988 Primaries* (Washington, D.C.: American Enterprise Institute for Public Policy Research and Center for Media and Public Affairs, 1988). For a discussion of data on news coverage of the 1984 nominations, see William C. Adams, "As New Hampshire Goes . . ." in *Media and Momentum: The New Hampshire Primary and Nomination Politics*, Gary R. Orren and Nelson W. Polsby, eds. (Chatham, N.J.: Chatham House, 1987), 42-59.

Table 2-6 Focus of Television News Coverage, 1988 Presidential
Election

Period	Horse race (percent)	Campaign issues (percent)	Policy issues (percent)	Number of stories
Primary				
1987 (2/8-12/31)	33	48	19	258
Iowa (1/1-2/8)	39	38	22	238
New Hampshire (2/9-2/16)	70	22	7	108
Super Tuesday (2/17-3/8)	58	23	18	130
Midwest (3/9-4/5)	82	8	10	148
New York (4/6-4/18)	56	22	22	59
California (4/19-6/7)	41	15	43	123
Primary total	50	29	20	1,064
General election				
Pre-convention (6/8-7/21)	11	55	33	248
Conventions (7/22-8/18)	18	43	38	200
First debate (8/19-9/25)	11	51	38	296
Second debate (9/26-10/13)	18	45	37	184
Final 25 days (10/14-11/7)	33	35	33	309
General election total	19	46	36	1,237
Primary and general election total	33	38	29	2,301

Note: "Horse race" coverage focuses on the contest—who's ahead, who's behind; "campaign issues" concern candidate character; "policy issues" involve concerns such as those detailed in Table 2-7.

Source: Center for Media and Public Affairs content analysis of the ABC, CBS, and NBC evening news from February 8, 1987, through November 7, 1988.

Table 2-7 Television Coverage of Issues during the 1988 Presidential Campaign

Issue	1987	Iowa	New Hampshire	Super Tuesday	Midwest	New York	California	General election[a]					Primary total	General election total	Primary and general election total	Number of stories
								1	2	3	4	5				
	2%	1%	3%	5%	3%	8%	4%	5%	10%	12%	5%	8%	3%	8%	6%	
Defense spending	2	2	5	6	7	7	4	5	7	4	1	6	4	5	5	235
General foreign policy	2	2	5	6	7	1	4	1	4	2	1	0	8	2	4	168
Iran-Contra	9	17	5	4	7	1	9	2	3	1	1	1	5	2	3	154
Central America	4	4	5	4	0	0	1	2	3	2	1	2	2	2	2	114
Arms control	6	1	8	1	2	2	2	1	2	2	0	3	2	2	2	84
Soviet relations	1	1	0	2	2	4	1	3	1	0	0	0	2	1	1	76
Middle East	1	1	0	0	6	21	1	1	2	3	0	1	1	1	1	51
SDI	0	2	0	0	1	0	0	1	3	3	2	0	1	2	1	49
Panama	2	0	0	0	0	0	0	0	1	1	1	1	0	1	1	39
Terrorism	0	0	2	3	0	0	3	2	1	1	0	1	1	1	1	35
South Africa	1	0	1	0	1	0	4	2	1	0	0	0	1	1	1	27
Persian Gulf	0	0	0	1	0	2	0	2	1	0	0	1	0	1	1	24
Dealing with allies	1	0	1	0	0	0	0	0	0	0	0	0	0	0	0	5
Human rights	0	0	0	0	0	0	0	0	0	0	0	0	0	0	0	4
Foreign policy total	29	31	34	26	33	45	31	26	36	31	13	24	31	27	29	1,065
General economy	4	7	5	5	5	6	7	9	10	8	7	11	6	9	8	296
Taxes	7	7	15	9	3	4	4	10	6	4	7	6	7	6	6	240

																Total
Unemployment/jobs	3	4	2	5	15	7	8	5	5	8	4	5	6	6	6	212
Budget deficit	5	5	2	4	3	0	3	3	2	3	3	4	4	3	3	125
Trade	4	5	7	9	8	0	3	1	2	3	2	2	5	2	3	123
Social welfare	4	4	5	2	0	0	3	2	0	3	4	2	3	2	2	79
Agriculture	4	7	0	3	4	1	1	1	2	1	2	2	3	1	2	78
Health/medical	2	2	2	2	2	0	1	2	2	1	3	1	2	2	2	68
Other budget	1	1	2	2	0	1	3	2	1	3	1	2	1	2	2	57
Energy	1	2	9	2	0	0	2	1	1	1	1	0	2	1	1	47
Industrial policy	0	0	0	1	3	0	4	1	2	1	1	1	1	1	1	43
Interest rates	0	1	0	1	0	0	0	0	2	1	1	0	1	1	1	22
Inflation	0	0	0	0	1	0	0	1	0	1	2	0	0	1	1	19
Economic total	35	46	47	45	44	19	37	39	36	35	38	36	40	37	38	1,409
Crime	0	0	0	1	1	2	1	5	2	5	13	15	1	8	5	186
Drugs	3	1	1	2	7	8	11	5	3	6	5	5	5	5	5	182
Civil rights	3	2	2	4	4	12	6	8	2	4	2	2	4	4	4	142
General social	6	3	3	7	1	4	2	4	5	2	5	2	4	4	4	135
Education	5	4	4	5	3	1	4	3	2	4	6	2	4	3	3	128
Abortion	4	1	2	2	0	0	0	2	2	2	2	2	2	2	2	72
Homeless	0	3	2	2	1	2	1	2	0	1	3	2	1	1	1	48
Women's issues	2	0	2	1	0	0	0	1	2	0	0	1	1	1	1	36
AIDS	1	0	1	0	1	1	1	1	0	0	0	0	1	0	0	15
Social total	24	15	15	24	17	31	25	31	20	23	37	32	21	28	25	944
Government ethics	2	2	1	0	2	2	4	3	4	1	1	2	2	2	2	82
Environment	1	0	1	1	0	0	2	1	2	4	3	4	1	3	2	78

(Table continues)

Table 2-7 (Continued)

Issue	1987	Iowa	New Hampshire	Super Tuesday	Midwest	New York	California	General election[a] 1	2	3	4	5	Primary total	General election total	Primary and general election	Number of stories
General governance	4%	4%	2%	3%	3%	1%	0%	0%	0%	0%	0%	0%	3%	0%	1%	43
Supreme Court	3	0	0	0	0	1	0	0	0	3	2	1	1	1	1	42
Other issues	1	0	0	1	1	0	0	0	0	2	3	1	0	1	1	35
Government management	0	1	0	0	0	0	1	0	0	0	0	0	0	0	0	10
Transportation	1	1	1	1	0	1	0	0	0	0	0	0	1	0	0	8
Space	0	0	0	0	0	0	0	0	0	0	1	0	0	0	0	6
Role of government	0	0	0	0	0	0	0	1	0	0	0	0	0	0	0	5
Other total	12	8	5	5	6	6	7	4	8	11	12	9	8	9	8	309
Number of stories	327	276	9	185	153	85	304	491	450	512	296	520	1,459	2,269	3,728	3,728

Note: Issues were coded if the story mentioned that particular issue. More than one issue could be coded for each story. Table entries give each issue's times mentioned as a percentage of all issues mentioned within each time period.

[a] Time periods for the general election are as follows: 1: 6/8-7/21; 2: 7/22-8/18; 3: 8/19-9/25; 4: 9/26-10/13; 5: 10/14-11/7.

Source: Center for Media and Public Affairs content analysis of the ABC, CBS, and NBC evening news from February 8, 1987, through November 7, 1988.

Table 2-8 Television News Coverage of the Candidates and Parties, 1987-1988 (percent)

Candidate	1987	Iowa	New Hampshire	Super Tuesday	Mid-west	New York	Cali-fornia	Total primary	General election[a]					Total general election
									1	2	3	4	5	
Democrats														
Babbitt	12	13	8	5	1	0	0	7	—	—	—	—	—	—
Bentsen	0	0	0	0	0	0	0	0	10	20	13	27	26	18
Biden	9	1	0	0	0	0	0	3	—	—	—	—	—	—
Dukakis	11	15	21	20	26	31	50	22	45	67	83	70	69	65
Gephardt	12	21	24	23	14	0	1	14	—	—	—	—	—	—
Gore	9	6	10	20	14	33	2	12	—	—	—	—	—	—
Hart	22	17	6	4	2	0	0	10	—	—	—	—	—	—
Jackson	13	8	8	19	34	33	47	21	45	13	4	3	5	17
Simon	12	19	23	11	9	2	0	11	—	—	—	—	—	—
Republicans														
Bush	31	33	27	24	29	25	91	35	100	81	70	67	87	79
Dole	24	31	24	24	57	25	3	27	—	—	—	—	—	—
du Pont	7	5	4	5	0	0	0	4	—	—	—	—	—	—
Haig	11	5	6	1	0	13	0	5	—	—	—	—	—	—
Kemp	13	11	13	11	3	13	0	10	—	—	—	—	—	—
Quayle	0	0	0	0	0	0	0	0	0	19	30	33	13	21
Robertson	14	14	26	35	10	25	5	18	—	—	—	—	—	—
Party														
Democrat	65	42	42	46	66	91	81	58	82	35	38	51	50	52
Republican	35	58	58	54	34	9	19	42	18	65	62	49	50	48

Note: The number of times each candidate appeared or was cited as a source. Table entries give each candidate's times mentioned as a percentage of all candidate mentions within each party for each time period. Table entries for the parties indicate the coverage of each party's presidential contest as a percentage of all mentions of either party's contest in each time period.

[a] Time periods for the general election are as follows: 1: 6/8-7/21; 2: 7/22-8/18; 3: 8/19-9/25; 4: 9/26-10/13; 5: 10/14-11/7.

Source: Center for Media and Public Affairs content analysis of the ABC, CBS, and NBC evening news from February 8, 1987, through November 7, 1988.

61

Table 2-9 Horse Race Judgments of the Presidential Candidates in Television News Coverage, 1987-1988

Party/candidate	1987 (2/8-12/31)		Iowa (1/1-2/8)		New Hampshire (2/9-2/16)		Super Tuesday (2/17-3/8)		Midwest (3/9-4/5)		New York (4/6-4/18)		New York to California (4/19-6/7)	
Democrats														
Babbitt	33%	(12)	25%	(24)	8%	(13)	0%	(10)	—		—		—	
Biden	30	(23)	—		—		—		—		—		—	
Dukakis	83	(41)	91	(47)	99	(72)	95	(80)	77%	(158)	90%	(59)	96%	(156)
Gephardt	64	(36)	92	(71)	70	(40)	49	(39)	13	(61)	—		—	
Gore	65	(26)	45	(11)	43	(7)	64	(25)	37	(43)	30	(40)	8	(25)
Hart	41	(150)	38	(63)	17	(12)	20	(10)	0	(13)	—		—	
Jackson	87	(47)	41	(22)	62	(21)	87	(70)	86	(164)	52	(42)	32	(60)
Simon	74	(38)	85	(41)	53	(30)	13	(24)	60	(42)	—		—	
Republicans														
Bush	73	(113)	72	(97)	49	(121)	92	(123)	90	(104)	100	(6)	48	(75)
Dole	82	(56)	92	(74)	88	(75)	52	(62)	14	(104)	—		—	
du Pont	10	(10)	11	(9)	0	(9)	11	(9)	—		—		—	
Haig	6	(18)	13	(8)	0	(16)	—		—		—		—	
Kemp	35	(20)	61	(31)	32	(22)	17	(30)	0	(10)	—		—	
Robertson	84	(50)	83	(54)	60	(60)	39	(56)	15	(13)	0	(2)	0	(4)

Party/candidate	Pre-convention (6/8-7/15)	Democratic convention (7/16-7/31)	Interlude (8/1-8/12)	Republican convention (8/13-8/28)	First debate (8/29-9/25)	Second debate (9/26-10/13)	Final 25 days (10/14-11/7)
Democrats							
Dukakis	66 (87)	86 (78)	72 (25)	34 (29)	22 (76)	31 (70)	45 (254)
Jackson	37 (19)	89 (18)	—[a]	—[a]	—[a]	—[a]	—[a]
Republicans							
Bush	29 (73)	20 (46)	46 (50)	40 (77)	79 (43)	83 (69)	80 (199)

Note: "—" indicates candidate was no longer an active presidential contender. Table entries are percent positive of all clearly positive and negative judgments by news sources about the probability the candidate will become president. This excludes positive and negative assessments of the candidate in other contexts (see Table 2-10). Total number of judgments about whether the candidate will become president are given in parentheses.
[a] No assessments coded for Jackson after July 21, 1988.

Source: Center for Media and Public Affairs content analysis of the ABC, CBS, and NBC evening news from February 8, 1987, through November 7, 1988.

Table 2-10 Assessments of the Presidential Candidates in Television News Coverage, 1987-1988

Party/candidate	1987 (2/8-12/31)		Iowa (1/1-2/8)		New Hampshire (2/9-2/16)		Super Tuesday (2/17-3/8)		Midwest (3/9-4/5)		New York (4/6-4/18)		New York to California (4/19-6/7)	
Democrats														
Babbitt	84%	(19)	91%	(11)	100%	(1)	100%	(2)	—		—		—	
Biden	54	(61)	—		—		—		—		—		—	
Dukakis	64	(22)	53	(15)	45	(20)	42	(52)	63%	(40)	53%	(36)	61%	(64)
Gephardt	78	(23)	48	(48)	40	(25)	41	(49)	38	(16)	—		—	
Gore	75	(4)	33	(3)	100	(3)	50	(14)	42	(12)	55	(20)	100	(1)
Hart	38	(151)	34	(32)	0	(1)	0	(1)	0	(1)	—		—	
Jackson	84	(31)	86	(7)	100	(3)	73	(41)	79	(85)	60	(47)	69	(35)
Simon	92	(13)	31	(16)	39	(23)	0	(1)	100	(4)	—		—	
Republicans														
Bush	48	(89)	41	(98)	67	(64)	44	(55)	67	(15)	14	(7)	61	(51)
Dole	80	(35)	54	(61)	66	(38)	56	(27)	75	(20)	—		—	
du Pont	40	(10)	75	(4)	—		—		—		—		—	
Haig	85	(7)	60	(5)	33	(3)	—		—		—		—	
Kemp	79	(19)	46	(24)	50	(2)	40	(5)	—		—		—	
Robertson	59	(29)	82	(11)	65	(26)	33	(52)	0	(4)	—		—	

Party/candidate	Pre-convention (6/8–7/15)	Democratic convention (7/16–7/31)	Interlude (8/1–8/12)	Republican convention (8/13–8/28)	First debate (8/29–9/25)	Second debate (9/26–10/13)	Final 25 days (10/14–11/7)
Democrats							
Bentsen	82 (17)[a]	73 (11)	100 (5)	88 (25)	50 (2)	55 (22)	96 (25)
Dukakis	43 (104)	64 (91)	24 (63)	29 (51)	28 (144)	31 (107)	38 (288)
Jackson	90 (48)	86 (35)[b]	[b]	[b]	[b]	[b]	[b]
Republicans							
Bush	63 (43)	39 (67)	37 (68)	79 (103)	23 (144)	28 (109)	36 (267)
Quayle	—	—	—	70 (137)[c]	38 (29)	46 (72)	25 (28)

Note: "—" indicates candidate was no longer an active presidential contender. Table entries are percent positive of all clearly positive and negative assessments by news sources, excluding horse race judgments (see Table 2-9). Total number of assessments about the candidate are given in parentheses.
[a] Assessments between July 12 and July 14 only.
[b] No assessments coded for Jackson after July 21.
[c] Assessments between August 16 and August 28 only.

Source: Center for Media and Public Affairs content analysis of the ABC, CBS, and NBC evening news from February 8, 1987, through November 7, 1988.

Table 2-11 Effectiveness of Presidential Candidate Television Ads, 1988

| | September-October | | | | | | | |
	9-11	16-18	23-25	30-2	7-9	14-16	21-23	28-30
Likely voters who saw candidate's TV ads in past week (percent)								
Bush	61.8	69.4	75.8	77.2	82.3	82.9	83.5	88.8
Dukakis	62.8	72.3	74.8	78.9	83.4	83.3	84.9	89.9
Likely voters more interested in candidate after seeing ad (percent)								
Bush	8.6	9.9	11.0	10.1	12.8	15.1	14.7	12.0
Dukakis	11.5	9.5	12.0	12.9	10.5	10.1	12.1	14.8
Likely voters less interested in candidate after seeing ad (percent)								
Bush	9.0	9.1	9.5	13.0	12.9	10.7	11.0	15.6
Dukakis	7.3	7.5	8.4	8.4	13.0	14.3	14.3	13.2
Index of Effectiveness[a]								
Bush	−0.4	+0.8	+1.6	−2.9	−0.1	+4.4	+3.7	−3.6
Dukakis	+4.2	+2.0	+3.6	+4.5	−2.5	−4.0	−2.1	+1.6
Likely voters who currently intend to vote for candidate (percent)								
Bush	39.4	46.8	45.0	41.6	45.3	49.4	49.2	48.8
Dukakis	44.2	37.5	39.3	42.4	40.6	37.7	33.9	37.7
Undecided	16.3	15.7	15.7	15.9	14.2	12.9	16.8	13.4
Likely voters	830	831	808	830	818	820	807	833
Sample	1,022	1,022	1,045	1,017	1,023	1,042	1,025	1,030

Note: Likely voters are those who said yes to the question, "Do you intend to vote in the presidential election in November?"

[a] The index of effectiveness is a net score: the percentage of likely voters who are more interested in voting for a candidate after seeing the candidate's ads minus the percentage of likely voters who are less interested after seeing the ads. A score of +100 indicates that every respondent who intends to vote saw a candidate's ad and became more interested in voting for the candidate. A score of −100 indicates that every likely voter saw the ad and became less interested.

Sources: ADWEEK (September 26, 1988), 34; (October 3), 24; (October 10), 24; (October 17), 19; (October 24), 30; (October 31), 19; (November 7), 38; and unpublished data. Reprinted with permission of ADWEEK.

Table 2-12 Public Use of Media to Follow Presidential Campaigns, 1952-1988 (percent)

Media	1952	1956	1960	1964	1968	1972	1976		1980	1984	1988
Read newspaper articles about the election											
regularly			44	40	37	26	28	good many	27	24	—
often	39[a]	69[b]	12	14	12	14	17	several	29	34	—
from time to time			16	18	19	16	24	one or two	17	19	—
once in a great while	40[c]		7	6	7	4	10				
no	21	31	21	22	25	40	22	no	27	23	—
Attention paid to newspaper articles about the presidential campaign											
great deal										8	6
quite a bit										14	12
some										28	22
very little										20	9
none										31	52
Listen to speeches or discussions on radio											
good many	34[a]	45[b]	15	12	12	8	12		14	10	5
several			17	23	16	21	20		22	20	10
one or two	35[c]		10	12	12	13	16		15	16	17
no	30	55	58	52	59	59	52		50	55	69
Watched programs about the campaign on television											
good many	32[a]	74[b]	47	41	42	33	37		28	25	—
several			29	34	34	41	38		37	37	—
one or two	19[c]		11	13	13	16	15		22	24	—
no	49	26	13	11	11	9	10		13	14	—

(Table continues)

Table 2-12 *(Continued)*

Media	1952	1956	1960	1964	1968	1972	1976	1980	1984	1988
Attention paid to television news about the presidential campaign										
great deal									17	15
quite a bit									24	26
some									28	29
very little									11	13
none									20	17
Read about the campaign in magazines										
good many	15[a]		12	10	9	7	12	7	7	—
several		31[b]	15	16	12	15	24	19	16	—
one or two	26[c]		13	13	15	14	15	12	11	—
no	60	69	59	61	64	64	49	62	66	—
Attention paid to magazine articles about the presidential campaign										
great deal									3	3
quite a bit									4	6
some									7	11
very little									2	3
none									84	76

Note: "—" indicates question not asked.

[a] Quite a lot, pretty much.

[b] Yes.

[c] Not very much.

Source: Calculated by the editors from the National Election Studies codebooks and data sets (Ann Arbor, Mich.: Center for Political Studies, University of Michigan).

Table 2-13 Use and Trustworthiness of Media, 1959-1988 (percent)

	1959	1961	1963	1964	1967	1968	1971	1972	1974	1976	1978	1980	1982	1984	1986	1988
Source of most news[a]																
Television	51	52	55	58	64	59	60	64	65	64	67	64	64	64	66	65
Newspapers	57	57	53	56	55	49	48	50	47	49	49	44	44	40	36	42
Radio	34	34	29	26	28	25	23	21	21	19	20	18	18	14	14	14
Magazines	8	9	6	8	7	7	5	6	4	7	5	5	6	4	4	4
People	4	5	4	5	4	5	4	4	4	5	5	4	4	4	4	5
Most believable[b]																
Television	29	39	36	41	41	44	49	48	51	51	47	51	53	53	55	49
Newspapers	32	24	24	23	24	21	20	21	20	22	23	22	22	24	21	26
Radio	12	12	12	8	7	8	10	8	8	7	9	8	6	8	6	7
Magazines	10	10	10	10	8	11	9	10	8	9	9	9	8	7	7	5
Don't know/no answer	17	17	18	18	20	16	12	13	13	11	12	10	11	9	12	13

[a] Question: "First, I'd like to ask you where you usually get most of your news about what's going on in the world today—from the newspapers or radio or television or magazines or talking to people or where?" (more than one answer permitted).
[b] Question: "If you got conflicting or different reports of the same news story from radio, television, the magazines, and the newspapers, which of the four versions would you be most inclined to believe—the one on the radio or television or magazines or newspapers?" (only one answer permitted).

Source: Television Information Office, "America's Watching 30th Anniversary 1959-1989" (New York: Television Information Office, 1989), 27, 28.

Table 2-14 National Nominating Conventions: Television Coverage and Viewership, 1952-1988

Year/party	TV households viewing some of convention	Average hours viewed by household	Network hours telecast
1952			
Republicans	—	10.5	57.5
Democrats	—	13.1	61.1
1956			
Republicans	—	6.4	22.8
Democrats	—	8.4	37.6
1960			
Republicans	—	6.2	25.5
Democrats	—	8.3	29.3
1964			
Republicans	—	7.0	36.5
Democrats	—	6.4	23.5
1968			
Republicans	83.5%	6.5	34.0
Democrats	89.7	8.5	39.1
1972			
Republicans	81.1	3.5	19.8
Democrats	86.1	5.8	36.7
1976			
Republicans	87.9	6.3	29.5
Democrats	88.5	5.2	30.4
1980			
Republicans	77.4	3.8	22.7
Democrats	81.5	4.4	24.1
1984			
Republicans	69.8	1.9	11.9
Democrats	73.2	2.5	12.9
1988[a]			
Republicans	68.0	2.2	12.6
Democrats	70.3	2.3	12.8

Note: "—" indicates not available.
[a] Preliminary figures.

Sources: 1952-1964: *Network Television Audiences to Primaries, Conventions, Elections* (Northbrook, Ill.: A. C. Nielsen, 1976), 8, 9, 21; 1968-1988: Data supplied by A. C. Nielsen Co.

Table 2-15 Newspaper Endorsements of Presidential Candidates, 1932-1988

	Papers		Circulation	
	Number	Percentage	Number	Percentage
1932				
Hoover (R)	656	52	—	—
Roosevelt (D)	511	41	—	—
Uncommitted	94	7	—	—
1936				
Landon (R)	727	57	—	—
Roosevelt (D)	459	36	—	—
Uncommitted	87	7	—	—
1940				
Willkie (R)	813	64	—	—
Roosevelt (D)	289	23	—	—
Uncommitted	171	13	—	—
1944				
Dewey (R)	796	60	26,654,996	69
Roosevelt (D)	291	22	6,902,243	18
Uncommitted	237	18	5,356,807	14
1948				
Dewey (R)	771	65	35,152,807	79
Truman (D)	182	15	4,489,851	10
Thurmond	45	4	537,730	1
Wallace	3	0	60,233	0
Uncommitted	182	15	4,454,557	10
1952				
Eisenhower (R)	933	67	40,129,237	80
Stevenson (D)	202	15	5,466,781	11
Uncommitted	250	18	4,417,102	9
1956				
Eisenhower (R)	740	62	34,538,755	72
Stevenson (D)	189	15	6,122,491	13
Uncommitted	270	23	7,079,846	15
1960				
Nixon (R)	731	58	38,006,203	71
Kennedy (D)	208	16	8,448,677	16
Uncommitted	328	26	7,135,954	13
1964				
Goldwater (R)	359	35	8,977,214	21
Johnson (D)	440	42	26,997,400	62
Uncommitted	237	23	7,638,727	18

(Table continues)

Table 2-15 *(Continued)*

	Papers		Circulation	
	Number	Percentage	Number	Percentage
1968				
Nixon (R)	634	61	34,559,385	70
Humphrey (D)	146	14	9,572,948	19
Wallace	12	1	159,524	0
Uncommitted	250	24	5,201,845	11
1972				
Nixon (R)	753	71	30,560,535	77
McGovern (D)	56	5	3,044,534	8
Uncommitted	245	23	5,864,548	15
1976				
Ford (R)	411	62	20,951,798	62
Carter (D)	80	12	7,607,739	23
Uncommitted	168	26	5,074,069	15
1980				
Reagan (R)	443	42	17,561,333	49
Carter (D)	126	12	7,782,078	22
Anderson	40	4	1,614,740	4
Uncommitted	439	42	9,131,940	25
1984				
Reagan (R)	381	58	18,357,512	52
Mondale (D)	62	9	7,568,639	21
Uncommitted	216	33	9,611,058	27
1988				
Bush (R)	241	31	18,186,225	40
Dukakis (D)	103	13	11,644,600	25
Uncommitted	428	55	16,224,807	35

Note: "−" indicates not available.

Sources: Editor & Publisher (October 26, 1940), 7; (November 4, 1944), 9; (October 30, 1948), 11; (November 1, 1952), 9; (November 3, 1956), 11; (November 5, 1960), 10; (October 31, 1964), 10; (November 2, 1968), 9; (November 7, 1972), 9; (October 30, 1976), 5; (November 1, 1980), 10; (November 3, 1984), 9; (November 5, 1988), 9.

Figure 2-2 Newspaper Endorsements of Presidential Candidates, 1932-1988: Democratic, Republican, and Neutral

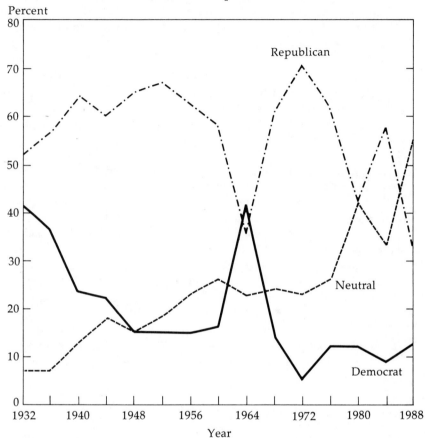

Sources: *Editor & Publisher* (October 26, 1940), 7; (November 4, 1944), 9; (October 30, 1948), 11; (November 1, 1952), 9; (November 3, 1956), 11; (November 5, 1960), 10; (October 31, 1964), 10; (November 2, 1968), 9; (November 7, 1972), 9; (October 30, 1976), 5; (November 1, 1980), 10; (November 3, 1984), 9; (November 5, 1988), 9.

Questions

1. What are the two biggest changes in media coverage in the 1980s (Table 2-1)? What implications do these developments have for political and news broadcasting?

2. If your target audience were young people, which particular media category would you use most (Table 2-2)? If your target were the middle-aged or elderly, what would your media strategy be? What if your purpose were to reach relatively well-educated and well-to-do people?

3. What explains the decline in newspaper circulation as a percentage of the population, which began in the late 1940s (Table 2-3)? (Hint: see Table 2-1.) In the twentieth century, circulation as a percentage of population rose considerably over what it had been in the nineteenth century. An obvious inference is that this made the electorate more informed about political matters. Yet some historians have argued that this was not the case. How might one support such an argument in the face of the figures in Table 2-3? (Hint: one clue—but only a very partial answer—is suggested in Figure 3-1.)

4. Why has the average number of press conferences declined since Franklin Roosevelt's time (Table 2-4)? (Hint: Figure 2-1 suggests one reason.) Why did Richard Nixon have especially few press conferences?

5. Why is there so much media coverage of the New Hampshire primary and the Iowa caucuses (Table 2-5)? Use Table 3-7 to determine whether states used caucuses or primaries in 1980 and 1984. (Separate out those few states in which one party used caucuses and the other a primary.) Based on percentage of news coverage in 1980 and 1984, did primary or caucus states receive more coverage? Answer both in terms of overall coverage in the primary versus caucus states and in terms of coverage per average state. There are at least two reasons for the difference. What are they?

6. It is frequently charged that the media today pay too much attention to the "horse race" aspects of political campaigns (who is ahead and who is behind) and too little attention to the issues. On the basis of Table 2-6, do you think this is true? Why or why not?

7. Given the large budget deficit, why do you think there was so little discussion of it during the general election campaign (Table 2-7)? Why was there so much discussion of crime in the last month of the campaign?

8. Did the candidates who received greater television news coverage (Table 2-8) typically fare well in the 1988 nomination contests? In what ways might more extensive news coverage help or hinder candidacies? Illustrate with examples from the 1988 contest (Tables 2-9 and 2-10 offer useful perspectives).

9. Do strongly positive assessments of a candidate in news coverage (Table 2-10) mean that the candidate's chances of winning the presidency are strong (Table 2-9)?

10. Considering the millions of dollars Bush and Dukakis spent on political advertising in 1988, do the numbers in the "index of effectiveness" row in Table 2-11 strike you as high, low, or unsurprising? Why?

11. In Tables 2-12 and 2-13 there are two almost contradictory trends with regard to the amount of television viewing. What are they?

12. Describe the trend in television viewership of the national nominating convention from 1952 to 1988 (Table 2-14). What are some of the factors that might account for this trend?

13. It is sometimes alleged that newspapers are more Republican than the general population. Based on newspaper endorsements (Table 2-15), presidential election outcomes (Table 3-13), and the population's party identification (Table 5-1), do you think that this allegation is valid? Explain your reasoning with numbers drawn from the three tables mentioned.

3

Elections and Campaigns

Campaigns and elections provide an abundance of numbers. Indeed, if asked for examples of political statistics, most people would think first of election results. But votes are only part of the numbers election campaigns generate: opinion surveys and exit polls, for example, offer a wealth of information about who the voters are and why they chose as they did; summary statistics show which party and which types of candidates won and lost; financial disclosure requirements furnish detailed information about campaign costs and contributions.

Not only are there a great many electoral statistics, but they extend back to the early years of the country. Consider the much-researched topic of partisan realignment. Long time series on voter turnout and the partisan breakdown of the vote have allowed researchers to comb the nation's past for realignments—fundamental shifts in support for parties and the coalitions supporting them. Election returns from localities dominated by different ethnic or economic groups also have been used to reveal the links between those groups and the parties. Thus, periods of realignment and the length of time between them— scholarly consensus holds that realignments occurred in the 1850s, 1890s, and between 1928 and 1932—are important for understanding our political history and the role of electoral statistics in uncovering that history. Realignment years are useful groupings for presenting data on partisan changes (Tables 3-14 and 3-15).

Available data also document more recent trends in campaigns and elections: the decline in presidential voter turnout after 1960 (Figure 3-1), the electoral advantages of incumbency (Table 3-17), the increasingly long quests for the presidential nominations (Figure 3-3), the greater emphasis on primaries (Table 3-7), the growing contributions from political action committees (Table 6-7), and the expense of political campaigns (Tables 7-7 and 8-5).

Added to the arsenal of statistics about elections in the past fifty years have been surveys of representative national, state, and local populations. These data have enlivened research on the identification and timing of electoral realignments. The partisan changes that have occurred since the mid-1960s are of particular interest. Most scholars see the period since the mid-1960s as one of "dealignment" rather than realignment—with voters more willing to vote for some nominees of both parties (Table 4-7) and with more frequent outcomes in which different parties carry the presidential and congressional vote in a district (Table 4-8). Public opinion surveys also allow researchers to move beyond reliance on the simple shape of overall election results. Extensive data on individual behavior and attitudes reveal patterns of voting turnout and support (Tables 3-1 and 3-11) and voters' opinions about the candidates, parties, and issues (for example, Tables 3-10 and 5-1) that are much more detailed than previously available.

Despite this volume of data there are some gaps: survey data is nonexistent before the mid-1930s, and reliable, consistent surveys date principally from the 1950s; until 1980, presidential primary surveys were limited; even official election returns below the state level are only now being made readily available (by the Inter-University Consortium for Political and Social Research); surveys emphasizing non-presidential voting are very limited prior to the mid-1970s; and campaign finance data are unavailable or uninformative in some states and systematically available for the federal level since the mid-1970s.

These are serious gaps, and they impose limits on what we know about campaigns, elections, and parties. The lack of survey data on earlier realignments, for example, is troublesome because it robs researchers of helpful historical comparisons. Nonetheless, in the area of campaigns and elections, more than anywhere, there is almost an embarrassment of riches.

Figure 3-1 Voter Turnout, Presidential and Midterm Elections,
1790-1988

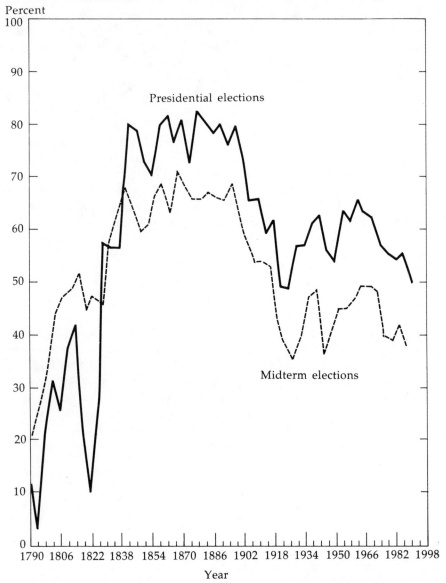

Percent

Year

Sources: 1790-1986: Walter Dean Burnham, "The Turnout Problem," in *Elections American Style,* ed. A. James Reichley (Washington, D.C.: Brookings, 1987), 113-114; 1988: calculated by the editors from *Congressional Quarterly Weekly Report* (1989), 139, and U.S. Bureau of the Census, Current Population Reports, "Projections of the Population of Voting Age," Series P-25, No. 1019 (Washington, D.C.: U.S. Government Printing Office, 1988), 11.

Figure 3-2 Voter Turnout, Presidential Elections, 1800-1988, South and Nonsouth

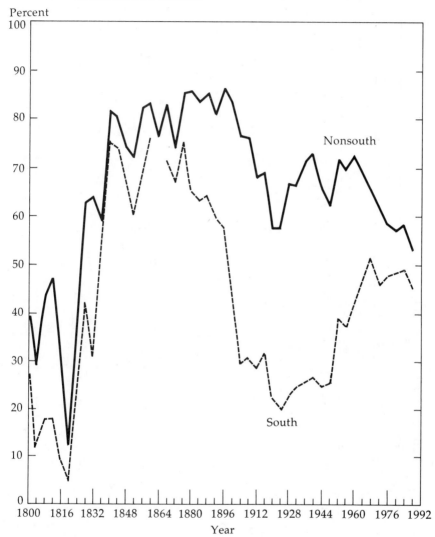

Sources: 1800-1984: Walter Dean Burnham, "The Turnout Problem," 113-114; 1988: calcu-lated by the editors from *Congressional Quarterly Weekly Report* (1989), 139, and U.S. Bureau of the Census, Current Population Reports, "Projections of the Population of Voting Age," Series P-25, No. 1019, 11.

Table 3-1 Citizens Registered and Voting, 1972-1988 (percent)

	Percentage reporting they registered									Percentage reporting they voted								
	Presidential election years					Congressional election years				Presidential election years					Congressional election years			
	1972	1976	1980	1984	1988	1974	1978	1982	1986	1972	1976	1980	1984	1988	1974	1978	1982	1986
Race/ethnicity																		
White	73	68	68	70	68	64	64	66	65	65	61	61	61	59	46	47	50	47
Black	66	59	60	66	65	55	57	59	64	52	49	51	56	52	34	37	43	43
Hispanic origin[a]	44	38	36	40	36	35	33	35	36	38	32	30	33	29	23	24	25	24
Sex																		
Male	73	67	67	67	65	63	63	64	63	64	60	59	59	56	46	47	49	46
Female	72	66	67	69	68	62	63	64	65	62	59	59	61	58	43	45	48	46
Region[b]																		
Northeast	—	66	65	67	65	62	62	63	62	—	60	59	60	57	49	48	50	44
Midwest	—	72	74	75	73	67	68	71	71	—	65	66	66	63	49	51	55	50
South	—	68	64	64	67	66	60	62	63	55	55	56	57	55	36	40	42	43
West	—	63	63	65	63	60	59	61	61	—	58	57	59	56	48	48	51	48
Age																		
18-20	58	47	45	47	45	36	35	35	35	48	38	36	37	33	21	20	20	19
21-24	60	55	53	54	51	45	45	48	47	51	46	43	44	38	26	26	28	24
25-34	68	62	62	63	58	55	56	57	56	60	55	55	55	48	37	38	40	35
35-44	75	70	71	71	69	67	67	68	68	66	63	64	64	61	49	50	52	49
45-64	80	76	76	77	76	74	74	76	75	71	69	69	70	68	57	59	62	59
65 and older	76	71	75	77	78	70	73	75	77	64	62	65	68	69	51	56	60	61

Employment																		
Employed	74	69	69	69	69	67	64	63	66	64	62	62	62	58	47	47	50	46
Unemployed	59	52	50	54	50	50	44	44	50	51	44	41	44	39	29	27	34	31
Not in labor force	70	65	66	68	66	67	61	63	64	65	57	57	59	57	43	46	49	48
Education																		
8 years or less	62	54	53	53	53	48	54	53	52	51	47	43	43	37	34	35	36	33
1-3 years high school	63	56	55	55	55	53	54	53	53	52	52	46	44	41	36	35	38	34
4 years high school	74	67	66	67	66	65	62	62	63	63	65	59	59	55	45	45	47	44
1-3 years college	82	75	74	76	74	74	67	69	70	70	75	67	68	65	50	52	53	50
4 or more years college	88	84	84	84	84	83	76	77	79	78	84	80	79	78	61	64	67	63
Total	72	67	67	68	67	67	62	62	64	64	63	59	60	57	45	46	49	46

Note: "—" indicates not available.

a Persons of Hispanic origin may be of any race.

b For composition of regions, see Appendix Table A-1.

Sources: U.S. Bureau of the Census, Current Population Reports, Series P-20, no. 435, *Voting and Registration in the Election of November 1988 (Advance Report)* (Washington, D.C.: U.S. Government Printing Office, 1989), 1-4; U.S. Bureau of the Census, *Statistical Abstract of the U.S., 1988* (Washington, D.C.: U.S. Government Printing Office, 1987), 249.

Table 3-2 Presidential General Election Returns by State, 1988

State	Electoral vote		Popular vote				Popular vote (percentage)	
	Republican	Democrat	Republican	Democrat	Other	Total	Republican	Democrat
Alabama	9		815,576	549,506	13,394	1,378,476	59.2	39.9
Alaska	3		118,817	72,105	8,186	199,108	59.7	36.2
Arizona	7		702,541	454,029	15,305	1,171,875	60.0	38.8
Arkansas	6		466,578	349,237	11,923	827,738	56.4	42.2
California	47		5,054,917	4,702,233	129,915	9,887,065	51.1	47.6
Colorado	8		728,177	621,453	22,763	1,372,393	53.1	45.3
Connecticut	8		750,241	676,584	16,569	1,443,394	52.0	46.9
Delaware	3		139,639	108,647	1,605	249,891	55.9	43.5
District of Columbia		3	27,590	159,407	5,880	192,877	14.3	82.6
Florida	21		2,616,597	1,655,851	26,701	4,299,149	60.9	38.5
Georgia	12		1,081,331	714,792	13,549	1,809,672	59.7	39.5
Hawaii		4	158,625	192,364	3,472	354,461	44.7	54.3
Idaho	4		253,881	147,272	7,815	408,968	62.1	36.0
Illinois	24		2,310,939	2,215,940	32,241	4,559,120	50.7	48.6
Indiana	12		1,297,763	860,643	10,215	2,168,621	59.8	39.7
Iowa		8	545,355	670,557	9,700	1,225,612	44.5	54.7
Kansas	7		554,049	422,636	16,339	993,024	55.8	42.5
Kentucky	9		734,281	580,368	7,868	1,322,517	55.5	43.9
Louisiana	10		883,702	717,460	27,040	1,628,202	54.3	44.1
Maine	4		307,131	243,569	4,335	555,035	55.3	43.9
Maryland	10		876,167	826,304	11,864	1,714,335	51.1	48.2
Massachusetts		13	1,194,635	1,401,415	36,751	2,632,801	45.4	53.2
Michigan	20		1,965,486	1,675,783	27,894	3,669,163	53.5	45.7
Minnesota		10	962,337	1,109,471	24,982	2,096,790	45.9	52.9
Mississippi	7		557,890	363,921	9,716	931,527	59.9	39.1
Missouri	11		1,084,953	1,001,619	6,656	2,093,228	51.8	47.9

State								
Montana	4		190,412	168,956	6,326	365,694	52.1	46.2
Nebraska	5		398,447	259,646	4,279	662,372	60.1	39.2
Nevada	4		206,040	132,738	11,289	350,067	58.9	37.9
New Hampshire	4		281,537	163,696	5,292	450,525	62.5	36.3
New Jersey	16		1,740,604	1,317,54	35,994	3,094,139	56.2	42.6
New Mexico	5		270,341	244,497	6,449	521,287	51.9	46.9
New York		36	3,081,871	3,347,882	55,930	6,485,683	47.5	51.6
North Carolina	13		1,237,258	890,167	6,945	2,134,370	58.0	41.7
North Dakota	3		166,559	127,739	2,963	297,261	56.0	43.0
Ohio	23		2,416,549	1,939,629	37,407	4,393,585	55.0	44.1
Oklahoma	8		678,367	483,423	9,246	1,171,036	57.9	41.3
Oregon		7	560,126	616,206	25,271	1,201,603	46.6	51.3
Pennsylvania	25		2,300,087	2,194,944	41,220	4,536,251	50.7	48.4
Rhode Island		4	177,761	225,123	1,685	404,569	43.9	55.7
South Carolina	8		606,443	370,554	9,012	986,009	61.5	37.6
South Dakota	3		165,415	145,560	2,016	312,991	52.9	46.5
Tennessee	11		947,233	679,794	9,223	1,636,250	57.9	41.5
Texas	29		3,036,829	2,352,748	37,833	5,427,410	56.0	43.3
Utah	5		428,442	207,352	11,222	647,016	66.2	32.0
Vermont	3		124,331	115,775	3,222	243,328	51.1	47.6
Virginia	12		1,309,162	859,799	22,648	2,191,609	59.7	39.2
Washington		10	903,835	933,516	27,902	1,865,253	48.5	50.0
West Virginia		5	310,065	341,016	2,230	653,311	47.5	52.2
Wisconsin		11	1,047,499	1,126,794	17,315	2,191,608	47.8	51.4
Wyoming	3		106,867	67,113	2,571	176,551	60.5	38.0
Total	426	111	48,881,278	41,805,374	898,168	91,584,820	53.4	45.6

Source: Congressional Quarterly Weekly Report (1989), 139.

Table 3-3 Democratic Presidential Primary Returns, 1988

State (date)	Turnout	Dukakis	Jackson	Gore	Gephardt	Simon	Others	Uncommitted
New Hampshire (2/16)	123,360	35.8%	7.8%	6.8%	19.8%	17.1%	12.8%	—
South Dakota (2/23)	71,606	31.2	5.4	8.4	43.5	5.6	5.9	—
Vermont (3/1)	50,791	55.8	25.7	—	7.7	5.2	5.6	—
Alabama (3/8)	405,642	7.7	43.6	37.4	7.4	0.8	2.7	0.4%
Arkansas (3/8)	497,544	18.9	17.1	37.3	12.0	1.8	5.7	7.1
Florida (3/8)	1,273,298	40.9	20.0	12.7	14.4	2.2	3.7	6.2
Georgia (3/8)	622,752	15.6	39.8	32.4	6.7	1.3	3.0	1.2
Kentucky (3/8)	318,721	18.6	15.6	45.8	9.1	2.9	4.6	3.3
Louisiana (3/8)	624,450	15.3	35.5	28.0	10.6	0.8	9.7	—
Maryland (3/8)	531,335	45.6	28.7	8.7	7.9	3.1	3.1	2.8
Massachusetts (3/8)	713,447	58.6	18.7	4.4	10.2	3.7	2.7	1.7
Mississippi (3/8)	361,811	8.3	44.4	33.3	5.4	0.6	4.6	3.5
Missouri (3/8)	527,805	11.6	20.2	2.8	57.8	4.1	2.3	1.3
North Carolina (3/8)	679,958	20.3	33.0	34.7	5.5	1.2	3.0	2.4
Oklahoma (3/8)	392,727	16.9	13.3	41.4	21.0	1.8	5.6	—
Rhode Island (3/8)	49,029	69.8	15.2	4.0	4.1	2.8	2.5	1.7
Tennessee (3/8)	576,314	3.4	20.7	72.3	1.5	0.5	1.1	0.5
Texas (3/8)	1,766,904	32.8	24.5	20.2	13.6	2.0	7.0	—
Virginia (3/8)	364,899	22.0	45.1	22.3	4.4	1.9	2.6	1.7
Illinois (3/15)	1,500,928	16.3	32.3	5.1	2.3	42.3	1.6	—
Puerto Rico (3/20)	356,178	22.9	29.0	14.4	3.0	18.2	12.5	—
Connecticut (3/29)	241,395	58.1	28.3	7.7	0.4	1.3	3.4	0.8
Wisconsin (4/5)	1,014,782	47.6	28.2	17.4	0.8	4.8	1.0	0.3
New York (4/19)	1,575,186	50.9	37.1	10.0	0.2	1.1	0.1	0.7
Pennsylvania (4/26)	1,507,690	66.5	27.3	3.0	0.5	0.6	2.2	—
District of Columbia (5/3)	86,052	17.9	80.0	0.8	0.3	0.9	0.1	—

Indiana (5/3)	645,708	69.6	22.5	3.4	2.6	1.9	—	—
Ohio (5/3)	1,376,135	62.7	27.5	2.2	—	1.1	6.6	—
Nebraska (5/10)	169,008	62.9	25.7	1.5	2.9	1.2	2.9	2.8
West Virginia (5/10)	322,148	78.9	14.0	3.6	—	0.7	2.8	—
Oregon (5/17)	388,932	56.8	38.1	1.4	1.7	1.2	0.7	—
Idaho (5/24)	51,370	73.4	15.7	3.7	—	2.7	—	4.5
California (6/7)	3,089,164	60.8	35.2	1.8	—	1.4	0.8	—
Montana (6/7)	120,962	68.7	22.1	1.8	2.8	1.3	—	3.2
New Jersey (6/7)	640,479	63.2	32.9	2.8	—	—	1.1	—
New Mexico (6/7)	188,610	61.0	28.1	2.5	—	1.5	5.2	1.7
North Dakota (6/14)	3,405	84.9	15.1	—	—	—	—	—
Total	23,230,525	42.4	29.1	13.7	6.0	4.7	3.1	1.0

Note: "—" indicates that the candidate or the uncommitted line was not listed on the ballot. No Democratic candidates filed to be on the ballot for the June 14 North Dakota primary; write-in votes only. Four states have both caucus and primary results. Idaho, North Dakota, and Vermont held nonbinding primaries and selected convention delegates through caucuses. Texas selected delegates through caucuses, but those delegates were bound to reflect voter preferences as revealed in the primary vote.

Source: Congressional Quarterly Weekly Report (1988), 1894, 1950.

Table 3-4 Republican Presidential Primary Returns, 1988

State (date)	Turnout	Bush	Dole	Robertson	Kemp	Others	Uncommitted
New Hampshire (2/16)	157,625	37.6%	28.4%	9.4%	12.8%	11.8%	—
South Dakota (2/23)	93,405	18.6	55.2	19.6	4.6	0.6	1.3%
Vermont (3/1)	47,832	49.3	39.0	5.1	3.9	2.7	—
South Carolina (3/5)	195,292	48.5	20.6	19.1	11.5	0.3	—
Alabama (3/8)	213,515	64.5	16.3	13.9	4.9	0.3	2.1
Arkansas (3/8)	68,305	47.0	25.9	18.9	5.1	1.0	—
Florida (3/8)	901,222	62.1	21.2	10.6	4.6	1.4	—
Georgia (3/8)	400,928	53.8	23.6	16.3	5.8	0.5	—
Kentucky (3/8)	121,402	59.3	23.0	11.1	3.3	1.4	1.8
Louisiana (3/8)	144,781	57.8	17.7	18.2	5.3	1.0	—
Maryland (3/8)	200,754	53.3	32.4	6.4	5.9	2.0	—
Massachusetts (3/8)	241,181	58.5	26.3	4.5	7.0	2.3	1.4
Mississippi (3/8)	158,872	66.0	16.9	13.5	3.4	0.2	—
Missouri (3/8)	400,300	42.2	41.1	11.2	3.5	0.7	1.4
North Carolina (3/8)	273,801	45.4	39.1	9.8	4.1	0.5	1.0
Oklahoma (3/8)	208,938	37.4	34.9	21.1	5.5	1.0	1.1
Rhode Island (3/8)	16,035	64.9	22.6	5.7	4.9	0.8	1.1
Tennessee (3/8)	254,252	60.0	21.6	12.6	4.3	0.6	0.9
Texas (3/8)	1,014,956	63.9	13.9	15.3	5.0	0.7	1.2
Virginia (3/8)	234,142	53.3	26.0	13.7	4.6	0.8	1.6
Illinois (3/15)	858,256	54.7	36.0	6.8	1.5	1.0	—
Puerto Rico (3/20)	3,973	97.1	2.7	0.1	—	0.1	—
Connecticut (3/29)	104,171	70.6	20.2	3.1	3.1	—	3.1
Wisconsin (4/5)	359,294	82.2	7.9	6.9	1.4	1.0	0.7
Pennsylvania (4/26)	870,549	79.0	11.9	9.1	—	—	—
District of Columbia (5/3)	6,720	87.6	7.0	4.0	—	1.4	—

	Votes					
Indiana (5/3)	437,655	80.4	9.8	6.6	3.3	—	—
Ohio (5/3)	794,904	81.0	11.9	7.1	—	—	—
Nebraska (5/10)	204,049	68.0	22.3	5.1	4.1	0.5	—
West Virginia (5/10)	143,140	77.3	10.9	7.3	2.7	1.8	—
Oregon (5/17)	274,451	72.9	17.9	7.7	—	1.5	—
Idaho (5/24)	68,275	81.2	—	8.6	—	—	10.2
California (6/7)	2,240,387	82.9	12.9	4.2	—	—	—
Montana (6/7)	86,380	73.0	19.4	—	—	—	7.5
New Jersey (6/7)	241,033	100.0	—	—	—	—	—
New Mexico (6/7)	88,744	78.2	10.5	6.0	—	2.4	2.9
North Dakota (6/14)	39,434	94.0	—	—	—	6.0	—
Total	12,169,003	67.9	19.2	9.0	2.7	0.7	0.5

Note: "—" indicates that the candidate or uncommitted line was not listed on the ballot. Montana, Vermont, and Virginia held nonbinding primaries but selected convention delegates through caucuses. Republicans did not hold a preference vote in New York; the April 19 primary was for election of delegates only.

Source: Congressional Quarterly Weekly Report (1988), 2254.

Table 3-5 Democratic Presidential Caucus Results, 1988

State (date)	Turnout	Dukakis	Jackson	Gore	Simon	Gephardt	Others	Uncommitted
Iowa (2/8)	126,000	22.1%	8.8%	0.0%	26.7%	31.3%	6.5%	4.6%
Minnesota (2/23)	100,000	33.3	19.8	1.0	17.9	7.1	2.3	18.6
Maine (2/28)	11,000	42.2	26.8	1.5	4.2	3.1	1.6	20.6
Wyoming (3/5)	2,968	26.1	12.9	26.9	3.4	23.1	0.3	7.3
Hawaii (3/8)	3,914	52.7	37.8	1.0	0.9	2.2	0.8	4.6
Idaho (3/8)	4,633	37.8	19.4	8.4	4.2	0.8	0.0	29.4
Nevada (3/8)	5,048	26.0	20.9	34.6	1.0	1.8	0.3	15.4
Texas (3/8)	100,000	31.4	36.4	17.0	0.5	2.5	0.2	11.9
Washington (3/8)	104,000	44.0	34.6	2.4	3.7	1.0	0.4	13.9
American Samoa (3/8)	36	38.9	5.6	0.0	0.0	22.2	0.0	33.3
Alaska (3/10)	2,600	29.6	34.6	1.9	0.7	1.1	0.3	31.8
South Carolina (3/12)	45,000	6.3	54.8	16.8	0.4	1.8	0.0	19.9
Kansas (3/19)	8,837	36.5	30.8	16.2	0.0	1.6	0.0	14.9
Democrats Abroad (3/22)	2,385	41.5	14.5	5.0	10.4	1.8	26.8	—
Michigan (3/26)	212,668	29.0	53.5	2.0	2.1	12.8	0.4	0.2
North Dakota (3/13-3/27)	2,530	27.4	18.9	5.4	5.9	17.5	4.2	20.7
Virgin Islands (4/2)	721	10.3	85.2	—	—	—	—	4.5
Colorado (4/4)	35,022	42.4	33.6	2.7	0.3	0.0	0.1	20.9
Arizona (4/16)	38,463	54.1	37.8	5.1	1.2	—	0.1	1.7
Delaware (4/18)	4,660	27.2	45.8	2.1	0.0	0.0	0.0	24.9
Vermont (4/19)	6,000	44.7	45.7	0.5	0.0	0.0	0.0	9.1
Utah (4/25)	11,097	71.6	15.4	—	—	—	1.6	11.4

Note: "—" indicates that the candidate was not listed on the caucus ballot or that his votes were not tabulated separately. For most states, percentages reflect share of delegates that each candidate won to the next stage of the caucus process rather than the presidential preferences of first-round caucus participants.

Source: Congressional Quarterly Weekly Report (1988), 1895.

Table 3-6 Republican Presidential Caucus Results, 1988

State (date)	Turnout	Bush	Dole	Robertson	Kemp	Others	Uncommitted
Michigan (1/14)	—	57.2%	2.6%	22.4%	17.1%	0.7%	0.0%
Hawaii (2/4)	4,000–5,000	8.7	9.1	81.3	0.6	0.3	0.0
Kansas (2/1–2/7)	25,431	0.0	98.7	0.5	0.0	0.0	0.8
Iowa (2/8)	108,838	18.6	37.3	24.6	11.1	7.7	0.7
Nevada (2/18)	5,038	26.6	22.4	14.6	12.8	0.9	22.7
Minnesota (2/23)	56,563	10.6	42.3	28.2	15.1	1.0	2.8
Wyoming (2/9–2/24)	794	36.6	36.6	9.2	7.1	0.0	10.5
Alaska (2/27–3/1)	4,000	24.2	19.7	46.8	6.9	2.4	0.0
Washington (3/8)	15,210	24.3	26.0	39.0	7.5	0.3	2.9
Colorado (4/4)	15,238	76.3		9.5		—	14.2

Note: "—" indicates not available. No first-round caucus results were available from Arizona, Delaware, Maine, Montana, Utah, Vermont, Virginia, Guam, or the Virgin Islands. Caucus activity in most of these states was held after active opposition to Bush had disappeared.

Source: Congressional Quarterly Weekly Report (1988), 1897.

Figure 3-3 Presidential Nominations, Campaign Lengths, 1968-1988

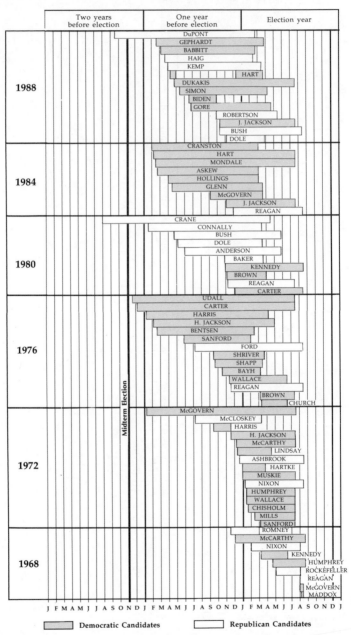

Note: Beginning of campaigns is determined by date of the formal announcement.

Sources: 1968-1984: Congressional Quarterly, *Elections '80* (Washington, D.C.: Congressional Quarterly, 1980), and Congressional Quarterly, *Congressional Quarterly's Guide to U.S. Elections*, 2d ed. (Washington, D.C.: Congressional Quarterly, 1985), 387; 1988: *Congressional Quarterly Weekly Report* (1987), 2732, (1988), 1894, 1896, 1899.

Table 3-7 State Methods for Choosing National Convention Delegates, 1968-1988

State	1968	1972	1976	1980	1984	1988
Alabama	DP	DP	OP	OP	CPI	CPI
Alaska	CC	CC	CC	CC	CC	CC
Arizona	(D)CO (R)CC	CC	CC	CC	CC	CC
Arkansas	CO	CC	OP	(D)OP (R)CC	CC	CPI
California	CP	CP	CP	CP	CP	CP
Colorado	CC	CC	CC	CC	CC	CC
Connecticut	CC	CC	CC	CP	(D)CP (R)CC	CP
Delaware	CC	CC	CC	CC	CC	CC
District of Columbia	CP	CP	CP	CP	CP	CP
Florida	CP	CP	CP	CP	CP	CP
Georgia	(D)CO (R)CC	CC	OP	OP	CPI	CPI
Hawaii	CC	CC	CC	CC	CC	CC
Idaho	CC	CC	OP	(D)CC (R)OP	(D)CPI	(D)X (R)OP
Illinois	DP,CC	CP	OP	OP	DP	DP
Indiana	OP	OP	OP	OP	CPI	CPI
Iowa	CC	CC	CC	CC	CC	CC
Kansas	CC	CC	CC	CPI	CC	CC
Kentucky	C	CC	CP	CP	CC	CP
Louisiana	CO	CC	CC	CP	CP	CP
Maine	CC	CC	CC	CC	CC	CC
Maryland	(D)CO (R)CC	CP	CP	CP	DP	CP
Massachusetts	CPI	CPI	CPI	CPI	CPI	CPI
Michigan	CC	OP	OP	(D)CC (R)OP	CC	(D)CC (R)X
Minnesota	CC	CC	CC	CC	CC	CC
Mississippi	CC	CC	CC	(D)CC (R)DP	CC	CPI
Missouri	(D)CC,CO (R)CC	CC	CC	CC	CC	CPI
Montana	CC	CC	OP	OP	DP	(D)CPI (R)X
Nebraska	OP	OP	OP	OP	CP	CP
Nevada	CC	CC	CP	CP	CC	CC
New Hampshire	CPI	CPI	CPI	CPI	CPI	CPI
New Jersey	CPI	CPI	CPI	CPI	DP	DP
New Mexico	CC	CP	CC	CP (R)CP	CP	CP

(Table continues)

Table 3-7 *(Continued)*

State	1968	1972	1976	1980	1984	1988
New York	DP,CO	DP,CO	DP	(D)CP	DP	CP
North Carolina	CC	CP	CP	CP	CP	CP
North Dakota	CC	CC	CC	CC	DP	(D)X (R)OP
Ohio	OP	OP	OP	OP	CPI	CPI
Oklahoma	CC	CC	CC	CC	CC	CP
Oregon	CP	CP	CP	CP	CP	CP
Pennsylvania	CP,CO	CP	CP	CP	DP	DP
Rhode Island	(D)CO (R)CC	CPI	CPI	CPI	CPI	CPI
South Carolina	CC	CC	CC	(D)CC (R)OP	CC	(D)CC (R)OP
South Dakota	CP	CP	CP	CP	CP	CP
Tennessee	CC	OP	OP	OP	CPI	CPI
Texas	CC	CC	OP	CP	(D)CC (R)OP	CPI
Utah	CC	CC	CC	CC	CC	CC
Vermont	CC	CC	X	X	X	X
Virginia	CC	CC	CC	CC	CC	(D)CPI (R)X
Washington	(D)CC,CO (R)CC	CC CP	CC CP	CC CP	CC	CC
West Virginia	CP	CP	CP	CP	CP	CP
Wisconsin	OP	OP	OP	OP	(D)X (R)OP	(D)CPI (R)OP
Wyoming	CC	CC	CC	CC	CC	CC
(Puerto Rico)	(D)C	CC	CC	OP	(D)CPI (R)CC	CPI

Notes: "CC" indicates delegates chosen by state and local caucuses and conventions; "CO" indicates delegates chosen by state party committee; "CP" indicates delegates chosen or bound by presidential preference primaries open only to voters preregistered as members of the particular parties; "CPI" indicates delegates chosen or bound by presidential preference primaries open only to voters preregistered as members of the particular parties or as independents; "D" indicates Democrats; "DP" indicates delegates chosen directly by voters in primaries—no binding presidential preference poll; "OP" indicates delegates chosen or bound by presidential preference primaries open to all registered voters without regard to party preregistration; "R" indicates Republicans; "X" indicates having nonbinding presidential preference primaries, but delegates are chosen by party caucuses and conventions.

Sources: 1968-1984: Austin Ranney, ed., *The American Elections of 1984* (Durham, N.C.: Duke University Press, 1985), 330-332, copyright © American Enterprise Institute for Public Policy Research, reprinted by permission; 1988: derived by the editors from Kevin Coleman, "A Summary of National and State Party Rules and State Laws Concerning the Election of Delegates to the 1988 Democratic and Republican National Conventions" (Washington, D.C.: Congressional Research Service, 1988), Report. no. 88-102 GOV.

Table 3-8 Vote by Groups in Democratic Presidential Primaries, 1984-1988

Group	1984 Percentage of primary electorate	Mondale	Hart	Jackson	1988 Percentage of primary electorate	Dukakis	Jackson	Others
Sex								
Men	46	38	36	17	47	41	29	30
Women	54	39	35	20	53	43	30	26
Race/ethnicity								
White	78	42	43	5	75	54	12	35
Black	18	19	3	77	21	4	92	4
Hispanic	—	—	—	—	3	48	30	20
Age								
Under 30	17	26	39	26	14	35	38	27
30-44	30	30	38	23	31	37	36	26
45-59	24	41	34	18	25	42	30	28
60 and older	28	52	31	10	30	53	19	29
Religion								
Catholic	—	—	—	—	30	60	18	22
White Protestant	—	—	—	—	36	43	10	47
Jewish	—	—	—	—	7	75	8	17
Party								
Democrat	74	42	33	20	72	43	33	24
Independent	20	28	44	16	20	44	20	34

(Table continues)

Table 3-8 (*Continued*)

Group	1984				1988			
	Percentage of primary electorate	Mondale	Hart	Jackson	Percentage of primary electorate	Dukakis	Jackson	Others
Ideology								
Liberal	27	34	36	25	27	41	41	19
Moderate	47	41	37	15	47	47	25	28
Conservative	21	37	34	16	22	38	23	38
Union household	33	45	31	19	—	—	—	—
Total	100	38	36	19	100	43	29	28

Note: "—" indicates not available. Entries are derived from exit poll data in twenty-four contested delegate selection primaries in 1984 and from thirty-three primary states in 1988. No exit poll in Louisiana in 1984 or in Montana, Oregon, or Washington, D.C., in 1988.

Sources: Adam Clymer, "The 1984 National Primary," *Public Opinion* (August/September 1984): 52-53 (reprinted with permission of the American Enterprise Institute for Public Policy Research); *New York Times*, June 13, 1988, B7 (copyright © 1988 by the New York Times Company, reprinted by permission).

Table 3-9 Convention Votes Presidential Candidates Received from Caucus State Delegates and Primary State Delegates, 1964-1988

Year/candidate	Caucus states	Primary states	Number of convention votes	Percentage of convention
1964 Republican convention				
Goldwater	74.5%	60.5%	883	67.5
Scranton	10.7	22.1	214	16.4
Rockefeller	0.6	16.8	114	8.7
Others	14.2	0.6	97	7.4
Total	N=655	N=653	1,308	100.0
1968 Democratic convention				
Humphrey	80.2	53.4	1,760.25	67.1
McCarthy	12.1	34.4	601	22.9
McGovern	3.8	7.5	146.5	5.6
Others	4.0	4.7	114.25	4.4
Total	N=1,346	N=1,276	2,622	100.0
1968 Republican convention				
Nixon	59.6	43.2	692	51.9
Rockefeller	14.4	27.9	277	20.8
Reagan	11.2	16.4	182	13.7
Others	14.7	12.4	182	13.7
Total	N=706	N=627	1,333	100.0
1972 Democratic convention				
McGovern	41.0	64.9	1,715.4	56.9
Jackson	30.0	11.5	534	17.7
Wallace	7.3	15.5	385.7	12.8
Others	21.7	8.1	380.9	12.6
Total	N=1,009	N=2,007	3,016	100.0
1976 Republican convention				
Ford	44.9	55.9	1,187	52.5
Reagan	55.1	43.9	1,070	47.4
Others	0.0	0.1	2	0.1
Total	N=693	N=1,566	2,259	100.0
1980 Democratic convention				
Carter	71.0	60.8	2,123	63.7
Kennedy	24.3	38.6	1,150.5	34.5
Others	4.7	0.5	57.5	1.7
Total	N=953	N=2,378	3,331	100.0

(Table continues)

Table 3-9 *(Continued)*

Year/candidate	Caucus states	Primary states	Number of convention votes	Percentage of convention
1984 Democratic convention				
Mondale	56.3%	55.6%	2,191	55.9
Hart	29.6	31.2	1,200.5	30.6
Jackson	11.9	11.9	465.5	11.9
Others	2.3	1.3	66	1.7
Total	N=1,460	N=2,463	3,923	100.0
1988 Democratic convention				
Dukakis	62.6	71.5	2,876.25	69.9
Jackson	36.2	28.1	1,218.50	29.6
Others	1.2	0.4	23	0.6
Total	N=766.75	N=3,351.00	4,117.75	100.0

Note: Shown are major presidential candidates with substantial opposition. The table is based on first ballot votes before switches. In 1984 and 1988, votes of Democratic superdelegates not chosen through caucuses or primaries are counted as if they were chosen by the delegate selection method in their state.

Sources: 1964-1980: Congressional Quarterly, *Elections '84* (Washington, D.C.: Congressional Quarterly, 1984), 50; 1984: compiled by the editors from Congressional Quarterly, *Congressional Quarterly Almanac, 1984* (Washington, D.C.: Congressional Quarterly, 1985), B68; 1988: *Congressional Quarterly Weekly Report* (1988), 2033, 1872-1892, 1894-1895.

Table 3-10 Election Year Candidate Preferences, 1948-1988 (percent)

Year/candidate	First poll of year	First poll after conventions	Early October	Final survey	Election results
1948					
Truman (D)[a]	46 (+ 5)	37	40	45	50 (+ 5)
Dewey (R)	41	48 (+11)	46 (+ 6)	50 (+ 5)	45
1952					
Eisenhower (R)	59 (+28)	50 (+ 7)	53 (+12)	51 (+ 2)	55 (+11)
Stevenson (D)	31	43	41	49	44
1956					
Eisenhower (R)[a]	61 (+26)	52 (+11)	51 (+10)	60 (+19)	57 (+15)
Stevenson (D)	35	41	41	41	42
1960					
Kennedy (D)	43	44	49 (+ 3)	51 (+ 2)	50 (+0.2)
Nixon (R)	48 (+ 5)	50 (+ 6)	46	49	50
1964					
Johnson (D)[a]	75 (+57)	65 (+36)	64 (+35)	64 (+28)	61 (+23)
Goldwater (R)	18	29	29	36	38
1968					
Nixon (R)	43 (+ 9)	43 (+12)	43 (+12)	43 (+ 1)	43 (+ 0.7)
Humphrey (D)	34	31	31	42	43
Wallace (AIP)[b]	9	19	20	15	14
1972					
Nixon (R)[a]	53 (+19)	64 (+34)	60 (+26)	62 (+24)	61 (+23)
McGovern (D)	34	30	34	38	38
1976					
Carter (D)	47 (+ 5)	51 (+15)	47 (+ 2)	48	50 (+ 2)
Ford (R)[a]	42	36	45	49 (+ 1)	48
1980					
Reagan (R)	33	38	40	47 (+ 3)	51 (+10)
Carter (D)[a]	62 (+29)	39 (+ 1)	44 (+ 4)	44	41
Anderson (I)		13	9	8	7
1984					
Reagan (R)[a]	48 (+ 1)	55 (+15)	56 (+17)	59 (+18)	59 (+18)
Mondale (D)	47	40	39	41	41
1988					
Bush (R)	52 (+ 12)	48 (+4)	49 (+6)	53 (+11)	54 (+8)
Dukakis (D)	40	44	43	42	46

[a] Incumbent.
[b] American Independent Party.

Sources: *Congressional Quarterly Weekly Report* (1984), 2648, (1988), 3245; 1984 final survey: *The Gallup Report* (November 1984), 31; 1988: The Gallup Poll, various press releases.

Table 3-11 Presidential Vote by Groups in General Elections, 1952-1988 (percent)

	1952		1956		1960		1964		1968			1972		1976			1980			1984		1988	
	D	R	D	R	D	R	D	R	D	R	Iᵃ	D	R	D	R	Iᵃ	D	R	Iᵃ	D	R	D	R
Sex																							
Male	47	53	45	55	52	48	60	40	41	43	16	37	63	53	45	1	38	53	7	36	64	44	56
Female	42	58	39	61	49	51	62	38	45	43	12	38	62	48	51	-	44	49	6	45	55	48	52
Race/ethnicity																							
White	43	57	41	59	49	51	59	41	38	47	15	32	68	46	52	1	36	56	7	34	66	41	59
Nonwhite	79	21	61	39	68	32	94	6	85	12	3	87	13	85	15	-	86	10	2	87	13	82	18
Education																							
Grade school	52	48	50	50	55	45	66	34	52	33	15	49	51	58	41	1	54	42	3	51	49	55	45
High school	45	55	42	58	52	48	62	38	42	43	15	34	66	54	46	-	43	51	5	43	57	46	54
College	34	66	31	69	39	61	52	48	37	54	9	37	63	42	55	2	35	53	10	39	61	42	58
Employment																							
Manual	55	45	50	50	60	40	71	29	50	35	15	43	57	58	41	1	48	48	5	46	54	—	—
White collar	40	60	37	63	48	52	57	43	41	47	12	36	64	50	48	2	40	51	9	47	53	—	—
Professional and business	36	64	32	68	42	58	54	46	34	56	10	31	69	42	56	1	33	55	10	34	66	—	
Age																							
Under 30	51	49	43	57	54	45	64	36	47	38	15	48	52	53	45	1	47	41	11	40	60	37	63
30-49	47	53	45	55	54	46	63	37	44	41	15	33	67	48	49	2	38	52	8	40	60	45	55
50 and older	39	61	39	61	46	54	59	41	41	47	12	36	64	52	48	-	41	54	4	41	59	49	51
Religion																							
Protestant	37	63	37	63	38	62	55	45	35	49	16	30	70	46	53	-	39	54	6	39	61	42	58
Catholic	56	44	51	49	78	22	76	24	59	33	8	48	52	57	41	1	46	47	6	39	61	51	49

Political affiliation

Democrat	77	23	85	15	84	16	87	13	74	12	14	67	33	82	18	-	69	26	4	79	21	85	15
Independent	35	65	30	70	43	57	56	44	31	44	25	31	69	38	57	4	29	55	14	33	67	43	57
Republican	8	92	4	96	5	95	20	80	9	86	5	5	95	9	91	-	8	86	5	4	96	7	93
Region[b]																							
East	45	55	40	60	53	47	68	32	50	43	7	42	58	51	47	1	43	47	9	46	54	51	49
Midwest	42	58	41	59	48	52	61	39	44	47	9	40	60	48	50	1	41	51	7	42	58	47	53
South	51	49	49	51	51	49	52	48	31	36	33	29	71	54	45	-	44	52	3	37	63	40	60
West	42	58	43	57	49	51	60	40	44	49	7	41	59	46	51	1	35	54	9	40	60	46	54
Union family	61	39	57	43	65	35	73	27	56	29	15	46	54	63	36	1	50	43	5	52	48	63	37
Total	45	55	42	58	50	50	61	39	43	43	14	38	62	50	48	1	41	51	7	41	59	46	54

Note: "_" indicates less than 0.5 percent. "—" indicates not available.

[a] "t" indicates the vote for George Wallace in 1968, for Eugene McCarthy in 1976, and for John Anderson in 1980. Table does not include votes for minor party candidates other than those shown for 1968, 1976, and 1980.

[b] For composition of regions, see Appendix Table A-2.

Source: The Gallup Report (November 1988), 6-7.

Table 3-12 Presidential Vote by Groups in General Elections, 1980-1988

Group	Percentage of 1988 voters	1980 Democrat	1980 Republican	1980 Independent	1984 Democrat	1984 Republican	1988 Democrat	1988 Republican
Sex								
Men	48	36	55	7	37	62	41	54
Women	52	45	47	7	44	56	49	50
Race/ethnicity								
White	85	36	55	7	35	64	40	59
Black	10	85	11	3	89	9	86	12
Hispanic	3	56	35	8	61	37	69	30
Age								
Under 30	20	44	43	11	40	59	47	52
30-44	35	36	54	8	42	57	45	54
45-59	22	39	55	5	39	59	42	57
60 and older	22	41	54	4	39	60	49	50
Education								
Not high school graduate	8	51	46	2	50	49	56	43
High school graduate	27	43	51	4	39	60	49	50
College incomplete	30	35	55	8	37	61	42	57
College graduate	35	35	52	11	41	58	43	56
Religion								
White Protestant	48	31	63	6	27	72	33	66
Catholic	28	42	49	7	45	54	47	52
Jewish	4	45	39	15	67	31	64	35
White fundamentalist	9	33	63	3	22	78	18	81
Union household	25	48	43	6	53	46	57	42

Income								
Under $12,500	12	51	42	6	54	45	62	37
$12,500-24,999	20	46	44	7	42	57	50	49
$25,00-34,999	20	39	52	7	40	59	44	56
$35,000-49,999	20	32	59	8	33	66	42	56
$50,000 and over	24	26	63	9	30	69	37	62
Region								
East	25	42	47	9	47	52	49	50
Midwest	28	40	51	7	40	58	47	52
South	28	44	52	3	36	64	41	58
West	19	34	53	10	38	61	46	52
Party								
Republican	35	8	86	4	6	93	8	91
Democrat	37	67	26	6	75	24	82	17
Independent	26	30	55	12	35	63	43	55
Ideology								
Liberal	18	60	25	11	70	28	81	18
Moderate	45	42	48	8	47	53	50	49
Conservative	33	23	72	4	17	82	19	80
1984 vote								
1984 Reagan voter	56	9	75	2	0	100	19	80
1984 Democratic Reagan voter	9	23	57	2	0	100	51	48
1984 Mondale voter	28	63	14	8	100	0	92	7
Total	100	41	51	7	40	59	45	53

Note: Income categories in 1980 were: less than $10,000; $10,000-14,999; $15,000-24,999; $25,000-49,999; and $50,000 and over.

Source: New York Times, November 10, 1988, B6 (copyright © 1988 by the New York Times Company, reprinted by permission).

Table 3-13 Popular and Electoral Votes, 1789-1988

Year	Number of states	Candidates		Electoral vote (number and percent)		Popular vote (number and percent)
		(Democrat-Republican)	*(Federalist)*	*(Democrat-Republican)*	*(Federalist)*	
1789[a]	10		Washington		69 / 100%	
1792[a]	15		Washington		132 / 98%	
1796[a]	16	Jefferson	Adams	68 / 49%	71 / 51%	
1800[a]	16	Jefferson	Adams	73 / 53%	65 / 47%	
1804	17	Jefferson / Clinton	Pinckney / King	162 / 92%	14 / 8%	
1808	17	Madison / Clinton	Pinckney / King	122 / 69%	47 / 27%	
1812	18	Madison / Genny	Clinton (Fusionist) / Ingersoll	128 / 59%	89 / 41%	
1816	19	Monroe (R) / Tompkins	King / Howard	183 / 83%	34 / 15%	
		(Democrat-Republican)	*(Independent Democrat-Republican)*	*(Democrat-Republican)*		
1820	24	Monroe / Tompkins	Adams / Stockton	231 / 98%	1 / 0%	
1824[b]	24	Jackson / Calhoun	Adams / Sanford	99 / 38%	84 / 32%	

Year	No.	(Democrat-Republican)	(National Republican)	(Democrat-Republican)	(National Republican)	(Democrat-Republican)	(National Republican)
1828	24	Jackson / Calhoun	Adams / Rush	178 / 68%	83 / 32%	642,553 / 56.1%	500,897 / 43.6%
1832	24	Jackson / Van Buren	Clay / Sergeant	219 / 76%	49 / 17%	701,780 / 54.2%	484,205 / 37.4%

Year	No.	(Democrat)	(Whig)	(Democrat)	(Whig)	(Democrat)	(Whig)
1836	26	Van Buren / Johnson	Harrison / Granger	170 / 58%	73[c] / 25%	764,176 / 50.8%	550,816 / 36.6%
1840	26	Van Buren / Johnson	Harrison / Tyler	60 / 20%	234 / 80%	1,128,854 / 46.8%	1,275,390 / 52.9%
1844	26	Polk / Dallas	Clay / Frelinghuysen	170 / 62%	105 / 38%	1,339,494 / 49.5%	1,300,004 / 48.1%
1848	30	Cass / Butler	Taylor / Fillmore	127 / 44%	163 / 56%	1,223,460 / 42.5%	1,361,393 / 47.3%
1852	31	Pierce / King	Scott / Graham	254 / 86%	42 / 14%	1,607,510 / 50.8%	1,386,942 / 43.9%

Year	No.	(Democrat)	(Republican)	(Democrat)	(Republican)	(Democrat)	(Republican)
1856	31	Buchanan / Breckinridge	Fremont / Dayton	174 / 59%	114 / 39%	1,836,072 / 45.3%	1,342,345 / 33.1%
1860	33	Douglas / Johnson	Lincoln / Hamlin	12 / 4%	180 / 59%	1,380,202 / 29.5%	1,865,908 / 39.8%
1864	36	McClellan / Pendleton	Lincoln / Johnson	21 / 9%	212 / 91%	1,812,807 / 45.0%	2,218,388 / 55.0%
1868	37	Seymour / Blair	Grant / Colfax	80 / 27%	214 / 73%	2,708,744 / 47.3%	3,013,650 / 52.7%
1872	37	Greeley / Brown	Grant / Wilson	d	286 / 78%	2,834,761 / 43.8%	3,598,235 / 55.6%

(Table continues)

Table 3-13 *(Continued)*

Year	Number of states	Candidates	Electoral vote (number and percent)	Popular vote (number and percent)
1876	38	Hayes	185 50%	4,034,311 47.9%
		Wheeler		
		Tilden	184 50%	4,288,546 51.0%
		Hendricks		
1880	38	Garfield	214 58%	4,446,158 48.3%
		Arthur		
		Hancock	155 42%	4,444,260 48.2%
		English		
1884	38	Blaine	182 45%	4,848,936 48.2%
		Logan		
		Cleveland	219 55%	4,874,621 48.5%
		Hendricks		
1888	38	Harrison	233 58%	5,443,892 47.8%
		Morton		
		Cleveland	168 42%	5,534,488 48.6%
		Thurman		
1892	44	Harrison	145 33%	5,179,244 43.0%
		Reid		
		Cleveland	277 62%	5,551,883 46.1%
		Stevenson		
1896	45	KcKinley	271 61%	7,108,480 51.0%
		Hobart		
		Bryan	176 39%	6,511,495 46.7%
		Sewall		
1900	45	McKinley	292 65%	7,218,039 51.7%
		Roosevelt		
		Bryan	155 35%	6,358,345 45.5%
		Stevenson		
1904	45	Roosevelt	336 71%	7,626,593 56.4%
		Fairbanks		
		Parker	140 29%	5,028,898 37.6%
		Davis		
1908	46	Taft	321 66%	7,676,258 51.6%
		Sherman		
		Bryan	162 34%	6,406,801 43.0%
		Kern		
1912	48	Taft	8 2%	3,486,333 23.2%
		Sherman		
		Wilson	435 82%	6,293,152 41.8%
		Marshall		
1916	48	Hughes	254 48%	8,546,789 46.1%
		Fairbanks		
		Wilson	277 52%	9,126,300 49.2%
		Marshall		
1920	48	Harding	404 76%	16,133,314 60.3%
		Coolidge		
		Cox	127 24%	9,140,884 34.2%
		Roosevelt		
1924	48	Coolidge	382	15,717,553
		Davis	136	8,386,169

Year	States	President	Vice President	Electoral Vote %	Electoral Votes	Popular Vote %	Popular Votes
(cont.)			Bryant	26%		28.8%	
(cont.)			Dawes	72%		54.1%	
1928	48	Smith	Robinson	16%	87	40.8%	15,000,185
1928		Hoover	Curtis	84%	444	58.2%	21,411,991
1932	48	Roosevelt	Garner	89%	472	57.4%	22,825,016
1932		Hoover	Curtis	11%	59	39.6%	15,758,397
1936	48	Roosevelt	Garner	90%	523	60.8%	27,747,636
1936		London	Knox	2%	8	36.5%	16,679,543
1940	48	Roosevelt	Wallace	85%	449	54.7%	27,263,448
1940		Willkie	McNary	15%	82	44.8%	22,336,260
1944	48	Roosevelt	Truman	81%	432	53.4%	25,611,936
1944		Dewey	Bricker	19%	99	45.9%	22,013,372
1948	48	Truman	Barkley	57%	303	49.5%	24,105,587
1948		Dewey	Warren	36%	189	45.1%	21,970,017
1952	48	Stevenson	Sparkman	17%	89	44.4%	27,314,649
1952		Eisenhower	Nixon	83%	442	55.1%	33,936,137
1956	48	Stevenson	Kefauver	14%	73	42.0%	26,030,172
1956		Eisenhower	Nixon	86%	457	57.4%	35,585,245
1960	50	Kennedy	Johnson	56%	303	49.7%	34,221,344
1960		Nixon	Lodge	41%	219	49.5%	34,106,671
1964	50	Johnson	Humphrey	90%	486	61.1%	43,126,584
1964		Goldwater	Miller	10%	52	38.5%	27,177,838
1968	50	Humphrey	Muskie	36%	191	42.7%	31,274,503
1968		Nixon	Agnew	56%	301	43.4%	31,785,148
1972	50	McGovern	Shriver	3%	17	37.5%	29,171,791
1972		Nixon	Agnew	97%	520	60.7%	47,170,179
1976	50	Carter	Mondale	55%	297	50.1%	40,830,763
1976		Ford	Dole	45%	240	48.0%	39,147,793

(Table continues)

Table 3-13 *(Continued)*

Year	Number of states	Candidates	Electoral vote (number and percent)		Popular vote (number and percent)	
1980	50	Carter	49		35,483,883	
				9%		41.0%
		Mondale				
		Reagan	489		43,904,153	
				91%		50.7%
		Bush				
1984	50	Mondale	13		37,577,137	
				2%		40.6%
		Ferraro				
		Reagan	525		54,455,074	
				98%		58.8%
		Bush				
1988	50	Dukakis	111		41,805,374	
				21%		45.6%
		Bentsen				
		Bush	426		48,881,278	
				79%		53.4%
		Quayle				

Note: For details of the electoral system as well as popular and electoral votes polled by minor candidates, see source. Popular vote returns are shown since 1824 because of availability and because by that time most electors were chosen by popular vote.
[a] The elections of 1789–1800 were held under different rules, which did not include separate voting for president and vice president. Scattered electoral votes are not shown.
[b] All candidates in 1824 represented factions of the Democratic-Republican party. Figures are for the two candidates with the highest electoral votes. The two other candidates were Crawford and Clay with 41 and 37 electoral votes, respectively.
[c] Three Whig candidates ran in 1836. Their electoral votes totalled 113.
[d] The Democratic presidential nominee, Horace Greeley, died between the popular vote and the meeting of presidential electors. Democratic electors split 63 votes among several candidates, Congress refused to count the three Georgians who insisted on casting their votes for Greeley, and an additional 14 electoral votes were not cast.

Source: Congressional Quarterly's Guide to U.S. Elections, 269ff, 329ff, 1220ff; Congressional Quarterly Weekly Report (1988), 3595, (1989), 139.

Table 3-14 Party Winning Presidential Election by State, 1789-1988

State	1789-1824			1828-1856			1860-1892			1896-1928			1932-1964			1968-1988		
	D	F	O	D	R	O	D	R	O	D	R	O	D	R	O	D	R	O
Alabama	2	0	0	8	0	0	6	2	0	9	0	0	7	1	1	1	4	1
Alaska	—	—	—	—	—	—	—	—	—	—	—	—	1	1	0	0	6	0
Arizona	—	—	—	—	—	—	—	—	—	2	3	0	5	4	0	0	6	0
Arkansas	—	—	—	6	0	0	6	1	0	9	0	0	9	0	0	1	4	1
California	—	—	—	2	0	0	2	7	0	1	7	1	6	3	0	0	6	0
Colorado	—	—	—	—	—	—	0	4	1	5	4	0	4	5	0	0	6	0
Connecticut	2	8	0	2	6	0	4	5	0	1	8	0	5	4	0	1	5	0
Delaware	2	8	0	2	6	0	7	1	1	1	8	0	5	4	0	1	5	0
District of Columbia[a]	—	—	—	—	—	—	—	—	—	—	—	—	1	0	0	6	0	0
Florida	—	—	—	2	1	0	4	3	1	8	1	0	6	3	0	1	5	0
Georgia	8	2	0	5	3	0	7	0	1	9	0	0	8	1	0	2	3	1
Hawaii	—	—	—	—	—	—	—	—	—	—	—	—	2	0	0	4	2	0
Idaho	—	—	—	—	—	—	—	—	1	4	5	0	6	3	0	0	6	0
Illinois	2	0	0	8	0	0	1	8	0	1	8	0	7	2	0	0	6	0
Indiana	3	0	0	6	2	0	3	6	0	1	8	0	3	6	0	0	6	0
Iowa	—	—	—	2	1	0	0	9	0	1	8	0	4	5	0	1	5	0
Kansas	—	—	—	—	—	—	0	7	1	3	6	0	3	6	0	0	6	0
Kentucky	8	1	0	2	6	0	8	0	1	6	3	0	7	2	0	1	5	0
Louisiana	4	0	0	6	2	0	5	1	1	9	0	0	6	2	1	1	4	1
Maine	2	0	0	5	3	0	0	9	0	1	8	0	1	8	0	1	5	0
Maryland	4	6	0	1	6	1	7	1	1	4	5	0	6	3	0	3	3	0
Massachusetts	3	7	0	0	8	0	0	9	0	2	7	0	7	2	0	4	2	0
Michigan	—	—	—	4	2	0	0	9	0	0	8	1	5	4	0	4	2	0

(Table continues)

Table 3-14 (Continued)

State	1789-1824 D	F	O	1828-1856 D	R	O	1860-1892 D	R	O	1896-1928 D	R	O	1932-1964 D	R	O	1968-1988 D	R	O
Minnesota	-	-	-	-	-	-	0	9	0	0	8	1	7	2	0	5	1	0
Mississippi	2	0	-	7	1	0	5	1	1	9	0	0	6	1	2	1	4	1
Missouri	-	-	-	8	0	0	7	2	0	4	5	0	8	1	0	1	5	0
Montana	-	-	-	-	-	-	0	1	0	4	5	0	6	3	0	0	6	0
Nebraska	-	-	-	-	-	-	0	7	0	4	5	0	3	6	0	0	6	0
Nevada	-	-	-	-	-	-	1	6	1	5	4	0	7	2	0	0	6	0
New Hampshire	4	6	0	6	2	0	0	9	0	2	7	0	4	5	0	0	6	0
New Jersey	5	5	0	3	5	0	7	2	0	1	8	0	6	3	0	0	6	0
New Mexico	-	-	-	-	-	-	-	-	-	2	3	0	7	2	0	0	6	0
New York	6	3	0	5	3	0	4	5	0	1	8	0	6	3	0	3	3	0
North Carolina	8	1	0	5	3	0	5	2	1	8	1	0	9	0	0	1	5	0
North Dakota	-	-	-	-	-	-	-	-	-	2	7	0	3	6	0	0	6	0
Ohio	6	0	0	4	4	0	0	9	0	2	7	0	5	4	0	1	5	0
Oklahoma	-	-	-	-	-	-	-	-	-	4	2	0	6	3	0	0	5	0
Oregon	-	-	-	-	-	-	1	8	0	1	8	1	5	4	0	1	5	0
Pennsylvania	8	2	0	6	2	0	0	9	0	0	8	0	5	4	0	2	4	0
Rhode Island	4	5	0	2	6	0	0	9	0	2	7	0	7	2	0	4	2	0
South Carolina	8	2	0	6	0	2	4	3	1	9	0	0	7	1	1	1	5	0
South Dakota	-	-	-	-	-	-	0	1	1	1	7	1	3	6	0	0	6	0
Tennessee	8	0	0	3	5	0	6	1	1	7	2	0	6	3	0	1	5	0
Texas	-	-	-	-	-	-	7	0	0	8	1	0	7	2	0	2	4	0
Utah	-	-	-	-	-	-	-	-	-	2	7	0	6	3	0	0	6	0
Vermont	6	3	0	7	1	0	0	9	0	0	9	0	1	8	0	0	6	0
Virginia	8	2	0	8	0	0	5	1	1	8	1	0	6	3	0	0	6	0
Washington	-	-	-	-	-	-	0	1	0	2	6	1	6	3	0	2	4	0

West Virginia	–	–	–	–	–	5	3	0	1	8	0	8	1	0	4	2	0
Wisconsin	–	–	2	1	–	8	0	1	1	7	1	5	4	0	2	4	0
Wyoming	–	–	–	–	–	0	1	3	3	6	0	5	4	0	0	6	0
Total[b]	113	61	136	79	3	118	189	15	170	244	7	274	158	5	63	238	5

Note: "D" is the Democratic-Republican party from 1796 to 1820 and in 1828, the Jackson faction in 1824, and the Democratic party in 1832 and later; "F" is the Federalists from 1792 to 1816, Independent Democrat-Republicans in 1820, and the Adams faction in 1824; "R" is the National Republicans in 1828 and 1832, Whigs from 1836 to 1852, and the Republican party in 1856 and later. The "O" column refers to other (third-party) parties. Southern Democrats in 1860 are counted as Democratic. "–" indicates that the state was not yet admitted to the Union.

[a] Residents of the District of Columbia received the presidential vote in 1961.

[b] Fewer total votes for a given state within a party system indicate admission of the state during the party system or nonvoting in certain southern states in 1864, 1868, and 1872.

Sources: Compiled by the editors from *Congressional Quarterly's Guide to U.S. Elections*, 269ff, 327; *Congressional Quarterly Weekly Report* (1988), 3245.

Table 3-15 Party Victories in U.S. House Elections by State, 1860-1988

State	1860-1895			1896-1931			1932-1965			1966-1988		
	Dem.	Rep.	Other	Dem.	Rep.	Other	Dem.	Rep.	Other	Dem.	Rep.	Other
Alabama	94	20	19	171	0	7	146	5	0	52	31	1
Alaska	-	-	-	-	-	-	4	0	0	3	11	0
Arizona	-	-	-	11	0	0	25	7	0	16	32	1
Arkansas	56	3	12	124	0	0	107	0	1	26	13	0
California[a]	27	45	11	10	86	80	178	146	121	286	206	4
Colorado	0	10	3	24	31	6	43	26	0	32	27	0
Connecticut	33	37	4	11	78	0	52	50	0	45	25	0
Delaware	15	2	2	5	14	0	9	8	0	4	8	0
Florida	18	9	1	61	0	0	111	8	0	108	55	0
Georgia	110	10	13	207	0	1	171	1	0	101	12	0
Hawaii	-	-	-	-	-	-	6	0	0	20	2	0
Idaho	0	4	0	0	25	3	20	14	0	2	20	0
Illinois	116	191	22	136	329	8	220	222	0	140	142	2
Indiana	107	99	19	96	139	1	84	109	0	66	57	0
Iowa	14	131	13	10	193	0	35	104	0	31	40	0
Kansas	0	64	12	23	114	8	16	91	0	15	44	1
Kentucky	143	19	31	149	54	0	122	25	0	50	29	1
Louisiana	69	25	2	136	0	2	140	0	0	66	17	3
Maine	1	76	9	4	71	0	8	41	0	9	14	0
Maryland	74	15	18	63	49	0	87	25	0	65	30	0
Massachusetts	22	166	21	60	208	5	102	134	3	103	31	2
Michigan	29	119	16	10	214	4	111	187	0	120	100	0
Minnesota	10	51	5	8	146	12	4	92	56	11	36	47
Mississippi	74	18	3	141	0	0	110	1	0	44	15	2
Missouri	142	42	40	202	89	0	159	48	0	87	27	0
Montana	1	3	0	13	13	2	24	11	0	13	10	0

State												
Nebraska	3	30	6	17	55	37	21	50	0	3	31	0
Nevada	4	9	4	3	9	6	14	3	0	11	4	1
New Hampshire	11	33	3	3	33	0	3	31	0	5	17	0
New Jersey	53	58	5	64	135	2	84	158	0	108	66	0
New Mexico	-	-	-	7	5	0	29	0	0	11	16	0
New York[b]	238	306	73	284	327	120	368	371	26	270	168	12
North Carolina	79	31	37	157	11	9	193	9	0	92	35	0
North Dakota	0	4	0	0	43	1	2	32	0	6	9	0
Ohio	145	185	40	127	265	0	163	238	2	103	165	2
Oklahoma	-	-	-	70	27	0	115	15	0	50	17	0
Oregon	7	13	2	2	38	6	22	42	0	34	17	0
Pennsylvania	157	296	41	71	524	31	253	292	0	130	112	2
Rhode Island	7	34	2	13	34	0	32	2	0	17	5	0
South Carolina	64	28	6	127	0	0	104	0	0	48	21	1
South Dakota	0	9	0	3	44	0	7	27	0	9	11	0
Tennessee	92	49	23	140	39	4	120	37	1	60	39	0
Texas	110	6	16	298	7	0	364	6	3	236	52	0
Utah	-	-	-	6	23	2	23	11	0	11	17	1
Vermont	1	42	4	0	36	0	1	16	0	0	11	1
Virginia	82	21	41	166	16	1	151	15	0	48	69	1
West Virginia	40	15	6	23	75	0	84	16	0	47	11	0
Washington	0	6	0	6	61	4	55	55	0	61	16	0
Wisconsin	45	93	5	17	176	5	47	105	21	60	47	1
Wyoming	1	2	0	1	17	0	4	13	0	4	8	0

Note: "–" indicates that the state was not yet admitted to the Union.
[a] The relatively high number of "other" victories between 1896 and 1965 stems from a law that allowed cross-filings such that many candidates ran as both Republican and Democrat or another combination of parties.
[b] In New York the large number of "other" victories represent candidates endorsed by both major and minor parties.

Sources: Inter-University Consortium for Political and Social Research, "Candidate and Constituency Statistics of Elections in the United States, 1788-1984," machine-readable data file (Ann Arbor, Mich.: Inter-University Consortium for Political and Social Research, 1986); Congressional Quarterly Weekly Report (1986), 2843, (1988), 3269.

Table 3-16 House and Senate Election Results by Congress, 1854-1988

		House			Gains/losses		Senate			Gains/losses		
Year	Congress	Dem.	Rep.	Other	Dem.	Rep.	Dem.	Rep.	Other	Dem.	Rep.	President
1854	34th	83	108	43			42	15	5			
1856	35th	131	92	14	+48	-16	39	20	5	-3	+5	Buchanan (D)
1858	36th	101	113	23	-30	+21	38	26	2	-1	+6	
1860	37th	42	106	28	-59	-7	11	31	7	-27	+5	Lincoln (R)
1862	38th	80	103		+38	-3	12	39		+1	+8	
1864	39th	46	145		-34	+42	10	42		-2	+3	Lincoln (R)
1866	40th	49	143		+3	-2	11	42		+1	0	A. Johnson (R)
1868	41st	73	170		+24	+27	11	61		0	+19	Grant (R)
1870	42d	104	139		+31	-31	17	57		+6	-4	
1872	43d	88	203		-16	+64	19	54		+2	-3	Grant (R)
1874	44th	181	107	3	+93	-96	29	46	1	+10	-8	
1876	45th	156	137		-25	+30	36	39		+7	-7	Hayes (R)
1878	46th	150	128	14	-6	-9	43	33		+7	-6	
1880	47th	130	152	11	-20	+24	37	37	2	-6	+4	Garfield (R)
1882	48th	200	119	6	+70	-33	36	40		-1	+3	Arthur (R)
1884	49th	182	140	2	-18	+21	34	41		-2	+2	Cleveland (D)
1886	50th	170	151	4	-12	+11	37	39		+3	-2	
1888	51st	156	173	1	-14	+22	37	47		0	+8	Harrison (R)
1890	52d	231	88	14	+75	-85	39	47	2	+2	0	
1892	53rd	220	126	8	-11	+38	44	38	3	+5	-9	Cleveland (D)
1894	54th	104	246	7	-116	+120	39	44	5	-5	+6	
1896	55th	134	206	16	+30	-40	34	46	10	-5	+2	McKinley (R)
1898	56th	163	185	9	+29	-21	26	53	11	-8	+7	
1900	57th	153	198	9	-10	+13	29	56	3	+3	+3	McKinley (R)
1902	58th	178	207	5	+25	+9	32	58		+3	+2	Roosevelt (R)

Year	Congress	House	House	House others	House gain	House gain	Senate	Senate	Senate others	Senate gain	Senate gain	President
1904	59th	136	250		−42	+43	32	58		0	0	Roosevelt (R)
1906	60th	164	222		+28	−28	29	61		−3	−3	
1908	61st	172	219		+8	−3	32	59		+3	−2	Taft (R)
1910	62d	228	162	1	+56	−57	42	49		+10	−10	
1912	63d	290	127	18	+62	−35	51	44	1	+9	−5	Wilson (D)
1914	64th	231	193	8	−59	+66	56	39	1	+5	−5	
1916	65th	210	216	9	−21	+23	53	42	1	−3	+3	Wilson (D)
1918	66th	191	237	7	−19	+21	47	48	1	−6	+6	
1920	67th	132	300	1	−59	+63	37	59		−10	+11	Harding (R)
1922	68th	207	225	3	+75	−75	43	51	2	+6	−8	Coolidge (R)
1924	69th	183	247	5	−24	+22	40	54	1	−3	+3	Coolidge (R)
1926	70th	195	237	3	+12	−10	47	48	1	+7	−6	
1928	71st	163	267	1	−32	+30	39	56	1	−8	+8	Hoover (R)
1930	72d	216	218	1	+53	−49	47	48	1	+8	−8	
1932	73d	313	117	5	+97	−101	59	36	1	+12	−12	Roosevelt (D)
1934	74th	322	103	10	+9	−14	69	25	2	+10	−11	
1936	75th	333	89	13	+11	−14	75	17	4	+6	−8	Roosevelt (D)
1938	76th	262	169	4	−71	+80	69	23	4	−6	+6	
1940	77th	267	162	6	+5	−7	66	28	2	−3	+5	Roosevelt (D)
1942	78th	222	209	4	−45	+47	57	38	1	−9	+10	
1944	79th	243	190	2	+21	−19	57	38	1	0	0	Roosevelt (D)
1946	80th	188	246	1	−55	+56	45	51		−12	+13	Truman (D)
1948	81st	263	171	1	+75	−75	54	42	1	+9	−9	Truman (D)
1950	82d	234	199	2	−29	+28	48	47		−6	+5	
1952	83d	213	221	1	−21	+22	47	48		−1	+1	Eisenhower (R)
1954	84th	232	203		+19	−18	48	47	1	+1	−1	
1956	85th	234	201		+2	−2	49	47	1	+1	0	Eisenhower (R)
1958	86th	283	154		+49	−47	64	34		+17	−13	
1960	87th	263	174		−20	+20	64	36		−2	+2	Kennedy (D)
1962	88th	258	176	1	−4	+2	67	33		+4	−4	

(Table continues)

Table 3-16 (Continued)

Year	Congress	House			Gains/losses		Senate			Gains/losses		President
		Dem.	Rep.	Other	Dem.	Rep.	Dem.	Rep.	Other	Dem.	Rep.	
1964	89th	295	140		+38	-38	68	32		+2	-2	L. Johnson (D)
1966	90th	248	187		-47	+47	64	36		-3	+3	
1968	91st	243	192		-4	+4	58	42		-5	+5	Nixon (R)
1970	92d	255	180		+12	-12	55	45		-4	+2	
1972	93d	243	192		-12	+12	57	43		+2	-2	Nixon (R)
1974	94th	291	144		+43	-43	61	38		+3	-3	
1976	95th	292	143		+1	-1	62	38		0	0	Carter (D)
1978	96th	277	158		-11	+11	59	41		-3	+3	
1980	97th	243	192		-33	+33	47	53		-12	+12	Reagan (R)
1982	98th	269	166		+26	-26	46	54		0	0	
1984	99th	253	182		-14	+14	47	53		+2	-2	Reagan (R)
1986	100th	258	177		+5	-5	55	45		+8	-8	
1988	101st	260	175		+3	-3	55	45		+1	-1	Bush (R)

Note: Because of changes in the overall number of seats in the Senate and House, in the number of seats won by third parties, and in the number of vacancies, a Republican loss is not always matched precisely by a Democratic gain, or vice versa. Gains/losses reflect preelection/postelection changes. Deaths, resignations, and special elections can cause further changes in party make-up. In the 1930 election, for example, Republicans won majority control, but when Congress organized, special elections held to fill fourteen vacancies resulted in a Democratic majority.

Sources: 1854: Congressional Quarterly, *Elections '84,* 106; 1856–1984: *Congressional Quarterly's Guide to U.S. Elections,* 1124; 1986: *Congressional Quarterly Weekly Report* (1986), 2811, 2843; 1988: *Congressional Quarterly Weekly Report* (1988), 3249, 3264, 3269.

Table 3-17   Advantages of Incumbency in Reelection: Representatives, Senators, and Governors, 1960-1988

Year/office	Number of incumbents			Winning election	Gaining over 60 percent of the vote
	Ran	Won	Lost		
1960					
House	400	374	26	93.5%	58.9%
Senate	29	28	1	96.6	41.3
Governor	13	7	6	53.8	15.4
1962					
House	396	381	15	94.3	63.6
Senate	34	29	5	85.3	26.4
Governor	24	15	9	62.5	12.5
1964					
House	389	344	45	88.4	58.5
Senate	32	28	4	87.5	46.8
Governor	14	12	2	85.7	42.9
1966					
House	402	362	40	90.1	67.7
Senate	29	28	1	96.6	41.3
Governor	21	14	7	66.7	23.8
1968					
House	401	396	5	98.8	72.2
Senate	24	20	4	83.3	37.5
Governor	13	9	4	69.2	15.4
1970					
House	391	379	12	96.9	77.3
Senate	29	23	6	79.3	31.0
Governor	24	17	7	70.8	4.2
1972					
House	380	367	13	95.6	77.8
Senate	25	20	5	80.0	52.0
Governor	9	7	2	77.8	44.5
1974					
House	383	343	40	89.6	66.4
Senate	25	23	2	92.0	40.0
Governor	22	17	5	77.3	36.4
1976					
House	381	368	13	96.6	69.2
Senate	25	16	9	64.0	40.0
Governor	7	5	2	71.4	28.6
1978					
House	378	359	19	95.0	76.6
Senate	22	15	7	68.1	31.8
Governor	21	16	5	76.2	28.6

(Table continues)

115

Table 3-17 *(Continued)*

Year/office	Number of incumbents			Winning election	Gaining over 60 percent of the vote
	Ran	Won	Lost		
1980					
House	392	361	31	90.7%	72.9%
Senate	25	16	9	55.2	40.0
Governor	10	7	3	70.0	30.0
1982					
House	381	352	29	92.4	68.9
Senate	30	28	2	93.3	56.7
Governor	24	19	5	79.2	41.7
1984					
House	407	391	16	96.1	78.9
Senate	29	26	3	89.7	65.5
Governor	6	4	2	66.7	50.0
1986					
House	391	385	6	98.5	84.5
Senate	28	21	7	75.0	50.0
Governor	17	15	2	88.2	52.9
1988					
House	408	402	6	99.0	87.3
Senate	27	23	4	85.0	60.9
Governor	9	8	1	89.0	37.5

Note: Includes general elections only. Percentage gaining over 60 percent of the vote is calculated on the basis of the vote for the two major parties. "Off-off" year gubernatorial elections, held in Kentucky, Louisiana, Mississippi, New Jersey, and Virginia, are not included in the above totals. For these gubernatorial election outcomes, see *Congressional Quarterly's Guide to U.S. Elections.*

Sources: House and Senate, 1960-1978: Congressional Quarterly, *Elections '80,* 14; House and Senate, 1980-1982, and governor, 1964-1966: Richard M. Scammon and Alice V. McGillivray, comps. and eds., *America Votes 16: A Handbook of Contemporary American Election Statistics* (Washington, D.C.: Elections Research Center, Congressional Quarterly, 1985); 1984: *Congressional Quarterly Almanac, 1984,* B7, B13, B19; House and Senate, 1986, and governor, 1968-1986: *Congressional Quarterly Weekly Report;* 1988: *Congressional Quarterly Weekly Report* (1988), 3249, 3266, 3296-3298, 3301-3307, (1989), 1074-1080, 1149.

Questions

1. Nationally, turnout fell sharply with the 1920 election (Figure 3-1). What could account for this decline?

2. Around the turn of the century, southern turnout dropped sharply and has approached the levels attained in the 1890s only since the 1960s (Figure 3-2). What accounts for the drop and recovery?

3. Which four groups generally register and vote at the lowest rates (Table 3-1)? What might account for the gap in participation between these groups and others? What political implications might flow from these low participation rates?

4. Which states gave more than 60 percent of their popular vote in 1988 to George Bush (Table 3-2)? Which gave 50 percent or more to Michael Dukakis? Which region is most supportive of Bush? (Use the four regions as defined by the Census Bureau—see the Appendix.)

5. On Super Tuesday (March 8, 1988), George Bush sewed up the Republican nomination by winning all sixteen Republican primaries (Table 3-4). In how many of these states did at least one Democratic candidate receive more votes in the Democratic primary (Table 3-3) held the same day than Bush received in the Republican primary? Which states were these?

6. Because it is the first major media event of the presidential nominating process, the Iowa caucus allows a candidate to establish momentum, and this has an enormous influence on who wins the presidential nominations. Looking at the 1988 Democratic and Republican primaries and caucuses (Tables 3-3 through 3-6), evaluate this statement.

7. In some years the Democrats have had considerably more candidates than the Republicans, while in other years the Republicans have had more (Figure 3-3). What explains these differences? In 1972, 1980, and 1984, the incumbent president announced his candidacy relatively late. Were the incumbents uncertain about whether they would run?

8. Which states did not use a presidential primary to select national

convention delegates at any time between 1968 and 1988 (Table 3-7)?

9. Contrast the bases of support for Michael Dukakis and Jesse Jackson in the 1988 Democratic primaries (Table 3-8). Do the same for Walter Mondale and Gary Hart in 1984.

10. Did Jimmy Carter in 1980, Walter Mondale in 1984, and Michael Dukakis in 1988 receive more of their convention votes from caucus states or primary states (Table 3-9)?

11. What is the average difference between the Republican "vote" in the final Gallup survey and the Republican vote in the election (Table 3-10)? The Gallup organization has tried to improve its procedures since the disastrous (for its image) incorrect "call" in 1948. Does the evidence suggest an improvement?

12. Support for third-party candidates George Wallace in 1968 and John Anderson in 1980 came from very different parts of the electorate (Table 3-11). Describe their differing bases of support.

13. Contrast the characteristics of voters in the Democratic presidential primaries of 1988 (Table 3-8) with those voting in the general election of 1988 (Table 3-12).

14. In what years has the winning presidential candidate received a minority of the *two-party* popular vote (Table 3-13)? Which winning candidate received the smallest percentage of the *total* popular vote?

15. Which fifteen states, excluding Hawaii, voted most heavily Democratic for president between 1932 and 1964 (Table 3-14)? Which of these states voted Democratic more often than the fifty-state national average of 1.26 times from 1968-1988?

16. Which five states have elected the highest percentage of Republican representatives from 1966-1988 (Table 3-15)? The highest percentage of Democratic representatives from 1966-1988? Which five states have elected Republican representatives over 100 times from 1966-1988?

17. Political scientists and historians speak of "realigning elections," elections in which there is a sharp shift in the partisanship or

long-term voting habits of the electorate. What do the results of House elections in the last decade of the nineteenth century suggest about the timing of the realignment in that period (Table 3-16)?

18. Except for 1986, there is a perfect pattern in Table 3-17: House incumbents most often get more than 60 percent of the vote, incumbent governors least often. What might explain this pattern?

4
Political Parties

Political parties live and die by the numbers—numbers of supporters, candidates, contributors, and especially voters. Therefore, it is not surprising that a book of statistics on American politics contains a great deal of data about parties or that these data appear throughout the volume.

Parties can be profitably viewed from three different perspectives: parties in the electorate, parties in government, and parties as organizations. As Chapter 3 is devoted entirely to elections, and Chapter 5 includes considerable data about elements of voting (partisanship and party evaluations), in this chapter only a portion of the material is devoted to parties in the electorate, despite the overwhelming importance to parties of gathering votes. Although no sharp distinction is possible or intended, the emphasis here is on aspects of voting that relate more closely to parties as organizations. Thus, for example, a number of tables concern the topics of party-line versus split-ticket voting and partisan versus split outcomes (Tables 4-4 through 4-8). Such topics are useful for assessing the strength of parties and of partisanship.

The party-line voting tables draw on two kinds of data—aggregate data (about collectivities such as states and congressional districts) and individual data (about individual voters, chiefly drawn from sample surveys). Although the two are likely to indicate the same sort of conclusions, they are independent of one another and each tells something distinct. It is possible, for example, for there to be a large amount of split-ticket voting by individuals and yet a small number of split district outcomes. For example, a very large majority may support the Democratic candidate for governor and a much narrower majority support the Democratic candidate for president. Likewise, it is possible for many individuals to split their tickets and still have winning candidates from the same party; if those who split their tickets do so in opposite ways, they will offset each others' votes.

Many of the tables in Chapters 7 and 8 concern parties in government. Voting in Congress frequently takes on partisan tones, as does support for or opposition to the president. Party unity and presidential support scores therefore offer important perspectives on the continuing or changing significance of political parties. Like voting by the electorate, congressional voting is viewed from both individual and aggregate perspectives. How individual representatives and senators vote is important to their constituents and to organized interests, so publications and tabulations showing individual voting behavior have become widespread (see Tables 7-15 and 7-16). How unified party members are in their voting, the degree to which the parties oppose each other, and the extent to which there are other cohesive groups—such as the so-called Conservative Coalition of Republicans and southern Democrats—are all important analytically for understanding congressional behavior and practically for those who wish to influence congressional action (Tables 7-9 through 7-11 and Figure 7-2).

In this chapter the emphasis is on parties as organizations, beginning simply with their organizational identities (Table 4-1). The growth of presidential primaries is also documented (Table 4-9). Two additional topics are covered principally since the 1970s when data collection began in earnest. First, as is discussed further in Chapter 6, the establishment of the Federal Election Commission in 1973 has led to more extensive and more revealing data about expenditures (Tables 4-12 and 4-13). Second, just as surveys have expanded the kind of material available about voters, they have been used to provide insight into party elites, especially national convention delegates. The data that have been systematically collected are largely limited to demographic information (Table 4-10). Nevertheless, data about national convention delegates are now available over an increasingly long period.

It is fortunate, in any event, that some information is available about party elites. In part because of the decentralized nature of American parties, scholars only recently have begun systematically to study parties as organizations.[1] Consequently data are scarce; what is available are from limited time periods and a restricted range of localities. This systematic study has occurred just as Republican and Democratic national party organizations have responded to the declining importance of parties in the electorate by stepping up the services they provide to local and state party organizations in areas such as candidate recruitment, media consulting, polling information, and fund raising.

How parties fare in the altered context of American politics depends partially upon how parties as organizations respond to changes such as the growth of political action committees, increased campaign costs, and the pervasive reach and use of media, particularly television. In doing so, the parties may add to scholarly efforts to increase available information about their activities and organizational efforts. Ironically, the much-heralded decline of parties in the electorate may make parties as organizations a growth area of data collection over the next decade.

Note

1. Cornelius P. Cotter, James L. Gibson, John F. Bibby, and Robert J. Huckshorn, *Party Organizations in American Politics* (New York: Praeger, 1984).

Figure 4-1   American Political Parties Since 1789

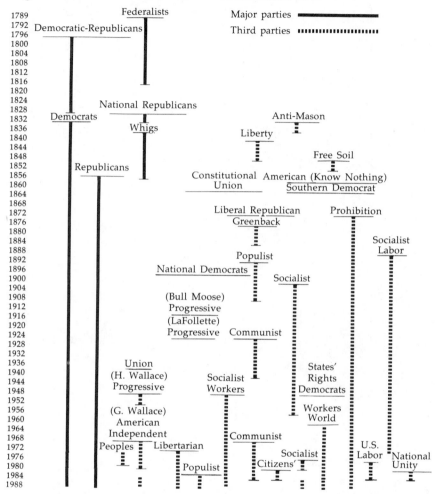

Note: The chart indicates the years parties either ran presidential candidates or held national conventions. The lifespan for many political parties can only be approximated because parties existed at the state or local level before they ran candidates in presidential elections, and parties continued to exist at local levels long after they ceased running presidential candidates. Not every party fielding a presidential candidate is represented in the chart. For instance, in 1988 at least nine other parties fielded such a candidate in at least one state.

Sources: Congressional Quarterly, Congressional Quarterly's Guide to U.S. Elections, 2d ed. (Washington, D.C.: Congressional Quarterly, 1985), 224; 1988: Congressional Quarterly Weekly Report (1988), 3184.

Table 4-1 Party Competition: The Presidency, 1968-1988

Number of times Republican presidential candidate carried the state
(based on electoral votes)

0	1	2	3	4	5	6
District of Columbia	Minnesota	Hawaii	Georgia	Alabama	Connecticut	Alaska
		Massachusetts	Maryland	Arkansas	Delaware	Arizona
		Rhode Island	New York	Louisiana	Florida	California
		West Virginia		Mississippi	Iowa	Colorado
				Pennsylvania	Kentucky	Idaho
				Texas	Maine	Illinois
				Washington	Michigan	Indiana
				Wisconsin	Missouri	Kansas
					North Carolina	Montana
					Ohio	Nebraska
					Oregon	Nevada
					South Carolina	New Hampshire
					Tennessee	New Jersey
						New Mexico
						North Dakota
						Oklahoma
						South Dakota
						Utah
						Vermont
						Virginia
						Wyoming

Sources: Compiled by the editors from Richard M. Scammon and Alice V. McGillivray, comps. and eds., *America Votes 16: A Handbook of Contemporary American Election Statistics* (Washington, D.C.: Elections Research Center, Congressional Quarterly, 1985), 31, 33, 35, 37, 41; *Congressional Quarterly Weekly Report* (1988), 3245.

Table 4-2   Party Competition in the States, 1968-1988

Percentage of Republican wins[a]				
0-20	21-40	41-60	61-80	81-100
Alabama	Alaska	Delaware	Arizona	Colorado
Arkansas	Illinois	Iowa	Kansas	Idaho
California	Montana	Maine	North Dakota	Indiana
Connecticut	Nebraska[b]	New York	South Dakota	New
Florida	Nevada	Ohio	Utah	Hampshire
Georgia	New Jersey	Pennsylvania	Vermont	Wyoming
Hawaii	Oregon			
Kentucky	Washington			
Louisiana	Wisconsin			
Maryland				
Massachusetts				
Michigan				
Minnesota				
Mississippi				
Missouri				
New Mexico				
North Carolina				
Oklahoma				
Rhode Island				
South Carolina				
Tennessee				
Texas				
Virginia				
West Virginia				

[a] The governorship, control of the lower chamber, and control of the upper chamber are figured separately. That is, if in a given year the Republicans won the governorship and control of one chamber, they had 66.7 percent of the wins.

[b] Results are for the governorship only because the legislature is nonpartisan.

Sources: Calculated by the editors. 1968-1986: Republican National Committee, *Republican Almanac, 1987: State Political Profiles* (Washington, D.C.: Republican National Committee, 1987); 1987-1988: *Congressional Quarterly Weekly Report* (1988), 3298; National Conference of State Legislatures, unpublished data.

Table 4-3 Party Competition by Region, 1860-1988 (percent)

	Party system			
Region/office	1860-1895	1896-1931	1932-1965	1966-1988
New England				
President	85.2	85.5	53.7	72.2
Governor	72.9	85.9	60.8	44.4
U.S. representative	76.7	82.7	57.7	36.4
U.S. senator	a	85.7	59.7	42.9
Middle Atlantic				
President	38.9	88.9	47.2	70.8
Governor	31.9	66.0	56.8	56.5
U.S. representative	53.1	63.4	52.8	40.4
U.S. senator	a	76.7	64.7	53.1
Midwest				
President	77.8	84.4	44.4	86.7
Governor	73.2	78.9	45.6	67.7
U.S. representative	55.8	73.5	57.1	50.7
U.S. senator	a	81.6	51.6	38.1
Plains				
President	88.9	77.8	57.4	83.3
Governor	86.7	73.6	64.1	46.8
U.S. representative	82.1	83.3	73.7	48.0
U.S. senator	a	76.2	73.1	50.0
South				
President	18.4	6.1	15.8	73.3
Governor	17.1	2.9	0.0	26.9
U.S. representative	17.6	4.0	4.5	28.5
U.S. senator	a	0.0	0.7	31.3
Border South				
President	8.6	56.8	22.2	63.6
Governor	14.0	38.6	16.7	34.5
U.S. representative	15.6	36.7	18.5	30.3
U.S. senator	a	41.2	24.6	40.0
Rocky Mountain				
President	73.3	57.8	35.2	97.9
Governor	63.0	44.7	40.0	34.0
U.S. representative	67.5	59.4	31.8	57.9
U.S. senator	a	44.3	30.5	56.3
Pacific Coast				
President	75.0	75.0	37.5	76.7
Governor	42.9	55.6	54.8	46.7
U.S. representative	57.1	63.1	38.6	38.4
U.S. senator	a	66.7	37.5	48.8

Note: Table entries are the percentages of all elections won by Republicans. For composition of regions, see Appendix Table A-3.

[a] Direct election of U.S. senators began after passage of the Seventeenth Amendment in 1913.

Sources: Calculated by the editors from Inter-University Consortium for Political and Social Research, "Candidate and Constituency Statistics of Elections in the United States, 1788-1987," machine-readable data file (Ann Arbor, Mich.: Inter-University Consortium for Political and Social Research, 1988); updated through 1988 from *Congressional Quarterly Weekly Report* (1988), 3245, 3264, 3269, 3298.

Table 4-4 Strength of Party Identification and the Presidential Vote, 1952-1988 (percent)

Year/candidate	Strong Democrat	Weak Democrat	Independent Democrat	Independent	Independent Republican	Weak Republican	Strong Republican	Total
1952								
Stevenson	84	62	61	20	7	6	2	42
Eisenhower	16	38	39	80	93	94	98	58
1956								
Stevenson	85	63	67	17	6	7	0	40
Eisenhower	15	37	33	83	94	93	100	60
1960								
Kennedy	91	72	90	46	12	13	2	49
Nixon	9	28	10	54	88	87	98	51
1964								
Johnson	95	82	90	77	25	43	10	68
Goldwater	5	18	10	23	75	57	90	32
1968								
Humphrey	92	68	64	30	5	11	3	46
Nixon	8	32	36	70	95	89	97	54
1972								
McGovern	73	48	61	30	13	9	3	36
Nixon	27	52	39	70	87	91	97	64
1976								
Carter	92	75	76	44	14	22	3	51
Ford	8	25	24	56	86	78	97	49
1980								
Carter	89	65	60	26	13	5	5	44
Reagan	11	35	40	74	87	95	95	56

(Table continues)

Table 4-4 (Continued)

Year/candidate	Strong Democrat	Weak Democrat	Independent Democrat	Independent	Independent Republican	Weak Republican	Strong Republican	Total
1984								
Mondale	89	68	79	28	7	6	3	42
Reagan	11	32	21	72	93	94	97	58
1988								
Dukakis	94	72	88	35	15	17	2	47
Bush	6	28	12	65	85	83	98	53

Note: Results are from surveys in which voters are asked which party they identify with and who they voted for. The exact question is as follows: "Generally speaking, do you consider yourself a Republican, a Democrat, an Independent, or what?" If Republican or Democrat: "Would you consider yourself a strong (R/D) or a not very strong (R/D)?" If Independent or other: "Do you think of yourself as closer to the Republican or Democratic party?" Votes for candidates other than the Democrat or Republican were excluded.

Source: Calculated by the editors from National Election Studies data (Ann Arbor, Mich.: Center for Political Studies, University of Michigan).

Table 4-5 Party-line Voting in Presidential and Congressional Elections, 1952-1988 (percent)

	Presidential elections			U.S. Senate elections			U.S. House elections		
Year	Party-line voters[a]	Defectors[b]	Independents	Party-line voters[a]	Defectors[b]	Independents	Party-line voters[a]	Defectors[b]	Independents
1952	77	18	5	79	16	5	80	15	5
1956	76	15	9	80	12	8	82	9	9
1958				84	11	5	84	11	5
1960	79	13	8	79	12	9	80	11	8
1962				—	—	—	83	11	6
1964	79	15	5	78	16	6	79	15	5
1966				76	17	7	76	17	7
1968	69	24	7	73	20	7	74	19	7
1970				77	13	10	76	16	9
1972	67	25	8	69	22	9	74	17	8
1974				74	18	8	74	18	8
1976	73	16	11	69	19	12	72	19	9
1978				71	20	9	67	23	10
1980	68	24	8	71	21	8	69	23	8
1982				77	17	6	76	17	6
1984	79	13	8	72	20	9	70	23	7
1986				76	20	4	72	22	6
1988	81	12	7	72	20	7	74	19	7

Note: "—" indicates not available. In presidential elections the base for percentages is all voters. In Senate and House elections the base for percentages is all voters supporting Democratic or Republican candidates.

[a] Democratic or Republican identifiers who vote for the candidate of their party. Party identification is based on surveys in which voters are asked which party they identify with (see Table 4-4 for exact question). "Independent partisans," or so-called "leaners," are included here as party-line voters or defectors.

[b] Democratic or Republican identifiers who do not vote for the candidate of their party.

Source: Calculated by the editors from the National Election Studies data set.

Table 4-6 Partisan Division of Governors and State Legislatures

| | Governor | | | Legislature | | | | |
| | | | | Upper house | | Lower house | | |
State	Name	Party	Next up for reelection	Democrats	Republicans	Democrats	Republicans	Next up for reelection
Alabama	Guy Hunt	R[a]	1990	30	5	89	16	1990
Alaska	Steve Cowper	D	1990	8	12	23	17	1990[b]
Arizona	Rose Mofford	D[a]	1990	13	17	26	34	1990
Arkansas	Bill Clinton	D	1990	31	4	88	11	1990[b]
California	George Deukmejian	R	1990	24	15	46	33	1990[b]
Colorado	Roy Romer	D	1990	11	24	26	39	1990[b]
Connecticut	William A. O'Neill	D	1990	23	23	88	63	1990
Delaware	Michael N. Castle	R	1992[c]	13	8	18	23	1990[b]
Florida	Bob Martinez	R[a]	1990	23	17	73	47	1990[b]
Georgia	Joe Frank Harris	D	1990[c]	45	11	144	36	1990
Hawaii	John Waihee	D	1990	22	3	45	6	1990[b]
Idaho	Cecil D. Andrus	D	1990	19	23	20	64	1990
Illinois	James R. Thompson	R	1990	31	28	67	51	1990[b]
Indiana	Evan Bayh	D[a]	1992	24	26	50	50	1990[b]
Iowa	Terry Branstad	R	1990	30	20	61	39	1990[d]
Kansas	Mike Hayden	R[a]	1990	18	22	58	67	1990[b]
Kentucky	Wallace Wilkinson	D	1991[c]	30	8	72	28	1991
Louisiana	Buddy Roemer	D	1991	34	5	86	18	1991
Maine	John McKernan, Jr.	R[a]	1990	20	15	97	54	1990
Maryland	William Schaefer	D	1990	40	7	125	16	1990
Massachusetts	Michael Dukakis	D	1990	32	8	128	32	1990
Michigan	James Blanchard	D	1990	18	20	61	49	1990
Minnesota	Rudy Perpich	D	1990	45	22	81	53	1990
Mississippi	Ray Mabus	D	1991	46	6	113	9	1991
Missouri	John Ashcroft	R	1992[c]	22	12	105	58	1990[b]
Montana	Stan Stephens	R[a]	1992	23	27	52	48	1990[b]

State	Governor	Party	Year					Year
Nebraska	Kay Orr	R[a]	1990	e	e	e	e	1990[b]
Nevada	Robert J. Miller	D	1990	8	13	30	12	1990[b]
New Hampshire	Judd Gregg	R	1990	8	16	119	281	1990
New Jersey	Thomas Kean	R	1989[c]	24	16	38	41	1989
New Mexico	Garrey Carruthers	R[a]	1990	26	16	45	25	1990[d]
New York	Mario Cuomo	D	1990	27	34	92	58	1990
North Carolina	James Martin	R	1992[c]	37	13	74	46	1990
North Dakota	George Sinner	D	1992	32	21	45	61	1990[b]
Ohio	Richard Celeste	D	1990[c]	14	19	59	40	1990[b]
Oklahoma	Henry Bellmon	R[a]	1990	33	15	69	32	1990[b]
Oregon	Neil Goldschmidt	D[a]	1990	19	11	32	28	1990[b]
Pennsylvania	Robert P. Casey	D[a]	1990	23	27	104	99	1990[b]
Rhode Island	Edward DiPrete	R	1990	41	9	82	18	1990
South Carolina	Carroll Campbell, Jr.	R[a]	1990	35	11	86	37	1990[d]
South Dakota	George Mickelson	R	1990	14	20	24	46	1990
Tennessee	Ned McWherter	D[a]	1990	22	11	59	40	1990[b]
Texas	William P. Clements	R[a]	1990	23	8	93	57	1990[b]
Utah	Norman Bangerter	R	1992	7	22	28	47	1990[b]
Vermont	Madeleine Kunin	D	1990	16	14	74	76	1990
Virginia	Gerald Baliles	D	1989[c]	30	9	64	34	1989[f]
Washington	Booth Gardner	D	1992	24	25	64	34	1990[b]
West Virginia	Gaston Caperton	D[a]	1992	30	4	79	21	1990[b]
Wisconsin	Tommy Thompson	R[a]	1990	20	13	56	43	1990[b]
Wyoming	Mike Sullivan	D	1990	11	19	23	41	1990[b]

Note: As of December 1988. Legislative divisions reflect seated members. Some vacancies exist.
[a] Change in party control from last election.
[b] Upper house elections are staggered so only some legislators are up for election in the year indicated.
[c] Barred by state law from seeking reelection.
[d] Lower house only, upper house in 1992.
[e] Nebraska's state legislature is nonpartisan and unicameral.
[f] Lower house only, upper house in 1991.

Sources: Governors: *Congressional Quarterly Weekly Report* (1988), 3298; state legislative divisions: National Conference of State Legislatures; next up for reelection: Council of State Governments, *Book of the States 1988-89* (Lexington, Ky.: Council of State Governments, 1987), 89, 182-183.

Table 4-7 Split-Ticket Voting, 1952-1988 (percent)

Year	President-House	Senate-House	State-local
1952	13	9	26
1956	16	10	29
1958		10	31
1960	14	9	27
1962		—	42
1964	14	18	41
1966		21	50
1968	17	21	47
1970		20	51
1972	30	22	58
1974		24	61
1976	25	23	—
1978		35	—
1980	28	31	59
1982		24	55
1984	25	20	52
1986		28	—
1988	25	27	—

Note: "—" indicates not available. Entries are the percentages of voters who "split" their ticket by supporting candidates of different parties for the offices indicated. Those who cast ballots for other than Democratic and Republican candidates are excluded in presidential and congressional calculations. The state-local figure is based on a general question: "Did you vote for other state and local offices? Did you vote a straight ticket, or did you vote for candidates from different parties?"

Source: Calculated by the editors from National Election Studies data.

Table 4-8 Split District Outcomes: Presidential and House Voting, 1900-1988

Year	Total number of districts[a]	Number of districts with split results[b]	Percentage of total
1900	295	10	3.4
1904	310	5	1.6
1908	314	21	6.7
1912	333	84	25.2
1916	333	35	10.5
1920	344	11	3.2
1924	356	42	11.8
1928	359	68	18.9
1932	355	50	14.1
1936	361	51	14.1
1940	362	53	14.6
1944	367	41	11.2
1948	422	90	21.3
1952	435	84	19.3
1956	435	130	29.9
1960	437	114	26.1
1964	435	145	33.3
1968	435	139	32.0
1972	435	192	44.1
1976	435	124	28.5
1980	435	143	32.8
1984	435	196	45.0
1988	435	148	34.0

[a] Before 1952 complete data are not available on every congressional district.
[b] Congressional districts carried by a presidential candidate of one party and a House candidate of another party.

Sources: 1900-1984: Norman J. Ornstein et al., eds., *Vital Statistics on Congress, 1987-1988* (Washington, D.C.: Congressional Quarterly, 1987), 62; 1988: calculated by the editors from Congressional Quarterly data.

Table 4-9   Presidential Primaries, 1912-1988

Year	Democratic party			Republican party		
	Number of primaries	Votes cast	Percentage of delegates from primary states	Number of primaries	Votes cast	Percentage of delegates from primary states
1912	12	974,775	32.9	13	2,261,240	41.7
1916	20	1,187,691	53.5	20	1,923,374	58.9
1920	16	571,671	44.6	20	3,186,248	57.8
1924	14	763,858	35.5	17	3,525,185	45.3
1928	17	1,264,220	42.2	16	4,110,288	44.9
1932	16	2,952,933	40.0	14	2,346,996	37.7
1936	14	5,181,808	36.5	12	3,319,810	37.5
1940	13	4,468,631	35.8	13	3,227,875	38.8
1944	14	1,867,609	36.7	13	2,271,605	38.7
1948	14	2,151,865	36.3	12	2,635,255	36.0
1952	16	4,928,006	39.2	13	7,801,413	39.0
1956	19	5,832,592	41.3	19	5,828,272	43.5
1960	16	5,686,664	38.4	15	5,537,967	38.6
1964	16	6,247,435	41.4	17	5,935,339	45.6
1968	17	7,535,069	48.7	17	4,473,551	47.0
1972	23	15,993,965	66.5	22	6,188,281	58.2
1976	30	16,052,652	76.1	29	10,374,125	70.4
1980	35	18,747,825	81.1	36	12,690,451	78.0
1984	30	18,009,217	67.1	29	6,575,651	66.6
1988	37	23,230,525	81.4	38	12,169,003	80.7

Note: Primaries include binding and nonbinding presidential preference primaries as well as primaries selecting national convention delegates only without indication of presidential preference. Prior to 1980, votes cast in the delegate-only primaries are not included in the total votes cast.

Sources: 1936 Democratic delegates: Democratic National Committee; 1964 Democratic delegates: *Congressional Quarterly Weekly Report* (1964), 1140; votes cast, number of primaries, and remaining delegates: Congressional Quarterly, *Congressional Quarterly's Guide to U.S. Elections*, 188-221, 387-441; 1988: *Congressional Quarterly Weekly Report* (1987), 1988, (1988), 1892, 1894-1897, 2033, 2254-2255.

Table 4-10 Profile of National Convention Delegates, 1944-1988 (percent)

	1944		1968		1972		1976		1980		1984		1988	
	D	R	D	R	D	R	D	R	D	R	D	R	D	R
Women	11	9	13	16	40	29	33	31	49	29	49	44	48	33
Black	—	—	5	2	15	4	11	3	15	3	18	4	23	4
Under thirty	—	—	3	4	22	8	15	7	11	5	8	4	4	3
Lawyer	38	37	28	22	12	—	16	15	13	15	17	14	16	17
Teacher	—	—	8	2	11	—	12	4	15	4	16	6	14	5
Union member	—	—	—	—	16	—	21	3	27	4	25	4	25	3
Attending first convention	63	63	67	66	83	78	80	78	87	84	78	69	65	68
Protestant	—	—	—	—	42	—	47	73	47	72	49	71	50	69
Catholic	—	—	—	—	26	—	34	18	37	22	29	22	30	22
Jewish	—	—	—	—	9	—	9	3	8	3	8	2	7	2
Liberal	—	—	—	—	—	—	40	3	46	2	48	1	43	0
Moderate	—	—	—	—	—	—	47	45	42	36	42	35	43	35
Conservative	—	—	—	—	—	—	8	48	6	58	4	60	5	58
Median age	—	—	49	49	42	—	43	48	44	49	43	51	46	51

Note: "—" indicates not available.

Sources: 1944: Barbara Farah, "Delegate Polls: 1944-1984," *Public Opinion* (August/September 1984): 43-45; 1968-1988: Martin Plissner and Warren J. Mitofsky, "The Making of the Delegates, 1968-1988," *Public Opinion* (September/October 1988): 47 (reprinted with permission of the American Enterprise Institute for Public Policy Research).

Table 4-11 Size of National Party Conventions, 1932-1988

| Year | Delegate votes | |
	Democrats	Republicans
1932	1,154	1,154
1936	1,100	1,003
1940	1,100	1,000
1944	1,176	1,056
1948	1,234	1,094
1952	1,230	1,206
1956	1,372	1,323
1960	1,521	1,331
1964	2,316	1,308
1968	2,622	1,333
1972	3,016	1,348
1976	3,008	2,259
1980	3,331	1,994
1984	3,933	2,235
1988	4,161	2,277

Note: The number of delegates (persons attending) may be larger because of fractional votes.

Sources: Democrats, 1932, 1940-1984: *Congressional Quarterly's Guide to U.S. Elections,* 115, 198-221; Democrats 1936, 1988: Democratic National Committee; Republicans (all years): Republican National Committee.

Table 4-12 Financial Activity of the National Political Parties, 1977-1988 (millions)

Party	1977-78	1979-80	1981-82	1983-84	1985-86	1987-88
Democrat						
Raised	$26.4	$37.2	$39.3	$98.5	$64.8	$127.9
Spent	26.9	35.0	40.1	97.4	65.9	121.9
Contributions	1.8	1.7	1.7	2.6	1.7	1.7
Coordinated expenditures[a]	0.4	4.9	3.3	9.0	9.0	17.9
Republican						
Raised	84.5	169.5	215.0	297.9	255.2	263.3
Spent	85.9	161.8	214.0	300.8	258.9	257.0
Contributions	4.5	4.5	5.6	4.9	3.4	3.4
Coordinated expenditures[a]	4.3	12.4	14.3	20.1	14.3	22.7

Note: Building funds and state and local election spending are not reported to the Federal Election Commission.

[a] Party committees are also allowed to spend money on behalf of federal candidates, in addition to the money party committees may contribute directly. This spending may be coordinated with a candidate.

Source: Federal Election Commission, "FEC Summarizes 1988 Political Party Activity," press release, March 27, 1989, 2.

Table 4-13   Party Contributions and Coordinated Expenditures by
Office and Party, 1975-1988

	Senate		*House*	
Year/party	Contributions	Expenditures	Contributions	Expenditures
1975-76				
Democrats	$468,795	$4,359	$1,465,629	$500
Republicans	930,034	113,976	3,658,310	329,583
1977-78				
Democrats	466,683	229,218	1,262,298	72,892
Republicans	703,204	2,723,880	3,621,104	1,297,079
1979-80				
Democrats	480,464	1,132,912	1,025,989	256,346
Republicans	677,004	5,434,758	3,498,323	2,203,748
1981-82				
Democrats	579,337	2,265,197	1,052,286	694,321
Republicans	600,221	8,715,761	4,720,959	5,293,260
1983-84				
Democrats	441,467	3,947,731	1,280,672	1,774,452
Republicans	590,922	6,518,415	4,060,120	6,190,309
1985-86				
Democrats	583,305	6,066,372	610,840	1,545,376
Republicans	629,472	9,959,330	1,655,250	4,098,389
1987-88				
Democrats	488,899	6,592,264	1,197,537	2,880,301
Republicans	721,237	10,260,600	2,650,569	4,162,644

Note: Includes direct contributions made by party committees to congressional candidates
and coordinated expenditures made on their behalf.

Sources: 1975-1984: Ornstein, *Vital Statistics on Congress, 1987-1988,* 102; 1985-1986: Federal
Election Commission, "FEC Final 1985-86 Report on Political Parties Shows Decline in
Financial Activity," press release, May 5, 1988, 2; 1987-1988: Federal Election Commission,
"FEC Summarizes 1988 Political Party Activity," press release, March 27, 1989, 4-5.

Questions

1. Which third party survived the longest (Figure 4-1)?

2. Using the Guide to References for Political Statistics, find a source of third party votes for president. Which third party received the greatest percentage of the popular vote in an election? Why?

3. Which party has dominated presidential elections since 1968 (Table 4-1)? Which party has dominated state elections since 1968 (Table 4-2)? What does this imply about voting behavior during this period?

4. Lyndon Johnson in 1964 was the first southerner to be elected president since before the Civil War. Why? Table 4-3 should help.

5. What does Table 4-4 suggest about the significance of party as a voting cue?

6. Compare the voting of weak and independent Democrats and of weak and independent Republicans (Table 4-4). What does this suggest about the strength of party identification among weak versus independent partisans?

7. Is the proportion of defectors consistently greater in House voting than in presidential voting (Table 4-5)? In the presidential election of 1972, are the defectors most likely to have been Republican identifiers voting for McGovern or Democratic identifiers voting for Nixon? What about 1984—Republicans for Mondale or Democrats for Reagan? What about 1960—Republicans for Kennedy or Democrats for Nixon?

8. In which states are the legislative parties fairly evenly matched in at least one house in 1988, in other words, states in which neither party has more than 55 percent of the legislators (Table 4-6)? In which state legislatures is one party completely dominant, in other words, states in which one party has more than two-thirds of the legislators in both houses? How does this "snapshot" of one aspect of partisan competition compare with the picture presented in Table 4-2?

9. What percentage of U.S. voters supported candidates of different parties for president and U.S. House of Representatives before the

mid-1960s (Table 4-7)? Since the mid-1960s? What does this difference suggest about the significance of party as a voting cue?

10. How can it be that only 14 percent of the voters split their ticket in presidential and House voting but in one-third of the districts candidates of different parties led the congressional and presidential voting, as happened in 1964 (Tables 4-7 and 4-8)? Explain your answer with a hypothetical example.

11. Presidential primaries are a more important part of the nomination process now than years ago. When do you think they became more important (Table 4-9)? Note that between 1968 and 1972 the number of Democratic primaries rose by just over 50 percent but that the number of votes cast more than doubled. Give two hypotheses that might explain this combination of results. Note that turnout in the Republican primaries was greater in 1976 than in 1984. Why? (Hint: see Figure 3-3.)

12. Contrast the ideology of Democratic and Republican national convention delegates (Table 4-10). Compare the delegates' ideology with that of the nation's population (Table 5-3).

13. Speculate on why the political parties have increased the size of national party conventions in the past two decades (Table 4-11) and why the Democrats have tended to have larger conventions than Republicans.

14. Which party raised the most money for its candidates between 1977 and 1988 (Table 4-12)? Has the ratio of the dollars raised by Republicans to dollars raised by Democrats increased steadily over the period shown?

15. In 1986 and 1988 the Republican party gave about $1.5 and $2.5 million, respectively, to its House candidates, far less than in previous years (Table 4-13). At the same time, the party increased its contributions to Senate candidates. Why? (Hint: Table 3-16 may help.)

5

Public Opinion

Public opinion data are everywhere. They are perhaps most prominent in preelection polls showing who is ahead and who is behind, but they are more important and more often used as guides by candidates and officeholders about what the public thinks and how it would react to changes in public policies. Surveys are also used, in a more partisan way, by politicians, journalists, and interest groups to support their positions. And, in a slightly different form, they are even more widely used by advertisers and manufacturers to gauge consumer reactions to new products and services. Reflecting this frequent and varied use, this book is interspersed with public opinion data. The present chapter includes what might be called general perspectives on public opinion.

Figures 5-1 through 5-3 and Tables 5-1 through 5-3 cover two of the most frequently cited components of public opinion—partisanship and political ideology. These characteristics merit emphasis due to their practical political significance. They are of interest not only to those who wish to understand scientifically why people behave as they do. They also attract the attention of those who analyze long-term political and social trends, and are of intense interest to those who track day-to-day politics.

From another perspective, these results are important because they illustrate the reliability and validity of public opinion polling as well as the hazards of gauging personal opinions. Figures 5-1 and 5-2, showing self-proclaimed party identification, are reasonably similar for the period they jointly cover. If public opinion data were totally unreliable, as some contend, such similarity would be unlikely. Moreover, these figures illustrate two aspects of reliability and validity. First, polling as few as fifteen hundred people tells something very real about the entire population; two separate organizations, as represented in Figures 5-1 and 5-2, would not obtain such similarity over several decades of interviewing if the results represented only those actually interviewed. (Of course, one must choose the fifteen hundred respondents according to scientific sampling procedures, as do all the major polling organizations.) Second, poll results are not completely dependent on exact question wording. The Gallup question focuses on the immediate situation ("In politics, as of today ..."), while the National Election Studies question is broader ("Generally speaking ..."), suggesting that the Gallup question might pick up more short-term fluctuations in partisanship. Yet the results are somewhat similar.

At the same time, differences between the two series indicate that we cannot consider one a mere clone of the other. The National Election Studies surveys probe those who claim to be independents to determine whether they lean toward one party or the other. The responses to this probe as well as other evidence (Table 4-4) raise the question of whether independents are really closet partisans. How we answer that question, as the contrast between the two plots in Figure 5-1 shows, has major implications for conclusions about the relative strengths of the parties. As has been emphasized in earlier introductions, even simple data descriptions involve interpretation.

Because surveys are not exact counts of the whole population, "sampling error" is often reported to convey the range within which the true population result lies. For example, results are said to be accurate to within plus or minus 3 percent. Yet even with greater precision (achieved by increasing the size of the sample), survey results still require interpretation. Suppose one could ask every American adult simultaneously whether he or she was a Democrat, an independent, or a Republican. There would then be no sampling error; because everyone was asked, the information would describe the entire U.S. population at that particular time. But that returns us to an equally vexing question: What does it mean to be an independent?

The "don't know" and "no opinion" responses to the liberal/conservative questions (Table 5-3)—and in the other public opinion tables—illustrate a similar point. Whether pollsters ask about a general position or a specific issue, some proportion of the sample—often as many as 15 percent and sometimes many more—respond "don't know." It is not immediately apparent how to interpret such responses; some people have information about the subject matter but no opinion, some have no information and no opinion, and a few have no information but have an opinion anyway—and the pollster's decision about how to treat such responses can make a large difference. For example, in a preelection poll, should a pollster assume that those who have not yet chosen whom to support will eventually (1) split votes between candidates in similar proportions as those who have already decided, (2) not vote, (3) divide evenly between the candidates, or (4) overwhelmingly support a particular candidate?

For public officials seeking guidance on public sentiment, no simple reading suffices because they must assess intensity as well as direction. Those seeking a theoretical understanding of politics face the same problem. For example, although more than public opinion accounted for the outcome, consider the Senate rejection of Judge Robert Bork's nomination to the Supreme Court (Table 9-4). Polls showed the public almost evenly divided on the matter, with a slight edge to those opposing the nomination. Such a close balance was misleading. Deeper political meaning turned on the intensity of those views. One senator said, "If you vote against Bork, those in favor of him will be mad at you for a week. But if you vote for him, those who don't like him will be mad at you for the rest of their lives." Understanding the importance of public opinion in politics requires more than a simple nose count. The salience of an opinion to the person holding it also counts.

In addition, a particular survey result usually tells little in isolation. The soundest interpretations depend upon several surveys stretching over time, often over a period of years. Consider the decline and partial recovery in public confidence in government (Figure 5-9). The confidence level at a particular time is a mere point, difficult or impossible to interpret. That point, when viewed with comparable points from similar surveys over the years, indicates a trend—decline, upsurge, constancy, whatever. Consequently, reports of public opinion increasingly emphasize long time series, as we do here and in other chapters (Figures 5-4 through 5-8). Such time series data can be usefully supplemented by cross-sections (Table 5-2); such within-survey contrasts convey whether and how groups differ in attitudes.

A final note. Even a firm understanding of public opinion can be contradicted by events, as one cannot blindly equate opinion with behavior. The growth of racial tolerance in the South, such as it is, is a telling counterpoint to a political atmosphere formerly committed to white supremacy. As one respondent, a segregationist, told a pollster in the mid-1960s: "You asked me what I favored, not what I will accept graciously, not what I thought was right." [1]

Note

1. Donald R. Matthews and James W. Prothro, *Negroes and the New Southern Politics* (New York: Harcourt, Brace & World, 1966), 363.

Table 5-1 Partisan Identification, National Election Studies, 1952-1988 (percent)

	1952	1954	1956	1958	1960	1962	1964	1966	1968	1970	1972	1974	1976	1978	1980	1982	1984	1986	1988
Strong Democrat	22	22	21	27	20	23	27	18	20	20	15	17	15	15	18	20	17	18	17
Weak Democrat	25	25	23	22	25	23	25	28	25	24	26	21	25	24	23	24	20	22	18
Independent Democrat	10	9	6	7	6	7	9	9	10	10	11	13	12	14	11	11	11	10	12
Independent	6	7	9	7	10	8	8	12	11	13	13	15	15	14	13	11	11	12	11
Independent Republican	7	6	8	5	7	6	6	7	9	8	10	9	10	10	10	8	12	11	13
Weak Republican	14	14	14	17	14	16	14	15	15	15	13	14	14	13	14	14	15	15	14
Strong Republican	14	13	15	11	16	12	11	10	10	9	10	8	9	8	9	10	12	10	14
Apolitical	3	4	4	4	2	4	1	1	1	1	1	3	1	3	2	2	2	2	2
Total	101	100	100	100	100	99	101	100	101	100	99	100	101	101	100	100	100	100	101
Number of interviews	1,784	1,130	1,757	1,808	1,911	1,287	1,550	1,278	1,553	1,501	2,694	2,505	2,850	2,283	1,613	1,418	2,236	2,166	2,032

Note: Question: "Generally speaking, do you consider yourself a Republican, a Democrat, an Independent, or what?" If Republican or Democrat: "Would you call yourself a strong (R/D) or a not very strong (R/D)?" If Independent or other: "Do you think of yourself as closer to the Republican or Democratic party?"

Source: Calculated by the editors from National Election Studies data (Ann Arbor, Mich.: Center for Political Studies, University of Michigan).

Figure 5-1 Partisan Identification, National Election Studies, 1952-1988

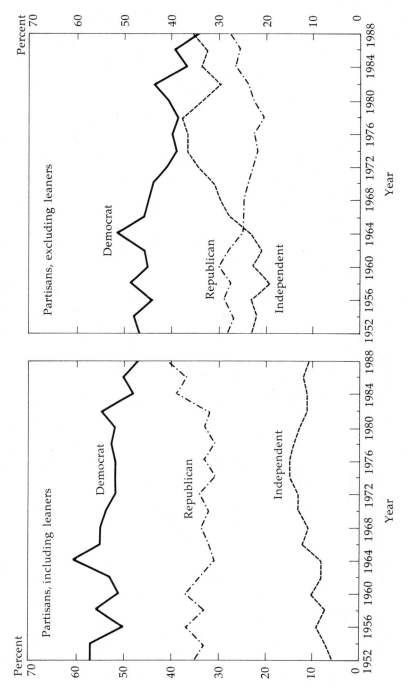

Note: See Table 5-1 for question. "Leaners" are independents who consider themselves closer to one party.

Source: National Election Studies data.

Figure 5-2   Partisan Identification, Gallup Poll, 1937-1988

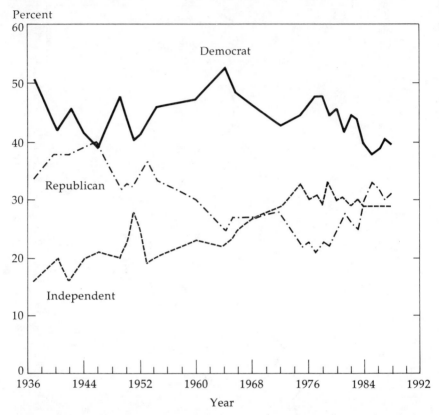

Note: Respondents who gave replies other than Democrat, Republican, or Independent are excluded. Question: "In politics, as of today, do you consider yourself a Republican, a Democrat, or an Independent?"

Sources: The Gallup Poll, "GOP Still Minority Party Despite Presidential Win Streak," press release, December 22, 1988; *The Gallup Report* (May 1987), 16-17, (January/February 1985), 21; *Gallup Opinion Index* (July 1979), 34, (October 1967), 6.

Table 5-2 Partisan Identification, Cross-Section, 1988 (percent)

	Republican	Democrat	Independent
Sex			
Men	31	37	32
Women	31	44	25
Age			
18-29	33	34	33
30-49	29	40	31
50 and over	31	46	23
Region[a]			
East	29	45	26
Midwest	32	32	36
South	32	43	25
West	30	43	27
Race/ethnicity			
White	34	36	30
Black	10	74	16
Hispanic	21	57	22
Education			
Not high school graduate	21	51	28
High school graduate	31	41	28
College incomplete	31	39	30
College graduate	38	32	30
Occupation of chief wage earner			
Blue collar	25	43	32
Unskilled worker	25	46	29
Skilled worker	26	39	35
Professional and business	36	36	28
Other white collar	36	38	26
Household income			
Under $15,000	27	49	24
$15,000-24,999	31	37	32
$25,000-39,999	31	38	31
$40,000 and over	36	37	27
Religion			
Protestant	36	38	26
Catholic	24	46	30
Labor union			
Labor union family	23	49	28
Nonunion family	32	39	29
Registered voters	32	43	25
National	31	40	29

Note: Question: "In politics, as of today, do you consider yourself a Republican, a Democrat, or an Independent?" Data are from pooled surveys conducted between July and September 1988 with 3,088 interviews.
[a] For composition of regions, see the Appendix, Table A-2.

Source: The Gallup Poll, "GOP Still Minority Party Despite Presidential Win Streak," press release, December 22, 1988.

Table 5-3 Liberal or Conservative Self-Identification, 1973-1988

Date	Extremely liberal	Liberal	Slightly liberal	Moderate	Slightly conservative	Conservative	Extremely conservative	Don't know	Number of interviews
March 1973	4%	14%	13%	36%	13%	13%	3%	6%	1,484
March 1974	1	14	14	38	15	11	2	5	1,480
March 1975	3	12	13	38	16	10	2	5	1,478
March 1976	2	13	12	37	15	13	2	6	1,494
March 1977	2	11	14	37	16	12	3	5	1,524
March 1978	1	9	16	36	17	12	2	5	1,505
March 1980	2	8	14	40	18	12	3	2	1,451
March 1982	2	9	15	39	14	13	4	4	1,495
March 1983	2	8	12	40	18	13	2	4	801
March 1984	2	9	12	39	19	13	3	4	1,462
March 1985	2	11	11	37	18	14	3	4	1,525
March 1986	2	9	12	39	16	14	3	5	1,468
March 1987	2	12	13	37	16	12	2	4	1,437
March 1988	2	12	13	35	17	15	2	4	1,472

Note: Question: "We hear a lot of talk these days about liberals and conservatives. I'm going to show you a seven-point scale on which the political views that people might hold are arranged from extremely liberal—point 1—to extremely conservative—point 7. Where would you place yourself on this scale?"

Source: General Social Survey, National Opinion Research Center, University of Chicago.

Figure 5-3 Ideological Self-Identification of College Freshmen, 1970-1988

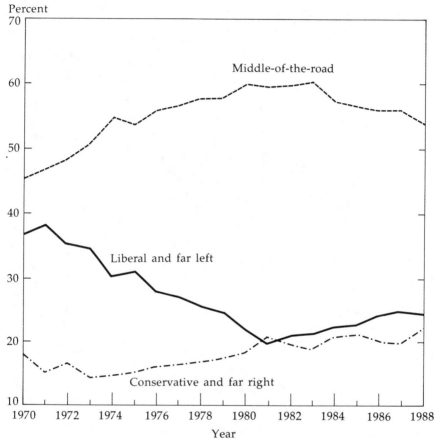

Note: Question: "How would you characterize your political views? Mark one: Far left, liberal, middle-of-the-road, conservative, far right."

Sources: Alexander W. Astin and others, *The American Freshman Twenty Year Trends, 1966-1985* (Los Angeles, The Higher Education Research Institute, Graduate School of Education, University of California, Los Angeles, 1987), 197; *The American Freshman National Norms for Fall 1986* (Los Angeles, The Higher Education Research Institute, Graduate School of Education, University of California, Los Angeles, 1986), 64; *Fall 1987* (1987), 61; *Fall 1988* (1988), 61.

Figure 5-4 The Most Important Problem: Domestic or Foreign, 1947-1987

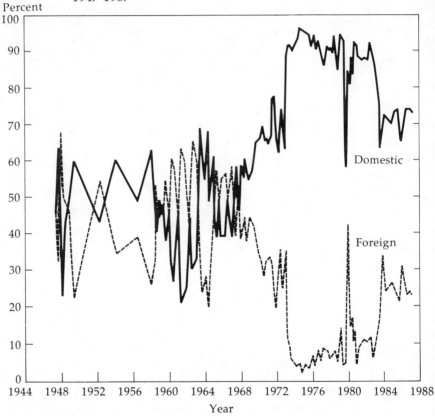

Note: For 1985-1987, "All other" responses were eliminated. Typical question: "What do you think is the most important problem facing this country today?"

Sources: 1947-1984: Gallup polls as reported in Tom W. Smith, "The Polls: America's Most Important Problems," *Public Opinion Quarterly* 49 (1985): 268-274; updated by the editors from *The Gallup Report* (December 1985), 13, (September 1986), 29, (May 1987), 7.

Figure 5-5 The Most Important Problem: Civil Rights, Vietnam, and Economics, 1947-1987

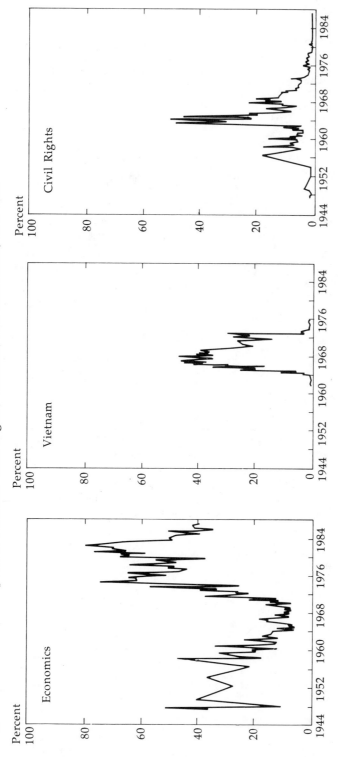

Note: For 1985-1987, "All other" responses were eliminated. Typical question: "What do you think is the most important problem facing this country today?"

Sources: 1947-1984: Gallup polls as reported in Tom W. Smith, "The Polls: America's Most Important Problems," *Public Opinion Quarterly* 49 (1985): 268-274; updated by the editors from *The Gallup Report* (December 1985), 13, (September 1986), 29, (May 1987), 7.

Figure 5-6 The Party Better Able to Handle the Most Important Problem, 1945-1988

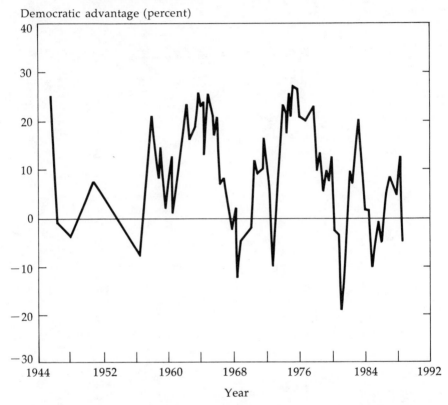

Democratic advantage (percent)

Year

Note: Question: "Which political party do you think can do a better job of handling the problems you have just mentioned—the Republican party or the Democratic party?" "Democratic advantage" is the percentage responding Democratic minus the percentage responding Republican.

Sources: The Gallup Report, May 1987, 9; The Gallup Poll, "Republicans Gain on Issue Barometers," press release, September 28, 1988.

Figure 5-7 The Party More Likely to Keep the United States
Out of War, 1951-1988

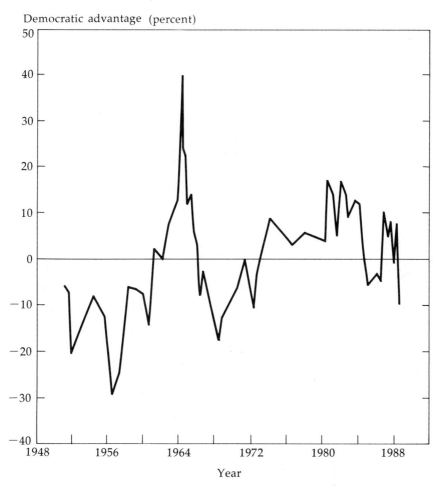

Democratic advantage (percent)

Year

Note: Question: "Looking ahead for the next few years, which political party would be more likely to keep the United States out of World War III—the Republican or the Democratic party?" "Democratic advantage" is the percentage responding Democratic minus the percentage responding Republican.

Sources: The Gallup Report, December 1987, 14; The Gallup Poll, "Republicans Gain on Issue Barometers," press release, September 28, 1988.

Figure 5-8   The Party Better Able to Keep the United States
Prosperous, 1951-1988

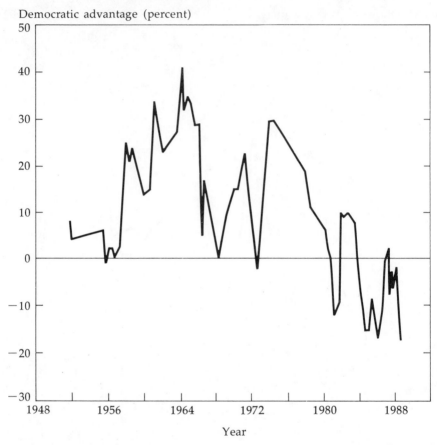

Year

Note: Question: "Which political party—the Republican or the Democratic party—would do a better job of keeping the country prosperous?" "Democratic advantage" is the percentage responding Democratic minus the percentage responding Republican.

Sources: The Gallup Report, December 1987, 14; The Gallup Poll, "Republicans Gain on Issue Barometers," press release, September 28, 1988.

Figure 5-9 Individual Confidence in Government, 1952-1988

Percentage difference index

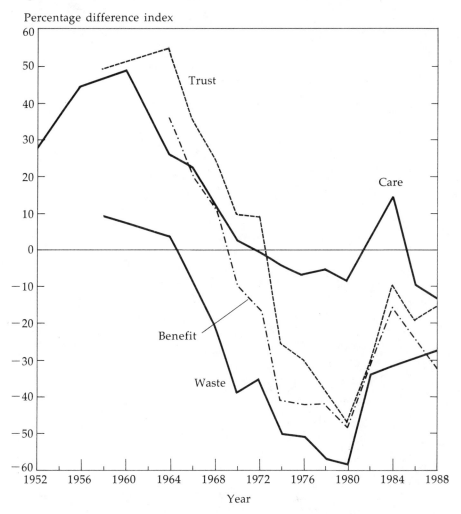

Year

Note: Questions: (Care) "I don't think public officials care much what people like me think." (Trust) "How much of the time do you think you can trust the government in Washington to do what is right—just about always, most of the time, or only some of the time?" (Benefit) "Would you say the government is pretty much run by a few big interests looking out for themselves or that it is run for the benefit of all people?" (Waste) "Do you think that people in the government waste a lot of money we pay in taxes, waste some of it, or don't waste very much of it?" The percentage difference index is calculated by subtracting the percentage giving a trusting response from the percentage giving a cynical response.

Source: Calculated by the editors from National Election Studies codebooks and data sets.

Figure 5-10 Satisfaction with "The Way Things Are," 1979-1988

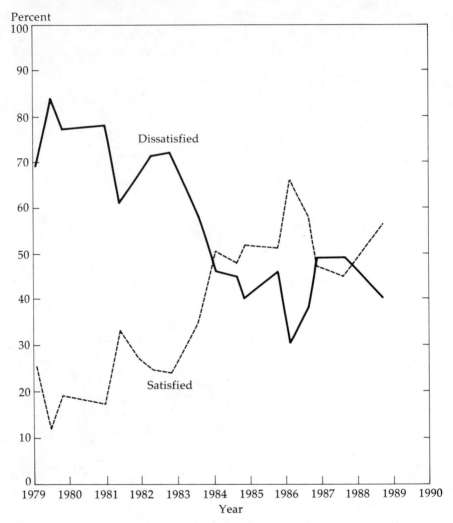

Note: Question: "In general, are you satisfied or dissatisfied with the way things are going in the United States at this time?"

Source: The Gallup Poll, "Public More Upbeat About State of Nation," press release, December 25, 1988, 1.

Questions

1. Compare the trends in party identification (for 1952-1988) in Figures 5-1 (partisans, excluding leaners) and 5-2. In what respects are the trends similar? How would the trends differ if you count "leaners" (those self-identified in Table 5-1 as "Independent Democrats" and "Independent Republicans") as partisans rather than independents?

2. What are the five most pro-Democratic groups in Table 5-2? The five most pro-Republican?

3. Have ideological trends among college freshmen mirrored trends in the adult population between 1973 and 1988 (Table 5-3 and Figure 5-3)?

4. Account for the gross contours of change in the most important problem series (Figure 5-4). (Hint: see Figure 5-5.)

5. Discuss briefly the major events that might have caused the public to upgrade or downgrade the importance of the economy, Vietnam, and civil rights as issues between 1946 and 1988 (Figure 5-5).

6. More often than not, the Democrats had the advantage in judgments about the party better able to handle the most important problem (Figure 5-6). What is it about the figure that nonetheless helps explain why the Republicans have won more than half of the post-World War II presidential elections?

7. Specific campaign statements or themes account for some of the features of Figures 5-7 and 5-8, especially the huge spike in 1964 in Figure 5-7 and the Republican advantages in 1980, 1984, and 1988 in Figure 5-8. What were these statements and themes? Based on these effects, how would you interpret the "party better able" responses? Are these responses long-term evaluations of parties?

8. What political events might explain the changes over time in individual confidence in government (Figure 5-7)? If someone wished to argue that the American public had lost confidence in its government, which facts and questions would be highlighted?

9. Do Figures 5-9 and 5-10 show similar changes in the public mood during the Reagan administration?

6

Interest Groups

When people think about interest groups, they think about dollars. Not surprisingly, then, most of the information in this chapter and in related tables in other chapters is about money—who gives it, who spends it, who regulates it, and what effect it has. Even more surprising is the huge quantity of information available, which results chiefly from the large number of elections in the United States and the collection and publication of data about them. For example, the most recent campaign expenditures are shown for all 435 representatives and 100 senators (Tables 7-15 and 7-16), as well as the amounts of money spent by individual presidential candidates (Table 8-5), and more aggregated information about expenditures by congressional candidates (Table 7-7). The present chapter concentrates on the sources of these funds, especially on funds derived from organized groups.

One could, in fact, easily be inundated by numbers relating to organized interests. The publications of the Federal Election Commission (FEC) alone run to multiple volumes every two years, with detailed accountings of receipts and expenditures of candidates in federal elections. More volumes are produced, though inconsistently and much less systematically, by various state agencies. Because such information is so voluminous, it is often summarized as it is here: how much money was contributed to incumbents versus challengers in congressional campaigns (Table 7-7), how much was spent by various types of political action committees (PACs) (Table 6-4), interest organizations (Table 6-10), and so on.

However, this wealth of information has not been collected for many U.S. elections. The FEC only began operations in the mid-1970s. Although there were studies of campaign costs before then, present time series are often limited to a span of no more than fifteen years. In addition, laws regulating campaign contributions, expenditures, and interest groups' activities change so frequently that long time series are often unobtainable and would be misleading if they could be compiled. For example, the growth of PACs dates from 1974 because changes in the laws at that time allowed their establishment (Table 6-1).

Concern about money is not limited to the sums spent by candidates. Indeed, there is probably more concern over interest group spending and about where candidates' funds come from and what, if anything, that money buys. Fortunately, data are increasingly available on interest group finances and on candidates' fund raising as well as expenditures. Much of the data concern PACs, the dominant organizations through which interest groups raise and spend money. The primary information is about general categories of PACs (Tables 6-1, 6-4, 6-5, and 6-7); the lists of PACs illustrate the variety of organizations that fall into these categories (Tables 6-2 and 6-6).

Because money is at the heart of interest group activities, matters of campaign finance law are directly relevant in this chapter. At the federal level these consist mainly of fairly straightforward contribution limits (Table 6-8). At the state level, there is a myriad of contribution and expenditure limits (Table 6-9).

Not all questions about interest groups involve money. Some other aspects of interest group activity that can be quantified are reflected in this volume, such as the growth and decline of labor unions (Table 6-10). For example, several interest groups rate members of Congress on how favorable their votes were to the groups' interests. A number of recent ratings of each representative and senator are provided in Tables 7-15 and 7-16.

Another perennial question about interest groups is whether such groups in the aggregate reflect the interests of the general population. This is a difficult question on which to collect data, but one perspective is given in Table 6-11. The listings of PAC types and of specific PACs also provide some understanding of the variety of organized interests.

For obvious reasons no one is able to collect systematically what would surely be the most captivating data on the activities of organized interests, that is, bribes, threats, blackmail, and so forth. But political analysts now have a larger body of material on interest groups than ever before. Although much of this information is buried in hard-to-digest volumes on campaign contributions and spending or in seemingly bland lists showing what interests are represented, the data provide more knowledge and more research capabilities than ever before about the scope and potential influence of organized interests.

Table 6-1   Number of Political Action Committees (PACs), 1974-1988

Date	Connected[a]					Noncon-nected[b]	Total
	Corpor-ate	Labor	Trade/member-ship/health	Cooper-ative	Corpor-ation without stock		
December 31, 1974	89	201	318[c]	—	—	—	608
November 24, 1975	139	226	357[c]	—	—	—	722
May 10, 1976	294	246	452[c]	—	—	—	992
December 31, 1976	433	224	489[c]	—	—	—	1,146
December 31, 1977	550	234	438	8	20	110	1,360
December 31, 1978	785	217	453	12	24	162	1,653
August, 1979	885	226	483	13	27	206	1,840
December 31, 1979	950	240	514	17	32	247	2,000
July 1, 1980	1,107	255	544	23	41	309	2,279
December 31, 1980	1,206	297	576	42	56	374	2,551
July 1, 1981	1,253	303	579	38	64	441	2,678
December 31, 1981	1,329	318	614	41	68	531	2,901
July 1, 1982	1,417	350	627	45	82	628	3,149
December 31, 1982	1,469	380	649	47	103	723	3,371
July 1, 1983	1,514	379	664	50	114	740	3,461
December 31, 1983	1,538	378	643	51	122	793	3,525
July 1, 1984	1,642	381	662	53	125	940	3,803
December 31, 1984	1,682	394	698	52	130	1,053	4,009
July 1, 1985	1,687	393	694	54	133	1,039	4,000
December 31, 1985	1,710	388	695	54	142	1,003	3,992
July 1, 1986	1,734	386	707	56	146	1,063	4,092
December 31, 1986	1,744	384	745	56	151	1,077	4,157
July 1, 1987	1,762	377	795	56	152	967	4,109
December 31, 1987	1,775	364	865	59	145	957	4,165
July 1, 1988	1,806	355	766	60	143	1,066	4,196
December 31, 1988	1,816	354	786	59	138	1,115	4,268

Note: "—" indicates not available.

[a] Connected PACs are associated with a sponsoring organization that may pay operating and fund-raising expenses. They are typically subdivided by the type of sponsor: corporate (with stockholders), labor (unions), membership/trade/health (professional groups and associations of corporations), cooperatives (primarily agricultural), and corporations without stock.

[b] Nonconnected PACs do not have a sponsoring organization.

[c] For the years 1974-1976, trade/membership/health category includes all PACs except corporate and labor; no further breakdown available.

Source: Federal Election Commission, press release, January 13, 1989.

Table 6-2 The Largest Washington-Based PACs

Type of PAC/name

Corporate PACs
  None

Labor PACs
  Active Ballot Club
    PAC of the United Food and Commercial Workers International Union
  AFL-CIO Committee on Political Education (COPE)
  American Federation of State, County, and Municipal Employees (PEOPLE)
  American Federation of Teachers Committee on Political Education
  Carpenters' Legislative Improvement Committee
  Committee on Letter Carriers Political Education
  Communications Workers of America-COPE Political Contributions
    Committee
  Democratic Republican Independent Voter Education Committee
    PAC of the International Brotherhood of Teamsters, Chauffeurs,
      Warehousemen, and Helpers of America
  International Brotherhood of Electrical Workers Committee on Political
    Education
  Machinists Non-Partisan Political League
  Marine Engineers Beneficial Association Political Action Fund
  National Education Association Political Action Committee
  Seafarers Political Activity Donation
  Sheet Metal Workers' International Association Political Action League

Trade/membership/health PACs
  American Bankers Association (BANKPAC)
  American Dental Political Action Committee
  American Medical Association Political Action Committee
  Association of Trial Lawyers of America Political Action Committee
  Build-Political Action Committee (BUILDPAC)
    PAC of the National Association of Home Builders
  Dealers Election Action Committee
    PAC of the National Automobile Dealers Association
  League of Conservation Voters
  National Association of Life Underwriters Political Action Committee
  National Association of Retired Federal Employees Political Action Committee
  Women's Campaign Fund

Nonconnected PACs
  American Citizens for Political Action
  Black Political Action Committees (Black PAC)
  Campaign America
    Supports Republican candidates

(Table continues)

Table 6-2 *(Continued)*

Type of PAC/name

Campaign for Prosperity
  Supports conservative candidates, especially those favoring free
    enterprise, traditional values, and a strong national defense
Congressional Majority Committee
  Supports conservative Republican and Democratic candidates for national
    office
Council for National Defense
  Supports candidates who favor a strong national defense
Fund for a Conservative Majority
Fund for America's Future
  Supports Republican candidates
National Committee for an Effective Congress
  Supports liberal or progressive candidates in marginal races
National Committee to Preserve Social Security
National Conservative Political Action Committee
National Political Action Committee
  Supports candidates who advocate close Israeli-American relations
National Security Political Action Committee
Ruff Political Action Committee
  Supports candidates who support a free market economic system and a
    strong national defense
Victory '88
  Formerly Jack Kemp Super Bowl Committee

Cooperative PACs
  None

Corporation without stock PACs
  None

Note: Listed are Washington-based political action committees with receipts or expenditures of $500,000 or more during 1986 and 1987.

Sources: Congressional Quarterly, *Washington Information Directory, 1988-1989* (Washington, D.C.: Congressional Quarterly, 1988), 652-655; type of PAC: Federal Election Commission.

Table 6-3 PACs: Receipts, Expenditures, Contributions, 1975-1988

Election cycle[a]	Adjusted receipts[b] (millions)	Adjusted expenditures[b] (millions)	Contributions to congressional candidates (millions)	Percentage contributed to congressional candidates
1975-1976	$54.0	$52.9	$22.6	42
1977-1978	80.0	77.4	34.1	43
1979-1980	137.7	131.2	55.2	40
1981-1982	199.5	190.2	83.6	42
1983-1984	288.7	266.8	105.3	36
1985-1986	353.4	340.0	132.7	38
1987-1988	369.5	349.6	151.3	41

[a] Data cover January 1 of the odd-numbered year to December 31 of the even-numbered year.
[b] Adjusted receipts and expenditures exclude funds transferred between affiliated committees.

Sources: 1975-1976: Joseph E. Cantor, "Political Action Committees: Their Evolution and Growth and Their Implications for the Political System" (Washington, D.C.: Congressional Research Service, 1982), Report no. 83, 87-88; 1977-1988: Federal Election Commission, "FEC Releases First PAC Figures for 1985-86," press release, May 21, 1987, 1, "FEC Finds Slower Growth of PAC Activity during 1988 Election," press release, April 19, 1989, 1, 7.

Table 6-4 Spending by Type of PAC, 1977-1988 (millions)

Election cycle	Corporate	Labor	Trade/ membership/ health	Non-connected	Other connected[a]	Total
1977-1978	$15.2	$18.6	$23.8	$17.4	$2.4	$77.4
1979-1980	31.4	25.1	32.0	38.6	4.0	131.2
1981-1982	43.3	34.8	41.9	64.3	5.8	190.2
1983-1984	59.2	47.5	54.0	97.4	8.7	266.8
1985-1986	79.3	57.9	73.3	118.4	11.1	340.0
1987-1988	89.0	70.4	81.6	97.0	11.6	349.6

Note: Adjusted expenditures exclude transfers of funds between affiliated committees. Detail may not add to totals because of rounding.
[a] This category combines the FEC categories of cooperatives and corporations without stock.

Sources: 1977-1978: Norman J. Ornstein et al., eds., *Vital Statistics on Congress, 1987-1988* (Washington, D.C.: Congressional Quarterly, 1987), 105; 1979-1988: Federal Election Commission, "FEC Finds Slower Growth of PAC Activity during 1988 Election Cycle," press release, April 9, 1989, 7.

Table 6-5 Contributions and Independent Expenditures by Type of PAC, 1987-1988

Type of PAC	Number[a]	Receipts[b]	Contributed to candidates[c]		Independent expenditures[d]	
			Amount	Percentage	Amount	Percentage
Corporate	1,613	$96,429,934	$56,254,449	58	$54,368	0.1
Labor	253	75,966,281	35,546,980	47	188,544	0.2
Trade/membership/health	626	86,406,330	41,210,121	48	3,893,403	5
Cooperative	51	4,632,632	2,740,732	59	4,550	0.1
Corporations without stock	121	8,634,276	3,316,674	38	288,450	3
Nonconnected	623	97,433,295	20,338,460	21	15,783,956	16
Total	3,287	369,502,748	159,407,416	43	20,213,271	5

[a] As of December 31, 1988. The numbers shown are those PACs that actually made contributions.

[b] Adjusted for money transferred between affiliated committees.

[c] Figures include contributions to all federal candidates, including those who did not run for office during 1987-1988.

[d] Independent expenditures include money spent on behalf of candidates and against candidates. Some independent expenditures made in 1987 pertained to candidates for previous elections.

Source: Federal Election Commission, "FEC Funds Slower Growth of PAC Activity during 1988 Election," press release, April 9, 1989, 3, 6.

Table 6-6   Top Twenty PACs in Overall Spending and in Contributions
to Federal Candidates, 1987-1988

PAC	Overall spending
1. National Security Political Action Committee	$10,279,012
2. Democratic Republican Independent Voter Education Committee	8,475,552
3. Realtors Political Action Committee	5,930,618
4. American Medical Association Political Action Committee	5,385,951
5. NRA Political Victory Fund	4,672,291
6. National Congressional Club	4,140,237
7. Campaign America	4,025,876
8. National Committee to Preserve Social Security PAC	4,013,264
9. American Citizens for Political Action	3,870,927
10. Association of Trial Lawyers of America Political Action Committee	3,870,741
11. Auto Dealers and Drivers for Free Trade PAC	3,849,920
12. National Education Association Political Action Committee	3,617,328
13. League of Conservation Voters	3,320,000
14. Voter Guide '88	3,297,422
15. UAW-V-CAP (UAW Voluntary Community Action Program)	3,141,909
16. American Federation of State, County, and Municipal Employees—PEOPLE, Qualified	3,037,105
17. Machinists Non-Partisan Political League	2,852,714
18. American Telephone and Telegraph Company Inc. PAC (AT&T PAC)	2,841,464
19. National Association of Retired Federal Employees Political Action Committee (NARFE-PAC)	2,533,093
20. Committee on Letter Carriers Political Education (Letter Carriers Political Action Fund)	2,501,529

PAC	Contributions to federal candidates
1. Realtors Political Action Committee	$3,040,969
2. Democratic Republican Independent Voter Education Committee	2,856,724
3. American Medical Association Political Action Committee	2,316,496
4. National Education Association Political Action Committee	2,104,689
5. National Association of Retired Federal Employees Political Action Committee (NARFE-PAC)	1,979,850
6. UAW-V-CAP (UAW Voluntary Community Action Program)	1,953,099
7. Association of Trial Lawyers of America Political Action Committee	1,913,558
8. Committee on Letter Carriers Political Education (Letter Carriers Political Action Fund)	1,737,982

(Table continues)

Table 6-6 *(Continued)*

PAC	Contributions to federal candidates
9. American Federation of State, County, and Municipal Employees—PEOPLE, Qualified	$1,663,386
10. Machinists Non-Partisan Political League	1,490,780
11. Build Political Action Committee of the National Association of Home Builders	1,448,560
12. Carpenters' Legislative Improvement Committee	1,363,498
13. National Association of Life Underwriters Political Action Committee	1,329,150
14. American Telephone and Telegraph Company Inc. PAC (AT&T PAC)	1,305,112
15. Air Line Pilots Association Political Action Committee	1,217,000
16. Dealers Election Action Committee of the National Automobile Dealers Association (NADA)	1,202,420
17. International Brotherhood of Electrical Workers Committee on Political Education	1,197,190
18. Auto Dealers and Drivers for Free Trade PAC	1,158,700
19. Active Ballot Club, A Department of United Food and Commercial Workers International Union	1,152,110
20. American Bankers Association BANKPAC	1,151,050

Source: Federal Election Commission, "FEC Finds Slower Growth of PAC Activity during 1988 Election Cycle," press release, April 9, 1989, 15-16.

Table 6-7 Political Action Committee (PAC) Congressional Campaign Contributions by Type of PAC and Incumbency Status of Candidate, 1977-1988 (millions)

Election cycle/ PAC type	House						Senate					
	Democrat	Republican	Incumbent	Challenger	Open seat[a]	Total	Democrat	Republican	Incumbent	Challenger	Open seat[a]	Total
1977-1978												
Corporate	$2.6	$3.4	$3.8	$1.1	$1.1	$6.0	$0.9	$2.6	$1.8	$0.9	$0.8	$3.5
Trade association	3.9	4.7	5.2	1.5	1.9	8.6	0.9	1.7	1.3	0.7	0.6	2.6
Labor	7.0	0.2	4.6	1.2	1.4	7.2	2.4	0.3	1.2	0.9	0.6	2.7
Nonconnected	0.4	1.4	0.5	0.8	0.5	1.8	0.2	0.5	0.2	0.3	0.2	0.7
Total	14.4	10.0	14.7	4.6	5.1	24.4	4.5	5.2	4.5	3.0	2.2	9.7
1979-1980												
Corporate	4.8	7.5	8.1	2.6	1.5	12.2	2.1	4.8	2.7	3.3	0.9	6.9
Trade association	5.1	6.6	8.0	2.2	1.5	11.7	1.9	2.2	2.2	1.4	0.5	4.1
Labor	8.9	0.4	6.6	1.5	1.2	9.4	3.4	0.4	2.7	0.7	0.4	3.8
Nonconnected	0.9	2.1	1.0	1.4	0.7	3.1	0.5	1.4	0.5	1.1	0.3	1.9
Total	20.5	17.2	24.9	7.9	5.1	37.9	8.4	9.0	8.6	6.6	2.1	17.3
1981-1982												
Corporate	7.0	12.0	14.4	2.0	2.6	18.9	2.4	6.2	5.5	1.7	1.4	8.6
Trade association	7.2	9.7	12.4	2.1	2.3	16.8	2.2	2.8	3.7	0.8	0.5	5.0
Labor	14.7	0.7	8.5	4.3	2.6	15.4	4.5	0.4	3.0	1.3	0.5	4.9
Nonconnected	3.9	3.5	3.4	2.5	1.6	7.4	1.6	1.7	1.5	1.3	0.5	3.3
Total	34.2	26.8	40.8	10.9	9.4	61.1	11.2	11.4	14.3	5.2	3.0	22.6

(Table continues)

167

Table 6-7 (Continued)

Election cycle/ PAC type	House						Senate					
	Democrat	Republican	Incumbent	Challenger	Open seat[a]	Total	Democrat	Republican	Incumbent	Challenger	Open seat[a]	Total
1983-1984												
Corporate	$10.4	$13.1	$18.8	$2.6	$2.0	$23.4	$3.2	$8.8	$8.8	$1.1	$2.2	$12.0
Trade association	10.5	9.9	16.5	2.1	1.7	20.4	2.7	3.7	4.5	0.9	1.0	6.3
Labor	18.8	1.0	14.3	3.5	2.0	19.8	4.7	0.3	1.6	2.3	1.2	5.0
Nonconnected	4.7	4.4	4.9	2.9	1.3	9.1	3.0	2.4	2.4	2.0	1.0	5.4
Total	46.3	29.3	57.2	11.3	7.2	75.7	14.0	15.6	17.9	6.3	5.4	29.7
1985-1986												
Corporate	12.8	14.0	22.8	1.0	3.0	26.8	4.8	14.4	11.7	2.6	4.8	19.1
Trade association	12.2	11.1	19.3	1.3	2.8	23.4	3.7	5.7	5.7	1.6	2.1	9.4
Labor	21.0	1.6	14.7	4.3	3.6	22.6	6.6	0.6	2.2	3.1	1.9	7.2
Nonconnected	6.6	4.5	6.1	2.6	2.6	11.1	4.2	3.4	3.1	2.4	2.1	7.6
Total	54.6	32.5	65.8	9.1	12.3	87.2	20.0	25.0	23.6	10.1	11.3	45.0
1987-1988												
Corporate	16.7	15.8	29.3	1.3	1.9	32.5	9.2	12.7	15.8	2.4	3.7	21.9
Trade association	16.8	12.3	25.1	1.6	2.5	29.1	5.8	5.9	8.5	1.3	2.0	11.8
Labor	25.2	2.1	18.7	5.2	3.4	27.2	7.0	0.7	4.2	2.2	1.3	7.7
Nonconnected	7.5	4.0	7.4	2.2	1.9	11.5	5.1	3.3	4.7	2.1	1.6	8.4
Total	68.6	35.6	83.9	10.5	9.9	104.2	28.3	23.4	34.5	8.2	8.9	51.7

Note: Figures are for amounts given to candidates in primary, general, run-off, and special elections during the two-year calendar period indicated. Totals include PACs classified by the Federal Election Commission as cooperatives and corporations without stock.

[a] Open seat refers to candidates in elections in which an incumbent did not seek reelection.

Sources: 1979-1984: *Statistical Abstract of the U.S., 1987* (Washington, D.C.: U.S. Government Printing Office, 1986), 246; 1985-1986: *Statistical Abstract of the U.S., 1988*, 254; 1987-1988: Federal Election Commission, "FEC Finds Slower Growth during 1988 Election," press release, April 9, 1989, 4.

Table 6-8   Contribution Limits under Federal Election Commission Act

Source	Candidate or his/her authorized committee	National party committee[a]	Any other committee	Total contributions
Individual	$1,000 per election[b]	$20,000	$5,000	$25,000
Multicandidate committee[c]	5,000 per election	15,000	5,000	NL
Party committee	1,000-5,000 per election[d]	NL	5,000	NL
Republican or Democratic Senatorial Campaign Committee,[e] or the National Party Committee, or a combination of both	17,500 to Senate candidate per calendar year in which candidate seeks election	NA	NA	NA
Any other committee or group[f]	1,000 per election	20,000	5,000	NL

Note: "NL" indicates no limit; "NA" indicates not applicable. Limits on contributions to national party committees and other committees and on total contributions are per calendar year.

[a] The following are considered national party committees: a party's national committee, the Senate campaign committees, and the national congressional committees, provided they are not authorized by any candidate. Individual contributions made or earmarked to influence a specific election of a clearly identified candidate are counted as if made during the year in which the election is held.

[b] The following are considered separate elections: primary election, general election, runoff election, special election, and party caucus or convention which has authority to select the nominee.

[c] A multicandidate committee is any committee with more than fifty contributors which has been registered for at least six months and, with the exception of state party committees, has made contributions to five or more federal candidates. Most PACs qualify as a multicandidate committee.

[d] Limit depends on whether party committee is a multicandidate committee.

[e] Republican and Democratic Senatorial Campaign committees are subject to all other limits applicable to a multicandidate committee.

[f] Group includes an organization, partnership, or group of persons.

Source: Federal Election Commission.

Table 6-9 State Campaign Finance: Tax Provisions, Public Funding, and Contribution and Expenditures Limits by State

State	Tax provisions[a]	Public funding	Limitations on	
			Individual contributions[b]	Expenditures
Alabama	Add-on, parties	none	No	No
Alaska	none	none	Yes	No
Arizona	Add-on, parties Deduction	none	Yes	No
Arkansas	none	none	Yes	No
California	Credit	none	Yes	No
Colorado	none	none	No	No
Connecticut	none	none	Yes	No
Delaware	none	none	Yes	No
Florida	none	Governor	Yes	Yes
Georgia	none	none	No	No
Hawaii	Checkoff, candidates Deduction	Governor, Legislature	Yes	Yes
Idaho	Checkoff, parties	none	No	No
Illinois	none	none	No	No
Indiana	none	none	No	No
Iowa	Checkoff, parties Deduction	none	No	No
Kansas	none	none	Yes	No
Kentucky	Checkoff, parties	none	Yes	No
Louisiana	none	none	No	No
Maine	Add-on, parties	none	Yes	No

State				
Maryland	none	Governor (terminates in 1990)	Yes	Yes
Massachusetts	Add-on, candidates	Governor	Yes	No
Michigan	Checkoff, candidates	Governor	Yes	Yes
Minnesota	Checkoff, candidates	Legislature	Yes	Yes
Mississippi	none	none	No	No
Missouri	none	none	No	Yes
Montana	Add-on candidates Deduction	Governor	Yes	No
Nebraska	none	none	No	No
Nevada	none	none	No	No
New Hampshire	none	none	Yes	No
New Jersey	Checkoff, candidates	Governor	Yes	Yes
New Mexico	none	none	No	No
New York	none	none	Yes	No
North Carolina	Add-on, candidates Deduction Checkoff, parties	Governor	Yes	Yes
North Dakota	none	none	No	No
Ohio	Checkoff, parties	none	No	No
Oklahoma	Deduction	none	Yes	No
Oregon	Add-on, parties	none	No	No
Pennsylvania	none	none	No	No
Rhode Island	Checkoff, parties	Governor	No	Yes
South Carolina	none	none	No	No
South Dakota	none	none	Yes	No
Tennessee	none	none	No	No
Texas	none	none	No	No

(Table continues)

171

Table 6-9 (Continued)

State	Tax provisions[a]	Public funding	Limitations on	
			Individual contributions[b]	Expenditures
Utah	Checkoff, parties	none	No	No
Vermont	none	none	Yes	No
Virginia	Add-on, parties	none	No	No
Washington	none	none	Yes	No
West Virginia	none	none	Yes	Voluntary
Wisconsin	Checkoff, candidates	Governor, legislature	Yes	Yes
Wyoming	none	none	Yes	No

[a] Tax add-on and checkoff provisions generally are for $1 or $2. Tax credits and deductions are more variable.
[b] Limits on individual contributions may be an aggregate contribution limit across candidates and contests or a limit on contributions to a candidate. For details, see sources.

Sources: Tax provisions, public funding, and limits on expenditures: Herbert E. Alexander and Mike Eberts, *Public Financing of State Elections: A Data Book on Tax-Assisted Funding of Political Parties and Candidates in Twenty States* (Los Angeles: Citizens' Research Foundation, 1986) and H. E. Alexander, personal communication; individual contributions: *Campaign Finance Law '88* (Washington, D.C.: D. T. Skelton Service Associates, Inc., Federal Election Commission's National Clearinghouse on Election Administration, 1988).

Table 6-10   Membership in Labor Unions, 1900-1984

Year	Membership (in thousands)	Percent in unions Nonagricultural employment	Percent in unions Labor force
1900	932.4	6.5	3.3
1905	1,947.1	10.8	6.0
1910	2,168.5	10.3	5.9
1915	2,597.6	11.5	6.6
1920	4,823.3	17.6	11.7
1925	3,685.1	12.8	8.2
1930	3,749.6	12.7	7.5
1935	3,649.6	13.5	6.9
1940	7,296.7	22.5	13.1
1945	12,254.2	30.4	22.8
1950	14,294.2	31.6	23.0
1955	16,126.9	31.8	24.8
1960	15,516.1	28.6	22.3
1965	18,268.9	30.1	24.5
1970	20,990.3	29.6	25.4
1971	20,711.1	29.1	24.5
1972	21,205.8	28.8	24.4
1973	21,881.3	28.5	24.5
1974	22,165.4	28.3	24.1
1975	22,207.0	28.9	23.7
1976	22,153.0	27.9	23.0
1977	21,632.1	26.2	21.8
1978	21,756.5	25.1	21.3
1979	22,025.4	24.5	21.0
1980	20,968.2	23.2	19.6
1981	20,646.8	22.6	19.0
1982	19,571.4	21.9	17.8
1983	18,633.6	20.7	16.6
1984	18,306.0	19.4	16.1

Source: Leo Troy and Neil Sheflin, *U.S. Union Sourcebook* (West Orange, N.J.: Industrial Relations Data and Information Services, 1985), A-1, A-2, 3-10.

Table 6-11 Organizational Focus of Groups in Comparison with Characteristics of U.S. Adults

Organizational focus	Percentage of organizations	Percentage of U.S. adults	Occupation or other characteristic
Trade, business, commercial, chambers of commerce, tourism	25	36	Managerial, professional, sales, supervisors
Agriculture	6	3	Farming, forestry, fishing
Legal, governmental, military	4	15-17	Governmental employees, military personnel
Science, engineering technical	9	5	Scientists, engineers, technicians
Education	8	5	Teachers, counselors, librarians
Social welfare	11	16	Social insurance recipients
Health and medical	13	5	Health and medical
Public affairs	14	a	
Religious	7	40-60	Church goers, members
Veterans, hereditary, patriotic	2	11	Veterans
Unions	1	16	Union member

Note: Percentages of organizations sum to 100 percent. Categories for adults are overlapping and do not include all types of workers; therefore they do not sum to 100 percent. Categories used for organizations are those of the first source. Excluded were approximately 5,800 (of about 23,000) groups; those excluded were cultural, ethnic, athletic, hobby, and Greek-letter organizations and fan clubs.

a This category of groups includes political parties and numerous special interest groups. Partly because of overlapping memberships, there is no clearly comparable set of individuals.

Sources: Organizational data: calculated by the editors from Karin E. Koek and Susan B. Martin, eds., *Encyclopedia of Associations* (Detroit, Mich.: Gale Research, Inc., 1988), Volume 1, parts 1 and 2, and Karin E. Koek, Susan B. Martin, and Annette Novallo, eds., *Encyclopedia of Associations* (Detroit, Mich.: Gale Research, Inc., 1989), Volume 3, part 3 (copyright © 1988, 1989 by Gale Research, Inc., reprinted by permission of the publisher); percentage of adults, occupational and other characteristics: U.S. Bureau of the Census, *Statistical Abstract of the U.S., 1988*, 52, 282, 323, 327, 376-377, and this volume, Tables 6-10, 12-9.

Questions

1. Was average PAC spending more in 1988 than in 1976? (Use the number of PACs from December 31, 1976, and December 31, 1988, from Table 6-1 and PAC spending [adjusted expenditures] for 1975-1976 and 1987-1988 from Table 6-3.) One measure of inflation, the Consumer Price Index (Table 13-2), rose 107.9 percent between 1976 and 1988 [(118.3-56.9)/56.9]. Did the increase in average PAC spending over the same period surpass the increase in the rate of inflation as measured by the Consumer Price Index?

2. Are there PACs whose goals you are likely to agree with (Table 6-2)? Any you would strongly oppose? Which ones are they? (There is no right and wrong answer.) Which category do these PACs fall under? Why would you agree or disagree with these particular PACs?

3. Which type of PAC spends the most money (Table 6-4)? Which type currently spends the most per PAC (Tables 6-4 and 6-1)? Corporate PACs spend relatively little per PAC and they are typically not based in Washington. How can it be, then, that corporations are thought to have considerable influence?

4. Do the different types of PACs follow roughly similar patterns in dividing their receipts between contributing to candidates and engaging in independent expenditures (Table 6-5)?

5. Did PACs give more money to incumbents or to challengers (Table 6-7)? Why? (Hint: see Table 3-17.)

6. How much can a PAC contribute to a single candidate in a single year (Table 6-8)? To multiple candidates?

7. How many states have tax provisions or other public funding for political candidates (Table 6-9)? Why are tax deductions and credits considered public funding?

8. Which states impose limits on campaign expenditures (Table 6-9)? In what circumstances do you think a state can impose expenditure requirements? Why do you think there is any kind of restriction about imposing expenditure limits?

9. In what year did union membership first surpass 20 percent of the nonagricultural workforce (Table 6-10)? In what year did this percentage peak? In what year did overall union membership (percent of labor force in unions) peak? Why is the latter year later than the former?

10. Though about half of the U.S. population attend church or are church members, less than 10 percent of the U.S. organizations are religious in nature. Why might this be so? Unions have a smaller ratio of organizations to adults than all other organizations shown, including churches. Why? Does the small number of union organizations mean that unions have little political power?

7
Congress

Statistics about Congress abound. Capsule descriptions of senators and representatives and their districts can easily run to over a thousand pages for each Congress (*Politics in America* and the *Almanac of American Politics*). Elections are held every two years, generating mounds of electoral and financial data. Recorded votes annually number more than four hundred in the House and more than three hundred in the Senate. It is thus hardly surprising that votes for Congress, votes in Congress, those who work for Congress, and those who benefit from (or are hurt by) congressional activities have been subject to extensive statistical scrutiny.

Congressional elections and roll call votes in Congress constitute the largest areas of research. Elections are covered in several other chapters, and the nature of electoral data is discussed in the introductions to Chapters 3 and 4. What is added here are a number of tables that pertain to hypotheses about congressional elections. Losses by the president's party in midterm elections (Table 7-4) have long been of interest because of a strong regularity and because the pattern has a variety of implications for the way voters evaluate their representatives. The same is true of incumbency; the results are interesting in and of themselves (Table 7-5) and because of what they suggest about how voters make choices. The electoral vulnerability of incumbents is reduced by their considerably greater ability to raise campaign funds (Table 7-7); PACs have been a large source of those funds in recent years (Table 7-8).

Congress generates other kinds of statistics. Simply apportioning members among the states (Table 7-1 and Figure 7-1) has led to a surprising amount of controversy and statistical calculation, which resulted in a fascinating, book-length treatment.[1] As the composition of

Congress changes to include more women and minorities, these and other characteristics have also been tabulated and analyzed (Tables 7-2 and 7-3).

Cohesion within and contrasts between the political parties were the topics of some of the first statistical treatments of political subjects.[2] Increased numbers of roll calls and other recorded votes (Table 7-11) have done nothing to dampen this tradition. Party unity and presidential support by individual representatives and senators (Tables 7-13 and 7-14) and for groups (Tables 7-7 through 7-9, Figure 7-2) have become a standard part of congressional analyses.

As Congress becomes a larger and more complex operation, more interest has been expressed in its workload and structure. These aspects of Congress are represented here with information about staff size (Figure 7-3), numbers of measures considered and passed (Table 7-10 and Figure 7-4), numbers of votes (Table 7-11), and numbers of and leadership of committees (Table 7-12). Although these, too, at first might be considered insignificant or analytically useless tabulations, analyses of the relationships among committee staffs, congressional voting, voter behavior, and legislative output suggest otherwise.

For the statistically minded, the study of Congress has long been an inviting prospect. The traditional topics are still interesting because the turnover of personnel, the constant change in congressional leadership and of the president, changes in regional strength, and so on, make Congress anything but static. In addition, reforms of congressional procedures and of campaign finance since Watergate, changing technologies that have resulted in electronic voting and the televising of proceedings in both chambers, and changes in the size and scope of the government bureaucracy Congress must deal with, are adequate reasons to scrutinize anew the data underlying one's understanding of Congress.

Notes

1. Michel Balinski and H.P. Young, *Fair Representation* (New Haven, Conn.: Yale University Press, 1982).
2. Stuart Rice, *Quantitative Methods in Politics* (New York: Knopf, 1928).

Table 7-1 Apportionment of Membership in the House of Representatives, 1789-1980

State	1789[a]	1790	1800	1810	1820	1830	1840	1850	1860	1870	1880	1890	1900	1910	1930[b]	1940	1950	1960	1970	1980
Alabama	-	-	-	1[c]	3	5	7	7	6	8	8	9	9	10	9	9	9	8	7	7
Alaska	-	-	-	-	-	-	-	-	-	-	-	-	-	-	-	-	1[c]	1	1	1
Arizona	-	-	-	-	-	-	-	-	-	-	-	-	-	1[c]	1	2	2	3	4	5
Arkansas	-	-	-	-	-	1[c]	1	2	3	4	5	6	7	7	7	7	6	4	4	4
California	-	-	-	-	-	-	-	2[c]	3	4	6	7	8	11	20	23	30	38	43	45
Colorado	-	-	-	-	-	-	-	-	-	1[c]	1	2	3	4	4	4	4	4	5	6
Connecticut	5	7	7	7	6	6	4	4	4	4	4	4	5	5	6	6	6	6	6	6
Delaware	1	1	1	2	1	1	1	1	1	1	1	1	1	1	1	1	1	1	1	1
Florida	3	-	-	-	-	-	1[c]	1	1	2	2	2	3	4	5	6	8	12	15	19
Georgia	3	2	4	6	7	9	8	8	7	9	10	11	11	12	10	10	10	10	10	10
Hawaii	-	-	-	-	-	-	-	-	-	-	-	-	-	-	-	-	1[c]	2	2	2
Idaho	-	-	-	-	-	-	-	-	-	-	1[c]	1	1	2	2	2	2	2	2	2
Illinois	-	-	-	1[c]	1	3	7	9	14	19	20	22	25	27	27	26	25	24	24	22
Indiana	-	-	-	1[c]	3	7	10	11	11	13	13	13	13	13	12	11	11	11	11	10
Iowa	-	-	-	-	-	-	2[c]	2	6	9	11	11	11	11	9	8	8	7	6	6
Kansas	-	-	-	-	-	-	-	-	1[c]	3	7	8	8	8	7	6	6	5	5	5
Kentucky	-	2	6	10	12	13	10	10	9	10	11	11	11	11	9	9	8	7	7	7
Louisiana	-	-	-	1[c]	3	3	4	4	5	6	6	6	7	8	8	8	8	8	8	8
Maine	-	-	-	7[c]	7	8	7	6	5	5	4	4	4	4	3	3	3	2	2	2
Maryland	6	8	9	9	9	8	6	6	5	6	6	6	6	6	6	6	7	8	8	8
Massachusetts	8	14	17	13[d]	13	12	10	11	10	11	12	13	14	16	15	14	14	12	12	11
Michigan	-	-	-	-	-	1[c]	3	4	6	9	11	12	12	13	17	17	18	19	19	18
Minnesota	-	-	-	-	-	-	-	2[c]	2	3	5	7	9	10	9	9	9	8	8	8
Mississippi	-	-	-	1[c]	1	2	4	5	5	6	7	7	8	8	7	7	6	5	5	5

(Table continues)

Table 7-1 (Continued)

State	1789[a]	1790	1800	1810	1820	1830	1840	1850	1860	1870	1880	1890	1900	1910	1930[b]	1940	1950	1960	1970	1980
Missouri	–	–	–	–	1	2	5	7	9	13	14	15	16	16	13	13	11	10	10	9
Montana	–	–	–	–	–	–	–	–	–	–	1[c]	1	1	2	2	2	2	2	2	2
Nebraska	–	–	–	–	–	–	–	–	1[c]	1	3	6	6	6	5	4	4	3	3	3
Nevada	–	–	–	–	–	–	–	–	1[c]	1	1	1	1	1	1	1	1	1	1	2
New Hampshire	3	4	5	6	6	5	4	3	3	3	2	2	2	2	2	2	2	2	2	2
New Jersey	4	5	6	6	6	6	5	5	5	7	7	8	10	12	14	14	14	15	15	14
New Mexico	–	–	–	–	–	–	–	–	–	–	–	–	–	1[c]	1	2	2	2	2	3
New York	6	10	17	27	34	40	34	33	31	33	34	34	37	43	45	45	43	41	39	34
North Carolina	5	10	12	13	13	13	9	8	7	8	9	9	10	10	11	12	12	11	11	11
North Dakota	–	–	–	–	–	–	–	–	–	–	1[c]	1	2	3	2	2	2	2	1	1
Ohio	–	–	1[c]	6	14	19	21	21	19	20	21	21	21	22	24	23	23	24	23	21
Oklahoma	–	–	–	–	–	–	–	–	–	–	–	–	5[c]	8	9	8	6	6	6	6
Oregon	–	–	–	–	–	–	–	1[c]	1	1	1	2	2	3	3	4	4	4	4	5
Pennsylvania	8	13	18	23	26	28	24	25	24	27	28	30	32	36	34	33	30	27	25	23
Rhode Island	1	2	2	2	2	2	2	2	2	2	2	2	2	3	2	2	2	2	2	2
South Carolina	5	6	8	9	9	9	7	6	4	5	7	7	7	7	6	6	6	6	6	6
South Dakota	–	–	–	–	–	–	–	–	–	–	2[c]	2	2	3	2	2	2	2	2	1
Tennessee	–	1	3	6	9	13	11	10	8	10	10	10	10	10	9	10	9	9	8	9
Texas	–	–	–	–	–	–	2[c]	2	4	6	11	13	16	18	21	21	22	23	24	27
Utah	–	–	–	–	–	–	–	–	–	–	–	1[c]	1	2	1	2	1	1	2	3
Vermont	–	2	4	6	5	5	4	3	3	3	2	2	2	2	1	1	1	1	2	1
Virginia	10	19	22	23	22	21	15	13	11	9	10	10	10	10	9	9	10	10	10	10
Washington	–	–	–	–	–	–	–	–	–	–	1[c]	2	3	5	6	6	7	7	7	8
West Virginia	–	–	–	–	–	–	–	–	–	3	4	4	5	6	6	6	6	5	4	4
Wisconsin	–	–	–	–	–	–	2[c]	3	6	8	9	10	11	11	10	10	10	10	9	9
Wyoming	–	–	–	–	–	–	–	–	–	–	1[c]	1	1	1	1	1	1	1	1	1

| Total | 65 | 106 | 142 | 186 | 213 | 242 | 232 | 237 | 243 | 293 | 332 | 357 | 391 | 435 | 435 | 435 | 435 | 437[e] | 435 | 435 | 435 |
| Apportionment ratio[f] | 30 | 33 | 33 | 35 | 40 | 48 | 71 | 93 | 127 | 131 | 152 | 174 | 194 | 211 | 281 | 301 | 345 | 410 | 469 | 521 | |

Note: "–" indicates state not yet admitted to Union. Apportionment effective with congressional election two years after census.
[a] Original apportionment made in Constitution, pending first census.
[b] No apportionment was made in 1920.
[c] Representation accorded newly admitted states by Congress, pending the next census.
[d] Twenty members were assigned to Massachusetts, but seven of these were credited to Maine when that area became a state.
[e] Normally 435, but temporarily increased two seats by Congress when Alaska and Hawaii became states.
[f] In thousands.

Sources: Congressional Quarterly, *Congressional Quarterly's Guide to Congress*, 3d ed. (Washington, D.C.: Congressional Quarterly, 1982), 699; U.S. Bureau of the Census, *Historical Statistics of the U.S.* (Washington, D.C.: U.S. Government Printing Office, 1975), 1085.

Figure 7-1 Apportionment of Membership in the House of Representatives by Region, 1910 and 1980

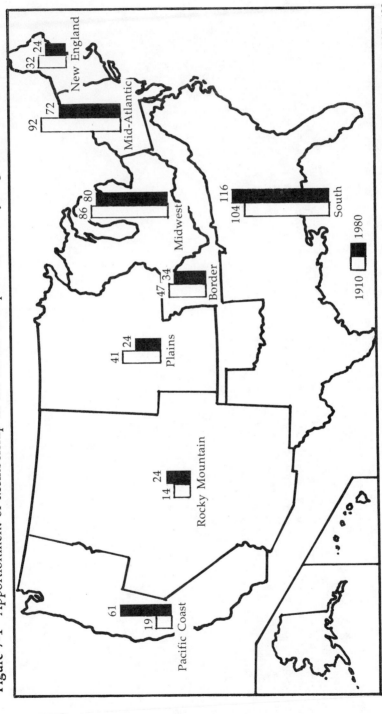

Source: Congressional Quarterly, *Congressional Quarterly's Guide to U.S. Elections,* 2d ed. (Washington, D.C.: Congressional Quarterly, 1985), 688.

Table 7-2 Members of Congress: Gender, Race, Marital Status, and Age, 1971-1989

Congress		Female	Black	Not married[a]	Age Under 40	Age 40-49	Age 50-59	Age 60-69	Age 70-79	Age 80 and over
Representatives										
92d	(1971)	12	12	26	40	133	152	86	19	3
93d	(1973)	14	15	34	45	132	154	80	20	2
94th	(1975)	19	15	54	69	138	137	75	14	2
95th	(1977)	18	16	56	81	121	147	71	15	0
96th	(1979)	16	16	69	86	125	145	63	14	0
97th	(1981)	19	17	86	94	142	132	54	12	1
98th	(1983)	21	21	68	86	145	132	57	13	1
99th	(1985)	22	20	69	71	154	131	59	17	2
100th	(1987)	23	23	64	63	153	137	56	24	2
101st	(1989)	25	24	—	38	165	131	79	20	2
Senators										
92d	(1971)	1	1	3	4	24	32	23	16	1
93d	(1973)	0	1	4	3	25	37	23	11	1
94th	(1975)[b]	0	1	6	5	21	35	24	15	0
95th	(1977)	0	1	9	6	26	35	21	10	2
96th	(1979)	1	0	5	10	31	33	17	8	1
97th	(1981)	2	0	7	9	35	36	14	6	0
98th	(1983)	2	0	10	7	28	39	20	3	3
99th	(1985)	2	0	8	4	27	38	25	4	2
100th	(1987)	2	0	11	5	30	36	22	5	2
101st	(1989)	2	0	—	0	29	41	22	6	2

Note: "—"indicates not available. As of beginning of first session of each Congress. Figures for representatives exclude vacancies.
[a] Single, widowed, or divorced.
[b] Includes Sen. John Durkin (D-N.H.), seated September 1975.

Sources: U.S. Bureau of the Census, *Statistical Abstract of the U.S., 1988* (Washington, D.C.: U.S. Government Printing Office, 1987), 244; 1989: *Congressional Quarterly Weekly Report* (1988), 3294.

Table 7-3 Members of Congress: Seniority and Occupation, 1981-1989

Representatives

Seniority and occupation	97th (1981)	98th (1983)[a]	99th (1985)	100th (1987) Total	Dem.	Rep.	101st (1989) Total	Dem.	Rep.
Seniority[b]									
Under 2 years	77	83	49	51	28	23	38	20	18
2-9 years	231	224	237	221	117	104	230	137	93
10-19 years	96	88	104	114	74	40	117	68	49
20-29 years	23	28	34	37	29	8	35	24	11
30 years or more	8	11	10	12	10	2	13	10	3
Occupation[c]									
Agriculture	28	29	24	20	10	10	19	8	11
Business or banking	134	139	144	142	66	76	138	66	72
Education	59	43	37	38	24	14	42	25	17
Journalism	21	21	21	20	11	9	17	9	8
Law	194	201	190	184	122	62	184	122	62
Public service/politics	52	49	65	94	59	35	94	58	36
Total	435	435[d]	435	435	258	177	435[e]	259	174

Senators

Seniority and occupation	97th (1981)	98th (1983)	99th (1985)	100th (1987) Total	Dem.	Rep.	101st (1989) Total	Dem.	Rep.
Seniority[b]									
Under 2 years	19	5	8	14	12	2	11	5	6
2-9 years	51	61	56	41	16	25	34	21	13
10-19 years	17	21	27	36	19	17	43	22	21
20-29 years	11	10	7	7	7	0	10	6	4
30 years or more	2	3	2	2	1	1	2	1	1
Occupation[c]									
Agriculture	9	9	7	5	2	3	4	1	3
Business or banking	28	35	30	28	13	15	28	13	15
Education	10	12	10	12	6	6	11	6	5
Journalism	7	7	8	8	6	2	8	5	3
Law	59	61	61	62	35	27	63	36	27
Public service/politics	13	2	11	20	13	7	20	14	6
Total	100	100	100	100	55	45	100	55	45

Note: Members of Congress may state more than one occupation; therefore, sum may be greater than total.
[a] Data have been adjusted for the subsequent switching of parties by one representative and the representative elected to fill the vacancy created by the death of Rep. Benjamin Rosenthal (D-N.Y.).
[b] Represents consecutive years of service.
[c] Not all occupations reported are listed.
[d] Includes one vacancy.
[e] Includes two vacancies.

Sources: Statistical Abstract of the U.S., 1988, 244, and Congressional Quarterly Weekly Report (1988), 3295, (1989), 41-44.

Table 7-4 Losses by President's Party in Midterm Elections, 1862-1986

Year	Party holding presidency	President's party: gain/loss of seats in House	President's party: gain/loss of seats in Senate
1862	R	−3	8
1866	R	−2	0
1870	R	−31	−4
1874	R	−96	−8
1878	R	−9	−6
1882	R	−33	3
1886	D	−12	3
1890	R	−85	0
1894	D	−116	−5
1998	R	−21	7
1902	R	9[a]	2
1906	R	−28	3
1910	R	−57	−10
1914	D	−59	5
1918	D	−19	−6
1922	R	−75	−8
1926	R	−10	−6
1930	R	−49	−8
1934	D	9	10
1938	D	−71	−6
1942	D	−55	−9
1946	D	−55	−12
1950	D	−29	−6
1954	R	−18	−1
1958	R	−48	−13
1962	D	−4	3
1966	D	−47	−4
1970	R	−12	2
1974	R	−48	−5
1978	D	−15	−3
1982	R	−26	1
1986	R	−5	−8

Note: Each entry is the difference between the number of seats won by the president's party in that midterm election and the number of seats won by that party in the preceding general election. Because of changes in the overall number of seats in the Senate and House, in the number of seats won by third parties, and in the number of vacancies, a Republican loss is not always matched precisely by a Democratic gain, or vice versa.

[a] Although the Republicans gained nine seats in the 1902 elections, they actually lost ground to the Democrats, who gained twenty-five seats after the increase in the overall number of representatives after the 1900 census.

Source: Norman J. Ornstein et al., eds., *Vital Statistics on Congress, 1987-1988* (Washington, D.C.: Congressional Quarterly, 1987), 51.

Table 7-5 House and Senate Incumbents Reelected, Defeated, or Retired, 1946-1988

			Defeated		Reelected	
Year	Retired[a]	Number seeking reelection	Primaries	General election	Total	Percentage of those seeking reelection
House						
1946	32	398	18	52	328	82.4
1948	29	400	15	68	317	79.3
1950	29	400	6	32	362	90.5
1952	42	389	9	26	354	91.0
1954	24	407	6	22	379	93.1
1956	21	411	6	16	389	94.6
1958	33	396	3	37	356	89.9
1960	26	405	5	25	375	92.6
1962	24	402	12	22	368	91.5
1964	33	397	8	45	344	86.6
1966	22	411	8	41	362	88.1
1968	23	409	4	9	396	96.8
1970	29	401	10	12	379	94.5
1972	40	390	12	13	365	93.6
1974	43	391	8	40	343	87.7
1976	47	384	3	13	368	95.8
1978	49	382	5	19	358	93.7
1980	34	398	6	31	361	90.7
1982	40	393	10	29	354	90.1
1984	22	409	3	16	390	95.4
1986	38	393	2	6	385	98.0
1988	26	409	1	6	402	98.3
Senate						
1946	9	30	6	7	17	56.7
1948	8	25	2	8	15	60.0
1950	4	32	5	5	22	68.8
1952	4	31	2	9	20	64.5
1954	6	32	2	6	24	75.0
1956	6	29	0	4	25	86.2
1958	6	28	0	10	18	64.3
1960	5	29	0	1	28	96.6
1962	4	35	1	5	29	82.9
1964	2	33	1	4	28	84.8
1966	3	32	3	1	28	87.5
1968	6	28	4	4	20	71.4
1970	4	31	1	6	24	77.4
1972	6	27	2	5	20	74.1

(Table continues)

Table 7-5 *(Continued)*

Year	Retired[a]	Number seeking reelection	Defeated		Reelected	
			Primaries	General election	Total	Percentage of those seeking reelection
1974	7	27	2	2	23	85.2
1976	8	25	0	9	16	64.0
1978	10	25	3	7	15	60.0
1980	5	29	4	9	16	55.2
1982	3	30	0	2	28	93.3
1984	4	29	0	3	26	89.6
1986	6	28	0	7	21	75.0
1988	6	27	0	4	23	85.2

[a] Does not include persons who died or resigned from office before the election.

Sources: Ornstein, *Vital Statistics on Congress, 1987-1988,* 56, 57; *Congressional Quarterly Weekly Report* (1988), 3249, 3266-3267.

Table 7-6   House and Senate Seats that Changed Party, 1954-1988

Year	Total changes	Incumbent defeated		Open seat	
		Democrat to Republican	Republican to Democrat	Democrat to Republican	Republican to Democrat
House					
1954	26	3	18	2	3
1956	20	7	7	2	4
1958	50	1	35	0	14
1960	37	23	2	6	6
1962	19	9	5	2	3
1964	57	5	39	5	8
1966	47	39	1	4	3
1968	11	5	0	2	4
1970	25	2	9	6	8
1972	23	6	3	9	5
1974	55	4	36	2	13
1976	22	7	5	3	7
1978	33	14	5	8	6
1980	41	27	3	10	1
1982	31	1	22	3	5
1984	22	13	3	5	1
1986	20	1	5	7	8
1988	9	2	4	1	2
Senate					
1954	8	2	4	1	1
1956	8	1	3	3	1
1958	13	0	11	0	2
1960	2	1	0	1	0
1962	8	2	3	0	3
1964	4	1	3	0	0
1966	3	1	0	2	0
1968	9	4	0	3	2
1970	6	3	2	1	0
1972	10	1	4	3	2
1974	6	0	2	1	3
1976	14	5	4	2	3
1978	13	5	2	3	3
1980	12	9	0	3	0
1982	4	1	1	1	1
1984	4	1	2	0	1
1986	10	0	7	1	2
1988	7	1	3	2	1

Note: This table reflects shifts in party control from immediately before to immediately after the November elections. It does not include party gains resulting from the creation of new districts and does not account for situations in which two districts were reduced to one, thus forcing incumbents to run against each other.

Sources: Ornstein, *Vital Statistics on Congress, 1987-1988,* 52, 54; *Congressional Quarterly Weekly Report* (1988), 3251, 3266-3267.

Table 7-7 Congressional Campaign Costs, by Party and Incumbency Status, 1983-1988

Year/party/status	House					Senate				
	Number of candidates	Receipts[a]	Percentage individual contributions	Percentage committee[b] contributions	Expenditures[a]	Number of candidates	Receipts[a]	Percentage individual contributions	Percentage committee[b] contributions	Expenditures[a]
1983-1984										
Democrats	434	$105.42	44.90	42.02	$95.30	33	$69.19	59.24	18.75	$67.15
Incumbents	258	80.87	44.78	46.48	71.13	12	22.24	62.32	29.05	21.06
Challengers	152	15.80	44.68	29.75	15.54	17	23.57	74.50	18.54	22.90
Open seats	24	8.75	46.40	22.97	8.63	4	23.38	40.93	9.15	23.19
Republicans	382	90.45	52.69	31.61	82.11	35	78.14	70.00	19.09	76.32
Incumbents	154	50.60	52.23	37.94	42.93	17	52.57	71.89	21.80	51.00
Challengers	204	30.00	53.83	20.27	29.55	13	8.18	66.87	18.70	8.32
Open seats	24	9.85	51.57	33.60	9.63	5	17.39	65.78	11.10	17.00
Other	192	0.19	52.63	0.00	0.19	33	0.20	60.00	5.00	0.20
Total	1,008	196.06	48.50	37.18	177.60	101	147.53	64.94	18.91	143.67
1985-1986										
Democrats	427	123.89	44.81	43.05	112.97	35	83.52	60.98	23.77	80.84
Incumbents	235	83.51	42.51	49.06	73.10	9	26.30	66.54	27.79	24.42
Challengers	147	21.32	51.22	30.07	21.10	19	37.04	55.05	21.11	36.48
Open seats	45	19.06	47.74	31.22	18.77	7	20.18	64.62	23.39	19.94
Republicans	383	104.35	55.18	30.58	97.27	34	108.38	68.63	22.81	108.84
Incumbents	160	65.78	53.79	37.75	58.98	18	64.00	68.11	25.59	64.88

(Table continues)

Table 7-7 (Continued)

Year/party/status	House					Senate				
	Number of candidates	Receipts[a]	Percentage individual contributions	Percentage committee[b] contributions	Expenditures[a]	Number of candidates	Receipts[a]	Percentage individual contributions	Percentage committee[b] contributions	Expenditures[a]
Challengers	182	$20.06	57.83	11.67	$19.97	9	$16.92	76.89	11.17	$16.88
Open seats	41	18.51	57.27	25.61	18.32	7	27.46	64.75	23.49	27.08
Other	152	0.11	36.36	0.00	0.10	31	0.05	80.00	0.00	0.05
Total	962	228.35	49.55	37.33	210.34	100	191.95	65.30	23.22	189.73
1987-1988										
Democrats	427	137.09	40.87	47.38	122.79	33	96.46	61.83	24.42	96.85
Incumbents	248	102.45	39.45	51.46	88.84	15	51.00	63.84	30.16	51.86
Challengers	153	22.37	48.06	33.21	21.95	12	26.11	73.88	17.92	25.81
Open seats	26	12.27	39.61	39.12	12.00	6	19.35	40.26	18.09	19.18
Republicans	382	104.72	54.54	32.43	98.72	33	86.11	68.12	24.67	88.09
Incumbents	164	72.42	52.43	39.69	67.03	12	47.27	66.91	28.35	49.41
Challengers	193	19.59	60.13	11.43	19.18	15	23.13	75.49	13.40	23.23
Open seats	25	12.71	57.91	23.45	12.51	6	15.71	60.92	30.17	15.45
Other	186	0.75	85.33	0.00	0.75	42	0.23	78.26	2.17	0.23
Total	995	242.56	46.91	40.78	222.26	108	182.80	64.81	24.51	185.17

Note: Figures are for general election candidates (primary and general election activity included) from January 1, 1983, to December 31, 1984; January 1, 1985, to December 31, 1986; and January 1, 1987, to December 31, 1988.

[a] In millions of dollars.

[b] "Committees" refers to contributions received mostly from PACs but also from other candidates' committees and some bodies not registered with the FEC.

Source: Federal Election Commission, "$458 Million Spent by 1988 Congressional Campaigns," press release, February 24, 1989, 8-9.

Table 7-8 Campaign Spending for Winning Congressional Candidates, 1975-1988

Chamber/years	Receipts[a]	Expenditures[a]	Political action committee contributions Total[a]	Political action committee contributions Percentage of receipts
House				
1975-1976	$42.5	$38.0	$10.9	25.6
1977-1978	60.0	55.6	17.0	28.3
1979-1980	86.0	78.0	27.0	31.4
1981-1982	123.1	114.7	42.7	34.7
1983-1984	144.8	127.0	59.5	41.1
1985-1986	172.7	154.9	72.8	42.2
1987-1988	190.8	170.8	86.1	45.1
Senate				
1975-1976	21.0	20.1	3.1	14.8
1977-1978	43.0	42.3	6.0	14.0
1979-1980	41.7	40.0	10.2	24.5
1981-1982	70.7	68.2	15.6	22.1
1983-1984	100.9	97.5	20.0	19.8
1985-1986	106.8	104.3	28.4	26.6
1987-1988	121.7	123.6	31.9	26.2

[a] In millions of dollars.

Source: Federal Election Commission, "$458 Million Spent by 1988 Congressional Campaigns," press release, February 24, 1989, 1.

Table 7-9 Party Unity and Polarization in Congressional Voting, 1953-1988 (percent)

Year	House	Senate
1953	52	—
1954	38	47
1955	41	30
1956	44	53
1957	59	36
1958	40	44
1959	55	48
1960	53	37
1961	50	62
1962	46	41
1963	49	47
1964	55	36
1965	52	42
1966	41	50
1967	36	35
1968	35	32
1969	31	36
1970	27	35
1971	38	42
1972	27	36
1973	42	40
1974	29	44
1975	48	48
1976	36	37
1977	42	42
1978	33	45
1979	47	47
1980	38	46
1981	37	48
1982	36	43
1983	56	44
1984	47	40
1985	61	50
1986	57	52
1987	64	41
1988	47	42

Note: "—" indicates not available. Data indicate the percentage of all recorded votes on which a majority of voting Democrats opposed a majority of voting Republicans.

Sources: 1953-1986: Ornstein, *Vital Statistics on Congress, 1987-1988,* 208; 1987-1988: *Congressional Quarterly Weekly Report* (1988), 101, 102, 3334.

Table 7-10   Party Support and Unity in Congressional Voting, 1954-1988 (percent)

	House			Senate		
Year	All Democrats	Southern Democrats	Repub-licans	All Democrats	Southern Democrats	Repub-licans
1954	80	—	84	77	—	89
1955	84	68	78	82	78	82
1956	80	79	78	80	75	80
1957	79	71	75	79	81	81
1958	77	67	73	82	76	74
1959	85	77	85	76	63	80
1960	75	62	77	73	60	74
1961	—	—	—	—	—	—
1962	81	—	80	80	—	81
1963	85	—	84	79	—	79
1964	82	—	81	73	—	75
1965	80	55	81	75	55	78
1966	78	55	82	73	52	78
1967	77	53	82	75	59	73
1968	73	48	76	71	57	74
1969	71	47	71	74	53	72
1970	71	52	72	71	49	71
1971	72	48	76	74	56	75
1972	70	44	76	72	43	73
1973	75	55	74	79	52	74
1974	72	51	71	72	41	68
1975	75	53	78	76	48	71
1976	75	52	75	74	46	72
1977	74	55	77	72	48	75
1978	71	53	77	75	54	66
1979	75	60	79	76	62	73
1980	78	64	79	76	64	74
1981	75	57	80	77	64	85
1982	77	62	76	76	62	80
1983	82	67	80	76	70	79
1984	81	68	77	75	61	83
1985	86	76	80	79	68	81
1986	86	76	76	74	59	80
1987	88	79	79	85	80	78
1988	88	81	80	85	78	74

Note: "—" indicates not available. Data show percentage of members voting with a majority of their party on party unity votes. Party unity votes are those roll calls on which a majority of Democrats vote against a majority of Republicans. Percentages are calculated to eliminate the impact of absences as follows: unity = (unity)/(unity + opposition).

Sources: 1954-1986: Ornstein, *Vital Statistics on Congress, 1987-1988,* 209; 1987-1988: *Congressional Quarterly Weekly Report* (1988), 105, 3339.

Figure 7-2 Party Votes in the House, 1887-1988

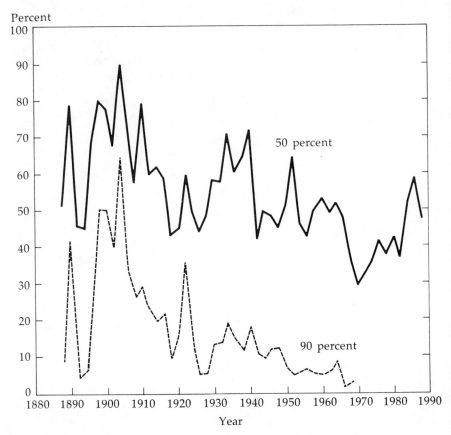

Note: A party vote occurs when the specified percentage (or more) of one party votes against the specified percentage (or more) of the other party. Figures for 90% party votes are unavailable between 1970 and 1986. In 1987-1988 the proportion of 90% party votes was 7 percent.

Sources: 1887-1969: Joseph Cooper, David William Brady, and Patricia A. Hurley, "The Electoral Basis of Party Voting: Patterns and Trends in the U.S. House of Representatives, 1887-1969," in *The Impact of the Electoral Process,* ed. Louis Maisel and Joseph Cooper (Beverly Hills: Sage, 1977), 139; 1970-1986: *Congressional Quarterly Almanac* (Washington, D.C.: Congressional Quarterly), annual volumes; 1988: *Congressional Quarterly Weekly Report* (1988), 3336.

Table 7-11 Conservative Coalition Votes and Victories, 1957-1988 (percent)

Year	House		Senate	
	Votes	Victories	Votes	Victories
1957	16	81	11	100
1958	15	64	19	86
1959	13	91	19	65
1960	20	35	22	67
1961	30	74	32	48
1962	13	44	15	71
1963	13	67	19	44
1964	11	67	17	47
1965	25	25	24	39
1966	19	32	30	51
1967	22	73	18	54
1968	22	63	25	80
1969	25	71	28	67
1970	17	70	26	64
1971	31	79	28	86
1972	25	79	29	63
1973	25	67	21	54
1974	22	67	30	54
1975	28	52	28	48
1976	17	59	26	58
1977	22	60	29	74
1978	20	57	23	46
1979	21	73	18	65
1980	16	67	20	75
1981	21	88	21	95
1982	16	78	20	90
1983	18	71	12	89
1984	14	75	17	94
1985	13	84	16	93
1986	11	78	21	93
1987	9	88	8	100
1988	8	82	10	97

Note: "Votes" is the percentage of all roll call votes on which a majority of voting southern Democrats and a majority of voting Republicans—the Conservative Coalition—opposed the stand taken by a majority of voting northern Democrats. "Victories" is the percentage of Conservative Coalition votes won.

Sources: 1957-1986: Ornstein, *Vital Statistics on Congress, 1987-1988,* 210; 1987-1988: *Congressional Quarterly Weekly Report* (1988), 110-113, 3343, 3347.

Figure 7-3 Congressional Staff, 1955-1986

Number of employees

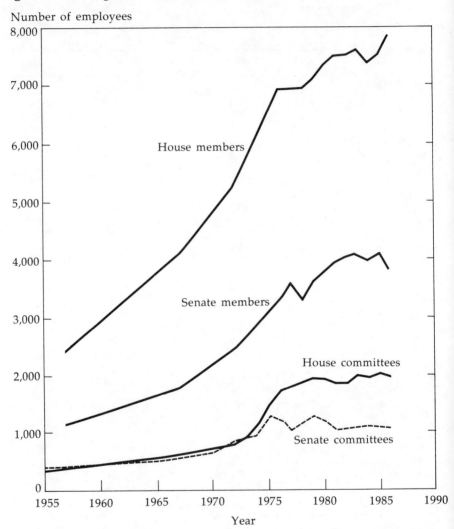

Year

Source: Ornstein, *Vital Statistics on Congress, 1987-1988,* 142, 146.

Table 7-12 Bills, Acts, and Resolutions, 1947-1988

Congress	Measures introduced			Measures enacted		
	Total	Bills	Joint resolutions	Total	Public	Private
80th (1947-1948)	10,797	10,108	689	1,363	906	457
81st (1949-1950)	14,988	14,219	769	2,024	921	1,103
82d (1951-1952)	12,730	12,062	668	1,617	594	1,023
83d (1953-1954)	14,952	14,181	771	1,783	781	1,002
84th (1955-1956)	17,687	16,782	905	1,921	1,028	893
85th (1957-1958)	19,112	18,205	907	1,720	936	784
86th (1959-1960)	18,261	17,230	1,031	1,292	800	492
87th (1961-1962)	18,376	17,230	1,146	1,569	885	684
88th (1963-1964)	17,480	16,079	1,401	1,026	666	360
89th (1965-1966)	24,003	22,483	1,520	1,283	810	473
90th (1967-1968)	26,460	24,786	1,674	1,002	640	362
91st (1969-1970)	26,303	24,631	1,672	941	695	246
92d (1971-1972)	22,969	21,363	1,606	768	607	161
93d (1973-1974)	23,396	21,950	1,446	774	651	123
94th (1975-1976)	21,096	19,762	1,334	729	588	141
95th (1977-1978)	19,387	18,045	1,342	803	633	170
96th (1979-1980)	12,583	11,722	861	736	613	123
97th (1981-1982)	11,490	10,582	908	529	473	56
98th (1983-1984)	11,156	10,134	1,022	677	623	54
99th (1985-1986)	9,885	8,697	1,188	688	664	24
100th (1987-1988)	11,282	8,515	1,073	761	713	48

Note: Excludes simple and concurrent resolutions.

Sources: United States Congress, *Calendars of the U.S. House of Representatives and History of Legislation,* 99th Cong., Final ed., 19-57 through 19-68; 1988: *Congressional Record,* Daily Digest, "Resume of Congressional Activity," 100th Cong. (2d sess., D1399).

Figure 7-4 Proportion of Measures Introduced that Were Passed, 1789-1988

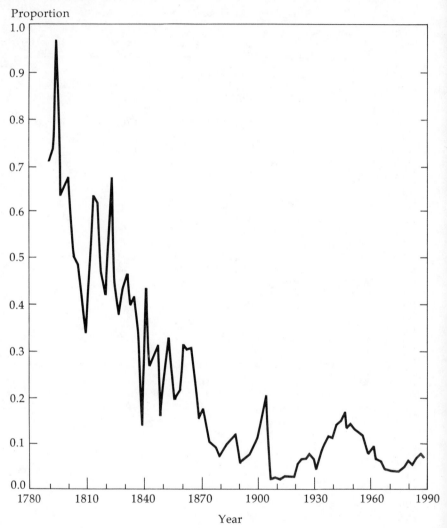

Proportion

Year

Note: Measures include acts, bills, and joint resolutions. Prior to 1824 only bills and acts are included.

Sources: 1789-1968: *Historical Statistics of the U.S.,* Series Y189-198, 1081-1082; 1969-1986: United States Congress, *Calendars of the U.S. House of Representatives and History of Legislation,* 99th Cong., Final ed., 19-57 through 19-68; 1987-1988: *Congressional Record,* Daily Digest, "Resume of Congressional Activity," 100th Cong. (2d sess., D1399).

Table 7-13 Recorded Votes in the House and the Senate, 1947-1988

Year	House	Senate
1947	84	138
1948	75	110
1949	121	226
1950	154	229
1951	109	202
1952	72	129
1953	71	89
1954	76	181
1955	73	88
1956	74	136
1957	100	111
1958	93	202
1959	87	215
1960	93	207
1961	116	207
1962	124	227
1963	119	229
1964	113	312
1965	201	259
1966	193	238
1967	245	315
1968	233	280[a]
1969	177	245
1970	266	422
1971	320	423
1972	329	532
1973	541	594
1974	537	544
1975	612	602
1976	661	688
1977	706	635
1978	834	516
1979	672	497
1980	604	531
1981	353	483
1982	459	465
1983	498	371
1984	408	275
1985	439	381
1986	451	354
1987	488	420
1988	451	379

[a] Does not include one "yea-and-nay" vote that was ruled invalid for lack of a quorum.

Sources: 1947-1971: Ornstein, *Vital Statistics on Congress, 1987-1988*, 168; 1972-1988: *Congressional Quarterly Weekly Report* (1988), 3119.

Table 7-14 Number of Committees and Majority Party Chairmanships, 1955-1989

Congress	Number of committees[a]	Party in majority	Number of majority party members	Number of majority party members chairing standing committees and subcommittees	Percentage of majority party members chairing standing committees and subcommittees	Number of majority party members chairing all committees and subcommittees	Percentage of majority party members chairing all committees and subcommittees
House							
84th (1955-1956)	130	D	232	63	27.2	75	32.3
90th (1967-1968)	185	D	247	111	44.9	117	47.4
92d (1971-1972)	175	D	254	120	47.2	131	51.6
94th (1975-1976)	204	D	289	142	49.1	150	51.9
96th (1979-1980)	193	D	276	144	52.2	149	54.0
97th (1981-1982)	174	D	243	121	49.8	125	51.4
98th (1983-1984)	172	D	267	124	46.4	127	47.6
99th (1985-1986)	191	D	253	129	51.0	131	51.8
100th (1987-1988)	192	D	258	128	49.6	132	51.2
101st (1989-1990)	182	D	260	133	51.2	137	52.7
Senate							
84th (1955-1956)	133	D	48	42	87.5	42	87.5
90th (1967-1968)	155	D	64	55	85.9	58	90.6
92d (1971-1972)	181	D	55[b]	51	92.7	52	94.5
94th (1975-1976)	205	D	62[b]	57	91.9	57	91.9
96th (1979-1980)	130	D	59[b]	58	98.3	58	98.3
97th (1981-1982)	136	R	53	51	96.2	52	98.1
98th (1983-1984)	137	R	54	52	96.3	52	96.3

99th (1985-1986)	120	R	53	49	92.4	49	92.4
100th (1987-1988)	118	D	54	47	87.0	47	87.0
101st (1989-1990)	115	D	55	46	83.6	46	83.6

Note: "—" indicates not available.

[a] Includes standing committees, subcommittees of standing committees, select and special committees, subcommittees of select and special committees, joint committees, and subcommittees of joint committees.

[b] Includes Harry Byrd, Jr. (I-Va.), elected as independent.

Sources: 84th-100th: Ornstein, *Vital Statistics on Congress, 1987-1988*, 127, 131, 132; 101st: calculated by the editors from *Congressional Quarterly Weekly Report,* supplement to vol. 47, no. 18 (May 6, 1989), 8-25, 31-84.

Table 7-15 The 101st Congress: House of Representatives

District/representative	Party	Year first elected	Year born	Percentage of 1988 vote	Campaign expenditures (1988)	Voting ratings[a]							
						VP	PS	PU	CC	ADA	ACU	AFL-CIO	CCUS
Alabama													
1. Callahan	R	1984	1932	59	$651,127	96	63	79	100	10	96	29	93
2. Dickinson	R	1964	1925	94	234,923	93	63	83	95	20	92	38	100
3. Browder	D	1989	1943	65	—	-	-	-	-	-	-	-	-
4. Bevill	D	1966	1921	96	130,642	89	31	71	71	45	50	100	46
5. Flippo	D	1976	1937	64	504,570	90	36	65	84	45	60	85	71
6. Erdreich	D	1982	1938	67	159,323	100	38	70	84	50	60	79	64
7. Harris	D	1986	1940	68	328,296	99	39	68	87	40	68	79	64
Alaska													
AL Young	R	1973	1933	63	626,377	93	49	64	71	30	63	64	69
Arizona													
1. Rhodes III	R	1986	1943	72	291,961	98	70	93	95	10	96	7	100
2. Udall	D	1961	1922	73	99,607	86	21	78	13	75	13	92	29
3. Stump	R	1976	1927	69	319,690	98	84	95	100	0	100	0	85
4. Kyl	R	1986	1942	87	316,476	97	78	93	97	0	100	8	93
5. Kolbe	R	1984	1942	68	434,665	97	58	88	89	20	80	14	93
Arkansas													
1. Alexander	D	1968	1934	U	640,427	88	18	83	26	80	5	100	17
2. Robinson	D	1984	1942	83	459,876	98	42	71	71	55	52	86	50
3. Hammerschmidt	R	1966	1922	75	159,221	95	64	72	97	10	96	29	86
4. Anthony, Jr.	D	1978	1938	69	570,155	93	28	81	55	80	16	92	46

California

1. Bosco	D	1982	1946	63	247,779	93	28	87	32	80	8	85	36
2. Herger	R	1986	1945	59	696,748	99	68	91	92	0	92	29	93
3. Matsui	D	1978	1941	71	638,688	93	20	88	16	90	4	86	36
4. Fazio	D	1978	1942	99	529,334	94	19	92	16	85	0	100	29
5. Pelosi	D	1987	1940	76	616,936	95	20	95	3	100	0	93	21
6. Boxer	D	1982	1940	73	351,687	89	17	86	8	80	5	93	27
7. Miller	D	1974	1945	68	269,887	92	18	85	5	95	4	93	31
8. Dellums	D	1970	1935	67	1,174,676	94	19	88	0	100	0	100	23
9. Stark	D	1972	1931	73	410,540	83	15	78	5	90	0	85	42
10. Edwards	D	1962	1915	86	173,537	96	18	94	5	100	0	100	23
11. Lantos	D	1980	1928	71	269,510	94	27	89	42	85	8	100	31
12. Campbell	R	1988	1952	52	1,440,639	-	-	-	-	-	-	-	-
13. Mineta	D	1974	1931	67	521,674	93	20	92	11	95	4	93	31
14. Shumway	R	1978	1934	63	492,349	98	83	79	92	0	100	0	92
15. Coelho[d]	D	1978	1942	70	972,235	96	21	95	29	90	12	100	23
16. Panetta	D	1976	1938	79	252,336	97	22	90	18	90	4	93	33
17. Pashayan, Jr.	R	1978	1941	71	206,677	97	46	73	68	35	64	71	57
18. Lehman	D	1982	1948	70	193,681	94	20	89	26	85	9	100	25
19. Lagomarsino	R	1974	1926	50	1,470,674	100	63	91	95	35	80	36	93
20. Thomas	R	1978	1941	71	329,354	96	60	81	87	25	78	43	100
21. Gallegly	R	1986	1944	69	465,310	96	68	94	95	15	96	21	100
22. Moorhead	R	1972	1922	70	234,920	98	73	98	97	10	96	7	100
23. Beilenson	D	1976	1932	63	140,486	93	26	89	11	95	8	77	50
24. Waxman	D	1974	1939	72	191,334	85	21	79	11	90	0	93	21
25. Roybal	D	1962	1916	85	67,957	96	20	89	5	95	0	100	23
26. Berman	D	1982	1941	70	409,233	92	23	90	5	95	4	85	36
27. Levine	D	1982	1943	68	398,597	94	21	92	8	95	4	86	36
28. Dixon	D	1978	1934	76	114,523	87	17	85	3	85	0	100	25
29. Hawkins	D	1962	1907	83	65,833	84	14	79	3	85	0	100	15

(Table continues)

Table 7-15 (Continued)

District/representative	Party	Year first elected	Year born	Percentage of 1988 vote	Campaign expenditures (1988)	VP	PS	PU	CC	ADA	ACU	AFL-CIO	CCUS
												Voting ratings[a]	
30. Martinez	D	1982	1929	60	$460,622	92	14	90	13	90	0	100	23
31. Dymally	D	1980	1926	72	481,799	87	16	83	0	90	0	100	23
32. Anderson	D	1968	1913	67	457,410	90	23	84	34	70	10	92	0
33. Dreier	R	1980	1952	69	186,183	98	80	95	91	4	96	0	100
34. Torres	D	1982	1930	63	227,098	93	16	90	11	90	0	100	23
35. Lewis	R	1978	1934	70	337,814	69	44	67	55	5	90	22	67
36. Brown, Jr.	D	1962	1920	54	532,897	85	13	80	8	80	5	100	25
37. McCandless	R	1982	1927	64	122,839	90	67	84	95	10	95	0	92
38. Dornan	R	1976	1933	60	1,755,892	92	65	84	84	0	100	7	91
39. Dannemeyer	R	1978	1929	74	250,737	92	69	93	89	0	100	0	92
40. Cox	R	1988	1952	67	1,110,126	-	-	-	-	-	-	-	-
41. Lowery	R	1980	1947	66	407,025	92	62	81	79	15	92	14	100
42. Rohrabacher	R	1988	1947	64	494,487	-	-	-	-	-	-	-	-
43. Packard	R	1982	1931	72	160,267	91	66	76	87	5	100	15	92
44. Bates	D	1982	1941	60	480,679	94	17	86	13	95	8	93	46
45. Hunter	R	1980	1948	74	489,395	94	65	89	95	0	100	15	77
Colorado													
1. Schroeder	D	1972	1940	70	217,503	96	20	70	29	95	0	100	31
2. Skaggs	D	1986	1943	63	721,647	97	29	81	47	95	16	86	57
3. Campbell	D	1986	1933	78	482,789	93	26	85	47	65	21	92	43
4. Brown	R	1980	1940	73	109,146	97	68	85	87	30	72	21	100
5. Hefley	R	1986	1935	75	183,229	98	60	91	92	5	100	7	100
6. Schaefer	R	1983	1936	63	636,204	98	56	82	87	15	83	50	71

District	Party	Elected	Born	%	Population								
Connecticut													
1. Kennelly	D	1982	1936	77	471,530	98	28	92	32	90	8	100	36
2. Gejdenson	D	1980	1948	64	727,919	96	19	93	8	95	0	92	29
3. Morrison	D	1982	1944	66	506,799	95	20	92	13	100	4	100	43
4. Shays	R	1987	1945	72	372,680	100	42	59	61	90	24	64	57
5. Rowland	R	1984	1957	74	375,660	96	54	72	79	45	60	57	54
6. Johnson	R	1982	1935	66	399,370	95	44	52	68	50	56	71	69
Delaware													
AL Carper	D	1982	1947	68	371,747	98	30	83	42	75	24	77	64
Florida													
1. Hutto	D	1978	1926	67	210,940	96	41	56	97	20	76	57	69
2. Grant	R	1986	1943	100	223,117	96	33	75	82	50	54	79	57
3. Bennett	D	1948	1910	U	19,500	100	35	82	66	65	28	79	43
4. James	R	1988	1941	50	313,415	-	-	-	-	-	-	-	-
5. McCollum	R	1980	1944	U	304,853	89	66	82	97	0	100	17	75
6. Stearns	R	1988	1941	53	408,292	-	-	-	-	-	-	-	-
7. Gibbons	D	1962	1920	U	382,889	93	35	74	55	60	35	71	64
8. Young	R	1970	1930	73	208,320	94	59	86	97	10	88	36	79
9. Bilirakis	R	1982	1930	100	193,901	96	67	87	89	10	96	14	93
10. Ireland	R	1976	1930	73	460,468	93	67	88	87	5	100	14	100
11. Nelson	D	1978	1942	61	565,632	93	43	67	76	45	56	71	43
12. Lewis	R	1982	1924	U	256,081	96	69	93	95	5	100	14	93
13. Goss	R	1988	1938	71	836,224	-	-	-	-	-	-	-	-
14. Johnston	D	1988	1931	55	971,883	-	-	-	-	-	-	-	-
15. Shaw, Jr.	R	1980	1939	66	455,578	94	65	70	100	5	96	21	92
16. Smith	D	1982	1941	69	555,473	92	23	83	21	85	17	100	23
17. Lehman	D	1972	1913	U	257,487	99	22	94	16	100	8	93	36
18. Pepper[e]	D	1962	1900	U	405,551	83	24	75	45	65	18	100	17
19. Fascell	D	1954	1917	72	337,596	96	28	88	42	75	17	93	36

(Table continues)

Table 7-15 (Continued)

District/representative	Party	Year first elected	Year born	Percentage of 1988 vote	Campaign expenditures (1988)	Voting ratings[a]							
						VP	PS	PU	CC	ADA	ACU	AFL-CIO	CCUS
Georgia													
1. Thomas	D	1982	1943	67	$337,048	99	38	77	95	50	48	64	64
2. Hatcher	D	1980	1939	62	368,470	89	31	72	84	50	43	62	64
3. Ray	D	1982	1927	U	256,751	70	22	48	37	20	53	56	56
4. Jones	D	1988	1941	60	516,737	-	-	-	-	-	-	-	-
5. Lewis	D	1986	1940	78	101,540	96	13	93	5	100	0	100	17
6. Gingrich	R	1978	1943	59	838,708	90	62	80	92	5	100	15	100
7. Darden	D	1983	1943	65	382,281	98	41	75	92	45	50	64	64
8. Rowland	D	1982	1926	U	195,895	97	36	79	82	55	46	57	69
9. Jenkins	D	1976	1933	63	405,040	93	38	68	87	45	54	64	71
10. Barnard, Jr.	D	1976	1922	64	193,123	80	38	56	82	25	64	54	67
Hawaii													
1. Saiki	R	1986	1930	55	686,165	94	41	42	71	50	39	77	50
2. Akaka	D	1976	1924	89	153,163	92	22	88	13	85	0	93	23
Idaho													
1. Craig	R	1980	1945	66	361,113	91	66	87	76	5	100	7	92
2. Stallings	D	1984	1940	63	502,083	92	35	71	79	55	48	71	71
Illinois													
1. Hayes	D	1983	1918	96	145,905	92	14	91	3	95	0	100	14
2. Savage	D	1980	1925	83	242,487	88	18	82	5	100	0	100	23
3. Russo	D	1974	1944	62	558,273	93	29	78	39	80	28	93	46
4. Sangmeister	D	1988	1931	50	359,942	-	-	-	-	-	-	-	-
5. Lipinski	D	1982	1937	61	165,144	88	33	68	47	55	35	100	45

6. Hyde	R	1974	1924	74	281,229	96	70	84	92	15	92	14	100
7. Collins	D	1973	1931	U	127,487	90	16	87	3	90	0	100	21
8. Rostenkowski	D	1958	1928	75	428,698	91	29	80	32	65	19	85	50
9. Yates	D	1948	1909	66	122,900	88	17	81	8	80	5	100	36
10. Porter	R	1980	1935	72	212,630	97	57	71	82	30	68	15	100
11. Annunzio	D	1964	1915	65	239,158	98	27	90	50	75	17	100	25
12. Crane	R	1969	1930	75	480,460	91	79	91	92	0	100	0	93
13. Fawell	R	1984	1929	70	289,190	98	61	80	92	40	64	14	92
14. Hastert	R	1986	1942	74	346,785	98	62	92	95	10	92	21	86
15. Madigan	R	1972	1936	72	374,760	90	59	81	89	15	77	27	85
16. Martin	R	1980	1939	64	329,598	91	56	83	82	30	76	46	69
17. Evans	D	1982	1951	65	471,233	99	17	97	8	100	0	100	14
18. Michel	R	1956	1923	55	861,969	92	64	76	82	10	92	31	85
19. Bruce	D	1984	1944	64	193,205	99	23	89	39	75	24	100	36
20. Durbin	D	1982	1944	69	251,634	98	24	88	18	90	16	100	36
21. Costello	D	1988	1949	53	394,412	99[b]	24	86	67	-	57	100	-
22. Poshard	D	1988	1945	65	392,791	-	-	-	-	-	-	-	-
Indiana													
1. Visclosky	D	1984	1949	77	141,855	99	22	91	18	100	0	100	36
2. Sharp	D	1974	1942	53	444,422	97	31	79	61	75	20	100	50
3. Hiler	R	1980	1953	54	1,085,140	95	63	89	89	95	4	100	21
4. Long	D	1989	1952	51	—	-	-	-	-	-	-	-	-
5. Jontz	D	1986	1951	56	689,086	99	16	91	26	95	4	100	21
6. Burton	R	1982	1938	73	333,723	98	84	96	95	15	100	0	93
7. Myers	R	1966	1927	62	157,671	94	57	60	82	15	83	15	92
8. McCloskey	D	1982	1939	62	551,484	98	20	91	29	75	16	100	21
9. Hamilton	D	1964	1931	71	333,957	99	25	88	47	85	8	100	36
10. Jacobs, Jr.	D	1964	1932	61	35,786	93[b]	26	58	26	95	12	100	42

(Table continues)

Table 7-15 (Continued)

District/representative	Party	Year first elected	Year born	Percentage of 1988 vote	Campaign expenditures (1988)	VP	PS	PU	CC	ADA	ACU	AFL-CIO	CCUS
Iowa
1. Leach	R	1976	1942	61	218,707	98	35	62	61	75	32	79	64
2. Tauke	R	1978	1950	57	581,514	96	54	80	87	45	67	23	85
3. Nagle	D	1986	1943	63	595,977	96	21	86	45	80	8	100	36
4. Smith	D	1958	1920	72	83,474	92	30	79	37	80	16	86	46
5. Lightfoot	R	1984	1939	64	420,730	88	63	76	92	10	90	15	85
6. Grandy	R	1986	1948	64	523,108	91	52	70	87	40	64	57	86
Kansas
1. Roberts	R	1980	1936	U	81,140	96	62	86	95	10	79	25	100
2. Slattery	D	1982	1948	73	388,866	96	32	78	61	55	33	85	38
3. Meyers	R	1984	1928	74	234,583	96	52	71	87	35	58	23	85
4. Glickman	D	1976	1944	64	545,755	98	32	75	61	80	16	86	43
5. Whittaker	R	1978	1939	70	117,312	95	61	84	89	10	88	29	100
Kentucky
1. Hubbard, Jr.	D	1974	1937	95	546,908	96	39	67	68	50	54	86	50
2. Natcher	D	1953	1909	61	8,397	100	26	94	42	75	16	100	21
3. Mazzoli	D	1970	1932	70	371,431	97	33	84	42	75	21	77	54
4. Bunning	R	1986	1931	74	468,870	96	65	92	97	0	100	8	100
5. Rogers	R	1980	1937	U	119,720	98	62	85	87	5	96	21	100
6. Hopkins	R	1978	1933	74	295,333	99	63	80	92	20	76	36	93
7. Perkins	D	1984	1954	59	411,699	100	20	95	26	85	12	100	14
Louisiana
1. Livingston	R	1977	1943	c	555,058	88	63	78	95	5	100	8	100
2. Boggs	D	1973	1916	c	252,835	94	27	83	39	80	5	100	18

3. Tauzin	D	1980	1943	c	707,085	99	45	61	97	45	64	86	62
4. McCrery	R	1988	1949	c	286,813	98[b]	61	80	94	12	94	20	100
5. Huckaby	D	1976	1941	c	194,021	91	44	56	84	40	65	57	77
6. Baker	R	1986	1948	c	270,899	93	63	80	97	5	100	15	100
7. Hayes	D	1986	1946	c	268,116	93	35	70	87	55	52	92	62
8. Holloway	R	1986	1943	57	629,950	88	65	76	92	0	96	36	92
Maine													
1. Brennan	D	1986	1934	63	464,541	99	22	91	29	90	12	100	29
2. Snowe	R	1978	1947	66	202,317	100	37	54	82	60	40	86	50
Maryland													
1. Dyson	D	1980	1948	50	684,204	92	29	71	63	55	50	92	36
2. Bentley	R	1984	1923	71	779,318	89	46	74	87	10	86	69	79
3. Cardin	D	1986	1943	73	354,701	98	22	93	18	90	4	93	36
4. McMillen	D	1986	1952	68	599,881	100	27	90	58	75	12	100	36
5. Hoyer	D	1981	1939	79	416,187	99	23	98	18	95	0	100	21
6. Byron	D	1978	1932	75	213,554	96	49	61	100	30	68	77	69
7. Mfume	D	1986	1948	U	110,565	98	23	93	21	95	4	100	21
8. Morella	R	1986	1931	63	821,574	96	28	30	32	90	8	79	46
Massachusetts													
1. Conte	R	1958	1921	83	131,566	96	29	30	29	90	8	93	46
2. Neal	D	1988	1949	80	268,094	—	—	—	—	—	—	—	—
3. Early	D	1974	1933	100	205,989	91	21	85	11	85	8	100	36
4. Frank	D	1980	1940	70	343,097	94	17	87	0	100	0	93	21
5. Atkins	D	1984	1948	84	344,930	96	16	96	3	100	0	100	23
6. Mavroules	D	1978	1929	70	337,199	94	24	87	26	90	8	100	23
7. Markey	D	1976	1946	U	134,388	96	17	93	3	90	0	100	23
8. Kennedy II	D	1986	1952	80	1,186,852	98	18	95	3	95	4	100	21
9. Moakley	D	1972	1927	100	273,488	98	21	95	5	90	8	100	21

(Table continues)

Table 7-15 (Continued)

| District/representative | Party | Year first elected | Year born | Percentage of 1988 vote | Campaign expenditures (1988) | Voting ratings[a] | | | | | | AFL-CIO | CCUS |
						VP	PS	PU	CC	ADA	ACU		
10. Studds	D	1972	1937	67	$235,946	97	16	94	0	100	0	100	21
11. Donnelly	D	1978	1947	81	167,960	84	15	86	18	80	8	100	23
Michigan													
1. Conyers, Jr.	D	1964	1929	91	124,823	86	13	83	3	90	0	100	21
2. Pursell	R	1976	1932	55	876,779	96	47	62	79	45	46	62	79
3. Wolpe	D	1978	1939	57	600,940	98	17	92	18	100	0	100	36
4. Upton	R	1986	1953	71	323,829	100	60	86	87	30	64	50	100
5. Henry	R	1984	1942	73	309,436	98	49	81	84	50	52	57	93
6. Carr	D	1974	1943	59	504,217	94	31	80	50	80	21	93	46
7. Kildee	D	1976	1929	76	150,594	100	17	95	11	95	4	100	14
8. Traxler	D	1974	1931	72	128,400	90	19	84	26	80	14	100	21
9. Vander Jagt	R	1966	1931	70	450,801	91	58	81	87	15	91	21	100
10. Schuette	R	1984	1953	73	728,533	97	52	81	84	40	63	50	93
11. Davis	R	1978	1932	60	680,819	95	35	43	66	60	42	100	29
12. Bonior	D	1976	1945	54	434,200	96	19	93	3	95	4	100	21
13. Crockett, Jr.	D	1980	1909	87	84,024	86	14	82	3	85	0	100	33
14. Hertel	D	1980	1948	63	137,560	99	22	92	24	95	4	100	21
15. Ford	D	1964	1927	64	234,435	87	13	83	5	100	0	100	23
16. Dingell	D	1955	1926	97	462,180	93	22	88	29	80	13	100	29
17. Levin	D	1982	1931	70	233,421	95	24	94	11	100	0	100	31
18. Broomfield	R	1956	1922	76	77,103	89	58	67	84	30	84	36	92
Minnesota													
1. Penny	D	1982	1951	70	165,016	99	37	59	66	60	36	71	64
2. Weber	R	1980	1952	58	623,776	97	61	84	92	15	96	14	93
3. Frenzel	R	1970	1928	68	381,646	93	64	70	63	35	57	23	92

4. Vento	D	1976	1940	72	216,172	98	21	94	11	90	4	100	36
5. Sabo	D	1978	1938	72	281,455	99	20	96	8	100	0	100	21
6. Sikorski	D	1982	1948	65	320,437	98	22	75	16	90	12	100	36
7. Stangeland	R	1977	1930	55	693,429	96	62	85	87	5	92	29	93
8. Oberstar	D	1974	1934	75	157,802	99	21	93	8	90	12	100	21
Mississippi													
1. Whitten	D	1941	1910	78	58,370	97	28	90	45	65	20	100	15
2. Espy	D	1986	1953	65	886,540	86	20	78	42	85	12	93	25
3. Montgomery	D	1966	1920	89	116,761	99	45	64	89	25	71	57	71
4. Parker	D	1988	1949	55	843,142	–	–	–	–	–	–	–	–
5. Smith	R	1988	1944	55	569,830	–	–	–	–	–	–	–	–
Missouri													
1. Clay	D	1968	1931	72	134,200	79	12	68	0	90	0	100	18
2. Buechner	R	1986	1940	66	693,066	95	57	82	97	15	88	31	79
3. Gephardt	D	1976	1941	63	512,206	80	18	73	16	75	10	92	20
4. Skelton	D	1976	1931	72	273,316	93	43	63	92	40	58	83	62
5. Wheat	D	1982	1951	70	240,623	98	15	79	5	100	0	93	21
6. Coleman	R	1976	1943	59	341,344	96	51	83	95	25	76	64	93
7. Hancock	R	1988	1929	53	338,125	–	–	–	–	–	–	–	–
8. Emerson	R	1980	1938	58	768,792	91	47	75	84	10	90	50	83
9. Volkmer	D	1976	1931	68	210,841	95	35	72	79	60	35	93	50
Montana													
1. Williams	D	1978	1937	61	250,276	85	14	70	13	85	0	100	15
2. Marlenee	R	1976	1935	56	380,928	93	68	85	92	0	96	7	86
Nebraska													
1. Bereuter	R	1978	1939	66	221,530	99[b]	56	79	87	20	76	57	93
2. Hoagland	D	1988	1941	51	858,762	–	–	–	–	–	–	–	–
3. Smith	R	1974	1911	79	229,109	99	53	64	92	25	80	43	93

(Table continues)

211

Table 7-15 (Continued)

| District/representative | Party | Year first elected | Year born | Percentage of 1988 vote | Campaign expenditures (1988) | Voting ratings[a] | | | | | | | |
						VP	PS	PU	CC	ADA	ACU	AFL-CIO	CCUS
Nevada													
1. Bilbray	D	1986	1938	64	$652,199	97	30	79	68	60	44	93	43
2. Vucanovich	R	1982	1921	57	614,853	97	68	92	92	10	92	14	77
New Hampshire													
1. Smith	R	1984	1941	60	333,695	99	73	97	95	5	100	14	93
2. Douglas	R	1988	1942	57	730,803	-	-	-	-	-	-	-	-
New Jersey													
1. Florio	D	1974	1937	70	924,427	90	23	83	24	80	9	100	21
2. Hughes	D	1974	1932	66	235,629	99	30	85	47	70	16	100	43
3. Pallone	D	1988	1951	52	678,647	-	-	-	-	-	-	-	-
4. Smith	R	1980	1953	66	252,823	98	40	44	68	60	48	100	43
5. Roukema	R	1980	1929	76	400,555	95	45	61	70	36	52	38	87
6. Dwyer	D	1980	1921	61	123,632	98	21	92	32	85	4	100	31
7. Rinaldo	R	1972	1931	75	370,387	99	48	44	71	45	54	100	36
8. Roe	D	1969	1924	U	267,609	94	29	84	50	70	13	100	21
9. Torricelli	D	1982	1951	67	403,059	93	23	88	39	85	4	100	25
10. Payne	D	1988	1934	77	413,338	-	-	-	-	-	-	-	-
11. Gallo	R	1984	1935	70	490,751	97	59	84	87	30	72	31	79
12. Courter	R	1978	1941	69	1,333,882	84	49	70	71	25	74	64	62
13. Saxton	R	1984	1943	69	411,620	99	57	80	82	30	72	50	79
14. Guarini	D	1978	1924	67	369,578	94	26	85	37	70	14	100	46
New Mexico													
1. Schiff	R	1988	1947	51	559,134	-	-	-	-	-	-	-	-
2. Skeen	R	1980	1927	U	67,727	99	56	80	89	5	100	29	93
3. Richardson	D	1982	1947	73	267,633	95	28	83	55	75	21	93	42

New York

		Party													
1.	Hochbrueckner	D	1988	1938	51	732,956	99	22	89	37	80	12	93	36
2.	Downey	D	1974	1949	62	627,584	98	23	93	8	100	0	86	36
3.	Mrazek	D	1982	1945	57	364,087	95	19	91	13	95	4	79	31
4.	Lent	R	1970	1931	70	436,310	94	48	61	76	25	68	62	69
5.	McGrath	R	1986	1942	65	337,792	88	46	62	74	25	55	83	82
6.	Flake	D	1986	1945	86	370,236	88	14	82	5	95	0	100	30
7.	Ackerman	D	1983	1942	U	142,041	91	15	93	3	95	0	100	23
8.	Scheuer	D	1964	1920	U	98,919	91	21	82	13	85	5	86	46
9.	Manton	D	1984	1932	U	256,832	93	24	89	32	60	18	100	23
10.	Schumer	D	1980	1950	78	87,129	96	20	90	5	100	4	86	36
11.	Towns	D	1982	1934	89	278,709	81	13	76	0	90	0	100	33
12.	Owens	D	1982	1936	93	189,684	85	13	79	3	95	4	93	33
13.	Solarz	D	1974	1940	75	553,532	95	24	88	11	95	4	93	33
14.	Molinari	R	1980	1928	63	206,796	88	53	74	76	30	63	73	91
15.	Green	R	1978	1929	61	602,942	98	37	38	29	75	25	50	64
16.	Rangel	D	1970	1930	97	479,427	87	14	80	5	85	0	100	31
17.	Weiss	D	1976	1927	84	170,567	85	15	80	5	75	0	100	21
18.	Garcia	D	1978	1933	91	448,391	84	13	77	5	85	4	100	31
19.	Engel	D	1988	1947	56	183,145	-	-	-	-	-	-	-	-
20.	Lowey	D	1988	1937	50	1,309,873	-	-	-	-	-	-	-	-
21.	Fish, Jr.	R	1968	1926	75	277,680	96	37	37	58	60	32	86	71
22.	Gilman	R	1972	1922	71	411,056	97	41	39	55	55	42	93	50
23.	McNulty	D	1988	1947	62	273,505	-	-	-	-	-	-	-	-
24.	Solomon	R	1978	1930	72	151,276	97	65	90	95	15	88	57	86
25.	Boehlert	R	1982	1936	U	145,883	96	37	58	58	65	24	86	64
26.	Martin	R	1980	1944	75	120,423	93	45	66	84	25	68	64	79
27.	Walsh	R	1988	1947	58	594,965	-	-	-	-	-	-	-	-
28.	McHugh	D	1974	1938	93	172,905	97	25	91	21	95	4	92	46
29.	Horton	R	1962	1919	69	130,597	90	30	28	55	65	22	92	50

(Table continues)

Table 7-15 (Continued)

District/representative	Party	Year first elected	Year born	Percentage of 1988 vote	Campaign expenditures (1988)	VP	PS	PU	CC	ADA	ACU	AFL-CIO	CCUS
30. Slaughter	D	1986	1929	57	$802,886	96	23	92	37	85	8	100	43
31. Paxton	R	1988	1954	53	688,382	-	-	-	-	-	-	-	-
32. LaFalce	D	1974	1939	73	133,738	96	24	85	32	80	8	93	38
33. Nowak	D	1974	1935	U	94,042	97	25	93	16	90	12	100	36
34. Houghton	R	1986	1926	96	319,098	96	52	61	92	45	56	57	100
North Carolina													
1. Jones	D	1966	1913	65	82,147	88	19	83	37	80	13	75	46
2. Valentine	D	1982	1926	U	84,671	96	40	70	95	45	48	71	62
3. Lancaster	D	1986	1943	U	98,956	98	38	78	84	60	40	71	64
4. Price	D	1986	1940	58	1,006,641	97	28	83	71	75	24	93	62
5. Neal	D	1974	1934	53	756,115	92	24	76	55	70	21	92	50
6. Coble	R	1984	1931	62	738,088	99	61	90	92	10	92	21	93
7. Rose	D	1972	1939	67	185,039	88	19	77	47	60	11	100	25
8. Hefner	D	1974	1930	51	581,888	91	29	76	68	65	25	92	50
9. McMillan	R	1984	1932	66	440,082	98	61	79	89	15	88	21	100
10. Ballenger	R	1986	1926	61	302,215	98	63	94	95	10	92	14	100
11. Clarke	D	1986	1917	50	494,092	95	29	82	71	60	29	86	57
North Dakota													
AL Dorgan	D	1980	1942	71	747,594	97	28	81	47	75	17	93	38
Ohio													
1. Luken	D	1976	1925	56	908,765	96	32	76	58	70	14	100	46
2. Gradison	R	1974	1928	72	125,682	95	61	62	66	35	62	21	83
3. Hall	D	1978	1942	77	182,889	89	24	79	37	75	17	93	23
4. Oxley	R	1981	1944	100	207,157	94	68	81	92	20	88	14	100

Voting ratings[a]

	Party	Born	Elected		Votes								
5. Gillmor	R	1939	1988	61	769,548	89	65	73	92	5	96	14	100
6. McEwen	R	1950	1980	74	884,754	99	69	92	89	5	100	14	93
7. DeWine	R	1947	1982	74	299,553	90	68	84	84	5	96	14	85
8. Lukens	R	1931	1986	76	147,712	89	21	86	45	0	13	100	43
9. Kaptur	D	1946	1982	81	244,030	98	62	85	95	75	92	100	93
10. Miller	R	1917	1966	72	99,247	97	21	88	37	15	8	43	29
11. Eckart	D	1950	1980	61	561,070	95	61	76	100	90	92	100	93
12. Kasich	R	1952	1982	79	351,517	97	29	88	24	15	8	29	50
13. Pease	D	1931	1976	70	157,632	99	24	94	18	90	4	86	36
14. Sawyer	D	1945	1986	75	419,005	92	54	61	84	95	80	93	92
15. Wylie	R	1920	1966	75	211,963	99	56	67	87	30	76	36	93
16. Regula	R	1924	1972	79	94,492	99	17	89	37	30	8	64	93
17. Traficant, Jr.	D	1941	1984	77	96,003	99	28	71	63	95	24	100	21
18. Applegate	D	1928	1976	77	86,061	95	17	86	18	70	0	100	29
19. Feighan	D	1947	1982	70	226,086	92	17	88	8	95	8	100	38
20. Oakar	D	1940	1976	83	783,180	91	19	88	8	90	8	100	17
21. Stokes	D	1925	1968	86	173,534	84	16	81	0	70	0	100	25
Oklahoma													
1. Inhofe	R	1934	1986	53	484,585	96	64	88	95	10	92	38	92
2. Synar	D	1950	1978	65	358,705	99	26	93	13	100	0	86	38
3. Watkins	D	1938	1976	U	174,437	98	35	75	87	50	46	79	57
4. McCurdy	D	1950	1980	U	251,956	94	33	73	79	60	30	71	64
5. Edwards	R	1937	1976	72	318,822	95	59	84	95	10	92	36	93
6. English	D	1940	1974	73	306,600	99	47	65	95	40	60	64	71
Oregon													
1. AuCoin	D	1942	1974	70	542,224	87	22	81	21	95	8	86	43
2. Smith	R	1931	1982	63	340,643	99	66	91	92	5	92	21	86
3. Wyden	D	1949	1980	99	287,996	99	29	87	34	90	16	86	43
4. DeFazio	D	1947	1986	72	279,809	95	20	86	24	80	13	86	25
5. Smith	R	1938	1980	50	559,616	92	65	89	79	5	96	14	92

(Table continues)

Table 7-15 *(Continued)*

District/representative	Party	Year first elected	Year born	Percentage of 1988 vote	Campaign expenditures (1988)	Voting ratings[a]							
						VP	PS	PU	CC	ADA	ACU	AFL-CIO	CCUS
Pennsylvania													
1. Foglietta	D	1980	1928	76	$234,957	90	16	83	8	90	4	92	42
2. Gray III	D	1978	1941	94	660,456	84	14	78	11	95	0	100	31
3. Borski	D	1982	1948	63	250,480	98	26	92	24	80	12	100	23
4. Kolter	D	1982	1926	70	90,710	88	26	78	45	60	22	100	17
5. Schulze	R	1974	1929	78	444,205	94	55	63	84	30	76	46	92
6. Yatron	D	1968	1927	63	121,435	96	23	87	44	84	13	100	33
7. Weldon	R	1986	1947	68	507,360	95	52	69	79	40	55	40	73
8. Kostmayer	D	1976	1946	57	1,089,612	96	21	89	16	85	4	100	31
9. Shuster	R	1972	1932	U	332,647	95	68	75	89	5	100	14	100
10. McDade	R	1962	1931	73	430,322	94	44	61	71	40	54	86	50
11. Kanjorski	D	1984	1937	U	310,305	99	32	88	50	70	20	100	36
12. Murtha	D	1974	1932	U	401,945	97	35	79	58	55	46	100	29
13. Coughlin	R	1968	1929	67	225,412	95	49	70	87	50	48	64	79
14. Coyne	D	1980	1936	79	80,730	93	19	92	11	95	0	100	31
15. Ritter	R	1978	1940	57	752,332	94	57	66	84	10	84	62	77
16. Walker	R	1976	1942	74	91,950	98	78	95	95	5	100	7	93
17. Gekas	R	1982	1930	U	97,611	99	72	93	97	10	92	21	93
18. Walgren	D	1976	1940	63	321,074	93	20	86	37	90	4	100	25
19. Goodling	R	1974	1927	77	57,091	94	50	77	84	30	63	50	93
20. Gaydos	D	1968	1926	98	137,023	93	26	80	63	65	24	100	25
21. Ridge	R	1982	1945	79	370,619	95	40	66	74	50	36	86	71
22. Murphy	D	1976	1927	72	183,335	88	28	50	47	60	24	100	33
23. Clinger, Jr.	R	1978	1929	62	336,675	95	47	67	76	25	63	62	86

Rhode Island													
1. Machtley	R	1988	1948	56	385,402	-	-	-	-	-	-	-	-
2. Schneider	R	1980	1947	72	443,267	93	24	31	50	80	17	100	38
South Carolina													
1. Ravenel	R	1986	1927	64	118,702	98	58	61	88	20	61	31	87
2. Spence	R	1970	1928	53	369,698	54	37	37	47	10	85	50	71
3. Derrick	D	1974	1936	54	641,429	95	33	76	66	70	36	71	54
4. Patterson	D	1986	1939	52	1,143,351	99	37	69	82	45	48	71	57
5. Spratt, Jr.	D	1982	1942	70	105,620	95	33	78	82	55	29	79	57
6. Tallon	D	1982	1946	76	243,559	98	42	63	82	40	60	79	62
South Dakota													
AL Johnson	D	1986	1946	72	632,105	99	25	77	66	70	28	93	36
Tennessee													
1. Quillen	R	1962	1916	80	227,503	88	48	59	82	15	91	36	100
2. Duncan	R	1964	1947	56	435,567	-	-	-	-	-	-	-	-
3. Lloyd	D	1974	1929	57	618,173	98	47	59	89	50	54	100	46
4. Cooper	D	1982	1954	U	234,375	98	34	84	66	70	28	79	69
5. Clement	D	1988	1943	U	291,818	93	31	79	63	75	20	93	36
6. Gordon	D	1984	1949	76	454,346	94	23	84	53	80	12	93	36
7. Sundquist	R	1982	1936	80	307,656	93	64	86	89	10	96	17	100
8. Tanner	D	1988	1944	62	863,425	-	-	-	-	-	-	-	-
9. Ford	D	1974	1945	82	364,330	70	12	61	5	85	0	100	36
Texas													
1. Chapman	D	1985	1945	62	505,611	93	36	70	87	50	52	71	64
2. Wilson	D	1972	1933	88	309,355	80	36	61	53	35	55	82	46
3. Bartlett	R	1982	1947	82	1,000,894	97	72	78	95	10	96	0	100
4. Hall	D	1980	1923	66	316,846	97	52	44	88	24	70	44	73
5. Bryant	D	1982	1947	61	646,218	94	19	87	42	85	9	100	27

(Table continues)

Table 7-15 (Continued)

District/representative	Party	Year first elected	Year born	Percentage of 1988 vote	Campaign expenditures (1988)	Voting ratings[a]							
						VP	PS	PU	CC	ADA	ACU	AFL-CIO	CCUS
6. Barton	R	1984	1949	68	$654,260	87	70	89	82	5	96	0	100
7. Archer	R	1970	1928	79	180,255	99	79	80	92	0	100	0	100
8. Fields	R	1980	1952	U	483,544	95	70	92	84	0	100	0	100
9. Brooks	D	1952	1922	U	226,581	86	24	82	26	75	9	100	23
10. Pickle	D	1963	1913	93	172,921	86	32	80	53	80	16	100	38
11. Leath	D	1978	1931	95	87,626	82	50	50	82	15	71	54	77
12. Wright[f]	D	1954	1922	99	940,760	-	-	-	-	-	-	-	-
13. Sarpalius	D	1988	1948	52	384,738	-	-	-	-	-	-	-	-
14. Laughlin	D	1988	1942	53	600,114	-	-	-	-	-	-	-	-
15. de la Garza	D	1964	1927	94	219,469	83	21	73	32	50	20	73	50
16. Coleman	D	1982	1941	U	317,444	96	27	89	37	80	17	93	29
17. Stenholm	D	1978	1938	U	342,766	96	57	45	87	20	78	46	77
18. Leland	D	1978	1944	93	534,732	83	15	77	5	100	0	100	27
19. Combest	R	1984	1945	68	244,821	97	68	75	97	0	92	21	93
20. Gonzalez	D	1961	1916	71	174,470	98	16	96	13	100	0	100	15
21. Smith	R	1986	1947	93	418,989	98	66	91	97	5	100	23	92
22. DeLay	R	1984	1947	67	361,255	94	78	88	97	0	100	0	92
23. Bustamante	D	1984	1935	65	187,302	93	25	88	45	70	8	100	21
24. Frost	D	1978	1942	93	438,949	90	21	84	37	70	9	92	23
25. Andrews	D	1982	1944	71	318,970	98	37	75	87	75	29	86	62
26. Armey	R	1984	1940	69	314,903	98	82	94	92	0	100	0	100
27. Ortiz	D	1982	1937	U	142,651	91	29	78	53	55	26	100	29
Utah													
1. Hansen	R	1980	1932	60	426,902	88	66	78	84	0	100	0	100
2. Owens	D	1986	1937	57	676,472	96	22	84	47	75	16	93	36
3. Nielson	R	1982	1924	67	102,055	98	74	83	95	5	92	21	100

		1988	1945	41	450,162	-	-	-	-	-	-	-	-

Vermont
| AL Smith | R | 1988 | 1945 | 41 | 450,162 | - | - | - | - | - | - | - | - |

Virginia
1. Bateman	R	1982	1928	73	284,702	98	64	68	92	20	84	14	85
2. Pickett	D	1986	1930	61	414,011	97	34	80	82	50	40	86	50
3. Bliley	R	1980	1932	100	366,816	98	61	86	89	10	96	21	93
4. Sisisky	D	1982	1927	100	93,232	94	38	77	76	55	40	86	50
5. Payne	D	1988	1945	54	274,442	99[b]	41	77	93	-	50	83	56
6. Olin	D	1982	1920	64	322,160	99	38	82	58	70	28	71	64
7. Slaughter, Jr.	R	1984	1925	100	87,195	99	63	86	97	10	92	14	93
8. Parris	R	1980	1929	62	689,035	94	57	78	87	15	96	29	93
9. Boucher	D	1982	1946	63	606,420	93	19	87	29	75	9	100	29
10. Wolf	R	1980	1939	68	758,365	99	59	82	87	25	88	43	86

Washington
1. Miller	R	1984	1938	55	1,321,021	96	44	50	66	60	38	64	79
2. Swift	D	1978	1935	U	301,229	94	23	92	16	90	0	85	36
3. Unsoeld	D	1988	1931	50	684,206	-	-	-	-	-	-	-	-
4. Morrison	R	1980	1933	75	194,505	98	47	59	87	55	65	36	93
5. Foley	D	1964	1929	76	476,460	94	23	91	21	85	4	86	38
6. Dicks	D	1976	1940	68	288,168	97	29	90	53	85	9	86	36
7. McDermott	D	1988	1936	76	348,082	-	-	-	-	-	-	-	-
8. Chandler	R	1982	1942	71	300,048	96	52	72	82	45	56	29	93

West Virginia
1. Mollohan	D	1982	1943	75	103,154	95	36	74	61	50	48	100	23
2. Staggers, Jr.	D	1982	1951	U	90,537	100	23	89	47	80	12	100	21
3. Wise	D	1982	1948	74	165,957	95	21	87	58	75	12	100	36
4. Rahall II	D	1976	1949	61	152,271	94	25	85	39	70	22	100	29

(Table continues)

Table 7-15 (Continued)

District/representative	Party	Year first elected	Year born	Percentage of 1988 vote	Campaign expenditures (1988)	Voting ratings[a]							
						VP	PS	PU	CC	ADA	ACU	AFL-CIO	CCUS
Wisconsin													
1. Aspin	D	1970	1938	76	$631,941	86	25	78	37	75	4	100	27
2. Kastenmeier	D	1958	1924	59	440,574	99	20	93	11	100	4	100	36
3. Gunderson	R	1980	1951	68	359,801	98	46	58	84	45	54	79	71
4. Kleczka	D	1984	1943	100	144,925	92	19	90	16	95	4	93	36
5. Moody	D	1982	1935	64	1,278,526	75	13	70	8	80	5	100	23
6. Petri	R	1979	1940	74	187,714	98	62	66	84	35	75	50	79
7. Obey	D	1969	1938	62	450,716	97	20	93	8	90	4	100	9
8. Roth	R	1978	1938	70	227,823	94	51	78	87	10	83	36	92
9. Sensenbrenner, Jr.	R	1978	1942	75	288,505	99	68	92	87	15	88	21	100
Wyoming													
AL Thomas	R	1989	1933	53	—	-	-	-	-	-	-	-	-

Note: "—" indicates not available. "-" indicates a newly elected representative (no basis for rating votes). Information as of June 7, 1989. "AL" indicates at large. "R" indicates Republican, "D" indicates Democrat, "U" indicates unopposed.

[a] "VP" indicates voting participation score (percentage of recorded votes on which a representative voted "yea" or "nay"). "PS" indicates presidential support score (percentage of the votes on which the president took a position that a member of Congress supported the president). "PU" indicates party unity score (percentage of the votes on which a member of Congress supported his or her party when a majority of voting Democrats opposed a majority of voting Republicans). "CC" indicates conservative coalition score (percentage of the votes on which a member of Congress voted in agreement with majorities of voting Republicans and southern Democrats against a majority of nonsouthern Democrats). Group ratings indicate the percentage of the time a member of Congress has supported the group-preferred position on votes the group selects. ADA (Americans for Democratic Action) is a liberal group, ACU (American Conservative Union) is a conservative group, AFL-CIO (American Federation of Labor-Congress of Industrial Organizations) is a labor group, and CCUS (Chamber of Commerce of the United States) is a business group.

[b] Not eligible for all recorded votes.

[c] Declared elected with more than 50.1 percent of the vote in an open primary.

[d] Rep. Tony Coelho resigned his seat effective June 15, 1989.

e Rep. Claude Pepper died May 30, 1989.
f Rep. Jim Wright announced on May 31, 1989, that he would resign his seat by the end of June. He resigned June 6, 1989, as Speaker of the House.

Sources: Campaign expenditures: Federal Election Commission, "$458 Million Spent by 1988 Congressional Campaigns," press release, February 24, 1989, 47-67; election vote percentage: *Congressional Quarterly Weekly Report* (1989), 1074-1080, 1149; year first elected: Congressional Quarterly, *Politics in America, The 100th Congress,* passim and *Congressional Quarterly Weekly Report* (1988, 1989), passim; all other data: "CQ's Member of Congress Data Diskette: The 101st Congress."

Table 7-16 The 101st Congress: Senate

State/senator	Party	Year first elected	Year born	Percentage of vote in last election	Campaign expenditures (most recent election)	Voting Ratings[a] VP	PS	PU	CC	ADA	ACU	AFL-CIO	CCUS
Alabama													
Heflin	D	1978	1921	63	$1,917,493	98	73	52	97	30	58	64	50
Shelby	D	1986	1934	50	2,259,167	99	57	56	92	35	60	71	57
Alaska													
Murkowski	R	1970	1933	54	1,387,756	90	65	81	89	15	79	23	85
Stevens	R	1980	1923	71	1,195,616	96	67	71	78	25	64	36	69
Arizona													
DeConcini	D	1976	1937	57	2,640,650	93	52	61	65	55	33	92	21
McCain	R	1986	1936	61	2,189,510	92	70	84	78	10	80	14	64
Arkansas													
Bumpers	D	1974	1925	62	1,672,432	93	44	84	41	80	12	79	33
Pryor	D	1978	1934	57	1,761,115	97	48	85	49	75	16	79	43
California													
Cranston	D	1968	1914	49	11,037,707	89	33	86	14	95	0	86	29
Wilson	R	1982	1933	53	12,969,294	85	64	65	68	15	75	27	77
Colorado													
Armstrong	R	1978	1937	64	2,993,045	96	83	89	84	5	96	7	93
Wirth	D	1986	1939	50	3,787,202	98	47	86	27	95	0	79	36
Connecticut													
Dodd	D	1982	1944	65	2,276,764	91	49	86	38	85	8	86	36
Lieberman	D	1988	1942	50	2,570,779	-	-	-	-	-	-	-	-
Delaware													
Biden, Jr.	D	1972	1942	60	1,439,310	18	13	13	3	15	0	80	67
Roth, Jr.	R	1970	1921	62	1,942,119	96	72	51	70	20	60	43	57

	Party												
Florida													
Graham	D	1986	1936	55	6,173,663	99	60	83	65	55	28	71	38
Mack	R	1988	1940	50	5,181,639	-	-	-	-	-	-	-	-
Georgia													
Fowler, Jr.	D	1986	1940	51	2,779,297	96	51	78	68	75	8	79	43
Nunn	D	1972	1938	80	729,843	93	63	68	92	40	42	54	50
Hawaii													
Inouye	D	1962	1924	74	1,039,418	91	42	87	24	85	4	92	38
Matsunaga	D	1976	1916	77	494,580	87	40	83	14	90	0	92	36
Idaho													
McClure	R	1972	1924	72	958,225	94	67	88	92	5	91	0	83
Symms	R	1980	1938	52	3,229,939	93	70	93	92	0	100	0	86
Illinois													
Dixon	D	1980	1927	65	1,928,750	93	56	60	89	45	44	69	57
Simon	D	1984	1928	50	4,578,703	72	31	70	0	85	0	91	42
Indiana													
Coats	R	1988	1943	b	—	-	-	-	-	-	-	-	-
Lugar	R	1976	1932	68	3,022,597	95	86	76	86	10	88	21	92
Iowa													
Grassley	R	1980	1933	66	2,513,319	99	78	87	86	5	88	21	93
Harkin	D	1984	1939	56	2,843,695	96	42	89	8	95	0	92	36
Kansas													
Dole	R	1968	1923	70	1,517,585	86	68	70	86	15	91	33	91
Kassebaum	R	1978	1932	76	360,964	93	69	61	81	30	61	23	71
Kentucky													
Ford	D	1974	1924	74	1,201,624	99	64	70	78	65	24	93	21
McConnell	R	1984	1942	50	1,776,128	98	85	80	92	5	92	29	93
Louisiana													
Breaux	D	1986	1944	53	2,948,313	94	61	73	92	50	44	85	43
Johnston	D	1972	1932	c	1,179,239	95	63	77	86	55	36	86	50

(Table continues)

223

Table 7-16 (Continued)

State/senator	Party	Year first elected	Year born	Percentage of vote in last election	Campaign expenditures (most recent election)	Voting Ratings[a]							
						VP	PS	PU	CC	ADA	ACU	AFL-CIO	CCUS
Maine													
Cohen	R	1978	1940	73	$1,022,134	97	52	39	41	35	46	57	57
Mitchell	D	1982	1933	81	1,340,157	99	43	95	5	95	0	100	21
Maryland													
Mikulski	D	1986	1936	61	2,057,216	96	40	93	5	95	0	100	29
Sarbanes	D	1976	1933	62	1,466,477	99	40	96	8	90	4	100	29
Massachusetts													
Kennedy	D	1962	1932	65	2,702,865	88	36	84	3	95	0	100	27
Kerry	D	1984	1943	55	2,070,000	93	40	88	0	90	0	93	36
Michigan													
Levin	D	1978	1934	52	3,504,962	97	42	91	14	80	0	92	21
Riegle, Jr.	D	1976	1938	60	3,383,849	97	41	94	24	90	4	93	36
Minnesota													
Boschwitz	R	1978	1930	58	6,022,365	91	73	68	76	20	70	38	69
Durenberger	R	1978	1934	56	5,410,783	88	57	43	32	60	26	77	43
Mississippi													
Cochran	R	1978	1937	61	2,791,749	89	70	66	97	5	96	15	100
Lott	R	1988	1941	54	3,405,242	-	-	-	-	-	-	-	-
Missouri													
Bond	R	1986	1939	53	5,376,255	92	75	73	89	0	88	23	86
Danforth	R	1976	1936	68	3,992,995	94	75	65	76	20	72	42	71
Montana													
Baucus	D	1978	1941	57	1,224,258	98	47	86	51	80	8	86	29
Burns	R	1988	1935	52	1,076,010	-	-	-	-	-	-	-	-

Nebraska													
Exon	D	1978	1921	52	843,393	95	65	66	86	35	48	71	50
Kerrey	D	1988	1943	57	3,461,148	-	-	-	-	-	-	-	-
Nevada													
Bryan	D	1988	1937	50	2,957,789	-	-	-	-	-	-	-	-
Reid	D	1986	1939	50	2,055,756	94	56	76	54	55	28	92	29
New Hampshire													
Humphrey	R	1978	1940	59	1,683,536	93	68	80	57	5	100	8	79
Rudman	R	1980	1930	63	831,098	93	65	58	68	15	68	29	93
New Jersey													
Bradley	D	1978	1943	64	4,566,758	91	48	81	22	75	9	75	25
Lautenberg	D	1982	1924	54	7,298,663	95	42	92	0	90	0	100	17
New Mexico													
Bingaman	D	1982	1943	63	2,808,659	96	52	71	68	70	20	77	43
Domenici	R	1972	1932	72	2,618,105	95	76	77	97	15	72	46	79
New York													
D'Amato	R	1980	1937	57	8,104,587	97	68	70	84	15	80	57	64
Moynihan	D	1976	1927	67	4,809,810	97	48	91	27	90	8	93	31
North Carolina													
Helms	R	1972	1921	52	16,499,387	85	60	72	81	5	100	23	75
Sanford	D	1986	1917	52	4,168,509	90	41	89	24	90	4	85	43
North Dakota													
Burdick	D	1960	1908	59	2,026,617	97	43	88	41	85	16	100	29
Conrad	D	1986	1948	50	908,374	99	48	78	35	80	24	93	29
Ohio													
Glenn	D	1974	1921	62	1,319,026	98	53	86	27	80	9	79	31
Metzenbaum	D	1976	1917	57	8,547,545	92	36	87	24	80	4	100	15
Oklahoma													
Boren	D	1978	1941	76	1,080,008	86	63	59	81	25	48	62	58
Nickles	R	1980	1948	55	3,252,964	96	80	92	100	0	92	7	86

(Table continues)

Table 7-16 (Continued)

State/senator	Party	Year first elected	Year born	Percentage of vote in last election	Campaign expenditures (most recent election)	VP	PS	PU	CC	ADA	ACU	AFL-CIO	CCUS
												Voting Ratings[a]	
Oregon													
Hatfield	R	1966	1922	67	$605,557	93	55	39	30	70	30	62	57
Packwood	R	1968	1932	63	6,523,492	96	58	41	54	55	40	64	57
Pennsylvania													
Heinz	R	1976	1938	66	5,151,512	90	55	40	59	55	41	79	46
Specter	R	1980	1930	56	5,993,230	97	63	48	59	60	33	83	62
Rhode Island													
Chafee	R	1976	1922	55	2,841,985	94	45	34	22	90	4	86	36
Pell	D	1960	1918	73	433,436	95	43	89	8	100	0	100	36
South Carolina													
Hollings	D	1966	1922	63	2,233,843	96	49	71	81	55	48	86	29
Thurmond	R	1954	1902	67	1,638,467	95	82	80	89	0	92	21	93
South Dakota													
Daschle	D	1986	1947	52	3,485,870	96	44	91	30	85	13	93	36
Pressler	R	1978	1942	74	938,709	96	73	88	97	0	96	29	79
Tennessee													
Gore, Jr.	D	1984	1948	61	3,180,975	61	33	57	11	60	9	83	45
Sasser	D	1976	1936	65	3,069,615	95	41	87	38	75	9	86	43
Texas													
Bentsen	D	1970	1921	59	8,829,361	74	61	55	78	40	42	89	25
Gramm	R	1984	1942	59	9,509,724	90	78	85	92	0	95	0	92
Utah													
Garn	R	1974	1932	72	741,645	90	77	88	73	0	96	7	92
Hatch	R	1976	1934	67	3,706,381	96	78	82	100	5	96	36	86

						VP	PS	PU	CC	ADA	ACU	AFL-CIO	CCUS
Vermont													
Jeffords	R	1988	1934	68	876,877	–	–	–	–	–	–	–	–
Leahy	D	1974	1940	63	1,705,099	97	34	93	8	100	0	86	36
Virginia													
Robb	D	1988	1939	71	2,881,666	–	–	–	–	–	–	–	–
Warner	R	1978	1927	70	2,786,140	96	74	71	95	5	87	36	86
Washington													
Adams	D	1986	1927	51	1,912,307	92	38	82	16	90	0	77	36
Gorton	R	1988	1928	51	2,851,591	–	–	–	–	–	–	–	–
West Virginia													
Byrd	D	1958	1917	65	1,099,709	100	56	81	49	55	36	86	29
Rockefeller IV	D	1984	1937	52	12,057,039	96	49	88	30	70	16	86	36
Wisconsin													
Kasten	R	1980	1942	51	3,433,870	95	74	78	84	10	84	43	71
Kohl	D	1988	1935	52	7,491,600	–	–	–	–	–	–	–	–
Wyoming													
Simpson	R	1978	1931	78	702,643	96	75	80	86	15	92	21	86
Wallop	R	1976	1933	50	1,344,185	83	72	85	89	0	100	11	91

Note: "—" indicates not available. "–" indicates a newly elected representative (no basis for rating votes). Information as of June 7, 1989. "AL" indicates at large, "R" indicates Republican, "D" indicates Democrat.

[a] "VP" indicates voting participation score (percentage of recorded votes on which a representative voted "yea" or "nay"). "PS" indicates presidential support score (percentage of the votes on which the president took a position that a member of Congress supported the president). "PU" indicates party unity score (percentage of the votes on which a member of Congress supported his or her party when a majority of voting Democrats opposed a majority of voting Republicans). "CC" indicates conservative coalition score (percentage of the votes on which a member of Congress voted in agreement with majorities of voting Republicans and southern Democrats against a majority of nonsouthern Democrats). Group ratings indicate the percentage of the time a member of Congress has supported the group-preferred position on votes the group selects. ADA (Americans for Democratic Action) is a liberal group, ACU (American Conservative Union) is a conservative group, AFL-CIO (American Federation of Labor-Congress of Industrial Organizations) is a labor group, and CCUS (Chamber of Commerce of the United States) is a business group.

[b] Appointed.

[c] Declared elected with more than 50.1 percent of the vote in an open primary.

(Table continues)

Table 7-16 (*Continued*)

Sources: Campaign expenditures: Federal Election Commission, "$458 Million Spent by 1988 Congressional Campaigns," press release, February 24, 1989, 40-46; election vote percentage: *Congressional Quarterly Weekly Report* (1989), 1074-1080, 1149; year first elected: Congressional Quarterly, *Politics in America, The 101th Congress,* passim and *Congressional Quarterly Weekly Report* (1988, 1989), passim; all other data: "CQ's Member of Congress Data Diskette: The 101st Congress."

Questions

1. Find the 1980 population of the state you are from (Table 1-1). Using the number of representatives from your state (Table 7-1), calculate the apportionment ratio (the number of citizens per House member). Why does it vary from the overall apportionment ratio (Table 7-1)?

2. Describe the changes in the characteristics of congressional representatives between 1971 and now (Table 7-2). Have these changes also occurred in the Senate? Why or why not?

3. There were considerably fewer new House members in 1985 and 1987 than in 1981 and 1983 (Table 7-3). Assuming this is not due to chance, why might this be the case? (Consider Table 7-5 in your answer.)

4. Note the pattern of seat changes for the president's party in midterm House elections (Table 7-4). Why does this pattern exist? An exception occurred in 1934. Why?

5. Speculate on why reelection rates to the House are almost always higher than to the Senate (Table 7-5). (Hint: one answer is suggested by data from within Table 7-5.)

6. In House elections, the number of seats that switch from Democratic to Republican and Republican to Democratic is usually more even in open-seat races (no incumbent running) than in those in which an incumbent is defeated (Table 7-6). For example, in 1954, 86 percent of the seats in which an incumbent was defeated changed from the Republicans to the Democrats, but this was true of only 60 percent of the open seats. Why is this the case? (Hint: think of the kinds of districts in which incumbents are defeated.)

7. Does the average challenger or incumbent spend more in congressional campaigns (Table 7-7)? How much did the average House candidate spend in 1987-1988? The average Senate candidate?

8. Do PACs contribute a larger proportion of the campaign expenditures for winning candidates to the House or to the Senate (Table 7-8)? Why do you think that is? (Hint: see Tables 6-8 and 7-7.)

9. Calculate and show the average party unity and polarization scores for each president, making separate calculations for the House and the Senate (Table 7-9, see Table 8-11 for presidential terms). Is there a general decline in the scores in the House (consider Figure 7-2)? In the Senate? Compare the pattern over time here with that for split-ticket voting by the electorate (Table 4-7). How would you interpret this difference?

10. In every instance but one (the Senate in 1957), southern Democrats are lower in party support than Republicans and nonsouthern Democrats (Table 7-10). How do we know from the table that southern Democrats are lower on party unity than nonsouthern Democrats? Why are they less loyal to the party?

11. In the Senate the percentage of Conservative Coalition victories is highest in 1957 and during the Reagan years, 1981-1988 (Table 7-11). Why? (Hint: see Table 3-16.)

12. What was the approximate size of the total congressional staff (House and Senate members' staffs and House and Senate committees) in 1960 (Figure 7-3)? What was the approximate size in 1986? About how many staff members did the average House member have in 1986?

13. Ronald Reagan argued that more activities ought to be left to private initiatives. The number of measures enacted by Congress during the Reagan administration was low (Table 7-12). Was this due primarily to his ideology? What evidence in the table would support or contradict such an explanation? What light does Figure 7-4 shed on this topic?

14. What modern technological development helps explain the increase in the number of recorded votes in the House in the mid-1970s (Table 7-13)? A larger number of recorded votes could have a number of effects on House members and on voters. What are some of the possible effects?

15. In both the House and the Senate, those who were rated very favorably (one hundred is the "best" score) by the AFL-CIO also tended to be rated favorably by the ADA (Tables 7-15 and 7-16). Why?

16. Six of the eight Democratic senators with a presidential support score of sixty or more were from which region of the country (Table 7-16)?

8

The Presidency and
the Executive Branch

The presidency poses special problems to those interested in the collection of statistical data. The scope and the variety of data available on the presidency are limited by the singularity of the president and the difference the individual president makes on the office's organization and operation. Moreover, the modern presidency has evolved since Franklin Roosevelt took office in the 1930s. Since then the emergence of the United States as a world power, the expansion of television, the growth of government, and the alteration of the presidential selection process have further changed the demands on and expectations of the presidency. Hence, for data on many points, the recent occupants of the Oval Office are just too few to sustain statistical analysis.

In spite of these seemingly insurmountable handicaps, the visibility of the president provides a considerable amount of relevant data. Of all elected officials, for example, only presidents have public judgments about how well they are doing prominently and repeatedly displayed: the twists and turns in the public approval ratings of a president's job performance are themselves news items. Consequently, in this book a series of figures are devoted to this subject alone— showing overall presidential approval scores for nine presidents (Figure 8-1), and detailed ratings for Jimmy Carter and Ronald Reagan (Figure 8-2). But presidents are not judged only by the public or only while they are in office. At various times and in various ways, historians and political scientists have rated all the U.S. presidents (Table 8-2).

Apart from approval ratings (and of course presidential elections), the presidency has not been subjected to extensive statistical scrutiny. However, perhaps because the number of presidents has now reached forty individuals, some additional areas are beginning to receive systematic study. The president's relationship with Congress is one such area. Information about presidential "victories" on votes in Congress (Table 8-11), the extent to which the president is supported by his own party and by the other party (Table 8-12), and success in having nominations approved (Table 8-14) are all regularly tabulated and increasingly analyzed.

Media coverage is also beginning to receive systematic study. In part this study results from the extreme visibility of the president and of the federal government in general (Figure 2-1); it is also due to changing relationships between the president and the press, as indicated, for example, by the considerable decline in press conferences since the 1930s (Table 2-4).

Compilations of various presidential characteristics and activities also have become more numerous or more meaningful with the larger number who have served as president. How individuals get to be president, for example, has been a subject of considerable interest (Tables 8-3 through 8-5). Presidential appointments have been checked for their partisan characteristics (Tables 8-15 and 9-3) and increasingly for their racial and gender distributions (Table 9-2).

The executive branch, apart from the president, has been subjected even less to statistical analysis. Yet here, too, there is ample opportunity for meaningful tabulations if not for t-tests and correlations. The tremendous size of the federal government (Table 8-8) necessitates such an interest. The expanded involvement of the government in regulation (Table 8-10), at least until the Reagan administration, also compels attention. But there are other more subtle and more significant messages in these data. For example, the changing emphases of the nation and of the priorities of particular presidents can be seen in such mundane listings as the size and composition of the White House staff (Table 8-7).

Thus, while the presidency provides data for conventional statistical analyses in only a few areas, a generous and increasing amount of numerical data provides considerable insight into what has traditionally been viewed as an office of impressive singularity.

Table 8-1 Presidents and Vice Presidents of the United States

President (political party)	Born	Died	Age at inauguration	Native of...	Elected from...	Term of service	Vice president
George Washington (F)	1732	1799	57	Va.	Va.	April 30, 1789-March 4, 1793	John Adams
George Washington (F)			61			March 4, 1793-March 4, 1797	John Adams
John Adams (F)	1735	1826	61	Mass.	Mass.	March 4, 1797-March 4, 1801	Thomas Jefferson
Thomas Jefferson (D-R)	1743	1826	57	Va.	Va.	March 4, 1801-March 4, 1805	Aaron Burr
Thomas Jefferson (D-R)			61			March 4, 1805-March 4, 1809	George Clinton
James Madison (D-R)	1751	1836	57	Va.	Va.	March 4, 1809-March 4, 1813	George Clinton
James Madison (D-R)			61			March 4, 1813-March 4, 1817	Elbridge Gerry
James Monroe (D-R)	1758	1831	58	Va.	Va.	March 4, 1817-March 4, 1821	Daniel D. Tompkins
James Monroe (D-R)			62			March 4, 1821-March 4, 1825	Daniel D. Tompkins
John Q. Adams (N-R)	1767	1848	57	Mass.	Mass.	March 4, 1825-March 4, 1829	John C. Calhoun
Andrew Jackson (D)	1767	1845	61	S.C.	Tenn.	March 4, 1829-March 4, 1833	John C. Calhoun
Andrew Jackson (D)			65			March 4, 1833-March 4, 1837	Martin Van Buren
Martin Van Buren (D)	1782	1862	54	N.Y.	N.Y.	March 4, 1837-March 4, 1841	Richard M. Johnson
W. H. Harrison (W)	1773	1841	68	Va.	Ohio	March 4, 1841-April 4, 1841	John Tyler
John Tyler (W)	1790	1862	51	Va.	Va.	April 6, 1841-March 4, 1845	
James K. Polk (D)	1795	1849	49	N.C.	Tenn.	March 4, 1845-March 4, 1849	George M. Dallas
Zachary Taylor (W)	1784	1850	64	Va.	La.	March 4, 1849-July 9, 1850	Millard Fillmore
Millard Fillmore (W)	1800	1874	50	N.Y.	N.Y.	July 10, 1850-March 4, 1853	
Franklin Pierce (D)	1804	1869	48	N.H.	N.H.	March 4, 1853-March 4, 1857	William R. King
James Buchanan (D)	1791	1868	65	Pa.	Pa.	March 4, 1857-March 4, 1861	John C. Breckinridge
Abraham Lincoln (R)	1809	1865	52	Ky.	Ill.	March 4, 1861-March 4, 1865	Hannibal Hamlin
Abraham Lincoln (R)			56			March 4, 1865-April 15, 1865	Andrew Johnson
Andrew Johnson (R)	1808	1875	56	N.C.	Tenn.	April 15, 1865-March 4, 1869	
Ulysses S. Grant (R)	1822	1885	46	Ohio	Ill.	March 4, 1869-March 4, 1873	Schuyler Colfax
Ulysses S. Grant (R)			50			March 4, 1873-March 4, 1877	Henry Wilson
Rutherford B. Hayes (R)	1822	1893	54	Ohio	Ohio	March 4, 1877-March 4, 1881	William A. Wheeler

President (Party)			Age			Term of Service	Vice President
James A. Garfield (R)	1881	1831	49	Ohio	Ohio	March 4, 1881-Sept. 19, 1881	Chester A. Arthur
Chester A. Arthur (R)	1886	1830	50	Vt.	N.Y.	Sept. 20, 1881-March 4, 1885	
Grover Cleveland (D)	1908	1837	47	N.J.	N.Y.	March 4, 1885-March 4, 1889	Thomas A. Hendricks
Benjamin Harrison (R)	1901	1833	55	Ohio	Ind.	March 4, 1889-March 4, 1893	Levi P. Morton
Grover Cleveland (D)	1908	1837	55			March 4, 1893-March 4, 1897	Adlai E. Stevenson
William McKinley (R)	1901	1843	54	Ohio	Ohio	March 4, 1897-March 4, 1901	Garret A. Hobart
William McKinley (R)			58			March 4, 1901-Sept. 14, 1901	Theodore Roosevelt
Theodore Roosevelt (R)	1919	1858	42	N.Y.	N.Y.	Sept. 14, 1901-March 4, 1905	
Theodore Roosevelt (R)			46			March 4, 1905-March 4, 1909	Charles W. Fairbanks
William H. Taft (R)	1930	1857	51	Ohio	Ohio	March 4, 1909-March 4, 1913	James S. Sherman
Woodrow Wilson (D)	1924	1856	56	Va.	N.J.	March 4, 1913-March 4, 1917	Thomas R. Marshall
Woodrow Wilson (D)			60			March 4, 1917-March 4, 1921	Thomas R. Marshall
Warren G. Harding (R)	1923	1865	55	Ohio	Ohio	March 4, 1921-Aug. 2, 1923	Calvin Coolidge
Calvin Coolidge (R)	1933	1872	51	Vt.	Mass.	Aug. 3, 1923-March 4, 1925	
Calvin Coolidge (R)			52			March 4, 1925-March 4, 1929	Charles G. Dawes
Herbert Hoover (R)	1964	1874	54	Iowa	Calif.	March 4, 1929-March 4, 1933	Charles Curtis
Franklin D. Roosevelt (D)	1945	1882	51	N.Y.	N.Y.	March 4, 1933-Jan. 20, 1937	John N. Garner
Franklin D. Roosevelt (D)			55			Jan. 20, 1937-Jan. 20, 1941	John N. Garner
Franklin D. Roosevelt (D)			59			Jan. 20, 1941-Jan. 20, 1945	Henry A. Wallace
Franklin D. Roosevelt (D)			63			Jan. 20, 1945-April 12, 1945	Harry S Truman
Harry S Truman (D)	1972	1884	60	Mo.	Mo.	April 12, 1945-Jan. 20, 1949	
Harry S Truman (D)			64			Jan. 20, 1949-Jan. 20, 1953	Alben W. Barkley
Dwight D. Eisenhower (R)	1969	1890	62	Texas	N.Y.	Jan. 20, 1953-Jan. 20, 1957	Richard M. Nixon
Dwight D. Eisenhower (R)			66		Pa.	Jan. 20, 1957-Jan. 20, 1961	Richard M. Nixon
John F. Kennedy (D)	1963	1917	43	Mass.	Mass.	Jan. 20, 1961-Nov. 22, 1963	Lyndon B. Johnson
Lyndon B. Johnson (D)	1973	1906	55	Texas	Texas	Nov. 22, 1963-Jan. 20, 1965	
Lyndon B. Johnson (D)			56			Jan. 20, 1965-Jan. 20, 1969	Hubert H. Humphrey

(Table continues)

Table 8-1 *(Continued)*

President (political party)	Born	Died	Age at inauguration	Native of...	Elected from...	Term of service	Vice president
Richard M. Nixon (R)	1913		56	Calif.	N.Y.	Jan. 20, 1969-Jan. 20, 1973	Spiro T. Agnew
Richard M. Nixon (R)			60		Calif.	Jan. 20, 1973-Aug. 9, 1974	Spiro T. Agnew
							Gerald R. Ford
Gerald R. Ford (R)	1913		61	Neb.	Mich.	Aug. 9, 1974-Jan. 20, 1977	Nelson A. Rockefeller
Jimmy Carter (D)	1924		52	Ga.	Ga.	Jan. 20, 1977-Jan. 20, 1981	Walter F. Mondale
Ronald Reagan (R)	1911		69	Ill.	Calif.	Jan. 20, 1981-Jan. 20, 1985	George Bush
Ronald Reagan (R)			73			Jan. 20, 1985-Jan. 20, 1989	George Bush
George Bush (R)	1924		64	Conn.	Texas	Jan. 20, 1989-	J. Danforth Quayle

Note: "D" indicates Democrat, "D-R" indicates Democrat-Republican, "F" indicates Federalist, "N-R" indicates National Republican, "R" indicates Republican, and "W" indicates Whig.

Source: Congressional Quarterly, *Presidential Elections Since 1789*, 4th ed. (Washington, D.C.: Congressional Quarterly, 1987), 4; updated by the editors.

Table 8-2 Ratings of U.S. Presidents

Schlesinger poll (1948)	Schlesinger poll (1962)	Dodder poll (1970)	DiClerico poll (1977)	Tribune poll (1982)	Murray poll (1982)
Great	**Great**	**Accomplishments of administration**	**Ten greatest presidents**	**Ten best presidents**	**Presidential rank**
1. Lincoln	1. Lincoln	1. Lincoln	1. Lincoln	1. Lincoln (best)	1. Lincoln
2. Washington	2. Washington	2. F. Roosevelt	2. Washington	2. Washington	2. F. Roosevelt
3. F. Roosevelt	3. F. Roosevelt	3. Washington	3. F. Roosevelt	3. F. Roosevelt	3. Washington
4. Wilson	4. Wilson	4. Jefferson	4. Jefferson	4. T. Roosevelt	4. Jefferson
5. Jefferson	5. Jefferson	5. T. Roosevelt	5. T. Roosevelt	5. Jefferson	5. T. Roosevelt
6. Jackson		6. Truman	6. Wilson	6. Wilson	6. Wilson
	Near great	7. Wilson	7. Jackson	7. Jackson	7. Jackson
Near great	6. Jackson	8. Jackson	8. Truman	8. Truman	8. Truman
7. T. Roosevelt	7. T. Roosevelt	9. L. Johnson	9. Polk	9. Eisenhower	9. J. Adams
8. Cleveland	8. Polk	10. Polk	10. J. Adams	10. Polk (10th best)	10. L. Johnson
9. J. Adams	Truman (tie)	11. J. Adams			11. Eisenhower
10. Polk		12. Kennedy		**Ten worst presidents**	12. Polk
	9. J. Adams	13. Monroe		1. Harding (worst)	13. Kennedy
Average	10. Cleveland	14. Cleveland		2. Nixon	14. Madison
11. J. Q. Adams		15. Madison		3. Buchanan	15. Monroe
12. Monroe	**Average**	16. Taft		4. Pierce	16. J. Q. Adams
13. Hayes	11. Madison	17. McKinley		5. Grant	17. Cleveland
14. Madison	12. J. Q. Adams	18. J. Q. Adams		6. Fillmore	18. McKinley
15. Van Buren	13. Hayes	19. Hoover		7. A. Johnson	19. Taft
16. Taft	14. McKinley	20. Eisenhower		8. Coolidge	20. Van Buren
17. Arthur	15. Taft	21. A. Johnson		9. Tyler	21. Hoover
	16. Van Buren	22. Van Buren			22. Hayes
	17. Monroe				23. Arthur

(Table continues)

Table 8-2 (Continued)

Schlesinger poll (1948)	Schlesinger poll (1962)	Dodder poll (1970)	DiClerico poll (1977)	Tribune poll (1982)	Murray poll (1982)
18. McKinley	18. Hoover	23. Arthur		10. Carter (10th worst)	24. Ford
19. A. Johnson	19. B. Harrison	24. Hayes			25. Carter
20. Hoover	20. Arthur	25. Tyler			26. B. Harrison
21. B. Harrison	Eisenhower (tie)	26. B. Harrison			27. Taylor
	21. A. Johnson	27. Taylor			28. Tyler
		28. Buchanan			29. Fillmore
Below average	Below average	29. Fillmore			30. Coolidge
22. Tyler	22. Taylor	30. Coolidge			31. Pierce
23. Coolidge	23. Tyler	31. Pierce			32. A. Johnson
24. Fillmore	24. Fillmore	32. Grant			33. Buchanan
25. Taylor	25. Coolidge	33. Harding			34. Nixon
26. Buchanan	26. Pierce				35. Grant
27. Pierce	27. Buchanan				36. Harding
Failure	Failure				
28. Grant	28. Grant				
29. Harding	29. Harding				

Note: These ratings result from surveys of scholars ranging in number from 55 to 950.

Sources: Henry J. Abraham, *Justices and Presidents: Appointments to the Supreme Court*, 2d ed. (New York: Oxford University Press, 1985), 380-383 (copyright © Henry J. Abraham, 1974, 1985, reprinted by permission of Oxford University Press, Inc.); Arthur Murphy, "Evaluating the Presidents of the United States," *Presidential Studies Quarterly* 14 (1984): 117-126 (permission granted by Center for the Study of the Presidency, publisher).

Table 8-3 Previous Public Positions Held by Presidents

Position	Number of presidents holding position prior to presidency	
	Pre-1900 (24)	Post-1900 (16)
Vice president	7	7
Cabinet member	7	3
U.S. representative	13	5
U.S. senator	9	5
U.S. Supreme Court justice	0	0
Federal judge	0	1
Governor	11	6
State legislator	16	5
State judge	1	2
Mayor	2	1
Diplomat, ambassador	7	2
Military general	11	1

Position	Last public position held before presidency	
	Pre-1900 (24)	Post-1900 (16)
Vice president		
Succeeded to presidency	4	5
Won presidency in own right	3	2
Congress		
House	1	0
Senate	3	2
Appointive federal office		
Military general	3	1
Cabinet secretary	3	2
Ambassador	2	0
Other civilian	1	0
Governor	4	4

Source: Compiled by the editors from Robert G. Ferris, *The Presidents,* rev. ed. (Washington, D.C.: National Park Service, 1977). In the list of generals, we have included Andrew Johnson (who had the rank of general when serving as military governor of Tennessee) and Chester A. Arthur (who held the rank of general when serving as quartermaster general); listed in various sources other than Ferris. Updated through President Bush.

Table 8-4 Latest Public Office Held by Candidates for Presidential Nominations, 1936-1988

Public office[a]	Percentage of all persons polling at least 1 percent in Gallup Poll	Percentage of all presidential nominees
President[b]	1	9
Vice president	1	27
U.S. senator	36	14
Governor	22	41
Cabinet officer	16	0
U.S. representative	8	0
Mayor	3	0
Supreme Court justice	1	0
All others	1	0
None	9	9
Total	98[c] (N=140)	100 (N=22)

[a] Last or current office at time person first polled at least one percent support for presidential nomination among fellow partisans or was first nominated.
[b] Presidents Truman and Ford received poll support for the presidential nomination only after they had actually served in the office.
[c] Less than 100 percent due to rounding.

Source: William R. Keech and Donald R. Matthews, *The Party's Choice: With an Epilogue on the 1976 Nominations* (Washington, D.C.: Brookings, 1976), 18; updated by the editors.

Table 8-5 Presidential Prenomination Campaign Finance, 1988

Party/candidate	Individual contributors	Federal matching funds	Receipts	Expenditures	Debts owed
Republicans					
Bush	$22,304,302	$8,313,986	$31,663,795	$29,279,286	$704,145
Dole	16,786,783	7,358,285	26,130,672	26,034,992	698,497
du Pont	5,417,829	2,550,952	8,059,211	7,998,816	0
Haig	1,369,100	526,069	1,975,172	1,963,707	340,320
Kemp	9,995,642	5,508,933	16,086,683	15,832,892	39,747
Robertson	19,478,733	8,870,209	28,819,032	28,790,864	1,182,019
Total	75,352,389	33,128,434	111,085,152	109,900,557	2,964,728
Democrats					
Babbitt	2,279,718	970,073	3,399,194	3,115,027	185,718
Dukakis	19,316,068	8,689,871	28,536,509	26,347,160	626,815
Gephardt	6,060,038	2,710,315	9,603,093	9,564,667	1,956,560
Gore	6,859,358	3,286,988	11,568,585	11,348,692	1,446,607
Hart	2,291,010	1,084,065	4,435,925	3,665,123	20,839
Jackson	11,692,089	4,749,461	17,224,469	17,209,154	769,078
LaRouche	2,822,699	662,667	3,490,376	3,445,277	276,140
Simon	5,852,422	2,997,588	9,150,752	8,786,544	467,234
Total	57,173,402	25,151,028	85,742,090	83,481,644	5,748,991
Grand total[a]	138,843,311	58,768,109	203,717,271	199,789,163	8,806,284

Note: Figures are for January 1, 1987, through June 30, 1988.

[a] Includes a nonmajor party candidate not shown separately (Fulani) and three inactive campaigns (Laxalt, Biden, and Schroeder).

Source: Federal Election Commission, "Presidential Primary Spending at $200 Million Mark," press release, August 18, 1988, 2-3.

Table 8-6 The President's Cabinet, 1989

Cabinet office	Year established[a]	Current secretary[b]	Date confirmed	Number of paid civilian employees		Number of noncivil service positions[c]	Percentage of all positions
				1980	1988[c]		
State	1789	James A. Baker III	1/25/89	23,497	25,634	21,049	82
Treasury	1789	Nicholas F. Brady	9/14/88	124,633	160,516	10,167	6
War	1789[d]						
Navy	1798[d]						
Interior	1849	Manuel Lujan, Jr.	1/1/89	77,357	78,216	20,285	26
Justice	1870	Richard L. Thornburgh	8/11/88	56,327	76,515	33,479	44
Post Office	1872[e]						
Agriculture	1889[f]	Clayton K. Yeutter	2/8/89	129,139	120,869	24,086	20
Commerce and Labor	1903[f]						
Commerce	1913	Robert A. Mosbacher	1/31/89	48,563[g]	52,819	24,127	46
Labor	1913	Elizabeth H. Dole	1/25/89	23,400	18,178	1,011	6
Defense	1947	Richard B. Cheney	3/17/89	960,116	1,049,619	169,794	16
Health, Education and Welfare	1953[h]						
Health and Human Services	1979	Louis W. Sullivan	3/1/89	155,662	123,270	18,984	15
Housing and Urban Development	1965	Jack F. Kemp	2/2/89	16,964[i]	13,342	1,036	8
Transportation	1966	Samuel K. Skinner	1/31/89	72,361	63,506	2,492	4
Energy	1977	James D. Watkins	3/1/89	21,557	17,031	1,654	10
Education	1979	Lauro Cavazos	9/20/88	7,364	4,542	662	15
Veterans Affairs	1989	Edward J. Derwinski	3/2/89	228,285[j]	245,467[j]	92,411[j]	38[j]

Note: The Cabinet also currently includes Vice President Dan Quayle and nondepartmental secretaries: U.S. Trade Representative Carla A. Hills and Director of the Office of Management and Budget Richard G. Darman. Offices of Attorney General and Postmaster General were created in 1789, but executive
[a] Dates are when the department achieved cabinet status.

departments were not created until later. A Department of Agriculture was established in 1862, but the commissioner did not achieve cabinet status until 1889.

[b] As of June 9, 1989.

[c] As of September 1988. Noncivil service positions include excepted and senior executive service.

[d] Incorporated into Defense Department in 1947.

[e] Independent agency as of 1971.

[f] Split into separate departments in 1913.

[g] Includes enumerators in 1970 and 1980 census.

[h] Split into Health and Human Services and Education in 1979.

[i] Number of civilian employees includes Housing and Home Finance Agency.

[j] Figures are for the Veterans Administration, the agency that was upgraded on March 15, 1989, to the Department of Veterans Affairs.

Sources: Ronald C. Moe, "The Federal Executive Establishment: Evolution and Trends," prepared for the U.S. Senate Commitee on Governmental Affairs by the Congressional Research Service (Washington, D.C.: U.S. Government Printing Office, 1980), 26-27; *Congressional Quarterly Weekly Report* (1988), 3059; U.S. Bureau of the Census, *Statistical Abstract of the U.S., 1988* (Washington, D.C.: U.S. Government Printing Office, 1987), 309; U.S. Office of Personnel Management, *Federal Civilian Workforce Statistics, Employment and Trends* (September 1988), 31-33.

Table 8-7 White House Staff and the Executive Office of the President, 1943-1988

Year	White House	OMB/ Bureau of Budget[a]	Council of Economic Advisers	National Security Council	Office of Economic Opportunity	Office of Science and Technology	Office of Adminis- tration	Special Representative for Trade Negotiations	Office of Policy Development/ Domestic Council	Total executive office[b]
1943[c]	51	543								703
1944[c]	58	542								683
1945[c]	64	705								820
1946[c]	216	692	26							1,034
1947[c]	228	549	26							1,077
1948[c]	209	521	38	20						1,205
1949	243	517	36	17						1,240
1950	313	509	38	17						1,408
1951	246	518	37	21						1,326
1952	248	470	31	22						1,296
1953	247	417	28	28						1,183
1954	262	430	34	26						1,078
1955	366	422	33	27						1,221
1956	392	443	38	25						1,228
1957	399	441	35	65						1,255
1958	395	424	33	61						2,605
1959	406	432	33	64						2,735
1960	423	441	31	64						2,779
1961	439	456	45	43						1,586
1962	338	465	65	39		63				1,492
1963	376	485	57	43		48		30		1,572
1964	328	493	46	41	1,768	57		29		1,478
1965	292	506	45	39		75		24		3,307

1966	270	592	62	40	2,319	105		26		4,050
1967	271	570	56	38	2,951	58		24		4,747
1968	261	550	74	35	3,211	62		22		4,964
1969	341	576	54	66	2,282	75		22		4,116
1970	491	636	57	82	2,633	77		26	26	4,808
1971	580	717	62	80	2,304	75		33	44	4,809
1972	583	703	58	80	2,066	76		38	53	5,721
1973	528	642	49	85	1,148			39	24	3,877
1974	560	646	46	87	1,090			45	32	2,868
1975	525	664	48	85				56	55	1,801
1976	534	694	39	79		19		55	43	1,796
1977	387	721	36	68		44		52	41	1,637
1978	381	617	35	76		46	197	58	55	1,679
1979	418	638	36	73		44	180	70	60	1,918
1980	426	631	38	74		50	182	131	68	2,013
1981	378	679	38	65		13	190	139	48	1,674
1982	374	617	35	59		20	196	138	46	1,608
1983	376	619	34	61		23	213	139	39	1,622
1984	371	605	28	63		21	196	147	40	1,593
1985	368	568	33	64		17	196	149	32	1,549
1986	360	541	35	66		12	198	143	44	1,525
1987	367	546	32	62		9	199	148	34	1,540
1988	366	552	29	60		11	212	158	38	1,554

Note: In almost all instances when no figures are shown, the office did not exist as a separate entity. Data as of December of the year indicated, except 1947 (January), 1960 (October), 1985 and 1986 (November), 1987 (July), and 1988 (September).
[a] The Bureau of the Budget became the Office of Management and Budget in 1970.
[b] Includes offices not shown separately.
[c] Total executive office excludes personnel in war establishments or emergency war agencies.

Source: U.S. Office of Personnel Management, *Federal Manpower Statistics, Federal Civilian Workforce Statistics,* monthly release.

Table 8-8 Number of Civilian Federal Government Employees and Percentage under Merit Civil Service, 1816-1988

Year	Total number of employees[a]	Percentage under merit	Year	Total number of employees	Percentage under merit
1816	4,837	—	1943	3,299,414	—
1821	6,914	—	1944	3,332,356	—
1831	11,491	—	1945	3,816,310	—
1841	18,038	—	1946	2,696,529	—
1851	26,274	—	1947	2,111,001	80.2
1861	36,672	—	1948	2,071,009	82.4
1871	51,020	—	1949	2,102,109	84.3
1881	100,020	—	1950	1,960,708	84.5
1891	157,442	21.5	1951	2,482,666	86.4
1901	239,476	44.3	1952	2,600,612	86.4
1908	356,754	57.9	1953	2,558,416	83.6
1909	372,379	63.1	1954	2,407,676	82.7
1910	388,708	57.2	1955	2,397,309	83.6
1911	395,905	57.5	1956	2,398,736	85.1
1912	400,150	54.3	1957	2,417,565	85.5
1913	396,494	71.3	1958	2,382,491	85.3
1914	401,887	72.8	1959	2,382,807	85.7
1915	395,429	73.9	1960	2,398,704	85.5
1916	399,381	74.3	1961	2,435,804	86.1
1917	438,500	74.5	1962	2,514,197	85.9
1918	854,500	75.2	1963	2,527,960	85.6
1919	794,271	86.6	1964	2,500,503	86.1
1920	655,265	75.9	1965	2,527,915	85.2
1921	561,142	79.9	1966	2,759,019	85.8
1922	543,507	77.4	1967	3,002,461	82.8
1923	536,900	76.6	1968	3,055,212	84.1
1924	543,484	76.5	1969	3,076,414	82.9
1925	553,045	76.6	1970	2,981,574	82.3
1926	548,713	77.0	1972[b]	2,608,000	65.6
1927	547,127	77.3	1973	2,667,000	61.6
1928	560,772	77.0	1974	2,724,000	62.6
1929	579,559	88.2	1975	2,741,000	62.5
1930	601,319	87.9	1976	2,725,000	62.0
1931	609,746	76.8	1977	2,724,000	62.6
1932	605,496	77.2	1978	2,752,000	63.5
1933	603,587	75.6	1979	2,763,000	55.7
1934	698,649	64.5	1980	2,772,000	61.0
1935	780,582	58.3	1981	2,722,000	61.1
1936	867,432	57.5	1982	2,733,000	61.3
1937	895,993	59.4	1983	2,754,000	61.2
1938	882,226	63.8	1984	2,824,000	60.1
1939	953,891	69.5	1985	2,902,000	58.9
1940	1,042,420	69.7	1986	2,895,000	58.0
1941	1,437,682	68.9	1987	3,090,699	56.7
1942	2,296,384	—	1988	3,112,822	55.7

(Notes follow)

Table 8-8 *(Continued)*

Note: "—"indicates not available.

[a] Excludes employees of the Central Intelligence Agency and the National Security Agency.

[b] Under Postal Reorganization Act of 1970, U.S. Postal Service employees were changed from competitive (merit) service to excepted service.

Sources: 1816-1970: U.S. Bureau of the Census, *Historical Statistics of the U.S.* (Washington, D.C.: U.S. Government Printing Office, 1975), 1102-1103; 1972-1986: U.S. Bureau of the Census, *Statistical Abstract of the U.S., 1977,* 268, *1980,* 279, *1987,* 309, *1988,* 307; 1987-1988: U.S. Office of Personnel Management, *Federal Civilian Workforce Statistics, Employment and Trends* (September 1988), 22.

Table 8-9 Major Regulatory Agencies

Agency	Year established	Agency head Number	Title	Number of employees[a]
Consumer Product Safety Commission	1972	5	commissioner	525
Environmental Protection Agency	1970	1	administrator	15,309
Equal Employment Opportunity Commission	1965	5	commissioner	3,229
Federal Communications Commission	1934	5	commissioner	1,887
Federal Deposit Insurance Corporation	1933	3	board of director	8,249
Federal Energy Regulatory Commission	1977	5	commissioner	—
Federal Reserve System	1913	7	governor	1,512
Federal Trade Commission	1914	5	commissioner	1,013
Food and Drug Administration	1906	1	commissioner	7,533
Interstate Commerce Commission	1887	5	commissioner	712
National Labor Relations Board	1935	5	board of director	2,374
Occupational Safety and Health Administration	1970	1	assistant secretary	69
Securities and Exchange Commission	1934	5	commissioner	2,188

Note: "—" indicates not available.

[a] As of September 1988.

Sources: Congressional Quarterly, *Federal Regulatory Directory* (Washington, D.C.: Congressional Quarterly, 1986), passim; U.S. Office of Personnel Management, *Federal Civilian Workforce Statistics, Employment and Trends* (September 1988), 12-14, 41.

Table 8-10 Number of Pages in the *Federal Register,* 1940-1988

Year	Pages	Year	Pages
1940	5,307	1975	60,221
1945	15,508	1976	57,072
1950	9,562	1977	63,629
1955	10,196	1978	61,261
1960	14,479	1979	77,497
1965	17,206	1980	87,012
1966	16,850	1981	63,554
1967	21,087	1982	58,493
1968	20,068	1983	57,703
1969	20,464	1984	50,997
1970	20,032	1985	53,479
1971	25,442	1986	47,418
1972	28,920	1987	49,653
1973	35,586	1988	53,375
1974	45,422		

Source: Compiled from successive volumes of the *Federal Register* (Washington, D.C.: U.S. Government Printing Office).

Table 8-11 Presidential Victories on Votes in Congress, 1953-1988

President/year	House and Senate	House	Number of votes	Senate	Number of votes
Eisenhower					
1953	89.2%	91.2%	34	87.8%	49
1954	82.8	—	—	—	—
1955	75.3	63.4	41	84.6	52
1956	69.2	73.5	34	67.6	65
1957	68.4	58.3	60	78.9	57
1958	75.7	74.0	50	76.5	98
1959	52.9	55.5	54	50.4	121
1960	65.1	65.0	43	65.1	86
Average	72.2	68.7		73.0	
Kennedy					
1961	81.5	83.1	65	80.6	124
1962	85.4	85.0	60	85.6	125
1963	87.1	83.1	71	89.6	115
Average	84.6	83.7		85.3	

(Table continues)

Table 8-11 *(Continued)*

President/year	House and Senate	House	Number of votes	Senate	Number of votes
Johnson					
1964	87.9%	88.5%	52	87.6%	97
1965	93.1	93.8	112	92.6	162
1966	78.9	91.3	103	68.8	125
1967	78.8	75.6	127	81.2	165
1968	74.5	83.5	103	68.9	164
Average	82.6	86.5		79.8	
Nixon					
1969	74.8	72.3	47	76.4	72
1970	76.9	84.6	65	71.4	91
1971	74.8	82.5	57	69.5	82
1972	66.3	81.1	37	54.3	46
1973	50.6	48.0	125	52.4	185
1974	59.6	67.9	53	54.2	83
Average	67.2	72.7		63.0	
Ford					
1974	58.2	59.3	54	57.4	68
1975	61.0	50.6	89	71.0	93
1976	53.8	43.1	51	64.2	53
Average	57.6	51.0		64.2	
Carter					
1977	75.4	74.7	79	76.1	88
1978	78.3	69.6	112	84.8	151
1979	76.8	71.7	145	81.4	161
1980	75.1	76.9	117	73.3	116
Average	76.4	73.2		78.9	
Reagan					
1981	82.3	72.4	76	87.3	128
1982	72.4	55.8	77	83.2	119
1983	67.1	47.6	82	85.9	85
1984	65.8	52.2	113	85.7	77
1985	59.9	45.0	80	71.6	102
1986	56.5	34.1	88	81.2	80
1987	43.5	34.3	99	56.4	78
1988	47.4	32.7	104	64.8	88
Average	61.9	46.8		77.0	

Note: "—" indicates not available. Percentages indicate number of congressional votes supporting the president divided by the total number of votes on which the president took a position.

Sources: 1969-1986: Norman J. Ornstein et al., eds., *Vital Statistics on Congress, 1987-1988* (Washington, D.C.: Congressional Quarterly, 1987), 203-204; 1987-1988: *Congressional Quarterly Weekly Report* (1988), 95, 97, 3323, 3325.

Table 8-12 Congressional Voting in Support of the President's Position, 1954-1988 (percent)

President/year	House			Senate		
	All Demo-crats	Southern Demo-crats	Repub-licans	All Demo-crats	Southern Demo-crats	Repub-licans
Eisenhower						
1954	54	—	—	45	—	82
1955	58	—	67	65	—	85
1956	58	—	79	44	—	80
1957	54	—	60	60	—	80
1958	63	—	65	51	—	77
1959	44	—	76	44	—	80
1960	49	—	63	52	—	76
Kennedy						
1961	81	—	41	73	—	42
1962	83	71	47	76	63	48
1963	84	71	36	77	65	52
Johnson						
1964	84	70	42	73	63	52
1965	83	65	46	75	60	55
1966	81	64	45	71	59	53
1967	80	65	51	73	69	63
1968	77	63	59	64	50	57
Nixon						
1969	56	55	65	55	56	74
1970	64	64	79	56	62	74
1971	53	69	79	48	59	76
1972	56	59	74	52	71	77
1973	39	49	67	42	55	70
1974	52	64	71	44	60	65
Ford						
1974	48	52	59	45	55	67
1975	40	48	67	53	67	76
1976	36	52	70	47	61	73
Carter						
1977	69	58	46	77	71	58
1978	67	54	40	74	61	47
1979	70	58	37	75	66	51
1980	71	63	44	71	69	50

(Table continues)

Table 8-12 *(Continued)*

President/year	House			Senate		
	House			*Senate*		
	All Demo-crats	Southern Demo-crats	Repub-licans	All Demo-crats	Southern Demo-crats	Repub-licans
Reagan						
1981	46	60	72	52	63	84
1982	43	55	70	46	57	77
1983	30	45	74	45	46	77
1984	37	47	64	45	58	81
1985	31	43	69	36	46	80
1986	26	37	69	39	56	90
1987	26	37	65	38	43	67
1988	28	34	61	51	58	73

Note: "−" indicates not available. Percentages indicate number of congressional votes supporting the president divided by the total number of votes on which the president took a position. The percentages are calculated to eliminate the effects of absences as follows: support = (support)/(support + opposition).

Sources: Ornstein, *Vital Statistics on Congress, 1987-1988,* 206-207; 1987-1988: *Congressional Quarterly Weekly Report* (1988), 94, 3326.

Table 8-13 Presidential Vetoes, 1789-1988

Years	President	Regular vetoes	Vetoes overridden	Pocket vetoes	Total vetoes
1789-1797	Washington	2	0	0	2
1797-1801	Adams	0	0	0	0
1801-1809	Jefferson	0	0	0	0
1809-1817	Madison	5	0	2	7
1817-1825	Monroe	1	0	0	1
1825-1829	J. Q. Adams	0	0	0	0
1829-1837	Jackson	5	0	7	12
1837-1841	Van Buren	0	0	1	1
1841-1841	Harrison	0	0	0	0
1841-1845	Tyler	6	1	4	10
1845-1849	Polk	2	0	1	3
1849-1850	Taylor	0	0	0	0
1850-1853	Fillmore	0	0	0	0
1853-1857	Pierce	9	5	0	9
1857-1861	Buchanan	4	0	3	7
1861-1865	Lincoln	2	0	5	7
1865-1869	A. Johnson	21	15	8	29
1869-1877	Grant	45	4	48	93
1877-1881	Hayes	12	1	1	13
1881-1881	Garfield	0	0	0	0
1881-1885	Arthur	4	1	8	12
1885-1889	Cleveland	304	2	110	414
1889-1893	Harrison	19	1	25	44
1893-1897	Cleveland	42	5	128	170
1897-1901	McKinley	6	0	36	42
1901-1909	T. Roosevelt	42	1	40	82
1909-1913	Taft	30	1	9	39
1913-1921	Wilson	33	6	11	44
1921-1923	Harding	5	0	1	6
1923-1929	Coolidge	20	4	30	50
1929-1933	Hoover	21	3	16	37
1933-1945	F. Roosevelt	372	9	263	635
1945-1953	Truman	180	12	70	250
1953-1961	Eisenhower	73	2	108	181
1961-1963	Kennedy	12	0	9	21
1963-1969	L. Johnson	16	0	14	30
1969-1974	Nixon	26[a]	7	17	43
1974-1977	Ford	48	12	18	66
1977-1981	Carter	13	2	18	31
1981-1989	Reagan	39	9	39	78
Total		1,419	103	1,050	2,469

[a] Two pocket vetoes, overruled in the courts, are counted here as regular vetoes.

Sources: Congressional Quarterly Weekly Report (1989), 7; Louis Fisher, *The Politics of Shared Power: Congress and the Executive*, 2d ed. (Washington, D.C.: CQ Press, 1987), 30.

Table 8-14 Senate Action on Nominations, 1929-1988

Congress		Number received	Senate action			
			Confirmed	Withdrawn	Rejected[a]	Unconfirmed
71st	(1929-1931)	17,508	16,905	68	5	530
72d	(1931-1933)	12,716	10,909	19	1	1,787
73d	(1933-1934)	9,094	9,027	17	3	47
74th	(1935-1936)	22,487	22,286	51	15	135
75th	(1937-1938)	15,330	15,193	20	27	90
76th	(1939-1941)	29,072	28,939	16	21	96
77th	(1941-1942)	24,344	24,137	33	5	169
78th	(1943-1944)	21,775	21,371	31	6	367
79th	(1945-1946)	37,022	36,550	17	3	452
80th	(1947-1948)	66,641	54,796	153	0	11,692
81st	(1949-1951)	87,266	86,562	45	6	653
82d	(1951-1952)	46,920	46,504	45	2	369
83d	(1953-1954)	69,458	68,563	43	0	852
84th	(1955-1956)	84,173	82,694	38	3	1,438
85th	(1957-1958)	104,193	103,311	54	0	828
86th	(1959-1960)	91,476	89,900	30	1	1,545
87th	(1961-1962)	102,849	100,741	1,279	0	829
88th	(1963-1964)	122,190	120,201	36	0	1,953
89th	(1965-1966)	123,019	120,865	173	0	1,981
90th	(1967-1968)	120,231	118,231	34	0	1,966
91st	(1969-1971)	134,464	133,797	487	2	178
92d	(1971-1972)	117,053	114,909	11	0	2,133
93d	(1973-1974)[b]	134,384	131,254	15	0	3,069
94th	(1975-1976)	132,151	131,378	6	0	3,801
95th	(1977-1978)	137,504	124,730	66	0	12,713
96th	(1979-1980)	154,797	154,665	18	0	1,458
97th	(1981-1982)	186,264	184,844	55	7	1,346
98th	(1983-1984)	97,893	97,262	4	0	610
99th	(1985-1986)	99,614	95,811	16	0	3,787
100th	(1987-1988)	89,193	88,721	23	1	5,922

[a] Includes only those nominations rejected outright by a vote of the Senate. Most nominations that fail to win approval of the Senate are unfavorably reported by committees and never reach the Senate floor, having been withdrawn. In some cases, the full Senate may vote to recommit a nomination to committee, in effect killing it.

[b] Forty-six nominations were returned to the president during the October-November 1974 recess in accordance with Senate Rule 38, which states: "[I]f the Senate shall adjourn or take a recess for more than thirty days, all nominations pending and not finally acted upon at the time of taking such adjournment or recess shall be returned by the Secretary to the President, and shall not again be considered unless they shall again be made to the Senate by the President."

Source: 1929-1980: Congressional Quarterly, *Congressional Quarterly's Guide to Congress,* 3d ed. (Washington, D.C.: Congressional Quarterly, 1982), 195; 1981-1986: Congressional Record (daily ed.), Daily Digest, "Resume of Congressional Activity," 97th Cong. (1st sess., D1613; 2d sess., D1499); 98th Cong. (2d sess., D1348); 99th Cong. (1st sess., D1565; 2d sess., D1343); 100th Cong. (2d sess., D1400).

Table 8-15 Senate Rejections of Cabinet Nominations

Nominee	Position	President	Date	Vote
Roger B. Taney	secretary of treasury	Jackson	6/23/1834	18-28
Caleb Cushing	secretary of treasury	Tyler	3/3/1843	19-27
Caleb Cushing	secretary of treasury	Tyler	3/3/1843	10-27
Caleb Cushing	secretary of treasury	Tyler	3/3/1843	2-29
David Henshaw	secretary of navy	Tyler	1/15/1844	6-34
James M. Porter	secretary of war	Tyler	1/30/1844	3-38
James S. Green	secretary of treasury	Tyler	6/15/1844	[a]
Henry Stanbery	attorney general	A. Johnson	6/2/1868	11-29
Charles B. Warren	attorney general	Coolidge	3/10/1925	39-41
Charles B. Warren	attorney general	Coolidge	3/16/1925	39-46
Lewis L. Strauss	secretary of commerce	Eisenhower	6/19/1959	46-49
John Tower	secretary of defense	Bush	3/9/1989	47-53

[a] Not recorded.

Source: Congressional Quarterly's Guide to Congress, 198; updated by the editors.

Table 8-16 Party Affiliation of Major Appointments, 1961-1984

Administration	Number of appointees	Affiliated with president's party	Party affiliated	Unaffiliated
Kennedy	430	63%	73%	27%
Johnson	524	47	58	42
Nixon	737	65	73	27
Ford	293	56	64	36
Carter (1977-1978)[a]	402	58	65	35
Reagan (1981-1984)	524	82	85	15

Note: Major appointments include cabinet, subcabinet, and lower policy-level positions in the executive branch, including ambassadorships and positions on various boards and commissions. In the case of some positions, particularly those on independent regulatory commissions, the ratio of party affiliation among appointees is legislatively prescribed. Therefore, these cases were not included in the annual totals. The Congressional Quarterly Almanac indicates the party affiliation for every appointee for whom that information is available. When not listed or listed as "independent," the appointee's affiliation was included here as "unaffiliated."

[a] Lists of major presidential appointees confirmed during the years 1979 and 1980 contained a high proportion of names for whom no information on party affiliation was made available by the Carter administration. In 1979, out of a total of 256 appointees listed, only 48 were assigned a party affiliation. For 1980, only 22 of 148 listed included this information.

Source: Roger G. Brown, "Party and Bureaucracy: From Kennedy to Reagan," Political Science Quarterly 97 (1982): 283. Data for 1981-1984 have been supplied by Professor Brown. Used by permission of Roger G. Brown, Department of Political Science, University of North Carolina-Charlotte.

Table 8-17 Treaties and Executive Agreements Approved by the
United States, 1789-1988

Year	Number of treaties	Number of executive agreements
1789-1839	60	27
1839-1889	215	238
1889-1929	382	763
1930-1932	49	41
1933-1944 (F. Roosevelt)	131	369
1945-1952 (Truman)	132	1,324
1953-1960 (Eisenhower)	89	1,834
1961-1963 (Kennedy)	36	813
1964-1968 (L. Johnson)	67	1,083
1969-1974 (Nixon)	93	1,317
1975-1976 (Ford)	26	666
1977-1980 (Carter)	79	1,476
1981-1988 (Reagan)	117	2,837

Note: Varying definitions of what comprises an executive agreement and their entry-into-force date make the above numbers approximate.

Sources: 1789-1980: *Congressional Quarterly's Guide to Congress,* 291; 1981-1988: Office of the Assistant Legal Adviser for Treaty Affairs, U.S. Department of State.

Figure 8-1 Presidential Approval, 1938-1988

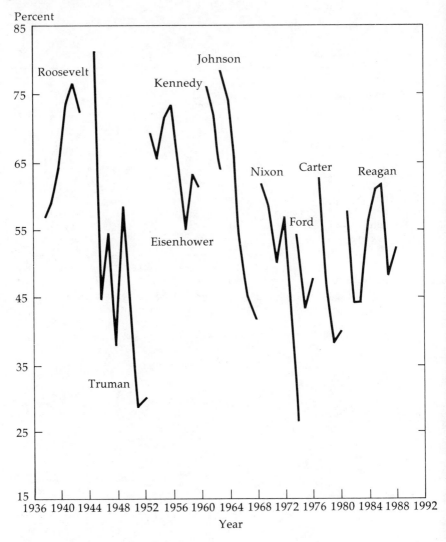

Percent

Year

Note: Averaged by year. Question: "Do you approve or disapprove of the way ____ (last name of president) is handling his job as president?"

Sources: Calculated by the editors; 1938-1980: *The Gallup Opinion Index* (October-November 1980), 13-38; 1981-1988: *The Gallup Report* (July 1988), 19-20; The Gallup Poll, "Reagan Regaining Public Confidence," press release, October 9, 1988, and the Gallup Library.

Figure 8-2   Presidential Approval, 1977-1988

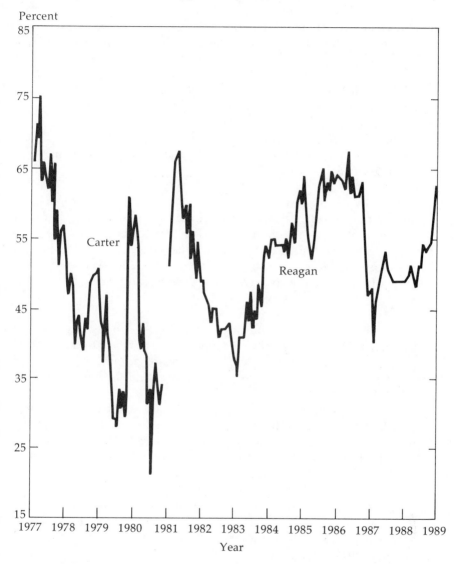

Percent

Year

Note: Question: "Do you approve or disapprove of the way Carter (Reagan) is handling his job as president?"

Sources: 1977-1980: *The Gallup Opinion Index* (October-November 1980), 13-14; 1981-1988: *The Gallup Report* (July 1988), 19-20; The Gallup Poll, "Reagan Regaining Public Confidence," press release, October 9, 1988, and the Gallup Library.

Questions

1. How many and which vice presidents were later elected president (Table 8-1)? How many were elected without first succeeding to the presidency because the president died?

2. Most presidents have been elected from large states. Why? (Hint: see the current state electoral votes in Table 3-2.)

3. Evaluations of presidents sometimes change over time. Which recent president "moved up" considerably between 1970 and later polls (Table 8-2)?

4. In the nineteenth century, compared to the twentieth, proportionately more presidents were at one time members of the House of Representatives (Table 8-3). What structural change near the turn of the century (Table 1-3) made the Senate more attractive, and therefore the House less so, as a source of presidential candidates? State officials were also a greater source of candidates during the nineteenth century. Why?

5. Comparing the last public position held by nineteenth century presidents, the last public position held by twentieth century presidents, and the latest public position of nominees since 1936 (Tables 8-3 and 8-4) reveals a strong trend. What is that trend?

6. Candidate differences in fund raising and campaign spending translate readily into differences in how well candidates fare at the polls. Evaluate the accuracy of this statement with respect to the overall standings of the candidates for each party's presidential nomination in 1988 (Tables 8-5, 3-3, and 3-4).

7. What are the three newest cabinet departments, and what department were two of them a part of (Table 8-6)? Besides Defense, which department was the largest in 1988 in the number of paid civilian employees? The smallest?

8. Which president began the Office of Economic Opportunity and what "war" was it associated with (Table 8-7)? The National Security Council was formed in connection with the formation of which cabinet-level department? Which office by itself constitutes about a third of the Executive Office of the President?

9. Did civilian employment by the federal government rise or fall between 1981, when President Ronald Reagan took office, and 1988 (Table 8-8)? By what percentage?

10. What is the oldest major federal regulatory agency and when was it established (Table 8-9)? Most agencies were formed in response to crises or major contemporary problems. Briefly, in response to what event or situation were the following formed: EPA, EEOC, FDIC, FERC, NLRB, and SEC?

11. Deregulation under President Reagan was intended to cut government bureaucracy. Based on the number of pages in the *Federal Register*, was it successful (Table 8-10)?

12. Democratic presidents since Dwight Eisenhower have been uniformly more successful than Republican presidents in obtaining legislation they favored (Table 8-11). Why? (Hint: see Table 3-16.) The president is said to enjoy a "honeymoon" period after each election. Does the evidence in Table 8-11 support the hypothesis that such a honeymoon period exists and has an effect on presidential victories on votes in Congress?

13. Which Democratic president received the lowest voting support from members of his own party in the House (Table 8-12)? Did President Jimmy Carter receive more or less support than other Democratic presidents from southern Democrats in the House?

14. Why is it important to distinguish regular vetoes from pocket vetoes? Apart from Franklin Roosevelt, who had slightly more than three terms to make his six hundred plus vetoes, which president vetoed the largest number of bills (Table 8-13)? Which president had the largest percentage of his vetoes overridden by Congress?

15. The Senate has rejected only nine individuals nominated to the cabinet. Indeed, over the past three decades, the Senate has rejected only a dozen nominations overall (Table 8-14). Does this mean that the Senate has abdicated its role in approving or disapproving the president's nominees?

16. Which president has been the most partisan in his appointments (Table 8-16)? Was this president more or less partisan in his appointments to federal courts (Tables 9-2 and 9-3)?

9

The Judiciary

The judiciary, although one of the three "separate but equal" branches of government, is often considered remote from the political push and pull that characterizes the other two. Preoccupation with process, precedent, and the meaning of the law gives the courts a strikingly different appearance. But grappling with the constitutionality of abortion or the death penalty and pouring practical meaning into ambiguous, generally worded statutes enacted by legislatures puts the courts squarely in the midst of the political process.

But even if courts can be considered political, are statistics essential to understanding the courts? They are for two reasons. First, the courts themselves have to deal with statistics. A 1987 Supreme Court decision, for example, considered the question of racially disparate patterns in the imposition of the death penalty—Georgia defendants who killed whites were eleven times more likely to be sentenced to die as those who killed blacks.[1] The Court held that the statistics were not relevant to this particular case. Although the numbers may have been accurate and meaningful, they did not show that there was racial discrimination against this defendant. This case serves as a pointed reminder of the distinction a court draws between general patterns and the facts of the specific case before it.

But this example should not give the impression that courts disdain statistics. In fact, as one federal judge wrote, "In the problem of racial discrimination, statistics often tell much, and Courts listen."[2] Cases often turn on conclusions drawn from numerical data—voting rights (Table 1-17), reapportionment (Table 1-16), and school desegregation (Table 12-12) are but three areas in which this is true.

Statistics also can promote understanding of the courts. A single case does not lend itself to statistical analysis, but the large number, the hierarchy (Figure 9-1), and the geographical spread (Figure 9-2) of the federal courts, and the even greater variety of state courts and appointment methods (Table 9-1) suggest that numerical summarization aids comprehension. In addition, precisely because of the judicial emphasis on precedents, there are perhaps better records of previous activities than in most other areas of government. A lengthy history by itself suggests statistical summation.

The characteristics of those on the federal bench are one area of interest. Although the nature of the courts might suggest that appointments are merely a matter of judicial qualifications, the record indicates otherwise. Federal judicial appointments have always been subject to partisan considerations (Tables 9-3 and 9-5), and other characteristics of federal judges have been shown to vary with the appointing president (Table 9-2). Partisan and ideological differences also explain part of the frustration presidents have encountered with nominations to the Supreme Court (Table 9-4). Nor are more subjective judgments ignored in characterizing court appointees. Just as historians have judged presidents, legal scholars have evaluated Supreme Court justices (Table 9-6).

The growing caseload of the courts has become a major concern in recent years, and, while individual "horror" stories may be more dramatic (when Chief Justice Warren E. Burger retired in 1986 he noted that in a recent week he had worked more than one hundred hours), statistical evidence tells an even more convincing story. The caseload of the courts has indeed climbed dramatically in recent years (Tables 9-7 through 9-10, Figure 9-3). Cases filed in the district courts rose by 59 percent between 1980 and 1985, while the number of judges rose by only 2 percent (Table 9-9).

There is also considerable information on the nature of judicial work. For example, civil rather than criminal cases account for the increased workload (Table 9-10). One can also see from the distribution of types of cases in the federal courts that a district court judge must be prepared to hear and decide cases on a wide range of topics (Table 9-11). Dramatic changes also have occurred in the kinds of cases courts must deal with and in the ways they have responded. The Supreme Court has struck down more federal, state, and local laws on constitutional grounds in this century than in the nineteenth (Table 9-12). Within this century, however, doctrinal trends have changed. For example, since the 1930s the Court has rejected far fewer economic regulatory laws and has increasingly struck down laws restricting civil liberties (Figure 9-4).

As they are with the executive and the legislature, statistics are a necessary component for understanding the courts and their decisions.

Notes

1. *McCleskey v. Kemp*, 481 U.S. —, decided April 22, 1987.
2. *Alabama v. United States*, 304 F.2d 201 (1961).

Figure 9-1 The United States Federal Court System

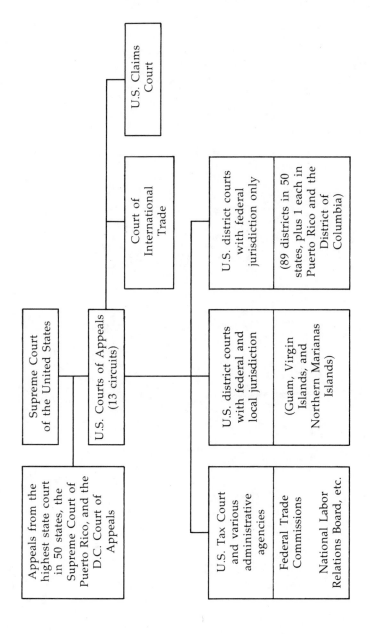

Source: Administrative Office of the United States Courts.

Figure 9-2 The Thirteen Federal Judicial Circuits and Ninety-four U.S. District Courts

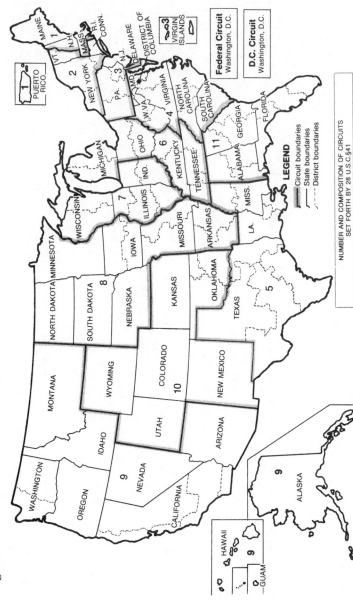

Source: Administrative Office of the United States Courts (January 1983).

Note: The remaining two circuit courts, the D.C. Circuit and Federal Circuit, are located in Washington, D.C.

Table 9-1 Principal Methods of Judicial Selection for State Courts

Partisan election	Nonpartisan election	Legislative election	Gubernatorial appointment	Merit plan
Alabama[a]	Georgia[a]	Connecticut[a]	California	Alaska[a]
Arkansas	Idaho[a]	Rhode Island[c]	Delaware	Arizona[a]
Illinois[a]	Kentucky	South Carolina[a]	Maine[a]	Colorado[a]
Mississippi[a]	Louisiana	Virginia	Massachusetts	Florida[a,b]
New Mexico	Michigan[a]		New Hampshire	Hawaii
North Carolina[b]	Minnesota		New Jersey[a]	Indiana[a]
Pennsylvania[a]	Montana		New York[a,d]	Iowa[a]
Tennessee[a,b]	Nevada			Kansas[a]
Texas[a]	North Dakota			Maryland
West Virginia	Ohio[a]			Missouri[a]
	Oregon[a]			Nebraska
	Washington[a]			Oklahoma[a,b]
	Wisconsin[a]			South Dakota[a]
				Utah
				Vermont
				Wyoming[a]

[a] Minor court judges chosen by other methods.
[b] Most but not all major judicial positions selected this way.
[c] Supreme Court justices only.
[d] Appellate judges only.

Source: Council of State Governments, *Book of the States, 1988-89* (Lexington, Ky.: Council of State Governments, 1987), 163-165.

Table 9-2 Characteristics of Federal District and Appellate Court Nominees, Presidents Johnson to Reagan (percent)

	Johnson nominees	Nixon nominees	Ford nominees	Carter nominees	Reagan nominees
District courts					
Occupation					
Politics/government	21.3	10.6	21.2	4.4	12.8
Judiciary	31.1	28.5	34.6	44.6	37.2
Large law firm[a]	2.4	11.3	9.7	14.0	17.6
Moderate firm[a]	18.9	27.9	25.0	19.8	19.3
Small/solo firm[a]	23.0	19.0	9.7	23.9	10.4
Other	3.3	2.8	0.0	3.5	2.8
Experience					
Judicial	34.4	35.2	42.3	54.5	46.6
Prosecutorial	45.9	41.9	50.0	38.6	44.1
Neither	33.6	36.3	30.8	28.2	28.3
Political affiliation					
Democrat	94.3	7.3	21.2	92.6	4.8
Republican	5.7	92.7	78.8	4.4	93.4
Independent	0.0	0.0	0.0	2.9	1.7
Past party activism	49.2	48.6	50.0	60.9	58.6
Religion					
Protestant	58.2	73.2	73.1	60.4	60.0
Catholic	31.1	18.4	17.3	27.7	30.4
Jewish	10.7	8.4	9.6	11.9	9.3
Race/ethnicity					
White	93.4	95.5	88.5	78.7	92.4
Black	4.1	3.4	5.8	13.9	2.1
Asian-American	0.0	0.0	3.9	0.5	0.7
Hispanic	2.5	1.1	1.9	6.9	4.8
Gender					
Female	1.6	0.6	1.9	14.4	8.3
Total number of nominees	122	179	52	202	290
Courts of Appeals					
Occupation					
Politics/government	10.0	4.4	8.3	5.4	6.4
Judiciary	57.5	53.3	75.0	46.4	55.1
Large law firm[a]	5.0	4.4	8.3	10.8	12.8
Moderate firm[a]	17.5	22.2	8.3	16.1	10.3
Small/solo firm[a]	7.5	6.7	0.0	5.4	1.3
Other	2.5	8.9	0.0	16.1	14.1
Experience					
Judicial	65.0	57.8	75.0	53.6	60.3
Prosecutorial	47.5	46.7	25.0	32.1	28.2
Neither	20.0	17.8	25.0	37.5	34.6

(Table continues)

Table 9-2 *(Continued)*

	Johnson nominees	Nixon nominees	Ford nominees	Carter nominees	Reagan nominees
Political affiliation					
Democrat	95.0	6.7	8.3	82.1	0.0
Republican	5.0	93.3	91.7	7.1	97.4
Independent	0.0	0.0	0.0	10.7	1.3
Other	0.0	0.0	0.0	0.0	1.3
Past party activism	57.5	60.0	58.3	73.2	69.2
Religion					
Protestant	60.0	75.6	58.3	60.7	55.1
Catholic	25.0	15.6	33.3	23.2	30.8
Jewish	15.0	8.9	8.3	16.1	14.1
Race/ethnicity					
White	95.0	97.8	100.0	66.7	97.4
Black	5.0	0.0	0.0	25.0	1.3
Asian-American	0.0	2.2	0.0	8.3	0.0
Hispanic	0.0	0.0	0.0	0.0	1.3
Gender					
Female	2.5	0.0	0.0	0.0	5.1
Total number of appointees	40	45	12	56	78

[a] Large: twenty-five or more partners and associates; moderate: five to twenty-four partners and associates; small: two to four partners and associates.

Source: Sheldon Goldman, "Reagan's Judicial Legacy: Completing the Puzzle and Summing Up," *Judicature* 72 (April-May 1989): 318-330.

Table 9-3   Federal Judicial Appointments of Same Party as President, Presidents Cleveland to Reagan

President	Party	Percentage
Cleveland	Democrat	97.3
Harrison	Republican	87.9
McKinley	Republican	95.7
T. Roosevelt	Republican	95.8
Taft	Republican	82.2
Wilson	Democrat	98.6
Harding	Republican	97.7
Coolidge	Republican	94.1
Hoover	Republican	85.7
F. Roosevelt	Democrat	96.4
Truman	Democrat	93.1
Eisenhower	Republican	95.1
Kennedy	Democrat	90.9
Johnson	Democrat	95.2
Nixon	Republican	93.7
Ford	Republican	81.2
Carter	Democrat	94.8
Reagan	Republican	97.8

Source: Henry J. Abraham, personal communication and *Justices and Presidents: Appointments to the Supreme Court,* 2d ed. (New York: Oxford University Press, 1985), 67 (copyright © Henry J. Abraham, 1974, 1985, reprinted by permission of Oxford University Press, Inc.).

Table 9-4 Supreme Court Nominations that Failed

Nominee	Year	President	Action
William Paterson	1793	Washington	withdrawn
John Rutledge	1795	Washington	rejected, 10-14
Alexander Wolcott	1811	Madison	rejected, 9-24
John Crittenden	1828	J. Q. Adams	postponed
Roger B. Taney	1835	Jackson	postponed
John Spencer	1844	Tyler	rejected, 21-26
R. Walworth	1844	Tyler	withdrawn
Edward King	1844	Tyler	withdrawn
Edward King	1844	Tyler	withdrawn
John Read	1845	Tyler	postponed
G. Woodward	1846	Polk	rejected, 20-29
Edward Bradford	1852	Fillmore	postponed
George Badger	1853	Fillmore	postponed
William Micou	1853	Fillmore	postponed
Jeremiah Black	1861	Buchanan	rejected, 25-26
Henry Stanbery	1866	A. Johnson	postponed
Ebenezer Hoar	1870	Grant	rejected, 24-33
George Williams	1874	Grant	withdrawn
Caleb Cushing	1874	Grant	withdrawn
Stanley Matteys	1881	Hayes	postponed
W. B. Hornblower	1894	Cleveland	rejected, 24-30
Wheeler H. Peckham	1894	Cleveland	rejected, 32-41
John J. Parker	1930	Hoover	rejected, 39-41
Abe Fortas[a]	1968	L. Johnson	withdrawn
Homer Thornberry	1968	L. Johnson	withdrawn
C. Haynsworth	1969	Nixon	rejected, 45-55
G. H. Carswell	1970	Nixon	rejected, 45-51
Robert Bork	1987	Reagan	rejected, 42-58
Douglas Ginsburg	1987	Reagan	not submitted[b]

Note: Twenty-nine of the 145 presidential nominations have failed to obtain Senate confirmation. However, five nominees declined appointment after having been nominated (Harrison, 1789; W. Cushing, 1796; Jay, 1800; Lincoln, 1811; Adams, 1811) and two withdrew after being confirmed (W. Smith, 1837; Conkling, 1882).

[a] In 1968, Fortas, an associate justice, was nominated for chief justice.

[b] Publicly announced but withdrawn before the president formally submitted his nomination to the Senate.

Source: Congressional Quarterly, *Congressional Quarterly's Guide to Congress,* 3d ed. (Washington, D.C.: Congressional Quarterly, 1982), 786-788; updated by the editors.

Table 9-5 Characteristics of Supreme Court Justices

Seat number and justice	Party	Home state	Years on Court	Age at nomination	Years of previous judicial experience
Washington appointees					
1 John Jay	Federalist	New York	1789-1795	44	2
2 John Rutledge	Federalist	South Carolina	1789-1791	50	6
3 William Cushing	Federalist	Massachusetts	1789-1810[a]	57	29
4 James Wilson	Federalist	Pennsylvania	1789-1798[a]	47	0
5 John Blair, Jr.	Federalist	Virginia	1789-1796	57	11
6 James Iredell	Federalist	North Carolina	1790-1799[a]	38	0.5
2 Thomas Johnson	Federalist	Maryland	1791-1793	59	1.5
2 William Paterson	Federalist	New Jersey	1793-1806[a]	47	0
1 John Rutledge	Federalist	South Carolina	1795	55	6[b]
5 Samuel Chase	Federalist	Maryland	1796-1811[a]	55	8
1 Oliver Ellsworth	Federalist	Connecticut	1796-1800	51	5
J. Adams appointees					
4 Bushrod Washington	Federalist	Virginia	1798-1829[a]	36	0
6 Alfred Moore	Federalist	North Carolina	1799-1804	44	1
1 John Marshall	Federalist	Virginia	1801-1835[a]	45	3
Jefferson appointees					
6 William Johnson	Jeffersonian	South Carolina	1804-1834[a]	32	6
2 H. Brockholst Livingston	Jeffersonian	New York	1806-1823[a]	49	0
7 Thomas Todd	Jeffersonian	Kentucky	1807-1826[a]	42	6
Madison appointees					
5 Gabriel Duvall	Jeffersonian	Maryland	1811-1835	58	6
3 Joseph Story	Jeffersonian	Massachusetts	1811-1845[a]	32	0
Monroe appointee					
2 Smith Thompson	Jeffersonian	New York	1823-1843[a]	55	16

J. Q. Adams appointee					
7 Robert Trimble	Jeffersonian	Kentucky	1826-1828[a]	49	11
Jackson appointees					
7 John McLean	Democrat	Ohio	1829-1861[a]	44	6
4 Henry Baldwin	Democrat	Pennsylvania	1830-1844[a]	50	0
6 James Wayne	Democrat	Georgia	1835-1867[a]	45	5
1 Roger B. Taney	Democrat	Maryland	1836-1864[a]	59	0
5 Philip P. Barbour	Democrat	Virginia	1836-1841[a]	52	8
Van Buren appointees					
8 John Catron	Democrat	Tennessee	1837-1865[a]	51	10
9 John McKinley	Democrat	Alabama	1837-1852[a]	57	0
5 Peter V. Daniel	Democrat	Virginia	1841-1860[a]	57	0
Tyler appointee					
2 Samuel Nelson	Democrat	New York	1845-1872	52	22
Polk appointees					
3 Levi Woodbury	Democrat	New Hampshire	1845-1851[a]	55	6
4 Robert C. Grier	Democrat	Pennsylvania	1846-1870	52	13
Fillmore appointee					
3 Benjamin R. Curtis	Whig	Massachusetts	1851-1857	41	0
Pierce appointee					
9 John A. Campbell	Democrat	Alabama	1853-1861	41	0
Buchanan appointee					
3 Nathan Clifford	Democrat	Maine	1858-1881[a]	54	0
Lincoln appointees					
7 Noah H. Swayne	Republican	Ohio	1862-1881	57	0
5 Samuel F. Miller	Republican	Iowa	1862-1890[a]	46	0

(Table continues)

Table 9-5 (Continued)

Seat number and justice	Party	Home state	Years on Court	Age at nomination	Years of previous judicial experience
Lincoln appointees (continued)					
9 David Davis	Republican	Illinois	1862-1877	47	14
10 Stephen J. Field	Democrat	California	1863-1897	46	6
1 Salmon P. Chase	Republican	Ohio	1864-1873[a]	56	0
Grant appointees					
4 William Strong	Republican	Pennsylvania	1870-1880	61	11
6 Joseph P. Bradley	Republican	New Jersey	1870-1892[a]	56	0
2 Ward Hunt	Republican	New York	1873-1882	62	8
1 Morrison R. Waite	Republican	Ohio	1874-1888[a]	57	0
Hayes appointees					
9 John M. Harlan	Republican	Kentucky	1877-1911[a]	44	1
4 William B. Woods	Republican	Georgia	1880-1887[a]	56	12
Garfield appointee					
7 Stanley Matthews	Republican	Ohio	1881-1889[a]	56	4
Arthur appointees					
3 Horace Gray	Republican	Massachusetts	1881-1902	53	18
2 Samuel Blatchford	Republican	New York	1882-1893[a]	62	15
Cleveland appointees (first term)					
4 Lucius Q. C. Lamar	Democrat	Mississippi	1883-1893[a]	62	0
1 Melville W. Fuller	Democrat	Illinois	1888-1910[a]	55	0
Harrison appointees					
7 David J. Brewer	Republican	Kansas	1889-1910[a]	52	19
5 Henry B. Brown	Republican	Michigan	1891-1906	54	16
6 George Shiras, Jr.	Republican	Pennsylvania	1892-1903	60	0

4 Howell E. Jackson	Democrat	Tennessee	1893-1895[a]	60	7
Cleveland appointees (second term)					
2 Edward D. White	Democrat	Louisiana	1894-1910[a]	48	1.5
4 Rufus W. Peckham	Democrat	New York	1895-1909[a]	57	9
McKinley appointee					
8 Joseph McKenna	Republican	California	1898-1925	54	5
T. Roosevelt appointees					
3 Oliver W. Holmes	Republican	Massachusetts	1902-1932	61	20
6 William R. Day	Republican	Ohio	1903-1922	53	7
5 William H. Moody	Republican	Massachusetts	1906-1910	52	0
Taft appointees					
4 Horace H. Lurton	Democrat	Tennessee	1909-1914[a]	65	26
7 Charles E. Hughes	Republican	New York	1910-1916	48	0
1 Edward D. White	Democrat	Louisiana	1910-1921[a]	65	1.5[b]
2 Willis Van Devanter	Republican	Wyoming	1910-1937	51	8
5 Joseph R. Lamar	Democrat	Georgia	1910-1916[a]	53	2
9 Mahlon Pitney	Republican	New Jersey	1912-1922	54	11
Wilson appointees					
4 James C. McReynolds	Democrat	Tennessee	1914-1941	52	0
5 Louis D. Brandeis	Republican	Massachusetts	1916-1939	59	0
7 John H. Clarke	Democrat	Ohio	1916-1922	59	2
Harding appointees					
1 William H. Taft	Republican	Ohio	1921-1930	63	13
7 George Sutherland	Republican	Utah	1922-1938	60	0
6 Pierce Butler	Democrat	Minnesota	1923-1939[a]	56	0
9 Edward T. Sanford	Republican	Tennessee	1923-1930[a]	57	14

(Table continues)

Table 9-5 (Continued)

Seat number and justice	Party	Home state	Years on Court	Age at nomination	Years of previous judicial experience
Coolidge appointee					
8 Harlan Fiske Stone	Republican	New York	1925–1941	52	0
Hoover appointees					
1 Charles E. Hughes	Republican	New York	1930–1941	67	0
9 Owens J. Roberts	Republican	Pennsylvania	1930–1945	55	0
3 Benjamin N. Cardozo	Democrat	New York	1932–1938[a]	61	18
F. Roosevelt appointees					
2 Hugo L. Black	Democrat	Alabama	1937–1971[a]	51	1.5
7 Stanley F. Reed	Democrat	Kentucky	1938–1957	53	0
3 Felix Frankfurter	Independent	Massachusetts	1939–1962	56	0
5 William O. Douglas	Democrat	Connecticut	1939–1975	40	0
6 Frank Murphy	Democrat	Michigan	1940–1949[a]	49	7
4 James F. Byrnes	Democrat	South Carolina	1941–1942	62	0
1 Harlan Fiske Stone	Republican	New York	1941–1946[a]	68	0[b]
9 Robert H. Jackson	Democrat	New York	1941–1954[a]	49	0
4 Wiley B. Rutledge	Democrat	Iowa	1943–1949[a]	48	4
Truman appointees					
9 Harold H. Burton	Republican	Ohio	1945–1958	57	0
1 Fred M. Vinson	Democrat	Kentucky	1946–1953[a]	56	5
6 Tom C. Clark	Democrat	Texas	1949–1967	49	0
4 Sherman Minton	Democrat	Indiana	1949–1956	58	8
Eisenhower appointees					
1 Earl Warren	Republican	California	1953–1969	62	0
8 John M. Harlan	Republican	New York	1955–1971	55	1
4 William J. Brennan	Democrat	New Jersey	1956–	50	7

7 Charles E. Whittaker	Republican	Missouri	1957-1962	56	3
9 Potter Stewart	Republican	Ohio	1958-1981	43	4
Kennedy appointees					
7 Byron R. White	Democrat	Colorado	1962-	44	0
3 Arthur J. Goldberg	Democrat	Illinois	1962-1965	54	0
L. Johnson appointees					
3 Abe Fortas	Democrat	Tennessee	1965-1969	55	0
6 Thurgood Marshall	Democrat	New York	1967-	59	4
Nixon appointees					
1 Warren E. Burger	Republican	Minnesota	1969-1986	61	13
3 Harry A. Blackmun	Republican	Minnesota	1970-	61	11
2 Lewis F. Powell, Jr.	Democrat	Virginia	1971-1987	64	0
8 William H. Rehnquist	Republican	Arizona	1971-1986	47	0
Ford appointee					
5 John Paul Stevens	Republican	Illinois	1976-	55	5
Reagan appointees					
9 Sandra Day O'Connor	Republican	Arizona	1981-	51	6.5
1 William H. Rehnquist	Republican	Arizona	1986-	61	0[b]
8 Antonin Scalia	Republican	Illinois	1986-	50	4
2 Anthony Kennedy	Republican	California	1988-	51	12

Note: Seat number 1 always held by the chief justice of the United States.

[a] Died in office.

[b] Prior to appointment to associate justice.

Sources: Sheldon Goldman, *Constitutional Law: Cases and Essays* (New York: Harper and Row, 1987); previous judicial experience: Abraham, *Justices and Presidents*, 56-58 (copyright © Henry J. Abraham, 1974, 1985, reprinted by permission of Oxford University Press, Inc.); *Congressional Quarterly's Guide to Congress*, 786-788; updated by the editors.

Table 9-6 Ratings of Supreme Court Justices

Great	Near great	Average			Below average	Failure
J. Marshall	W. Johnson	Jay	McKinley	Shiras	T. Johnson	Van Devanter
Story	Curtis	J. Rutledge	Daniel	Peckham	Moore	McReynolds
Taney	Miller	Cushing	Nelson	McKenna	Trimble	Butler
Harlan I	Field	Wilson	Woodbury	Day	Barbour	Byrnes
Holmes	Bradley	Blair	Grier	Moody	Woods	Burton
Hughes	Waite	Iredell	Campbell	Lurton	H. E. Jackson	Vinson
Brandeis	E. D. White	Paterson	Clifford	J. R. Lamar		Minton
Stone	Taft	S. Chase	Swayne	Pitney		Whittaker
Cardozo	Sutherland	Ellsworth	Davis	J. H. Clarke		
Black	Douglas	Washington	S. P. Chase	Sanford		
Frankfurter	R. H. Jackson	Livingston	Strong	Roberts		
Warren	W. B. Rutledge	Todd	Hunt	Reed		
		Harlan II	Duvall	Matthews		
		Brennan	Thompson	Gray		
		Fortas	McLean	Blatchford		
		Murphy	Brewer	Baldwin		
		T. C. Clark	B. R. White	Wayne		
		Stewart	Goldberg	Catron		
		L. Q. C. Lamar	T. Marshall	Brown		
		Fuller				

Note: Ratings reflect evaluations made in June 1970 by sixty-five law school deans and professors of law, history, and political science with expertise in the judicial process.

Source: Albert P. Blaustein and Roy M. Mersky, *The First One Hundred Justices: Statistical Studies on the Supreme Court of the United States* (Hamden, Conn.: Shoe String Press, Archon Books, 1978), 37–40.

Table 9-7 Caseload of the U.S. Supreme Court, 1970-1987

Action	1970	1971	1972	1973	1974	1975	1976	1977	1978	1979	1980	1981	1982	1983	1984	1985	1986	1987
Appellate cases on docket	1,903	2,070	2,183	2,480	2,308	2,352	2,324	2,341	2,383	2,509	2,749	2,935	2,710	2,688	2,575	2,571	2,547	2,577
From prior term	325	362	442	412	540	431	452	472	434	425	527	522	545	520	539	400	476	440
Docketed during present term	1,578	1,708	1,741	2,068	1,768	1,921	1,872	1,869	1,949	2,084	2,222	2,413	2,165	2,168	2,036	2,171	2,071	2,137
Cases acted upon	1,613	1,752	1,834	1,948	1,967	1,900	2,019	1,979	2,023	2,050	2,324[a]	2,513[a]	2,279[a]	2,220[a]	2,253[a]	2,185[a]	2,189[a]	2,224[a]
Granted review	214	238	217	229	235	244	237	224	210	199	167	203	169	140	167	166	152	157
Denied, dismissed, or withdrawn	1,285	1,409	1,397	1,572	1,594	1,538	1,620	1,676	1,734	1,776	1,999	2,100	1,892	1,902	1,953	1,863	1,876	1,919
Summarily decided	114	105	220	147	138	118	162	79	79	75	90	114	113	71	59	78	71	66
Cases not acted upon	290	318	349	532	341	452	305	362	360	459	425	422	413	468	322	386	358	353
Pauper cases on docket	2,289	2,445	2,436	2,585	2,348	2,395	2,398	2,349	2,331	2,249	2,371	2,354	2,352	2,394	2,416	2,577	2,564	2,675
Cases acted upon	1,802	2,023	1,982	2,013	1,976	1,997	2,083	1,960	1,996	1,838	2,027[a]	2,039[a]	2,013[a]	1,992[a]	2,067[a]	2,189[a]	2,250[a]	2,263[a]
Granted review	41	61	35	30	28	28	30	24	27	32	17	7	10	9	18	20	15	23
Denied, dismissed, or withdrawn	1,683	1,781	1,902	1,942	1,914	1,903	2,013	1,899	1,938	1,757	1,968	2,014	1,995	1,968	2,050	2,136	2,186	2,210
Summarily decided	78	181	45	41	34	66	40	37	31	49	32	12	6	10	14	24	38	21
Cases not acted upon	487	422	454	572	372	398	315	389	335	411	344	315	339	402	329	388	314	412
Original cases on docket	20	18	21	14	12	14	8	14	17	23	24	22	17	18	15	10	12	16
Cases disposed of during term	7	8	8	4	4	7	2	3	0	1	7	6	3	7	8	2	1	5
Total cases available for argument	267	280	256	261	278	280	269	260	249	238	264	318	312	269	271	276	270	280
Cases disposed of	160	181	180	172	178	181	181	185	170	160	162	192	199	189	184	175	179	175
Cases argued	151	176	177	170	175	179	176	172	168	156	154	184	183	184	175	171	175	167
Cases dismissed or remanded without argument	9	5	3	2	3	2	5	13	2	4	8	8	16	5	9	4	4	8
Cases remaining	107	99	76	89	100	99	88	75	79	78	102	126	113	80	87	101	91	105
Cases decided by signed opinion	126	143	159	161	144	160	154	153	143	143	144	170	174	174	159	161	164	151

(Table continues)

277

Table 9-7 (*Continued*)

Action	1970	1971	1972	1973	1974	1975	1976	1977	1978	1979	1980	1981	1982	1983	1984	1985	1986	1987
Cases decided per curiam opinion	22	24	18	8	20	16	22	8	8	12	8	10	6	6	11	10	10	9
Number of signed opinions	109	129	140	140	123	138	126	129	130	130	123	141	151	151	139	146	145	139
Total cases on docket	4,212	4,533	4,640	5,079	4,668	4,761	4,731	4,704	4,731	4,781	5,144	5,311	5,079	5,100	5,006	5,158	5,123	5,268

[a] Includes cases granted review and carried over to next term, not shown separately.

Sources: U.S. Bureau of the Census, *Statistical Abstract of the U.S., 1977* (Washington, D.C.: U.S. Government Printing Office, 1976), 184, 1979, 191, 1987, 168; 1986-1987: reprinted with permission from *The United States Law Week* (Washington, D.C.: The Bureau of National Affairs), vol. 56, 3102; vol. 57, 3074 (copyright © by The Bureau of National Affairs).

Figure 9-3 Cases Filed in the U.S. Supreme Court, 1938-1988

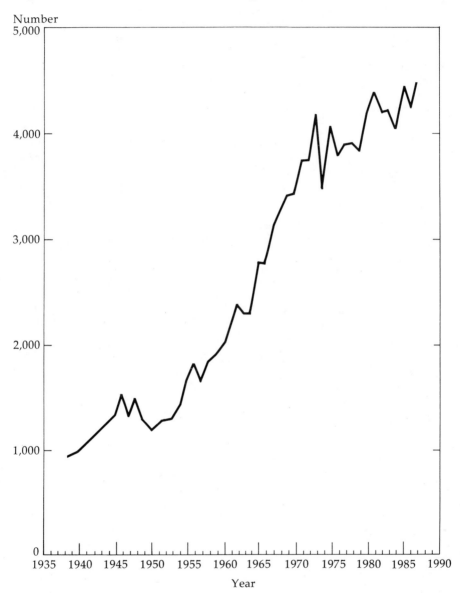

Number

Year

Source: 1938-1969: successive volumes of *Statistical Abstract of the U.S.;* 1970-1983: Office of the Clerk of the Supreme Court; 1984-1987: reprinted with permission from *The United States Law Week,* vol. 56, 3102, vol. 57, 3074 (copyright © by the Bureau of National Affairs).

Table 9-8 Caseloads of U.S. Courts of Appeals, 1980-1988

	1980	1984	1985	1986	1987	1988
Number of judgeships	132	132	156	156	156	156
Number of sitting senior judges	42	50	45	41	50	50
Number of vacant judgeship months	217.1	23.9	275.0	163.0	123.4	122.9
Appeals filed						
Prisoner	3,704	5,964	6,532	6,992	8,488	9,256
All other civil	12,141	17,600	18,660	18,979	18,705	19,213
Criminal	4,405	4,881	4,989	5,134	5,260	6,012
Administrative	2,950	3,045	3,179	3,187	2,723	3,043
Total	23,200	31,490	33,360	34,292	35,176	37,524
Appeals terminated						
Consolidations and cross appeals	2,704	3,953	2,669	2,848	2,689	2,698
Procedural	6,170	12,905	12,349	12,727	13,253	14,012
On the merits						
Prisoner	2,267	2,163	2,835	3,345	3,631	4,455
Other civil	5,861	7,916	9,208	9,853	9,996	9,989
Criminal	2,718	2,927	3,070	3,540	3,308	3,493
Administrative	1,167	1,321	1,256	1,461	1,567	1,241
Total on the merits	12,013	14,327	16,369	18,199	18,502	19,178
Total	20,887	31,185	31,387	33,774	34,444	35,888
Pending appeals	20,252	22,785	24,758	25,276	26,008	27,644
Per active judge[a]						
Termination on the merits	227	276	308	330	323	335
Procedural terminations	—	116	103	90	87	93

Note: "—" indicates not available.
[a] Includes only judges active during the entire twelve-month period.

Source: Director of the Administrative Office of the United States Courts, Federal Court Management Statistics 1985 (Washington, D.C.: U.S. Government Printing Office, 1985), 29-30; 1988, 29.

Table 9-9   Caseloads of U.S. District Courts, 1980-1988

	1980	1984	1985	1986	1987	1988
Overall						
Filings	188,487	285,563	299,164	282,074	268,023	269,174
Terminations	180,245	266,304	293,545	292,092	265,728	265,916
Pending	199,019	267,020	272,636	262,637	264,953	268,070
Number (and percentage) of civil cases over three years old	20,592	15,646	16,726	18,235	19,782	21,487
	(11.7)	(6.3)	(6.6)	(7.6)	(8.1)	(8.8)
Number of judgeships	516	515	575	575	575	575
Vacant judgeship months	956.2	246.8	895.8	669.9	495.4	485.2
Per judgeship						
Civil filings	327	508	476	444	416	417
Criminal felony filings	38	46	44	47	50	51
Total filings	365	554	520	491	466	467
Pending cases	386	518	474	457	461	466
Terminations	349	517	511	508	462	462
Trials completed	38	40	36	35	35	35
Median time from filing to disposition (months)						
Criminal felony	3.7	3.5	3.7	3.9	4.1	4.3
Civil	8	7	7	7	8	8
Median time from issue to trial (months)						
Civil only[a]	15	14	14	14	14	14

[a] Time is computed from the date that the answer or response is filed to the date trial begins.

Source: Director of the Administrative Office of the United States Courts, *Federal Court Management Statistics 1985,* 167; *1988,* 167.

Table 9-10 Number of Civil and Criminal Cases Filed in U.S. District
Courts, 1950-1987

	Civil cases		Criminal cases	
Year	Commenced	Terminated	Commenced	Terminated
1950	44,454	42,482	36,383	37,675
1955	48,308	47,959	35,310	38,990
1960	49,852	48,847	28,137	30,512
1965	67,678	63,137	31,569	33,718
1970	87,321	79,466	38,102	36,356
1975	117,320	103,787	41,108	49,212
1980	168,789	160,481	28,932	29,297
1981	180,576	177,975	31,328	30,221
1982	206,193	189,473	32,682	31,889
1983	241,842	215,356	35,913	33,985
1984	261,485	243,113	36,845	35,494
1985	273,670	269,848	39,500	37,139
1986	254,828	266,765	41,490	39,328
1987	238,982	238,000	43,292	42,287

Sources: 1950-1975: *Statistical Abstract of the U.S., 1971,* 152, *1976,* 168; 1980-1987: Director of
the Administrative Office of the United States Courts, *Annual Report of the Director of the
Administrative Office of the United States Courts* (Washington, D.C.: U.S. Government Printing
Office, 1987), 7, 13.

Table 9-11 Types of Civil and Criminal Cases in the Federal District Courts, 1987

Civil cases	Percentage	Criminal cases	Percentage
Contract actions	29.1	Embezzlement and fraud	22.4
Recovery of overpayments		Drunk driving and traffic	18.8
and enforcement of		Narcotics	12.1
judgments	(10.1)	Larceny and theft	8.2
Other contract actions	(19.0)	Marijuana	7.0
Liability	18.0	Homicide, robbery, assault,	
Product liability	(5.9)	and burglary	5.4
Motor vehicle personal		Forgery and counterfeiting	5.1
injury	(3.0)	Weapons and firearms	4.6
Marine personal injury	(1.5)	Immigration	3.9
Other personal injury	(6.0)	Controlled substances	2.0
Personal property damage	(1.6)	Escape	1.9
Statutory	48.1	Auto theft	0.6
State prisoner petitions	(13.7)	All other	8.2
Civil rights	(8.3)		
Social security	(5.6)	Total number of	
Labor laws	(5.3)	criminal cases	42,156
Federal prisoner petitions	(1.9)		
Tax suits	(1.2)		
Antitrust	(0.3)		
Other statutory	(11.8)		
Real property	4.8		
Total number of			
civil cases	238,982		

Source: Director of the Administrative Office of the United States Courts, *Annual Report of the Director of the Administrative Office of the United States Courts* (1987), 12, 17.

Table 9-12 Federal, State, and Local Laws Declared Unconstitutional by the Supreme Court by Decade, 1789-1987

Years	Federal	State and local
1789-1799	0	0
1800-1809	1	1
1810-1819	0	7
1820-1829	0	8
1830-1839	0	3
1840-1849	0	9
1850-1859	1	7
1860-1869	4	23
1870-1879	8	36
1880-1889	4	46
1890-1899	5	36
1900-1909	9	40
1910-1919	5	118
1920-1929	15	139
1930-1939	13	93
1940-1949	2	58
1950-1959	4	60
1960-1969	16	149
1970-1979	19	193
1980-1987	14	125
Total	120	1,151

Source: Lawrence Baum, *The Supreme Court,* 3d ed. (Washington, D.C.: CQ Press, 1989), 177, 180.

Figure 9-4 Economic and Civil Liberties Laws Overturned by the Supreme Court in the Twentieth Century

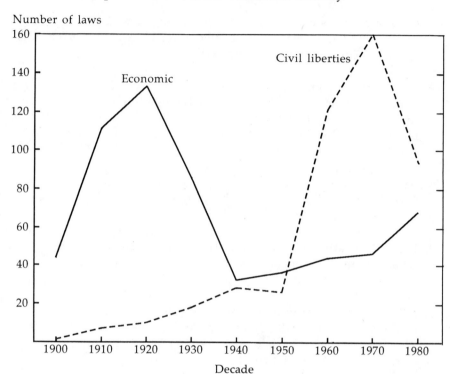

Number of laws

Note: Civil liberties category does not include laws supportive of civil liberties. Laws include federal, state, and local. The figures for the 1980s are based on the actual numbers for 1980-1987, multiplied by 1.25 to create a ten-year "rate" for that decade.

Source: Baum, *The Supreme Court,* 188.

Questions

1. Generally, cases can be appealed to the Supreme Court only after they have been heard by one of two other high-level courts. What are these kinds of courts (Figure 9-1)?

2. Six of the ten youngest states use a merit plan to elect most of their judges for state courts (Table 9-1 and Table 1-1). This would suggest that as states update their constitutions, many might adopt this method. Is this true? Use the states that have adopted new constitutions since 1945 (Table 1-2).

3. Are district and appellate court judges chosen on a nonpartisan basis (Tables 9-2 and 9-3)? Is the proportion of blacks, Hispanics, and women steadily rising?

4. Using the ratings in the 1982 *Tribune* poll (Table 8-2), ascertain whether the worst presidents had more trouble with their Supreme Court nominees than the best presidents.

5. A historical curiosity: two people were rejected for positions both in the cabinet (Table 8-15) and on the Supreme Court (Table 9-4). Who were they? Which of them subsequently served for nearly thirty years as chief justice?

6. Who were the youngest appointees to the Supreme Court (Table 9-5)? Who was the oldest? The one with the longest previous judicial experience? The first from west of the Mississippi?

7. Ratings of the sort in Table 9-6 are a subjective and imperfect guide. Looking at the year of appointment of the Supreme Court justices (Table 9-5) rated as "great" and as "failures," state a hypothesis about why these justices stand out as especially good or bad. Evaluate the following: the great justices compared to those below average and failures (1) were more often chief justice; (2) had, on average, more years of previous judicial experience; (3) served longer on the Court.

8. Warren E. Burger, former chief justice of the United States, argued frequently that the caseload of the Supreme Court was too great and that some intermediate court needs to be established to deal

with the overload. Drawing on Table 9-7 and Figure 9-3, construct an argument to support Burger's contention that the Court is overburdened. If an intermediate court is not established, how else could the Court reduce its load?

9. What happens to most cases that reach the Supreme Court (Table 9-7)? How can there be more cases decided by signed opinion than there are signed opinions, something that has happened every year since 1970?

10. With the increase in the number of judges in 1985, on average how many authorized judgeships are there per circuit in the U.S. courts of appeals (Table 9-8 and Figure 9-2)? Average, per district in the ninety-four district courts (Table 9-9)?

11. What kinds of cases—civil or criminal—account for the considerable increase in the caseload of district courts and courts of appeals (Tables 9-8 through 9-10)? Has the time taken to dispose of cases increased since 1980 (Table 9-9)?

12. From Table 9-12 and Figure 9-4, are you able to determine the subject matter of most laws declared unconstitutional in this century? If so, what are they?

13. The note to Figure 9-4 seems almost self-contradictory at first reading. What kinds of civil liberties laws were in fact overturned? Since most civil liberties laws were overturned in the 1950s, 1960s, and 1970s, what is likely to have been the subject matter of many of these laws?

10

Federalism

From a statistical point of view, a major problem in studying American government below the federal level is that there are fifty state governments and thousands of local governmental units (Table 10-1). Among other things, this often makes it difficult to get accurate, up-to-date information about all relevant jurisdictions. Even for state-level data, a researcher often must turn to each of the fifty state capitals, or to fifty-one units if data about the District of Columbia are needed, or even more if Puerto Rico and areas such as the Northern Marianas Islands are included, as might be necessary for studying delegates to the national party conventions. If the researcher's interest is in counties, cities, school districts, and the like, the data collection task can be enormous—well beyond the capacity of one person.

Fortunately, organizations and publications devoted to data collection have stepped to the fore. Some, such as the Council of State Governments and the International City Management Association, are well established. The former has published the *Book of the States* since 1935, and the latter the *Municipal Year Book* since 1934. Other sources are brand new, such as Congressional Quarterly's magazine *Governing*, which began publication in 1987. The U.S. Census Bureau also offers systematic collections of data covering increasingly longer spans. Two examples are the *State and Metropolitan Area Data Book* (published biennially since 1980) and the *County and City Data Book* (published, though with varying frequency, since 1952). Such groups and publications make data collection far easier, more systematic, and ensure higher quality than in the past.

Even when data are available, a researcher still can be frustrated by the inevitable variety that occurs across units. Simple tables or one-sentence summaries are often inadequate. Table 6-9, which concerns financing state election campaigns, for example, shows enormous variation among states. Similarly, the listing of state fiscal discipline measures (Table 10-9) notes that provisions for overriding gubernatorial vetoes vary, without giving the exact requirement in each state. So much variation exists on this single point—a two-thirds majority of the legislators present and voting, two-thirds of the total number of legislators, 60 percent of the legislators present, and so on—that this book leaves it to the original sources to present the particulars.

Therefore, in studying state and local governments, their interrelationships, and their relations with the federal government, a researcher must pay attention to details. Even more than usual it is essential to read footnotes and check several sources. Differences in data collection procedures, the timing of data collection, and variations in detail of reports all become important. The user must also keep in mind the purpose for examining the data. It takes a careful researcher to know when variations can be ignored and when they become so frequent or so large that they must be an explicit part of the analysis.

Despite improvements in data collection, it is still necessary to go directly to states and localities for some information. Fortunately, this too has become easier. Publications such as the *National Directory of State Agencies* and the *State Information Book* give names and titles of specific individuals and offices, typically with addresses and phone numbers. While this will still not make a project involving twenty-five or fifty states easy, at least one can gather missing information or exact details about specific states and localities.

The recent surge in availability of information has now made possible a serious look at cities, counties, states, regions, and the relationships among all of these governments. The tables in this book emphasize three topics. First, data are provided about states and localities as a whole and how they differ from the federal government and from each other (Tables 10-1 and 10-3, Figure 10-1). Second, information is given about specific states, often with an eye toward how states rank relative to one another (Tables 10-2 and 10-12). Third, considerable emphasis is given to intergovernmental relationships because of the growing fiscal interdependence between federal and state governments, state and local units, and even directly between federal and local governments (Tables 10-4 through 10-8).

As these tables amply demonstrate, students as well as professionals now have access to systematic information about all fifty states and increasingly about localities. Although users may have to make extra effort to absorb all the details provided by these tables, they are rewarded by the new possibilities for research and understanding.

Table 10-1 Federal, State, and Local Governmental Units, Number and Employees, 1942-1987

| Year | Federal | State | Local government | | | | | | Total |
			County	Municipal	School district	Township and town	Special district[a]	Total	
1942									
Number	1	48	3,050	16,220	108,579	18,919	8,299	155,067	155,116
Employees (thousands)[b]	2,664	503[c]	333[c]	872[c]	—	223[c,d]	[d]	1,428[c]	5,915
1952[d]									
Number	1	50	3,052	16,807	67,355	17,202	12,340	116,756	116,807
Employees (thousands)	2,583	1,060	573	1,341	1,234	312[c]	[c]	3,461	7,105
1957[d]									
Number	1	50	3,050	17,215	50,454	17,198	14,424	102,341	102,392
Employees (thousands)[e]	2,439	1,300	726	1,539	1,651	394[c]	[c]	4,307	8,047
1962									
Number	1	50	3,043	18,000	34,678	17,142	18,323	91,186	91,237
Employees (thousands)	2,539	1,680	862	1,696	2,161	449[c]	[c]	5,169	9,388
1967									
Number	1	50	3,049	18,048	21,782	17,105	21,264	81,248	81,299
Employees (thousands)	2,993	2,335	1,077	1,993	2,919	549[c]	[c]	6,539	11,867
1972									
Number	1	50	3,044	18,517	15,781	16,991	23,885	78,218	78,269
Employees (thousands)	2,832	2,957	1,369	2,376	3,587	348	327	8,007	13,759
1977									
Number	1	50	3,042	18,862	15,174	16,822	25,962	79,862	79,913
Employees (thousands)	2,839	3,491	1,761	2,469	4,127	361	402	9,120	15,459

1982									
Number	1	50	3,041	19,076	14,851	16,734	28,078	81,780	81,831
Employees (thousands)	2,862	3,744	1,824	2,397	4,194	356	478	9,249	15,841
1987									
Number	1	50	3,042	19,200	14,721	16,691	29,532	83,186	83,217
Employees (thousands)[f]	3,019	4,068	1,926	2,494	4,502	400	524	9,846	16,933

Note: "—" indicates not available.
[a] Special districts include independent public housing authorities, local irrigation units, power authorities, and other such bodies.
[b] Month for employee counts varies across years. For details, see sources.
[c] Employees in other than education.
[d] Townships and special districts are combined.
[e] Adjusted to include units in Alaska and Hawaii.
[f] For 1986.

Sources: 1942-1967: U.S. Bureau of the Census, *Historical Statistics of the U.S.* (Washington, D.C.: U.S. Government Printing Office, 1975), 1086, 1100; 1972-1987 governmental units: U.S. Bureau of the Census, *Census of Governments, 1987,* preliminary report (Washington, D.C.: U.S. Government Printing Office, 1987), 1; 1972-1986 employees: U.S. Office of Personnel Management, *Federal Manpower Statistics, Federal Civilian Workforce Statistics;* U.S. Bureau of the Census, *Public Employment in 1985* (Washington, D.C.: U.S. Government Printing Office, 1986), 2; *Public Employment in 1986,* x, 2.

Figure 10-1 Number of Government Employees: Federal, State, and Local, 1929-1986

Number of employees

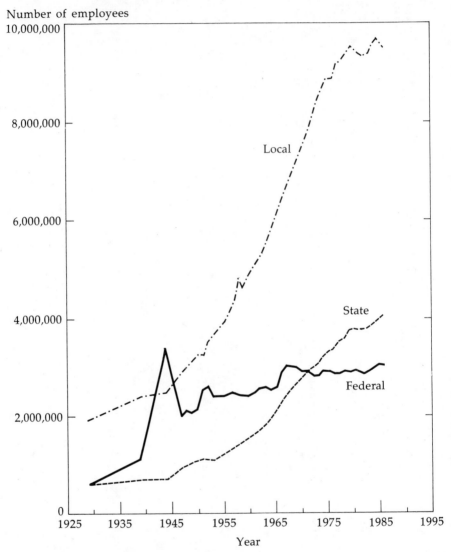

Year

Sources: 1929-1944, 1949, 1954, 1959, 1964, 1969-1986: U.S. Advisory Commission on Intergovernmental Relations, *Significant Features of Fiscal Federalism, 1988,* vol. 2 (Washington, D.C.: U.S. Advisory Commission on Intergovernmental Relations, 1988), 93; other years: *Historical Statistics of the U.S.,* 1100.

Table 10-2 Tax Capacity and Tax Efforts of the States, 1967-1985

State	1967 TC	1967 TE	1975 TC	1975 TE	1980 TC	1980 TE	1981 TC	1981 TE	1982 TC	1982 TE	1983 TC	1983 TE	1984 TC	1984 TE	1985 TC	1985 TE
Alabama	70	89	77	79	76	85	74	91	74	87	75	87	73	90	75	87
Alaska	99	104	155	76	260	166	324	184	313	180	272	166	250	141	259	128
Arizona	95	109	92	108	89	117	89	106	96	92	97	91	99	95	99	97
Arkansas	77	83	78	78	79	86	82	79	79	81	78	83	75	87	74	91
California	124	108	110	119	117	102	115	100	116	99	119	92	119	93	120	94
Colorado	104	106	106	90	113	90	113	84	121	81	122	79	121	82	118	85
Connecticut	117	93	110	99	112	100	110	103	117	99	124	96	124	99	127	99
Delaware	123	90	124	84	111	89	111	87	115	84	118	82	123	77	123	80
District of Columbia	121	90	118	94	111	131	111	145	115	145	117	146	120	139	123	138
Florida	104	84	102	74	100	74	101	73	104	72	103	75	105	74	103	76
Georgia	80	92	86	89	82	96	81	97	84	96	87	93	89	89	90	90
Hawaii	99	135	109	119	107	124	105	126	117	105	114	108	118	99	117	99
Idaho	91	105	89	90	87	88	87	87	86	85	83	87	78	91	78	90
Illinois	114	84	112	99	108	102	104	105	99	107	98	107	97	110	96	106
Indiana	99	95	98	92	92	84	91	88	89	88	86	89	87	95	87	96
Iowa	104	104	106	93	105	96	102	98	96	105	91	109	87	112	84	112
Kansas	105	96	109	85	109	88	109	87	106	88	102	92	100	95	99	96
Kentucky	80	85	85	84	83	89	82	88	82	88	79	91	77	89	78	87
Louisiana	94	90	97	87	109	78	117	77	113	82	107	81	102	81	97	93
Maine	81	105	84	104	80	111	79	113	84	107	90	100	88	105	89	104
Maryland	101	103	101	106	99	109	98	107	100	106	99	107	105	100	105	101
Massachusetts	98	121	98	129	96	135	96	134	101	119	107	112	111	105	113	106

(Table continues)

293

Table 10-2 (*Continued*)

State	1967 TC	1967 TE	1975 TC	1975 TE	1980 TC	1980 TE	1981 TC	1981 TE	1982 TC	1982 TE	1983 TC	1983 TE	1984 TC	1984 TE	1985 TC	1985 TE
Michigan	104	100	101	106	97	116	96	116	93	120	90	128	93	129	94	120
Minnesota	95	119	97	117	102	111	100	109	99	111	97	124	101	124	101	119
Mississippi	64	98	70	96	69	96	72	95	71	92	68	95	70	95	69	93
Missouri	97	86	96	84	94	84	92	81	91	82	89	87	89	85	91	84
Montana	105	93	103	92	112	92	114	92	110	97	105	94	95	101	91	107
Nebraska	110	78	106	85	97	102	97	95	97	93	101	94	93	99	94	93
Nevada	171	71	145	70	154	60	148	62	151	63	147	64	146	65	146	64
New Hampshire	110	81	102	75	97	75	95	74	100	75	108	69	110	69	112	65
New Jersey	107	97	109	103	105	112	105	112	106	113	112	109	114	109	117	105
New Mexico	94	92	97	85	107	83	114	89	115	82	108	79	103	85	99	86
New York	108	138	98	160	90	167	89	171	92	170	95	163	98	158	101	156
North Carolina	78	94	85	86	80	97	80	95	82	94	87	88	87	89	86	93
North Dakota	92	97	101	92	108	79	123	74	115	83	111	81	106	93	102	92
Ohio	100	82	104	80	97	87	94	89	92	94	89	103	90	105	91	103
Oklahoma	102	80	98	73	117	72	127	73	126	78	115	80	113	76	105	84
Oregon	106	101	100	96	103	93	99	101	99	95	95	103	94	103	95	101
Pennsylvania	91	99	98	93	93	104	90	105	89	106	88	105	88	105	89	102
Rhode Island	91	105	88	112	84	123	80	130	81	133	86	126	86	123	88	118
South Carolina	64	97	77	85	75	95	75	95	74	96	76	96	77	95	77	95
South Dakota	91	107	94	87	90	88	86	93	87	91	87	85	83	87	82	87
Tennessee	78	87	84	79	79	84	79	87	77	86	80	82	81	81	83	82
Texas	98	75	111	68	124	65	132	65	130	66	124	67	117	69	111	76
Utah	87	111	86	89	86	101	86	97	86	97	82	98	81	106	81	109
Vermont	88	119	94	108	84	104	84	105	89	102	94	95	95	94	97	93
Virginia	86	90	93	87	95	88	94	90	94	90	96	89	96	88	98	87

Washington	112	106	98	101	103	94	99	92	102	93	101	104	99	103	101	95
West Virginia	75	96	89	85	94	82	90	83	92	86	87	88	79	100	77	103
Wisconsin	94	124	98	115	95	116	91	120	87	128	87	137	89	133	89	128
Wyoming	141	79	154	70	196	74	216	73	201	105	182	113	181	105	169	108

Note: Tax capacity (TC) measures a state's underlying economic resources and speaks to the ability to raise revenue. The tax capacity is the amount of revenue each state would raise if it applied a national average set of tax rates for twenty-six commonly used tax bases. The index above is the per capita tax capacity divided by the per capita average for all states, with the index for the average set at 100. Tax effort (TE) is the ratio of a state's actual tax collections to its tax capacity. The relative index of tax effort is created by dividing each state's tax effort by the average for all states. One hundred is the index for the U.S. average. For a more complete explanation, see the source.

Source: U.S. Advisory Commission on Intergovernmental Relations, *Significant Features of Fiscal Federalism, 1988,* vol. 2, 91-92.

Table 10-3 Federal, State, and Local Taxes by Source, 1957-1986
(percent)

Jurisdiction/ year	Property taxes	Sales, gross receipts and customs	Individual and corporate income taxes	All other taxes
Federal				
1957		15.9	81.3	2.7
1967		13.7	83.0	3.3
1972		13.1	82.5	4.4
1977		9.5	86.8	3.7
1979		8.4	88.9	2.7
1981		12.0	85.5	2.5
1982		11.3	85.7	3.0
1983		11.7	85.5	2.8
1984		11.9	85.1	3.0
1985		10.8	86.4	2.8
1986		10.0	87.3	2.7
State				
1957	3.3	58.1	17.5	21.1
1967	2.7	58.2	22.4	16.8
1972	2.1	55.5	29.1	13.3
1977	2.2	51.8	34.3	11.7
1979	2.0	51.0	35.8	11.2
1981	2.0	48.6	36.8	12.6
1982	1.9	48.4	36.7	12.9
1983	1.9	48.9	36.7	12.4
1984	2.0	48.7	37.8	11.5
1985	1.9	48.9	37.7	11.5
1986	1.9	49.3	37.6	11.2
Local				
1957	86.7	7.2	1.3	4.8
1967	86.6	6.7	3.2	3.5
1972	83.7	8.6	4.5	3.3
1977	80.5	11.1	5.0	3.4
1979	77.5	13.1	5.3	4.0
1981	76.0	13.9	5.8	4.3
1982	76.0	14.3	5.9	3.9
1983	76.0	14.5	5.7	3.9
1984	75.0	14.8	5.8	4.3
1985	74.2	15.6	5.9	4.3
1986	74.0	15.6	5.9	4.5

Source: U.S. Advisory Commission on Intergovernmental Relations, *Significant Features of Fiscal Federalism, 1988,* vol. 2, 66.

Table 10-4 Flow of Federal Funds to and from the States, 1965-1984

State	1965-1967	1969-1971	1974-1976	1982-1984
Alabama	1.52	1.49	1.31	1.29
Alaska	1.01	2.76	1.82	1.01
Arizona	1.33	1.19	1.18	1.14
Arkansas	1.29	1.20	1.19	1.27
California	1.32	1.24	1.15	1.09
Colorado	1.33	1.24	1.05	0.91
Connecticut	0.92	0.88	0.92	1.02
Delaware	0.54	0.60	0.71	0.83
District of Columbia	2.16	2.99	3.23	—
Florida	1.15	1.09	0.96	1.09
Georgia	1.52	1.29	1.08	1.09
Hawaii	1.38	1.53	1.56	1.38
Idaho	1.15	0.96	1.03	1.13
Illinois	0.59	0.63	0.70	0.70
Indiana	0.75	0.81	0.74	0.83
Iowa	1.00	0.83	0.81	0.80
Kansas	1.44	1.14	0.96	1.02
Kentucky	1.32	1.14	1.17	1.10
Louisiana	1.33	1.19	1.07	0.90
Maine	1.14	1.04	1.19	1.30
Maryland	1.34	1.39	1.31	1.27
Massachusetts	0.90	0.95	1.04	1.10
Michigan	0.58	0.61	0.76	0.78
Minnesota	0.93	0.89	0.87	0.85
Mississippi	1.68	1.73	1.65	1.61
Missouri	1.09	1.10	1.12	1.43
Montana	1.53	1.18	1.17	1.07
Nebraska	1.26	0.91	0.91	0.95
Nevada	0.86	0.75	0.85	0.92
New Hampshire	0.83	0.97	0.90	0.98
New Jersey	0.71	0.75	0.79	0.70
New Mexico	1.68	1.67	1.47	1.80
New York	0.62	0.78	0.93	0.92
North Carolina	1.21	0.99	1.00	0.95
North Dakota	2.04	1.51	1.32	1.06
Ohio	0.70	0.75	0.76	0.85
Oklahoma	1.36	1.35	1.23	0.88
Oregon	0.80	0.84	0.91	0.89
Pennsylvania	0.71	0.85	0.95	0.96
Rhode Island	1.17	1.14	1.07	1.05
South Carolina	1.58	1.25	1.22	1.25
South Dakota	1.67	1.26	1.33	1.24

(Table continues)

Table 10-4 *(Continued)*

State	1965-1967	1969-1971	1974-1976	1982-1984
Tennessee	1.12	1.01	0.98	1.20
Texas	1.35	1.31	0.96	0.78
Utah	1.32	1.53	1.28	1.27
Vermont	1.11	1.02	1.16	1.10
Virginia	1.73	1.68	1.46	1.52
Washington	1.24	1.10	1.20	1.09
West Virginia	1.02	1.09	1.21	1.07
Wisconsin	0.67	0.71	0.76	0.82
Wyoming	1.50	1.10	1.00	0.75

Note: "—" indicates not available. Numbers are the estimated amount of federal expenditures in each state for each $100 of federal taxes paid by residents of each state. Includes all federal expenditures that can be allocated by state. All figures adjusted proportionally so that overall there is $1.00 of revenue for each $1.00 of expenditure. Three-year averages for expenditures and revenue were used to ensure that unusually high or low figures in a particular state in any single year would not unduly influence the flow-of-fund ratios.

Source: U.S. Advisory Commission on Intergovernmental Relations, *Significant Features of Fiscal Federalism, 1985-86,* 178.

Table 10-5 Federal Grants-in-Aid Outlays, 1950-1994

		Federal grants as a percentage of			
		Federal outlays[a]		State and local	Gross
	Total grants-in-aid		Domestic	expendi-	national
Year	(billions)	Total	programs[b]	tures[c]	product
1950	$2.3	5.3	11.6	10.4	0.8
1955	3.2	4.7	17.2	10.1	0.8
1960	7.0	7.6	20.6	14.6	1.4
1965	10.9	9.2	20.3	15.2	1.6
1970	24.1	12.3	25.3	19.2	2.4
1975	49.8	15.0	23.1	22.7	3.3
1980	91.5	15.5	23.3	25.8	3.4
1981	94.8	14.0	21.6	24.6	3.2
1982	88.2	11.8	19.0	21.6	2.8
1983	92.5	11.4	18.6	21.3	2.8
1984	97.6	11.5	19.6	20.9	2.6
1985	105.9	11.2	19.3	20.9	2.7
1986	112.4	11.3	19.8	20.5	2.7
1987	108.4	10.8	19.0	18.3	2.4
1988	115.3	10.8	18.9	18.2	2.4
1989 est.	123.6	10.9	18.7	—	2.4
1990 est.	123.6	10.7	18.7	—	2.3
1991 est.	126.1	10.4	17.8	—	2.2
1992 est.	129.7	10.4	17.4	—	2.1
1993 est.	134.0	10.5	17.2	—	2.0
1994 est.	138.1	10.5	17.1	—	2.0

Note: "—" indicates not available. Fiscal years.
[a] Includes off-budget outlays; all grants are on-budget.
[b] Excludes outlays for national defense, international affairs, and net interest.
[c] As defined in the national income and product accounts.

Source: Office of Management and Budget, *Budget of the United States Government, Fiscal Year 1990, Special Analyses* (Washington, D.C.: U.S. Government Printing Office, 1989), Table H-7.

Table 10-6   Fiscal Dependency of Lower Levels on Higher Levels of Government, 1955-1986 (percent)

| Year | Intergovernmental revenue as a percentage of general revenue from own sources | | |
	State from federal	Local from federal[a]	Local from state[b]
1955	20.9	2.5	40.6
1960[c]	31.0	2.6	41.6
1965[c]	32.3	3.6	43.3
1970[c]	33.5	5.1	52.4
1972	37.9	7.1	54.5
1974	35.5	13.3	58.1
1975	37.3	12.9	60.5
1976	39.1	14.6	60.3
1977	37.9	16.3	59.1
1978	37.0	17.5	58.4
1979	36.1	17.6	63.3
1980	36.6	16.3	62.5
1981	36.2	15.4	61.1
1982	32.1	12.8	58.2
1983	31.7	11.7	54.9
1984	30.5	10.6	53.9
1985	30.7	10.1	53.8
1986	31.4	8.8	54.3

[a] Local governments include townships and special districts.
[b] Includes indirect federal aid passed through the states; duplicate intergovernmental transfers are excluded.
[c] Partially estimated.

Source: U.S. Advisory Commission on Intergovernmental Relations, *Significant Features of Fiscal Federalism, 1988,* vol. 2, 81.

Table 10-7 Variations in Local Dependency on State Aid, 1986-1987 (percent)

State	Percentage	State	Percentage
1. New Mexico	49.8	27. Michigan	32.9
2. West Virginia	44.9	28. Utah	32.9
3. California	44.2	29. Oklahoma	32.7
4. Delaware	43.6	30. Maine	32.1
5. North Carolina	43.3	31. Pennsylvania	31.1
6. Wisconsin	42.1	32. Georgia	30.7
7. Kentucky	41.3	33. Louisiana	30.0
8. Washington	40.6	34. Florida	28.8
9. Arkansas	39.7	35. Tennessee	28.5
10. Indiana	39.1	36. Rhode Island	28.2
11. Massachusetts	39.0	37. Missouri	27.5
12. Idaho	38.9	38. Maryland	27.4
13. Minnesota	38.9	39. Illinois	27.0
14. Mississippi	38.9	40. Vermont	26.5
15. Alaska	37.9	41. Connecticut	25.0
16. North Dakota	37.4	42. Montana	24.9
17. Nevada	37.2	43. Colorado	24.5
18. Arizona	36.3	44. Texas	24.5
19. South Carolina	35.3	45. Oregon	24.3
20. New York	35.0	46. South Dakota	22.0
21. Iowa	34.2	47. Kansas	21.0
22. Wyoming	34.1	48. Nebraska	19.5
23. Ohio	34.0	49. New Hampshire	12.5
24. New Jersey	33.6	50. Hawaii	9.4
25. Alabama	33.5		
26. Virginia	33.4	Total	33.9

Note: Percentages reflect state transfers (including "pull-through" monies from the federal government) as a percentage of total local revenues.

Source: U.S. Bureau of the Census, *Governmental Finances in 1986-87* (Washington, D.C.: U.S. Government Printing Office, 1988), 22-23.

Table 10-8 Federal Grants-in-Aid to State and Local Governments by Function, 1940-1994 (percent)

Function	1940	1945	1950	1955	1960	1965	1970	1975	1980	1985	1988	1990 (est.)	1994 (est.)
Health	2	11	5	4	3	6	16	18	17	23	28	31	38
Income security	39	52	59	54	38	32	24	19	20	26	27	27	27
Education, training, employment, and social services	3	14	7	10	8	10	27	24	24	17	17	18	17
Transportation	19	4	21	19	43	38	19	12	14	16	16	15	12
Natural resources and environment	-	1	1	1	2	2	2	5	6	4	3	3	2
Community and regional development	32	14	-	2	2	6	7	6	7	5	4	4	2
General purpose fiscal assistance	1	1	2	3	2	2	2	14	9	7	2	2	1
Agriculture	3	3	5	7	4	5	3	1	1	2	2	1	1
Other	1	-	-	-	-	-	-	1	2	-	-	-	-
Total	100	100	100	100	102	101	100	100	100	100	99	101	100

Note: "-" indicates 0.5 percent or less.

Source: Office of Management and Budget, *Budget of the U.S. Government, Fiscal Year 1990, Historical Tables* (Washington, D.C.: U.S. Government Printing Office, 1989), Table 12-2, 243-249.

Table 10-9 State Fiscal Discipline Measures

State	Tax and expenditure limitations	Balanced budget requirement	Require super-majority vote to pass tax	Index income tax	Gubernatorial line-item veto	Fiscal note review procedure	Program evaluation and sunset	"Rainy day" funds
Alabama		X			X	X	X	
Alaska	X	X			X		X	X
Arizona	X	X		X	X	X	X	X
Arkansas		X	X		X	X		
California	X	X	X	X	X	X		X
Colorado	X	X	X	X	X	X		X
Connecticut		X			X	X	X	X
Delaware		X	X		X		X	X
Florida		X	X		X	X		X
Georgia		X			X	X	X	X
Hawaii	X	X			X	X	X	X
Idaho	X	X			X			
Illinois	X	X			X	X	X	X
Indiana		X			X	X	X	X
Iowa		X		X	X	X		
Kansas		X			X	X		
Kentucky	X	X			X	X	X	X
Louisiana	X	X	X		X	X		X
Maine		X		X	X		X	
Maryland		X			X	X	X	
Massachusetts		X			X	X	X	
Michigan	X	X			X			
Minnesota		X		X	X	X		X
Mississippi		X	X		X	X		X
Missouri	X	X			X	X		X
Montana	X	X		X	X	X	X	X

(Table continues)

303

Table 10-9 (Continued)

State	Tax and expenditure limitations	Balanced budget requirement	Require super-majority vote to pass tax	Index income tax	Gubernatorial line-item veto	Fiscal note review procedure	Program evaluation and sunset	"Rainy day" funds
Nebraska		x			x	x		x
Nevada	x	x				x		
New Hampshire		x				x	x	
New Jersey		x			x	x		
New Mexico		x			x	x	x	x
New York		x			x			x
North Carolina		x			x	x		
North Dakota		x			x	x		x
Ohio		x			x	x		x
Oklahoma		x			x		x	
Oregon	x	x		x	x	x	x	
Pennsylvania		x			x	x	x	x
Rhode Island	x	x			x	x	x	x
South Carolina	x	x	x	x	x	x	x	x
South Dakota		x			x	x		
Tennessee	x	x			x	x	x	x
Texas	x	x			x	x	x	
Utah	x	x			x	x	x	
Vermont							x	
Virginia		x			x	x		
Washington	x	x			x	x	x	x
West Virginia		x		x	x	x	x	x
Wisconsin		x			x	x	x	
Wyoming		x			x	x	x	x
Total	18	49	7	10	43	41	29	24

Note: Considerable detail about each mechanism can be found in the source.

Source: U.S. Advisory Commission on Intergovernmental Relations, *Significant Features of Fiscal Federalism, 1985-86,* 145; 1988, vol. 2, 135.

Table 10-10 State Lottery Revenues, 1980 and 1986

State/year	Date established	Gross revenue (millions)	Net proceeds (millions)	Net proceeds as a percentage of state revenue[a]	Annual bet per capita	Where the revenues go
Arizona	July 1981					
1980		-	-	-	-	
1986		$113.6	$42.2	1.1	$34.25	Transportation
California	October 1985					
1980		-	-	-	-	
1986		1,675.7	685.6	1.8	62.11	Education
Colorado	January 1983					
1980		-	-	-	-	Parks and recreation,
1986		102.4	26.1	0.8	31.34	capital construction
Connecticut	February 1972					
1980		129.9	60.8	2.6	41.80	General fund
1986		406.6	165.6	3.2	127.50	
Delaware	October 1975					
1980		15.9	6.3	0.9	26.79	General fund
1986		37.7	15.5	1.2	59.51	
Illinois	July 1974					
1980		91.0	35.8	0.4	7.97	Education
1986		1,199.9	545.1	4.5	103.86	
Iowa	August 1985					
1980		-	-	-	-	
1986		77.2	26.3	0.8	27.08	Economic development

(Table continues)

305

Table 10-10 (Continued)

State/year	Date established	Gross revenue (millions)	Net proceeds (millions)	Net proceeds as a percentage of state revenue[a]	Annual bet per capita	Where the revenues go
Maine	June 1974					
1980		$6.0	$0.7	[b]	$5.36	General fund
1986		36.2	13.7	1.0	30.82	
Maryland	May 1973					
1980		372.3	185.4	5.1	88.32	General fund
1986		689.5	323.4	5.3	154.49	
Massachusetts	March 1972					
1980		192.5	92.5	2.0	33.55	Local government
1986		910.9	318.4	3.3	156.19	
Michigan	November 1972					
1980		487.9	236.0	3.2	52.70	Education
1986		931.0	403.2	3.3	101.80	
Missouri	January 1986					
1980		-	-	-	-	General fund
1986		196.5	80.0	1.7	38.79	
New Hampshire	March 1964					
1980		9.0	3.7	0.9	9.72	Education
1986		33.8	10.2	1.2	32.91	
New Jersey	January 1970					
1980		331.9	142.4	2.7	45.07	Education, institutions
1986		937.1	416.1	3.6	122.98	
New York	1967–1975, September 1976					
1980		182.8	83.3	0.6	10.41	Education
1986		1,204.7	567.2	2.1	67.79	

State / Year	Start date					Purpose
Ohio	August 1974					
1980		57.2	35.7	0.6	5.30	
1986		888.3	380.9	3.2	82.62	Education
Oregon	April 1985					
1980		-	-	-	-	
1986		83.1	21.3	0.7	30.80	Economic development
Pennsylvania	March 1972					
1980		194.7	158.0	1.9	16.40	
1986		1,234.2	539.2	4.1	103.81	Senior citizens programs
Rhode Island	May 1974					
1980		33.4	16.6	2.0	35.24	
1986		50.0	20.7	1.4	51.24	General fund
Vermont	February 1978					
1980		2.9	0.2	b	5.58	
1986		11.8	2.7	0.4	21.79	General fund
Washington	November 1982					
1980		-	-	-	-	
1986		181.5	65.0	1.0	40.67	General fund
Washington, D.C.	August 1982					
1980		-	-	-	-	
1986		112.3	41.4	2.0	179.39	General fund
West Virginia	January 1986					
1980		-	-	-	-	
1986		53.0	22.1	1.0	27.60	General fund

Note: "-" indicates lottery not in operation. In addition to the states listed above, in which lotteries were in operation in 1986, Florida, Idaho, Kansas, Kentucky, Minnesota, Montana, South Dakota, Virginia, and Wisconsin have adopted lotteries.

[a] Excludes federal grants-in-aid.

[b] Less than one-tenth of one percent.

Source: U.S. Advisory Commission on Intergovernmental Relations, *Significant Features of Fiscal Federalism, 1985–86,* 126; *1988,* vol. 2, 88–90.

Figure 10-2   Government Spending as a Percentage of GNP, 1929-1988

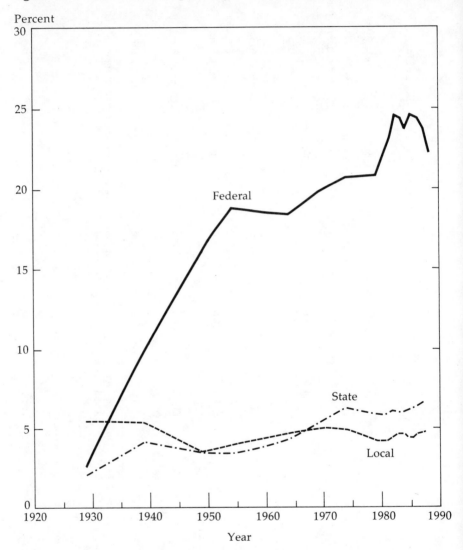

Percent

Year

Note: State and local figures unavailable for 1988.

Sources: 1929-1987: U.S. Advisory Commission on Intergovernmental Relations, *Significant Features of Fiscal Federalism, 1988,* vol. 2, 22-23; 1988: Office of Management and Budget, *Budget of the U.S. Government, Fiscal Year 1990, Historical Tables,* Table 15-3, 361-362.

Table 10-11 State and Local Government Expenditures by Function, 1902-1987 (percent)

Function	1902	1940	1952	1962	1972	1977	1982	1986	1987
Education	23.3	23.5	27.0	31.5	34.6	31.7	29.4	29.4	29.3
Highways	16.0	14.0	15.1	14.7	10.0	7.1	6.6	6.9	6.8
Public welfare	3.4	10.3	9.0	7.2	11.1	11.1	11.1	10.4	10.5
Health	1.6	1.4	1.4	0.9	1.4	1.7	2.0	2.2	2.2
Hospitals	3.9	4.0	5.7	5.2	5.5	5.4	5.8	5.3	5.2
Police protection	4.6	3.2	3.0	3.0	3.2	3.2	3.2	3.2	3.2
Fire protection	3.7	2.1	1.9	1.6	1.4	1.4	1.3	1.3	1.4
Natural resources	0.8	1.9	2.5	1.9	1.6	1.3	1.3	1.3	1.3
Corrections	—	—	1.1	1.1	1.1	1.3	1.6	2.1	2.2
Sanitation and sewerage	4.7	1.8	3.2	2.8	2.5	2.9	2.9	2.7	2.8
Housing and community development	—	—	2.0	1.6	1.4	1.0	1.6	1.6	1.5
Parks and recreation	2.6	1.4	1.0	1.3	1.2	1.5	1.4	1.4	1.4
Financial administration	12.9	5.0	3.9	1.5	1.3	1.4	1.5	1.7	1.7
Other government administration				1.8	1.8	1.9	2.7	2.8	2.9
Social insurance administration									
Interest on general debt	6.2	0.6	0.6	0.6	0.6	0.5	0.4	0.4	0.4
Utilities	7.5	5.8	1.8	2.9	3.2	3.5	3.8	5.2	5.4
Liquor store expenditures	—	11.8	9.9	7.7	6.0	7.5	9.2	8.7	8.5
Insurance trust expenditure	—	6.1	5.5	6.9	5.5	8.1	7.5	6.5	6.6
Other	8.9	5.0	4.2	4.8	6.7	7.7	6.7	6.6	6.8
Total direct expenditure (millions)	$1,095	$11,240	$30,863	$70,547	$190,496	$324,554	$524,817	$716,211	$772,864

Note: "—" indicates not available. For 1902-1952, financial administration includes other government administration. For 1902-1982, utilities includes liquor store expenditures.

Sources: U.S. Bureau of the Census, *Census of Governments, 1982* (Washington, D.C.: U.S. Government Printing Office, 1985), 32-33; U.S. Bureau of the Census, *Governmental Finances in 1985-86* (Washington, D.C.: U.S. Government Printing Office, 1987), 13; *1986-87*, 13.

Figure 10-3   Surpluses and Deficits in Government Finances, 1947-1988

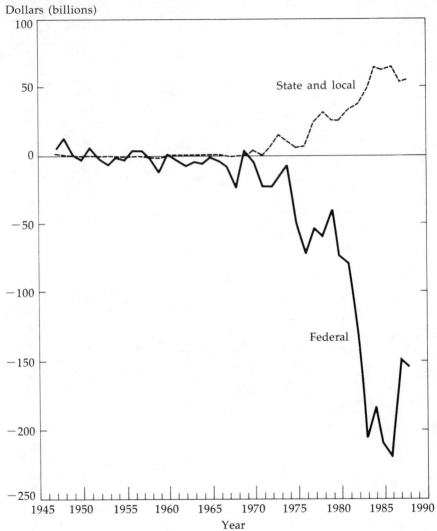

Source: Office of Management and Budget, *Budget of the U.S. Government, Fiscal Year 1990, Historical Tables,* Table 15-6, 367-368.

Figure 10-4 State and Local Government Surpluses Compared to Federal Grants-in-Aid, 1947-1988

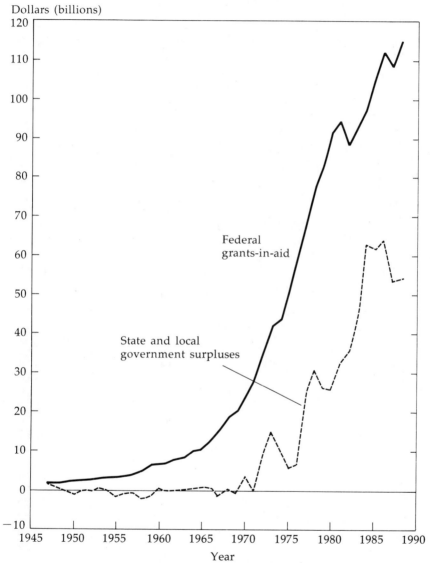

Dollars (billions)

Federal grants-in-aid

State and local government surpluses

Year

Source: Office of Management and Budget, *Budget of the U.S. Government, Fiscal Year 1990, Historical Tables*, Table 12-1 (grants-in-aid), 239-240, and Table 15-6 (surpluses), 367-368.

Table 10-12 Benefits (1988) and Recipients (1986) of Aid to Families with Dependent Children (AFDC) and Food Stamps by State

State	Maximum AFDC grant (per month)[a]	Food stamp benefit (per month)[b]	Combined benefits as a percentage of 1987 poverty threshold[c]	Public aid recipients (percentage of population)	Food stamp recipients (percentage of population)
Alabama	$118	$228	46	6.8	11.9
Alaska	779	201	104	4.0	5.1
Arizona	293	219	68	3.3	6.1
Arkansas	202	228	57	5.9	9.7
California	633	117	99	8.7	6.0
Colorado	356	201	74	3.5	5.6
Connecticut	601	127	96	4.5	3.9
Delaware	319	212	70	4.6	4.9
District of Columbia	379	194	76	11.3	10.4
Florida	275	225	66	3.9	5.2
Georgia	263	228	65	6.4	8.1
Hawaii	515	308	95	5.4	8.4
Idaho	304	216	69	2.6	5.6
Illinois	342[d]	210	73	7.6	9.5
Indiana	288	221	67	3.8	6.3
Iowa	381	193	76	5.4	7.2
Kansas	409[d]	195	80	3.7	4.8
Kentucky	207	228	58	7.0	13.9
Louisiana	190	228	55	8.2	15.6
Maine	416	183	79	6.9	8.9
Maryland	359[d]	217	76	5.5	5.9
Massachusetts	510	154	88	5.9	5.4
Michigan[e]	528[d]	171	93	8.7	9.8
Minnesota	532	148	90	4.6	5.5
Mississippi	120	228	46	10.4	18.9
Missouri	282	223	67	5.5	7.4
Montana	359	200	74	4.2	7.1
Nebraska	350	202	73	3.9	5.9
Nevada	325	210	71	2.5	3.6
New Hampshire	486	162	86	1.9	2.0
New Jersey	424[d]	188	81	5.8	5.2
New Mexico	264	228	65	5.3	10.3
New York[f]	539[d]	162	93	8.2	9.4
North Carolina	266	228	65	5.0	6.7
North Dakota	371	196	75	3.0	5.2
Ohio	309[d]	219	70	7.5	10.3

(Table continues)

Table 10-12   *(Continued)*

State	Maximum AFDC grant (per month)[a]	Food stamp benefit (per month)[b]	Combined benefits as a percentage of 1987 poverty threshold[c]	Public aid recipients (percentage of population)	Food stamp recipients (percentage of population)
Oklahoma	$310	$214	69	4.5	8.1
Oregon	412[d]	219	84	4.2	8.0
Pennsylvania	402	187	78	6.3	8.4
Rhode Island	503[d]	195	92	6.2	6.5
South Carolina	200	228	57	6.5	9.2
South Dakota	366	198	75	3.7	7.5
Tennessee	159	228	51	6.1	10.4
Texas	184	228	55	4.1	8.2
Utah	376	195	76	3.0	4.8
Vermont	603	126	97	5.6	6.3
Virginia	354	201	74	4.1	5.7
Washington	492[d]	174	88	5.6	6.6
West Virginia	249	228	63	8.2	13.9
Wisconsin	517	152	89	7.8	7.5
Wyoming	360	199	74	2.7	5.5

Note: The first two columns are maximum potential AFDC and food stamp benefits for a one-parent family of three persons. In most states the AFDC and food stamps amounts apply also to two-parent families of three (where the second parent is incapacitated or, as permitted in almost half the states, unemployed). Some, however, increase benefits for such families.

[a] In states with area differentials, figure shown is for areas with highest benefit.

[b] Food stamp benefits are based on maximum AFDC benefits shown. For assumptions about deductions, see the source.

[c] Based on the Census Bureau's 1987 poverty threshold for a family of three persons, $9,056, converted to a monthly rate of $755. For Alaska, this threshold was increased by 25 percent; for Hawaii, by 15 percent, following the practice of the Office of Management and Budget.

[d] Part of the AFDC cash benefit has been designated as energy aid and is disregarded by the state in calculating food stamp benefits. The amounts disregarded vary by state. See the source for further details.

[e] Wayne County only.

[f] New York City only.

Sources: Benefits: U.S. Congress, House, *Background Material and Data on Programs Within the Jurisdiction of the Committee on Ways and Means, 1988 Edition,* 100th Cong., 2d session, March 24, 1988 (Washington, D.C.: U.S. Government Printing Office, 1988), 408-410; recipients: *Statistical Abstract of the U.S., 1988* (Washington, D.C.: U.S. Government Printing Office, 1987), xxii.

Questions

1. Which component of local government accounts for the largest decline in the number of governments between 1942 and 1982 (Table 10-1)? Federal, state, local—which level had the greatest numerical increase in employees from 1984 to 1986? The greatest percentage increase between 1942 and 1986?

2. Surely Wyoming cannot raise more revenue than large states such as California and New York. Yet Wyoming consistently has one of the greatest tax capacities of the fifty states (Table 10-2). How do you explain this apparent anomaly? (Hint: read the table note.)

3. Do tax capacity and tax effort "go together"; specifically, for 1985 where do the five highest states (exclude Washington, D.C.) in tax capacity rank in terms of tax effort?

4. Describe the differences in the sources of federal, state, and local taxes (Table 10-3). How has the source of state taxes changed over the period shown?

5. Which state received the most federal funds relative to federal taxes in 1982-1984 (Table 10-4)? The least? Find the states with a value of 1.5 or more in 1965-1967. What happened to their value in 1982-1984? What about states with a value of .75 or below? What could account for this pattern?

6. From 1983 to 1984 and from 1985 to 1986, federal grants went up as a percentage of federal outlays but went down as a percentage of state and local expenditures (Table 10-5). What does this imply about federal versus state and local expenditures?

7. There has been great growth in intergovernmental revenue since 1955 (despite the decline since the mid- to late-1970s) (Table 10-6). Say in different words what this growth means. What social or political implications might follow from this growth?

8. Are states in which localities are most dependent on state aid (Table 10-7) typically those states making the greatest tax effort (Table 10-2)?

9. In which function has there been the largest increase in federal grants-in-aid (Table 10-8)?

10. How many states have all of the fiscal discipline mechanisms listed in Table 10-9? How many states have none? Indexing income taxes means that as prices go up, tax brackets change so that individuals whose income goes up only as much as prices will not pay any more in taxes. In what way is this a fiscal discipline measure?

11. What is the highest percentage of state revenue raised by lottery proceeds (Table 10-10)? In what state and year was this? Are lotteries becoming more or less successful as fund raisers? Explain your reasoning.

12. Of the "program" expenditures (education through parks and recreation) for which function was the ratio of 1987 to 1962 expenditures the greatest (Table 10-11)? Between 1987 and 1902? Which function saw the biggest decline between 1902 and 1987?

13. Do the farm belt states of Illinois, Iowa, Minnesota, Kansas, Nebraska, South Dakota, and North Dakota have lower percentages of food stamp recipients than other states do (Table 10-12)? Which farm state has the higher percentage of food stamp recipients? Why?

11

Foreign and Military Policy

Even if one sought to understand only U.S. domestic politics, data on international relations would be essential. In the 1960 presidential campaign, for example, John Kennedy made the "missile gap" a major issue: the United States was falling behind the Soviet Union in its missile arsenal, and this imperiled the defense of the free world. The actual existence of that missile gap has been disputed, but the charge fit in with Kennedy's pledge to get the country moving again and played well to the public in the aftermath of Sputnik and the U-2 incident. Similarly, Ronald Reagan made increased military spending a cornerstone of his campaign platform in 1980.

One might think that statistics relating to foreign policy, especially the military aspects, are difficult or impossible to find, that secrecy prevents publication of important information about our defense capabilities. There are instances in which this is the case. Performance capabilities of spy satellites and the "stealth" bomber are understandably kept secret. There are also secret diplomatic and military initiatives undertaken by the Central Intelligence Agency and other organizations that the public learns about only when something goes wrong. The sale of weapons to Iran while the United States was publicly declaring that it would have nothing to do with that country, and the use of profits from these sales to support the Nicaraguan Contras, is a case in point.

Despite these examples and the obvious need for secrecy in defense-related areas, a surprisingly wide array of data is available, in part because details about military hardware are not the only kinds of relevant information. In fact, the first table in this chapter deals with public opinion data. As was evident during the 1960s, public opinion about foreign policy is extraordinarily relevant and powerful informa-

316

tion. Public opinion on U.S involvement in Vietnam reveals a great deal about why President Lyndon Johnson declined to run for reelection in 1968 and why U.S. forces began to withdraw from Vietnam shortly thereafter (Figure 11-1). Public opinion on defense spending has been politically relevant, although the pattern of changes in the late 1970s and 1980s suggests that Ronald Reagan was leading as well as responding to changes in public sentiments (Table 11-11).

A great deal of other information closely relates to both defense and domestic policy, and this kind of data is emphasized here. Defense spending, for example, involves more than whether the United States has spent enough to defend itself. Elementary economics courses use the phrase "guns or butter" to express the tradeoff between defense spending and nondefense spending. Every dollar spent for weaponry means a dollar less that can be spent for social programs, tax reductions, and other politically worthy causes. Therefore information on defense spending (Table 11-10) is doubly relevant.

In presenting information about defense spending, two elements arise. The first is the concept of "constant" versus "current" dollars. Current dollars are what people deal with every day. The price asked for goods is the price paid; whether the price has gone up more or less than other prices is not especially relevant. People may be aware that prices of some goods have gone up (for example, oil and gasoline in the 1970s) or down (for example, many electronic products) more than others, but the price quoted is what is most significant. Constant dollars, in contrast, take into account what has happened to prices more generally (see Table 13-2 for the Consumer Price Index). Thus, for example, most food clearly costs more in current dollars than it did years ago; in the 1960s one never heard of a loaf of bread that cost $1.00. Yet relative to other prices, the cost of bread has been reduced. Its price may have only doubled in a given period of time while other prices have tripled. In a very meaningful sense, therefore, bread and other foods are cheaper than they used to be; the "real" cost of bread has been reduced.

Another, perhaps simpler, way to express this is to say that constant dollar calculations take inflation into account. For defense spending, therefore, the question is: after taking inflation into account, has spending increased? If spending has risen only as fast as inflation, the new budget will buy only as much as the previous budget, even though nominally, that is, in current dollars, it is larger. Because this issue of real versus current dollars is so significant, Table 11-10 and many of the tables in Chapter 13 express expenditures both ways.

The second new element in presenting information about defense spending is that it is especially relevant to see what other countries are doing as well. Whether the United States is spending a lot or a little is a relative question. If foreign adversaries raise their spending, then perhaps the United States must do the same. As a consequence, information is presented on worldwide military expenditures (Table 11-12) even though the focus in this volume is on the United States.

Economic and social dimensions are also relevant to U.S. foreign and military policy, and data about these are widely available. The slippage of the U.S. trade balance (Table 11-16) and the increasing foreign investment in the United States and U.S. investment abroad (Table 11-15) are two aspects of the economic context of recent foreign policy discussions. Foreign aid, whether in the form of military (Table 11-13) or nonmilitary (Table 11-14) assistance, is another part of economic foreign policy. Immigration policy has social and economic implications, and changes in the flow of immigrants, along with future prospects, make it a most significant aspect of U.S. foreign relations (Table 11-17).

The statistical picture would be incomplete without information about military weapons and forces. Here, too, information is needed about more than just the United States. Therefore, one of many possible comparisons between Soviet and American military strength is presented (Table 11-5) as well as existing bilateral and multilateral arms control agreements (Table 11-4). In both a contemporary and historical vein, information is given about military conflicts and personnel. Even here, however, it is impossible to avoid domestic aspects of these data. One of the tables on military personnel reports information by sex, race, and Hispanic origin (Table 11-9). This classification of personnel is obviously more relevant to U.S. domestic policy than to the question of whether the country is sufficiently prepared to meet a challenge from abroad.

The emergence of the United States as a world power in the twentieth century has elevated the political significance of international relations so that no overview of American politics would be complete without a look at foreign and military policy. Foreign policy has often proved critical in domestic politics, and that accounts for the array of numbers presented here.

Table 11-1   Public Opinion on U.S. Involvement in World Affairs, 1945-1988 (percent)

Date	Active part	Stay out	No opinion
October 1945	70	19	11
September 1947	65	26	9
September 1949	67	25	8
November 1950	64	25	11
December 1950	66	25	9
October 1952	68	23	9
February 1953	73	22	5
September 1953	71	21	8
April 1954	69	25	6
March 1955	72	21	7
November 1956	71	25	4
June 1965	79	16	5
March 1973	66	31	3
March 1975	61	36	4
March 1976	63	32	5
March 1978	64	32	4
December 1978	59	29	12
March 1982	61	34	5
November 1982	53	35	12
March 1983	65	31	4
March 1984	65	29	6
March 1985	70	27	2
March 1986	65	32	4
March 1988	65	32	4

Note: Question: "Do you think it would be best for the future of this country if we take an active part in world affairs, or if we stay out of world affairs?"

Sources: 1945, 1947, November 1950, December 1978, November 1982: Gallup surveys; 1949, December 1950, 1952-1965: National Opinion Research Center; all others: General Social Survey, National Opinion Research Center, University of Chicago.

Table 11-2   U.S. Diplomatic and Consular Posts, 1781-1988

Year	Diplomatic	Consular
1781	4	3
1790	2	10
1800	6	52
1810	4	60
1820	7	83
1830	15	141
1840	20	152
1850	27	197
1860	33	282
1870	36	318
1880	35	303
1890	41	323
1900	41	318
1910	48	324
1920	45	368
1930	57	299
1940	58	264
1950	74	179
1960	99	166
1970	117	122
1980	133	100
1988	168	102

Note: 1988 figures are as of May. For that year, diplomatic posts include embassies, countries with ambassadors without physical missions, branch offices, missions, and interest sections. Consular posts include consulates general and consulates.

Source: U.S. Department of State, Office of Public Communication, *A Short History of the U.S. Department of State 1781-1981* (Washington, D.C.: U.S. Government Printing Office, 1981), 35. Updated from U.S. Department of State, *Key Officers of Foreign Service Posts* (Washington, D.C.: U.S. Government Printing Office, May 1988), vii.

Table 11-3 U.S.-Soviet Summit Meetings, 1945-1988

Date	Location	Leaders	Topic
July-August 1945	Potsdam	President Harry S Truman, Soviet leader Josef Stalin, British prime ministers Winston Churchill and Clement R. Attlee	Partition and control of Germany
July 1955	Geneva	President Dwight D. Eisenhower, Soviet leader Nikolai A. Bulganin, British prime minister Anthony Eden, French premier Edgar Faure	Reunification of Germany, disarmament, European security
September 1959	Camp David, Md.	President Dwight D. Eisenhower, Soviet leader Nikita S. Khrushchev	Berlin problem
May 1960	Paris	President Dwight D. Eisenhower, Soviet leader Nikita S. Khrushchev, French president Charles de Gaulle, British prime minister Harold Macmillan	U-2 incident
June 1961	Vienna	President John F. Kennedy, Soviet leader Nikita S. Khrushchev	Berlin problem
June 1967	Glassboro, N.J.	President Lyndon B. Johnson, Soviet leader Aleksei N. Kosygin	Middle East
May 1972	Moscow	President Richard M. Nixon, Soviet leader Leonid I. Brezhnev	SALT I, antiballistic missile limitations
June 1973	Washington, D.C.	President Richard M. Nixon, Soviet leader Leonid I. Brezhnev	Détente
June-July 1974	Moscow and Yalta	President Richard M. Nixon, Soviet leader Leonid I. Brezhnev	Arms control
November 1974	Vladivostok	President Gerald R. Ford, Soviet leader Leonid I. Brezhnev	Arms control
June 1979	Vienna	President Jimmy Carter, Soviet leader Leonid I. Brezhnev	SALT II

(Table continues)

Table 11-3 *(Continued)*

Date	Location	Leaders	Topic
November 1985	Geneva	President Ronald Reagan, Soviet leader Mikhail Gorbachev	Arms control
October 1986	Reykjavik	President Ronald Reagan, Soviet leader Mikhail Gorbachev	Arms control
December 1987	Washington, D.C.	President Ronald Reagan, Soviet leader Mikhail Gorbachev	Arms control
May 1988	Moscow	President Ronald Reagan, Soviet leader Mikhail Gorbachev	Human rights Arms control
December 1988	New York	President Ronald Reagan, Soviet leader Mikhail Gorbachev	[a]

[a] Short meeting after Gorbachev's U.N. address, with Reagan and Vice President/President-Elect George Bush. Gorbachev announced unilateral troop reductions.

Source: Congressional Quarterly Weekly Report (1987), 667; updated by the editors.

Table 11-4 Arms Control and Disarmament Agreements

Issue	Participants
Nuclear weapons	
To prevent the spread of nuclear weapons	
Antarctic Treaty, 1959	32 states[a]
Outer Space Treaty, 1967	125 states[a]
Latin American Nuclear-Free Zone	
Treaty, 1967	31 states[a]
Nonproliferation Treaty, 1968	136 states[a]
Seabed Treaty, 1971	108 states[a]
To reduce the risk of nuclear war	
Hot Line and Modernization	
Agreements, 1963	United States and Soviet Union
Accidents Measures Agreement, 1971	United States and Soviet Union
Prevention of Nuclear War Agreement,	
1973	United States and Soviet Union
To limit nuclear testing	
Limited Test Ban Treaty, 1963	127 states[a]
Threshold Test Ban Treaty, 1974[b]	United States and Soviet Union
Peaceful Nuclear Explosions Treaty,	
1976[b]	United States and Soviet Union
To limit nuclear weapons	
ABM Treaty (SALT I) and Protocol, 1972	United States and Soviet Union
SALT I Interim Agreement, 1972[c]	United States and Soviet Union
SALT II, 1979[d]	United States and Soviet Union
Intermediate Range Nuclear Force	
(INF) Missiles Treaty, 1988	United States and Soviet Union
Other weapons	
To prohibit use of gas	
Geneva Protocol, 1925	130 states
To prohibit biological weapons	
Biological Weapons Convention, 1972	131 states
To prohibit techniques changing the	
environment	
Environmental Modification	
Convention, 1977	73 states
To control use of inhumane weapons	
Inhumane Weapons Convention, 1981	22 states[e]
To reduce risk of war	
Notification of Military Activities, 1986	35 states

[a] Number of parties and signatories as of December 1986.
[b] Not yet ratified.
[c] Expired by its terms on October 3, 1977.
[d] Never ratified. If the treaty had entered into force, it would have expired by its terms on December 31, 1985.
[e] Convention entered into force December 1983. The United States is not a signatory.

Sources: U.S. Arms Control and Disarmament Agency, *World Military Expenditures and Arms Transfers* (Washington, D.C.: U.S. Government Printing Office, 1983), 28, and unpublished data from Arms Control and Disarmament Agency.

Table 11-5 Strategic Offensive Forces of the Superpowers, 1988

	United States		Soviet Union	
Classification	Weapon	Number	Weapon	Number
ICBMs	Minuteman II	450	SS-11	420
	Minuteman III	523	SS-13	60
	Peacekeeper	27	SS-17	145
			SS-18	308
			SS-19	350
			SS-25	~100
Total		1,000		~1,380
SLBMs	Poseidon (C-3)	256	SS-N-5	39
	Trident 1 (C-4)[a]	384	SS-N-6	256
			SS-N-8	286
			SS-N-17	12
			SS-N-18	224
			SS-N-20[a]	100
			SS-N-23[a]	64
Total		640		981
Bombers	B-52G	167	Bear	160
	B-52H	96	Bison	15
	FB-111	61	Backfire	305
	B-1B	66		
Total		390		480
Delivery vehicles				
	Missiles	1,640	Missiles	2,361
	Bombers	390	Bombers	480
Total		2,030		2,841

Note: Data as of September 30, 1987. "ICBM" refers to intercontinental ballistic missile, "SLBM" refers to submarine-launched ballistic missile.
[a] Includes SLBMs potentially carried on U.S. Trident and on Soviet Typhoon and Delta-IV submarines on sea trials.

Source: Joint Chiefs of Staff, *Military Posture for Fiscal Year 1989* (Washington, D.C.: U.S. Government Printing Office, 1988), 39.

Table 11-6 U.S. Personnel in Major Military Conflicts

Item	Civil War[a]	Spanish-American War	World War I	World War II	Korean conflict	Vietnam conflict
Personnel serving (thousands)	2,213	307[b]	4,744	16,354[c]	5,764[d]	8,811[e]
Average duration of service (months)	20	8	12	33	19	23
Casualties (thousands)						
Battle deaths	140	[f]	53	292	34	47[g]
Wounds not mortal	282	2	204	671	103	304[g]
Draftees: classified (thousands)	777	0	24,234	36,677	9,123	75,717[e]
Examined	522	0	3,764	17,955	3,685	8,611[e]
Rejected	160	0	803	6,420	1,189	3,880[e]
Inducted	46	0	2,820	10,022	1,560	1,759[e]
Cost (millions)[h]						
Current	$2,300	$270	$32,700	$360,000	$50,000	$140,600
Constant (1967)	8,500	1,100	100,000	816,300	69,300	148,800

Note: For Revolutionary War, number of personnel serving not known, but estimates range from 184,000 to 250,000; for Mexican War, 78,718 served. Dates of the major conflicts may differ from those specified in various laws providing benefits for veterans.

[a] Union forces only. Estimates of the number serving in Confederate forces range from 600,000 to 1.5 million; cost for the Confederacy estimated at $1 million (current dollars) and $3.7 million (constant dollars).

[b] Covers April 21, 1898, to August 13, 1898.

[c] Covers December 1, 1941, to December 31, 1946.

[d] Covers June 25, 1950, to July 27, 1953.

[e] Covers August 4, 1964, to January 27, 1973.

[f] Fewer than 500.

[g] Covers January 1, 1961, to January 27, 1973.

[h] Original direct costs only. Excludes service-connected veterans' benefits and interest payments on war loans.

Source: U.S. Bureau of the Census, *Statistical Abstract of the U.S., 1988* (Washington, D.C.: U.S. Government Printing Office, 1987), 320, 324.

Table 11-7 U.S. Military Forces and Casualties in Vietnam, 1957-1986

Year	Military forces (thousands)	Battle deaths				Wounded, nonfatal[a]	
		Total[a]	Killed	Died of wounds	Died while missing[b]	Hospital care (thousands)	No hospital care (thousands)
1957-1964	23.3[c]	279	197	10	72	0.8	0.8
1965	184.3	1,432	1,124	111	197	3.3	2.8
1966	385.3	5,047	4,142	579	326	16.5	13.6
1967	485.6	9,463	7,525	979	959	32.4	29.7
1968	536.1	14,623	12,624	1,598	401	46.8	46.0
1969	475.2	9,426	8,117	1,168	141	32.9	37.3
1970	234.6	4,230	3,486	555	189	15.2	15.4
1971	156.8	1,376	1,082	160	134	4.8	4.2
1972	24.2	361	205	28	128	0.6	0.6
1973-1986[b]	0.0	1,141	28	8	1,105	[d]	[d]
Total	[e]	47,378	38,530	5,196	3,652	153.3	150.3

Note: Military forces as of December 31. All U.S. forces withdrawn by January 27, 1973.
[a] Casualties from enemy action. Deaths exclude 10,752 servicemen who died in accidents or from disease.
[b] Includes servicemen who died while captured.
[c] For 1964 only.
[d] Fewer than fifty.
[e] Not applicable.

Sources: Military forces, battle deaths: *Statistical Abstract of the U.S., 1988,* 324; wounded, nonfatal: *Statistical Abstract of the U.S., 1987,* 328.

Figure 11-1 Public Opinion on Vietnam War, 1965-1973

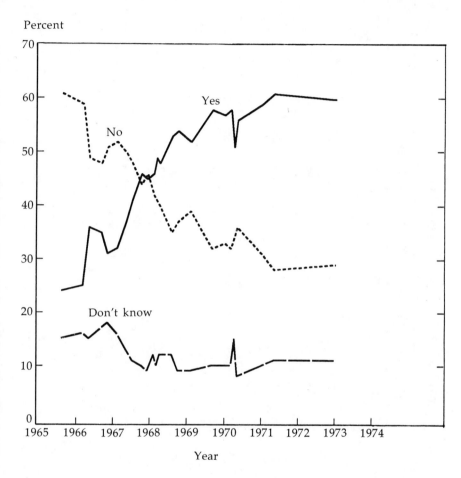

Percent

Note: Question: "In view of the developments since we entered the fighting in Vietnam, do you think the United States made a mistake sending troops to fight in Vietnam?"

Source: Gallup polls as cited in John E. Mueller, *War, Presidents and Public Opinion* (New York: Wiley, 1973), 54-55 (reprinted in 1985 by University Press of America, Lanham, Md.); *The Gallup Poll, 1972-1975*, vol. I (Wilmington, Del.: Scholarly Resources, 1977), 87.

Table 11-8 U.S. Military Personnel Abroad or Afloat by Country, 1972-1986 (thousands)

Country	1972	1973	1974	1975	1976	1977	1978	1979	1980	1981	1982	1983	1984	1985	1986
Outside United States[a]	628	585	519	517	464	483	494	481	502	502	528	520	511	515	500
Europe[b]	298	319	297	314	297	313	330	325	332	337	356	342	352	358	345
Germany, Federal Republic	210	229	208	220	209	224	234	239	244	248	256	254	254	247	247
Greece	3	5	4	4	3	3	4	3	4	3	4	4	4	4	3
Iceland	3	3	3	3	3	3	3	3	3	3	3	3	3	4	3
Italy	10	10	12	12	12	10	12	12	12	12	13	14	15	15	15
Spain	9	9	10	9	9	9	9	9	9	9	5	9	5	9	9
Turkey	7	7	6	7	4	5	5	5	5	5	5	5	5	5	5
United Kingdom	22	21	21	21	20	21	22	23	24	25	26	28	29	30	29
Other countries	8	6	6	7	6	6	6	6	7	7	7	7	8	9	10
Afloat	28	26	26	30	29	32	35	25	22	25	33	18	25	36	24
Asia and Pacific	275	199	169	156	123	130	129	122	115	125	139	137	121	125	131
Japan[c]	65	57	58	48	45	46	46	46	46	46	51	49	46	47	49
Philippines	17	16	17	15	15	14	14	14	13	15	14	15	15	15	16
South Korea	41	42	38	42	40	40	42	39	39	38	39	39	41	42	43
Thailand	47	42	31	20	1	[d]	[d]	[d]	[d]	[d]	[d]	[d]	[d]	[d]	[d]
South Vietnam	47	[d]	0	0	0	0	0	0	0	0	0	0	0	0	0
Afloat	51	33	20	28	19	29	26	22	16	25	33	34	18	20	22
U.S. outlying areas[e]	29	33	26	25	24	23	22	22	2	13	13	13	13	14	13
Troop dependents	342	341	347	365	334	322	318	383	369	347	368	386	399	385	—

Note: "—" indicates not available. As of September 30, except for 1986, which is as of December 31.
[a] Includes troops in countries not shown.
[b] Western Europe and related areas.
[c] Includes Okinawa.
[d] Fewer than 500.
[e] Primarily Guam, Panama Canal Zone, Puerto Rico, and Midway Islands.

Sources: 1972-1985: *Statistical Abstract of the U.S., 1977,* 370, *1981,* 364, *1982-1983,* 361, *1986,* 343, *1987,* 328; 1986: U.S. Department of Defense, *Military Manpower Statistics, December 31, 1986* (Washington, D.C.: U.S. Government Printing Office, 1987), 34-41.

Table 11-9 U.S. Active Duty Forces by Sex, Race, and Hispanic Origin, 1965-1988

Year	Female			Black			Hispanic[a]			Total[b]	
	Officers	Enlisted	Total	Officers	Enlisted	Total	Officers	Enlisted	Total	Officers (thousands)	Enlisted (thousands)
1965	3.1%	0.9%	1.2%	1.9%	10.5%	9.5%	—	—	—	339	2,317
1966	3.2	0.8	1.1	—	—	—	—	—	—	349	2,745
1967	3.3	0.8	1.0	2.1	9.9	8.9	—	—	—	385	2,992
1968	3.2	0.8	1.1	2.1	10.2	9.2	—	—	—	416	2,132
1969	3.1	0.9	1.1	2.1	9.6	8.7	—	—	—	419	3,041
1970	3.3	1.1	1.4	2.2	11.0	9.8	—	—	—	402	2,664
1971	3.5	1.3	1.6	2.3	12.1	10.7	1.3%	3.4%	3.1%c	371	2,329
1972	3.8	1.6	1.9	2.4	13.5	11.9	1.2	4.0	3.6	336	1,987
1973	4.0	2.2	2.5	2.7	14.9	13.2	1.2	4.5	4.0	321	1,932
1974	4.3	3.3	3.5	3.0	16.2	14.4	1.3	4.5	3.9	303	1,860
1975	4.6	4.5	4.6	3.2	16.2	14.4	1.4	4.6	4.2	292	1,836
1976	5.0	5.3	5.2	3.6	17.1	15.2	1.3	4.6	4.2	281	1,801
1977	5.4	5.8	5.7	3.9	17.4	15.6	1.5	4.5	4.1	276	1,798
1978	6.2	6.5	6.5	4.3	19.3	17.3	1.6	4.5	4.1	274	1,788
1979	6.9	7.5	7.4	4.7	21.2	19.0	1.6	4.4	3.8	274	1,753
1980	7.7	8.5	8.4	5.0	21.9	19.6	1.2	4.0	3.6	278	1,759
1981	8.1	9.0	8.9	5.3	22.1	19.8	1.2	4.1	3.7	285	1,783
1982	8.6	9.0	9.0	5.3	22.0	19.7	1.2	4.1	3.7	292	1,804
1983	9.0	9.3	9.3	5.8	21.6	19.4	1.4	4.1	3.7	301	1,811
1984	9.4	9.5	9.5	6.2	21.1	19.0	1.4	3.9	3.6	304	1,820
1985	9.8	9.8	9.8	6.4	21.1	18.9	1.5	3.9	3.6	309	1,828

(Table continues)

Table 11-9 (*Continued*)

Year	Female			Black			Hispanic[a]			Total[b]	
	Officers	Enlisted	Total	Officers	Enlisted	Total	Officers	Enlisted	Total	Officers (thousands)	Enlisted (thousands)
1986	10.1%	10.0%	10.1%	6.5%	21.2%	19.1%	1.7%	4.1%	3.7%	311	1,845
1987	10.4	10.2	10.2	6.5	21.5	19.4	1.7	4.3	3.9	308	1,856
1988[d]	10.7	10.4	10.4	6.7	22.0	19.8	1.8	4.5	4.1	305	1,819

Note: "—" indicates not available.

[a] Hispanics may be of any race.

[b] Includes other races not shown separately.

[c] Data on percent Hispanic origin from 1971-1979 is based on male armed forces members only.

[d] September 1988.

Sources: 1965-1985: *Statistical Abstract of the U.S.*, 1976, 336, 1980, 375-376, 1984, 353, 1986, 341, 1987, 327; 1986-1988: Department of Defense, unpublished data.

Table 11-10   U.S. Defense Spending, 1940-1994

| Year | Annual percentage change[a] | | Defense outlays as a percentage of | |
	Current dollars	Constant dollars	Federal outlays	Gross national product
1940	—	—	17.5	1.7
1941	276.5	239.1	47.1	5.7
1942	301.6	241.2	73.0	18.0
1943	159.5	137.4	84.9	37.9
1944	18.6	25.9	86.7	39.2
1945	4.9	13.3	89.5	39.1
1946	−48.6	−42.5	77.3	20.0
1947	−70.0	−73.5	37.1	5.7
1948	−28.9	−37.9	30.6	3.7
1949	45.1	38.7	33.9	5.0
1950	3.8	8.4	32.2	5.1
1951	72.3	79.1	51.8	7.5
1952	95.3	72.3	68.1	13.5
1953	14.5	4.9	69.4	14.4
1954	−6.6	−7.9	69.5	13.3
1955	−13.4	−15.6	62.4	11.1
1956	−0.5	−5.9	60.2	10.2
1957	6.8	2.5	59.3	10.3
1958	3.1	−2.6	56.8	10.4
1959	4.7	−1.2	53.2	10.2
1960	−1.8	−2.0	52.2	9.5
1961	3.1	1.6	50.8	9.6
1962	5.4	3.6	49.0	9.4
1963	2.1	−2.5	48.0	9.1
1964	2.6	0.9	46.2	8.7
1965	−7.7	−8.8	42.8	7.5
1966	14.8	9.1	43.2	7.9
1967	22.9	18.8	45.4	9.0
1968	14.7	8.4	46.0	9.6
1969	0.7	−4.5	44.9	8.9
1970	−1.0	−7.3	41.8	8.3
1971	−3.4	−10.2	37.5	7.5
1972	0.4	−5.8	34.3	6.9
1973	−3.2	−8.3	31.2	6.0
1974	3.4	−6.7	29.5	5.6
1975	9.1	−2.1	26.0	5.7
1976	3.6	−3.9	24.1	5.3
TQ[b]	c	c	23.2	5.0
1977	8.5	0.5	23.8	5.0

(Table continues)

Table 11-10 *(Continued)*

| Year | Annual percentage change[a] | | Defense outlays as a percentage of | |
	Current dollars	Constant dollars	Federal outlays	Gross national product
1978	7.5	0.5	22.8	4.8
1979	11.3	2.6	23.1	4.8
1980	15.2	3.1	22.7	5.0
1981	17.5	4.5	23.2	5.3
1982	17.7	8.1	24.9	5.9
1983	13.3	8.6	26.0	6.3
1984	8.3	5.0	26.7	6.2
1985	11.1	8.8	26.7	6.4
1986	8.2	6.0	27.6	6.5
1987	3.1	2.7	28.1	6.4
1988	3.0	1.0	27.3	6.1
1989	2.7	−1.1	26.2	5.8
1990	1.6	−2.2	26.3	5.5
1991	3.8	0.4	26.0	5.4
1992	3.8	1.1	26.2	5.3
1993	4.1	1.9	26.6	5.2
1994	4.2	2.5	27.0	5.1

[a] Change from prior year.
[b] Transition quarter, July-September.
[c] Not applicable.

Sources: Annual percentage change calculated from actual dollar amounts of defense spending in Table 13-3; percent of federal outlays and GNP: Office of Management and Budget, *Budget of the U.S. Government, Fiscal Year 1990, Historical Tables* (Washington, D.C.: U.S. Government Printing Office, 1989), Table 6-2, 132-141.

Table 11-11 Public Opinion on U.S. Defense Spending, 1960-1987
(percent)

Year	Too much	About right	Too little	No opinion
1960	18	45	21	16
1969	52	31	8	9
1971	50	31	11	8
1973	46	30	13	11
1974	44	32	12	12
1976	36	32	22	10
1977	23	40	27	10
1979	21	33	34	12
1980	14	24	49	13
1981	15	22	51	12
1982	41	31	16	12
1983	37	36	21	6
1985	46	36	11	7
1986	47	36	13	4
1987	44	36	14	6

Note: Question: "There is much discussion as to the amount of money the government in Washington should spend for national defense and military purposes. How do you feel about this? Do you think we are spending too little, too much, or about the right amount?"

Sources: Gallup Opinion Index (February 1980), 10; *The Gallup Report* (March 1985), 4, (April 1986), 15, and (May 1987), 3.

Table 11-12 Worldwide Military Expenditures, 1975-1985

Country group	1975	1976	1977	1978	1979	1980	1981	1982	1983	1984	1985	Per capita (in 1984 dollars) 1975	1985
Current dollars (billions)													
Worldwide, total[a]	$363.4	$389.2	$420.8	$461.5	$509.8	$578.3	$654.6	$730.9	$780.6	$827.5	$880.2	$161	$175
NATO countries[b]	133.1	137.0	151.0	164.4	183.0	212.3	246.1	280.0	306.3	331.0	364.7	434	589
United States	90.9	91.0	100.9	109.2	122.3	144.0	169.9	196.4	217.2	237.1	265.8	765	1,077
Warsaw Pact countries[c]	150.0	161.1	174.1	189.6	208.7	232.9	256.1	277.8	292.3	308.7	322.5	756	800
Soviet Union[d]	128.0	138.0	149.0	163.0	180.0	210.0	221.0	237.0	250.0	264.0	275.0	914	956
Constant (1984) dollars (billions)													
Worldwide, total[a]	660.2	664.9	673.9	688.4	699.0	726.8	750.5	787.4	809.7	827.5	853.0	—	—
NATO countries	241.8	234.0	241.8	245.3	250.9	266.8	282.2	301.6	317.7	331.0	353.4	—	—
United States	165.2	155.5	161.6	163.0	167.7	181.0	194.8	211.6	225.3	237.1	257.6	—	—
Warsaw Pact countries	272.5	275.2	278.8	282.9	286.1	292.7	293.6	299.3	303.2	308.7	312.5	—	—
Soviet Union[d]	232.5	235.7	238.6	243.2	246.8	252.6	253.4	255.3	259.3	264.0	266.5	—	—
Percentage of GNP[e]													
Worldwide, total[a]	6.2	6.0	5.8	5.7	5.6	5.7	5.8	6.1	6.2	6.0	6.1	—	—
NATO countries	4.8	4.4	4.4	4.3	4.2	4.5	4.7	5.1	5.2	5.2	5.4	—	—
United States	5.7	5.1	5.1	4.9	4.9	5.3	5.6	6.2	6.4	6.3	6.6	—	—

Warsaw Pact countries	11.4	11.1	10.9	10.7	10.8	10.9	10.8	10.8	10.7	10.7	10.7	—	—
Soviet Union	13.7	13.3	13.0	12.8	12.9	13.0	12.9	12.7	12.6	12.6	12.5	—	—

Note: "—" indicates not applicable.

[a] Includes countries not shown separately.

[b] Current members of NATO (North Atlantic Treaty Organization) are Belgium, Canada, Denmark, France, Iceland, Great Britain, Greece, Italy, Luxembourg, The Netherlands, Norway, Portugal, Spain, Turkey, the United States, and West Germany.

[c] The Warsaw Pact countries include Bulgaria, Czechoslovakia, East Germany, Hungary, Poland, Romania, and the Soviet Union.

[d] Estimate based on partial or uncertain data.

[e] The meaning of military expenditures as a percentage of GNP differs between most Communist countries and non-Communist countries because of different estimating procedures.

Source: U.S. Arms Control and Disarmament Agency, *World Military Expenditures and Arms Transfers, 1987,* 43, 47, 77, 81.

Table 11-13 U.S. Military Sales and Military Assistance to Foreign Governments, Principal Recipients, 1950-1986 (millions)

Country	Military sales				Military assistance			
	1950-1983	1984	1985	1986	1950-1983	1984	1985	1986
Australia	$2,438.0	$441.1	$448.5	$350.0	$0.0	$0.0	$0.0	$0.0
Belgium	1,462.9	195.6	119.5	28.1	1,203.8	0.0	0.0	0.0
Canada	1,699.0	139.4	73.8	116.4	0.0	0.0	0.0	0.0
China (Taiwan)	2,370.0	275.0	341.7	253.3	2,554.6	0.0	0.0	0.0
France	418.1	45.3	45.9	145.9	4,045.1	0.0	0.0	0.0
Germany, Federal Republic	7,459.7	339.1	224.8	218.2	884.8	0.0	0.0	0.0
Greece	1,749.4	106.8	126.0	77.6	1,665.7	1.0	0.5	0.4
Indochina	8.5	0.0	0.0	0.0	709.0	0.0	0.0	0.0
Iran	10,669.6	0.0	0.0	0.0	766.7	0.0	0.0	0.0
Israel	8,291.2	216.1	484.1	222.1	0.0	0.0	0.0	0.0
Italy	830.3	54.0	58.4	68.8	2,243.7	0.0	0.0	0.0
Korea	2,334.0	258.4	258.6	397.8	5,470.0	1.3	0.3	0.1
The Netherlands	2,021.5	432.4	394.0	380.0	1,178.0	0.0	0.0	0.0
Saudi Arabia	12,379.8	1,940.4	1,783.4	1,803.3	23.9	0.0	0.0	0.0
Thailand	1,023.6	166.4	123.3	125.1	1,167.6	0.9	0.2	0.2
Turkey	1,128.9	306.0	392.0	295.8	3,134.1	3.1	0.5	0.2
United Kingdom	3,597.9	461.1	377.1	381.5	1,012.9	0.0	0.0	0.0
Vietnam	1.2	0.0	0.0	0.0	14,773.9	0.0	0.0	0.0
Total	77,213.2	8,195.0	7,720.8	7,165.5	54,392.5	128.7	23.2	28.0

Note: Figures exclude training.

Source: U.S. Defense Security Assistance Agency, *Foreign Military Sales, Foreign Military Construction Sales, and Military Assistance Facts, September 30, 1986* (Washington, D.C.: U.S. Government Printing Office, 1987), 10-13, 60-61.

Table 11-14   U.S. Foreign Aid, Principal Recipients, 1962-1986 (millions)

Region/country	1962-1982	1983	1984	1985	1986
Near East and					
South Asia[a]	$23,235	$2,400	$2,474	$3,867	$3,728
Egypt	5,905	750	853	1,065	1,069
India	3,448	89	88	89	94
Israel	6,075	785	910	1,950	1,898
Jordan	1,010	20	20	100	95
Pakistan	2,141	200	225	250	263
Turkey	1,859	285	139	175	120
East Asia[a]	9,444	216	230	313	518
Indonesia	1,187	72	75	72	66
Korea	1,080	0	0	0	0
Philippines	692	87	84	183	351
Vietnam	4,490	0	0	0	0
Europe	825	45	62	94	131
Latin America[a]	8,515	842	912	1,506	1,124
Brazil	1,480	0	0	0	0
Costa Rica	193	184	146	196	139
Dominican Republic	514	35	64	126	67
El Salvador	398	199	164	376	268
Honduras	327	87	71	205	112
Jamaica	270	82	88	115	85
ROCAP[b]	306	19	16	107	63
Africa[a]	5,331	636	728	900	766
Cameroon	78	19	23	24	24
Chad	37	2	11	16	16
Kenya	251	61	53	40	43
Morocco	226	11	26	38	37
Niger	84	21	26	28	24
Senegal	91	19	35	44	50
Somalia	135	48	51	51	45
Sudan	355	115	146	149	71
Zaire	324	15	26	36	48
Zambia	146	16	21	42	20
Zimbabwe	125	60	41	41	13
Oceania and other	11	0	0	6	8
Total	58,639	5,244	5,684	8,132	6,783

[a] Includes countries not shown separately.
[b] Regional programs covering Costa Rica, El Salvador, Guatemala, Honduras, Nicaragua, and Panama.

Source: U.S. Agency for International Development, *U.S. Overseas Loans and Grants and Assistance from International Organizations 1987* (Washington, D.C.: U.S. Government Printing Office, 1987), 4-175.

Table 11-15 Foreign Investment in the United States and U.S. Investment Abroad, 1950-1987 (millions)

Year	All areas	Canada	Europe	Japan
Foreign direct investment in the United States				
1950	$3,391	$1,029	$2,228	—
1960	6,910	1,934	4,707	$88
1970	13,270	3,117	9,554	229
1980	83,046	12,162	54,688	4,723
1981	108,714	12,116	72,377	7,697
1982	124,677	11,708	83,193	9,677
1983	137,061	11,434	92,936	11,336
1984	164,583	15,286	108,211	16,044
1985	184,615	17,131	121,413	19,313
1986	220,414	20,318	144,181	26,824
1987	261,927	21,732	177,963	33,361
U.S. investment abroad				
1950	11,788	3,579	1,733	19
1960	32,778	11,198	6,681	254
1970	78,178	22,790	24,516	1,483
1980	215,578	44,978	96,539	6,243
1981	227,342	46,957	101,318	6,807
1982	221,343	44,509	99,877	6,872
1983	207,203	44,339	92,178	7,661
1984	211,480	46,730	91,589	7,936
1985	230,250	46,909	105,171	9,235
1986	259,562	49,994	122,165	11,332
1987	308,793	56,879	148,954	14,270

Note: "—" indicates not available.

Sources: 1950-1960: U.S. Department of Commerce, Foreign Business Investments in the United States: A Supplement to Survey of Current Business (Washington, D.C.: U.S. Government Printing Office, 1962), 34; Survey of Current Business, August 1962, 22; others from Survey of Current Business: August 1973, 50; September 1973, 24; August 1982, 21-22; August 1983, 24; August 1985, 63; August 1988, 65, 80.

Table 11-16   U.S. Balance of Trade, 1946-1988 (millions)

Year	Merchandise trade balance[a]	Balance on current account[b]	Year	Merchandise trade balance[a]	Balance on current account[b]
1946	$6,697	$4,885	1968	$635	$611
1947	10,124	8,992	1969	607	399
1948	5,708	2,417	1970	2,603	2,331
1949	5,339	873	1971	−2,260	−1,433
1950	1,122	−1,840	1972	−6,416	−5,795
1951	3,067	884	1973	911	7,140
1952	2,611	614	1974	−5,505	1,962
1953	1,437	−1,286	1975	8,903	18,116
1954	2,576	219	1976	−9,483	4,207
1955	2,897	430	1977	−31,091	−14,511
1956	4,753	2,730	1978	−33,947	−15,427
1957	6,271	4,762	1979	−27,536	−991
1958	3,462	784	1980	−25,480	1,873
1959	1,148	−1,282	1981	−27,978	6,884
1960	4,892	2,824	1982	−36,444	−8,679
1961	5,571	3,822	1983	−67,080	−46,246
1962	4,521	3,387	1984	−112,522	−107,077
1963	5,224	4,414	1985	−122,148	−115,103
1964	6,801	6,823	1986	−144,547	−138,828
1965	4,951	5,431	1987	−160,280	−153,964
1966	3,817	3,031	1988	−126,525	−135,332
1967	3,800	2,583			

[a] "Merchandise trade balance" measures the difference between the value of goods the United States imports and the goods the United States exports.
[b] "Balance on current account" is the broadest trade gauge, measuring the difference in imports and exports of merchandise trade and trade in services; also includes certain one-way flows of money into the United States, such as pension payments.

Sources: U.S. President, *The Economic Report of the President* (Washington, D.C.: U.S. Government Printing Office, 1989), 424; 1988: U.S. Department of Commerce, *News,* press release, "Summary of U.S. International Transactions: Fourth Quarter and Year 1988," March 14, 1989, 6.

Table 11-17 Immigrants by Country, 1820-1987

Year	Europe Northwestern[a]	Central[b]	Southern[c]	Eastern[d]	Asia[e]	Canada	Other western hemisphere[f]	All other[g]	Total number (thousands)
1820-1830	62.8%	5.1%	2.1%	0.1%	—	1.6%	6.2%	22.0%	151.8
1831-1840	56.3	25.5	1.0	-	—	2.3	3.3	11.7	599.1
1841-1850	67.6	25.4	0.3	-	—	2.4	1.2	3.1	1,713.3
1851-1860	56.9	36.7	0.8	-	1.6%	2.3	0.6	1.1	2,598.2
1861-1870	53.7	34.4	0.9	0.1	2.8	6.6	0.5	0.8	2,314.8
1871-1880	48.1	28.6	2.7	1.4	4.4	13.6	0.7	0.4	2,812.2
1881-1890	44.3	35.4	6.3	4.2	1.3	7.5	0.6	0.3	5,246.6
1891-1900	30.9	32.4	19.1	14.2	1.9	0.1	1.0	0.5	3,687.6
1901-1910	17.8	28.2	26.4	20.1	2.8	2.0	2.1	0.2	8,795.4
1911-1920	14.9	18.3	25.5	17.7	3.4	12.9	7.0	0.4	5,735.8
1921-1930	21.2	20.8	14.0	4.3	2.4	22.5	14.4	0.4	4,107.2
1931-1940	15.9	30.8	15.9	3.3	3.0	20.5	9.8	0.9	528.4
1941-1950	25.4	26.3	7.7	0.6	3.5	16.6	17.7	2.1	1,035.0
1951-1960	17.7	26.0	10.6	2.9	6.1	10.9	22.5	3.1	2,515.5
1961-1970	12.2	11.2	12.2	1.3	13.2	8.6	38.9	2.3	3,321.7
1971-1980	4.3	4.0	8.0	1.8	35.9	2.6	40.4	3.1	4,493.3
1981-1987	4.1	3.3	2.4	1.7	46.1	2.3	36.9	3.3	4,067.6

Note: "—" indicates less than 0.1 percent.

[a] Great Britain, Ireland, Norway, Sweden, Denmark, Iceland, The Netherlands, Belgium, Luxembourg, Switzerland, and France.

[b] Germany, Poland, Czechoslovakia, Yugoslavia, Hungary, and Austria.

[c] Italy, Spain, Portugal, and Greece.

[d] USSR, Finland, Romania, Bulgaria, and Turkey.

[e] Cambodia, China, Taiwan, Hong Kong, India, Iran, Iraq, Israel, Japan, Jordan, Korea, Laos, Lebanon, Pakistan, Philippines, Thailand, and Vietnam.

[f] Mexico, Caribbean, Central and South America.

[g] Africa, Australia, New Zealand.

Sources: U.S. Department of Justice, Immigration and Naturalization Service, *Statistical Yearbook of the Immigration and Naturalization Service, 1986* (Washington, D.C.: U.S. Government Printing Office, 1987), 2-5; U.S. Immigration and Naturalization Service, *Immigration Statistics: Fiscal Year 1987 Advance Report* (Washington, D.C.: U.S. Government Printing Office, 1988), Table 4.

Questions

1. Although the change has been small and possibly has run its course, there seems to have been a shift away from public support for active U.S. involvement in world affairs (Table 11-1). Based on its timing, why do you think this change occurred?

2. A considerable increase in the number of countries in the world accounts for the rise in the number of diplomatic posts (Table 11-2). Yet the number of consular posts has dropped sharply. Why?

3. How many of the nine U.S. postwar presidents have held a summit meeting with the Soviet leader (Table 11-3)? What was the topic of four of the first five meetings? Of most of the meetings since 1972?

4. When was the first multinational arms control agreement reached (Table 11-4)? What was it about?

5. Does the United States or the Soviet Union have the greater number of weapons (Table 11-5)? The number of weapons alone does not determine the balance of power. Why not?

6. Which U.S. war cost the most lives (Table 11-6)? The second most? In which war was the casualty rate (battle deaths per person served) the greatest?

7. What feature of public opinion about the Vietnam War (Figure 11-1) coincided almost perfectly with the maximum number of battle deaths in Vietnam (Table 11-7)?

8. As of 1986 about how many military personnel were overseas or on board ship (Table 11-8)? Where were most of these troops stationed? Of our Asian and Pacific troops, where were most of these stationed?

9. Blacks, women, and Hispanics make up increasingly larger shares of active duty forces, both officers and enlisted personnel (Table 11-9). If proportional representation—equality between the proportion of military personnel and voting-age population (VAP is shown in Table 12-17)—were the criterion, how have these groups fared?

10. The defense budget has changed dramatically at times (Table 11-10). How much are the biggest increase and decrease (in percentage of constant dollars) and when did they occur? Apart from the buildup for World War II and the war in Vietnam (1966-1968), in what year was the increase the greatest?

11. In 1980 Ronald Reagan campaigned in part on the theme that the United States was spending too little on national defense. Looking at Table 11-11, do you think he was following or leading public opinion? Throughout his terms, President Reagan continued to support a defense buildup, and in fact spending increased (Table 11-10). Did he continue to follow or lead public opinion?

12. Which defense group—NATO or the Warsaw Pact—has had higher military expenditures in current dollars (Table 11-12)? Which in terms of spending as a percentage of GNP? In constant dollars, which group or country (NATO, the United States, the Warsaw Pact, the Soviet Union) increased its spending by the largest percentage between 1984 and 1985? What was the percentage?

13. Since 1984 which country has been the principal recipient of U.S. military sales (Table 11-13)? Another country among the top buyers of military materiel was also the largest recipient of U.S. foreign aid (Table 11-14). What was that country?

14. What region of the world has had the largest increase in U.S. foreign aid since 1983 (Table 11-14)? Large increases have gone to what East Asian country and what Central American countries? Why?

15. By what percentage did U.S. investment abroad grow between 1980 and 1987 (Table 11-15)? By what percentage did foreign investment in the United States grow during the same period?

16. What was the first year in which the United States imported more goods than it exported (Table 11-16)? What was the most recent year in which the United States exported more goods than it imported?

17. Only one area—Central Europe—has sent a large, steady stream of immigrants to the United States. All other groups came in waves (Table 11-17). Describe when and where these waves came from. Note that 22 percent came from "all other" areas of the world in the 1820s. Who were they? Make and justify a projected distribution of immigrants for the 1990s.

12

Social Policy

The study of social policies might fairly be described as controversies informed by, but not settled by, statistics. No matter what the area, those on all sides of an issue try to support their arguments with relevant data.

The data are of many kinds and can be characterized in a variety of ways. First, there is factual information showing, for example, how many whites, blacks, and Hispanics are below the poverty line (Table 12-2), how much money is spent on social welfare (Tables 12-4 and 12-5), and how many crimes were committed in a given year (Table 12-20). Second, there are data about public opinion and social policy. Social policy concerns not only the actual crime rate but what people think about crime—for example, whether the courts are too easy on criminals (Table 12-22) and whether the death penalty is acceptable and desirable (Table 1-11). It matters not only what abortion rates are (Table 1-12) but also what people think and say about abortion (Table 1-13). One might also distinguish between data about the past or present and projections about the future. Much of the concern about Social Security payments and about health care costs are not about present payments but about what to expect in the future (Tables 12-7 and 12-8, Figure 12-2).

Social policies are inherently controversial, and so too are data relevant to such policies. Often, for example, analysts agree on a set of facts but disagree on the relevance of the material and on its interpretation. Information about numbers of people on welfare (Table 12-9), about the proportion of women and minorities elected to political office (Table 12-17), about the extent of crime and the cost of prisons (Tables 12-20 and 12-21), and so on, do not automatically answer causal questions (why the situation is as it is) any more than they answer normative questions (whether the existing situation is good and what should be done). Moreover, the importance of future projections often leads to special problems of inference. Any projection must be based on assumptions about what the future will be like. A footnote in Table 12-8, for example, should underscore the fact that no one can be certain in 1989 what health or Social Security costs will be in 2065.

In the face of enormous problems of inference, of controversy about almost every fact, and of the need to deal with future unknowns, one might well ask whether all these numbers are useful or necessary when discussing social policies. There are at least two answers to this question. The first is highly pragmatic. Some analysts will surely have factual information at their disposal; those who do not or cannot understand data and are unable or unwilling to provide any of their own will be hostage to others' information and interpretations.

From a more theoretical perspective, one can note that although data are always subject to some error and interpretation, people often do agree on the facts and on roughly how they should be interpreted. There is no disagreement, for example, that—barring major unforeseen catastrophes or extremely large and unlikely changes in immigration— there will be a considerably smaller ratio of young people to old people in the first half of the next century. Knowing this does not solve the problems implicit in this fact, but it tells analysts that there will be problems and that the country needs to be thinking of solutions. It also suggests possible solutions—raising the retirement age, lowering Social Security payments or raising Social Security taxes, encouraging private pension plans so that the elderly need less government support, and so on.

In the area of social policy, then, as in other areas, data do not speak for themselves. They must be analyzed and interpreted. The facts alone will settle few arguments about causality or about normative questions. Still, data and an ability to interpret them are an essential ingredient in the arsenal of any well-educated social analyst, commentator, or student.

Figure 12-1   U.S. Population: Total, Urban, and Rural, 1790-2020

Population
(millions)

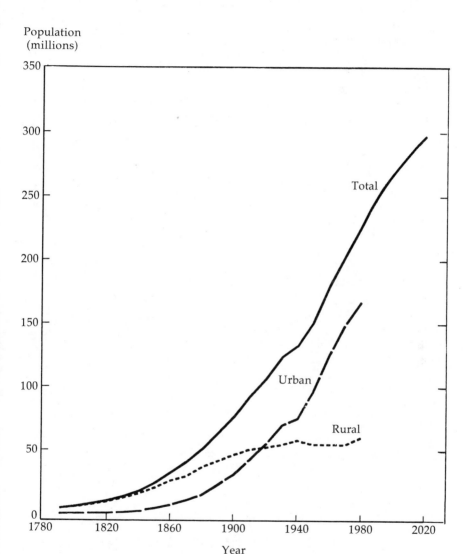

Year

Note: Urban places, in general, are those with a population of 2,500 or more. A change in definition in 1950 resulted in about 5 percent more individuals being classified as urban than under the old definition. For details on definitions and projections, see sources.

Source: Total population: U.S. Bureau of the Census, *Statistical Abstract of the U.S., 1987* (Washington, D.C.: U.S. Government Printing Office, 1986), 8, 15; urban and rural populations: U.S. Bureau of the Census, *Historical Statistics of the U.S.* (Washington, D.C.: U.S. Government Printing Office, 1975), 11.

Table 12-1 Median Family Income by Race and Hispanic Origin, 1950-1987

Year	Median income in current dollars				Median income in constant (1987) dollars				Annual percentage change in median income of all families	
	All families[a]	White	Black	Hispanic origin[b]	All families[a]	White	Black	Hispanic origin[b]	Current dollars	Constant dollars
1950	$3,319	$3,445	$1,869[c]	—	$15,689	$16,284	$8,835	—	—	—
1955	4,418	4,613	2,544[c]	—	18,773	19,601	10,810	—	6.6[d]	3.9[d]
1960	5,620	5,835	3,230[c]	—	21,546	22,371	12,383	—	5.4[d]	3.0[d]
1965	6,957	7,251	3,993[c]	—	25,041	26,099	14,372	—	4.8[d]	3.2[d]
1970	9,867	10,236	6,279	—	28,880	29,960	18,378	—	8.4[d]	3.1[d]
1971	10,285	10,672	6,440	—	28,822	29,907	18,047	—	4.2	−0.2
1972	11,116	11,549	6,864	$8,183	30,216	31,393	18,658	$22,243	8.1	4.8
1973	12,051	12,595	7,269	8,715	30,820	32,211	18,590	22,288	8.4	2.0
1974	12,902	13,408	8,006	9,540	29,735	30,901	18,451	21,967	7.1	−3.5
1975	13,719	14,268	8,779	9,551	28,970	30,129	18,538	20,168	6.3	−2.6
1976	14,958	15,537	9,242	10,259	29,863	31,019	18,451	20,482	9.0	3.1
1977	16,009	16,740	9,563	11,421	30,025	31,396	17,935	21,420	7.0	0.5
1978	17,640	18,368	10,879	12,566	30,730	31,998	18,952	21,891	10.2	2.3
1979	19,587	20,439	11,574	14,169	30,669	32,003	18,122	22,185	11.0	−0.2
1980	21,023	21,904	12,674	14,716	28,996	30,211	17,481	20,297	7.3	−5.5
1981	22,388	23,517	13,266	16,401	27,977	29,368	16,578	20,495	6.5	−3.5
1982	23,433	24,603	13,598	16,227	27,591	28,969	16,011	19,106	4.7	−1.4
1983	24,674	25,837	14,561	16,930	28,147	29,474	16,610	19,313	5.3	2.0
1984	26,433	27,686	15,431	18,832	28,923	30,294	16,884	20,606	7.1	2.8
1985	27,735	29,152	16,786	19,027	29,302	30,799	17,734	20,102	4.9	1.3
1986	29,458	30,809	17,604	19,995	30,524	31,935	18,247	20,726	6.2	4.2
1987	30,853	32,274	18,098	20,306	30,853	32,274	18,098	20,306	4.7	1.1

Note: "—" indicates not available.

[a] Includes other races not shown separately.

[b] Persons of Hispanic origin may be of any race.

[c] For 1950-1965, black and other races.

[d] Calculated by annualizing the five-year change.

Sources: 1950-1965, 1971-1972: *Statistical Abstract of the U.S., 1987*, 436; 1970, 1973-1987: U.S. Bureau of the Census, Current Population Reports, "Money Income and Poverty Status in the United States: 1987" (Washington, D.C.: U.S. Government Printing Office, 1988), Series P-60, no. 161, 15-16, 42; median income in constant dollars for 1950-1965, 1971-1972, and annual percentage changes calculated by the editors.

Table 12-2 Persons Below the Poverty Level by Race and Hispanic Origin, 1959-1987 (percent)

Year	White	Black	Hispanic origin[a]	Total[b]
1959	18.1	55.1	—	22.4
1960	17.8	—	—	22.2
1965	13.3	—	—	17.3
1966	11.3	41.8	—	14.7
1969	9.5	32.2	—	12.1
1970	9.9	33.5	—	12.6
1971	9.9	32.5	—	12.5
1972	9.0	33.3	—	11.9
1973	8.4	31.4	21.9	11.1
1974	8.6	30.3	23.0	11.2
1975	9.7	31.3	26.9	12.3
1976	9.1	31.1	24.7	11.8
1977	8.9	31.3	22.4	11.6
1978	8.7	30.6	21.6	11.4
1979	9.0	31.0	21.8	11.7
1980	10.2	32.5	25.7	13.0
1981	11.1	34.2	26.5	14.0
1982	12.0	35.6	29.9	15.0
1983	12.1	35.7	28.0	15.2
1984	11.5	33.8	28.4	14.4
1985	11.4	31.3	29.0	14.0
1986	11.0	31.1	27.3	13.6
1987	10.5	33.1	28.2	13.5

Note: "—" indicates not available.
[a] Persons of Hispanic origin may be of any race.
[b] Includes other races not shown separately.

Source: U.S. Bureau of the Census, Current Population Reports, "Money Income and Poverty Status in the United States: 1987," Series P-60, no. 161, 28-29.

Table 12-3   Persons Below the Poverty Line, 1987

Group	Percentage of group that is poor	Group as a percentage of all poor people
Race/ethnicity		
White	10.5	65.8
Black	33.1	29.8
Hispanic origin[a]	28.2	16.8
Family status		
Female householder, no husband present		
White	26.4	29.5
Black	53.8	21.0
Hispanic	53.0	7.2
All other families		
White	7.1	36.3
Black	17.2	8.7
Hispanic	20.8	9.6
Age		
Under 15	21.4	34.5
65 or over	12.2	10.7
Dwelling		
Metropolitan residents	12.5	72.0
Nonmetropolitan residents	16.9	28.0
Region		
Northeast	11.0	16.8
Midwest	12.7	23.0
South	16.1	40.8
West	12.6	19.3

[a] Persons of Hispanic origin may be of any race.

Source: U.S. Bureau of the Census, Current Population Reports, "Money Income and Poverty Status in the United States: 1987," Series P-60, no. 161, 27, 29-31.

Table 12-4   Social Welfare Expenditures, 1960-1986

	Federal		State and local		Total expenditures	
Year	Total (billions)	Percentage of total federal outlays	Total (billions)	Percentage of total state and local outlays	Total (billions)	Percentage of total GNP
1950	$10.5	26.2	$13.0	59.2	$23.5	8.2
1955	14.6	22.3	18.0	55.3	32.6	8.2
1960	25.0	28.1	27.3	60.1	52.3	10.3
1965	37.7	32.6	39.5	60.4	77.2	11.5
1970	77.3	40.1	68.5	64.0	145.9	14.7
1975	167.4	52.0	122.7	65.3	290.1	19.0
1976	197.1	57.0	135.0	66.2	332.1	19.5
1977	218.4	54.7	142.2	66.3	360.6	18.6
1978	239.8	55.3	154.6	66.6	394.4	18.1
1979	263.0	54.6	167.2	62.4	430.3	17.5
1980	302.6	54.3	189.9	60.8	492.5	18.5
1981	344.1	53.9	206.4	61.9	550.5	18.4
1982	367.6	52.6	227.2	60.0	594.9	18.9
1983	398.7	52.2	242.4	59.9	641.2	19.3
1984	419.4	50.2	251.6	58.6	670.9	18.2
1985	452.9	48.6	277.5	59.0	730.4	18.5
1986[a]	472.4	48.4	298.2	58.2	770.5	18.4

[a] Preliminary.

Source: U.S. Department of Health and Human Services, Social Security Administration, *Social Security Bulletin,* November 1988 (Washington, D.C.: U.S. Government Printing Office, 1988), 27-28.

Table 12-5 Social Welfare Expenditures By Category, 1950-1986

Year	Social insurance	Public aid	Health and medical programs[a]	Veterans programs	Education	Housing	Other social welfare[b]	All health and medical care[c]	Total social welfare outlays
Federal (millions)									
1950	$2,103	$1,103	$604	$6,386	$157	$15	$174	$1,362	$10,541
1955	6,385	1,504	1,150	4,772	485	75	252	1,948	14,623
1960	14,307	2,117	1,737	5,367	868	144	417	2,918	24,957
1965	21,807	3,594	2,781	6,011	2,470	238	812	4,625	37,712
1970	45,246	9,649	4,775	8,952	5,876	582	2,259	16,600	77,337
1975	99,715	27,186	8,521	16,570	8,629	2,541	4,264	33,013	167,426
1980	191,162	48,666	12,703	21,254	13,452	6,608	8,786	68,801	302,631
1985	313,108	61,985	18,630	26,704	13,796	11,088	7,548	118,955	452,860
1986[d]	326,588	65,615	19,926	27,072	15,022	10,164	7,977	125,730	472,364
State and local (millions)									
1950	2,844	1,393	1,460	480	6,517	—	274	1,704	12,967
1955	3,450	1,499	1,953	62	10,672	15	367	2,473	18,017
1960	4,999	1,984	2,727	112	16,758	33	723	3,478	27,337
1965	6,316	2,690	3,466	20	25,638	80	1,254	4,911	39,464
1970	9,446	6,839	5,132	127	44,970	120	1,886	8,791	68,519
1975	23,298	14,122	9,267	449	72,205	631	2,683	18,249	122,654
1980	38,592	23,133	14,948	212	107,597	601	4,813	31,492	189,897
1985	59,420	34,792	22,430	338	152,622	1,540	6,398	48,587	277,540
1986[d]	63,816	37,464	24,408	373	163,495	1,872	6,728	53,884	298,158

(Table continues)

351

Table 12-5 (*Continued*)

Year	Social insurance	Public aid	Health and medical programs[a]	Veterans programs	Education	Housing	Other social welfare[b]	All health and medical care[c]	Total social welfare outlays
Total (millions)									
1950	$4,947	$2,496	$2,064	$6,866	$6,674	$15	$448	$3,065	$23,508
1955	9,835	3,003	3,103	4,834	11,157	89	619	4,421	32,640
1960	19,307	4,101	4,464	5,479	17,626	177	1,139	6,395	52,293
1965	28,123	6,283	6,246	6,031	28,108	318	2,066	9,535	77,175
1970	54,691	16,488	9,907	9,078	50,845	701	4,145	25,391	145,856
1975	123,013	41,308	17,788	17,019	80,834	3,172	6,947	52,063	290,084
1980	229,754	71,799	27,650	21,466	121,050	7,210	13,599	100,294	492,528
1985	372,529	96,777	41,060	27,042	166,418	12,627	13,946	167,542	730,399
1986[d]	390,404	103,079	44,334	27,445	178,518	12,036	14,705	179,614	770,522
Percentage of total expenditures									
1950	21.0	10.6	8.8	29.2	28.4	0.1	1.9	13.0	100.0
1955	30.1	9.2	9.5	14.8	34.2	0.3	1.9	13.5	100.0
1960	36.9	7.8	8.5	10.5	33.7	0.3	2.2	12.2	100.0
1965	36.4	8.1	8.1	7.8	36.4	0.4	2.7	12.4	100.0
1970	37.5	11.3	6.8	6.2	34.9	0.5	2.8	17.4	100.0
1975	42.4	14.2	6.1	5.9	27.9	1.1	2.4	17.9	100.0
1980	46.6	14.6	5.6	4.4	24.6	1.5	2.8	20.4	100.0
1985	51.0	13.2	5.6	3.7	22.8	1.7	1.9	22.9	100.0
1986[d]	50.7	13.4	5.8	3.6	23.2	1.6	1.9	23.3	100.0

Percentage federal of total

1950	42.5	44.2	29.2	93.0	2.3	100.0	38.9	44.4	44.8
1955	64.9	50.1	37.1	98.7	4.3	84.3	40.7	44.1	44.8
1960	74.1	51.6	38.9	98.0	4.9	81.4	36.6	45.6	47.7
1965	77.5	57.2	44.5	99.7	8.8	74.9	39.3	48.5	48.9
1970	82.7	58.5	48.2	98.6	11.6	82.9	54.5	65.4	53.0
1975	81.1	65.8	47.9	97.4	10.7	80.1	61.4	65.1	57.7
1980	83.2	67.8	45.9	99.0	11.1	91.7	64.6	68.1	61.4
1985	84.0	64.0	45.4	98.8	8.3	87.8	54.1	71.0	62.0
1986[d]	83.6	63.7	44.9	98.6	8.4	84.4	54.2	70.0	61.3

Note: "—" indicates not available. Figures for fiscal years ending in year shown.

[a] Excludes medical services parts of social insurance, public aid, veterans, and other social welfare.

[b] Includes outlays for vocational rehabilitation, institutional care, child nutrition and welfare, and social welfare expenditures not elsewhere classified.

[c] Combines health and medical programs with medical services included in social insurance, public aid, veterans, vocational rehabilitation, and antipoverty programs.

[d] Preliminary figures.

Source: U.S. Department of Health and Human Services, Social Security Administration, *Social Security Bulletin,* November 1988, 27-28.

Table 12-6 Private Social Welfare Expenditures by Category and as a Percentage of Gross National Product, 1972-1985 (millions)

| Year | Private[a] | | | | | Public Total[d] | Percentage of gross national product | | |
	Health	Income maintenance[b]	Education	Welfare services[c]	Total		Private[e]	Public[f]	Total[g]
1972	$58,500	$15,955	$12,677	$7,457	$94,589	$191,357	7.7	16.6	23.8
1973	64,000	17,087	13,610	8,245	102,942	213,942	7.6	16.6	23.7
1974	69,100	19,753	15,004	8,906	112,763	239,397	7.7	16.9	24.1
1975	76,400	21,910	16,626	9,990	124,926	290,080	7.8	19.0	26.3
1976	88,000	25,004	18,120	11,657	142,781	331,956	8.0	19.5	26.9
1977	100,100	30,662	19,927	13,424	164,113	360,925	8.2	18.6	26.2
1978	110,100	36,743	21,379	16,168	184,390	394,377	8.2	18.1	25.8
1979	124,200	42,628	23,361	18,717	208,906	430,280	8.3	17.6	25.0
1980	142,900	51,504	26,751	21,455	242,610	492,528	8.9	18.5	26.4
1981	165,800	59,095	30,062	23,827	278,784	550,545	9.1	18.4	26.5
1982	188,499	70,450	32,697	25,362	316,909	594,876	10.0	18.9	27.8
1983	209,700	82,783	35,911	27,624	356,018	641,169	10.5	19.3	28.7
1984	231,300	91,812	38,722	30,307	392,141	670,945	10.4	18.2	27.5
1985	246,600	106,110	42,735	33,819	429,264	727,861	10.7	18.4	28.0

[a] Calendar year basis.
[b] These expenditures represent outlays for private employee benefit plans including private pension plans, group life insurance, sickness and disability insurance, paid sick leave, and supplemental unemployment benefits.
[c] Expenditures include individual and family social services, adoption services, emergency and disaster services, child day care centers, senior citizen centers, residential care, recreation and group work, civic, social, and fraternal organizations, job training, and vocational rehabilitation.
[d] Fiscal year basis.
[e] Calendar year expenditures as a percentage of calendar year gross national product.
[f] Fiscal year expenditures as a percentage of federal fiscal year gross national product.
[g] The sum of public and private expenditures as a percentage of gross national product, after adjustment to eliminate overlap that occurs when public or private income maintenance payments are used to purchase medical care, educational services, or residential care.

Source: U.S. Department of Health and Human Services, Social Security Administration, *Social Security Bulletin*, August 1988. 4.

Table 12-7   Federal Pension and Health Spending as a Percentage of GNP and the Budget, 1965-2040

Year	Pension spending as a percentage of GNP[a]	Health spending as a percentage of GNP[a]	Total as a percentage of GNP[a]	Total as a percentage of budget[b]
1965	4.1	0.3	4.4	24.9
1970	4.7	1.4	6.1	30.0
1975	6.4	2.0	8.4	37.1
1980	6.5	2.3	8.8	38.2
1982	7.1	2.7	9.7	39.6
1984	7.0	2.8	9.8	39.7
1986	6.6	3.0	9.6	39.4
1988	6.4	3.2	9.6	39.4
1990	6.6	3.1	9.7	40.4
1995	6.2	3.7	9.9	41.3
2000	5.8	4.0	9.8	40.8
2005	5.6	4.4	10.0	41.7
2010	6.0	4.7	10.7	44.6
2015	6.0	5.0	11.0	45.8
2020	6.5	5.4	11.9	49.6
2025	7.0	5.9	12.9	53.9
2030	7.1	6.4	13.5	56.3
2035	7.1	7.0	14.1	58.8
2040	7.0	7.5	14.5	60.4

[a] Estimates for 1984-1988 are based on Congressional Budget Office baseline assumptions (August 1983); forecasts for 1990 and beyond are based on intermediate assumptions of the Social Security and Medicare actuaries.
[b] Forecasts for 1990 and beyond are based on the assumption that the budget accounts for 24 percent of GNP.

Source: United States, Congress, Senate, Special Committee on Aging, "Developments in Aging: 1986," 100th Cong., 1st sess., S. Rep. 100-4, vol. 3, February 27, 1987, 107.

Table 12-8 Social Security (OASDI) Covered Workers and Beneficiaries, 1945-2065

Year	Covered workers[a] (thousands)	Beneficiaries[b] OASI	DI	Total	Covered workers per OASDI beneficiary	Beneficiaries per 100 covered workers
1945	46,930	1,106	—	1,106	42.4	2
1950	48,280	2,930	—	2,930	16.5	6
1955	65,200	7,563	—	7,563	8.6	12
1960	72,530	13,740	522	14,262	5.1	20
1965	80,680	18,509	1,648	20,157	4.0	25
1970	93,090	22,618	2,568	25,186	3.7	27
1975	100,200	26,998	4,125	31,123	3.2	31
1980	112,980	30,385	4,734	35,119	3.2	31
1985	121,300	32,776	3,874	36,650	3.3[c]	30[c]
1986	124,500	33,349	3,972	37,321	3.3[c]	30[c]
1987	127,917	33,917	4,034	37,952	3.4[c]	30[c]
1990	132,396	35,581	4,203	39,784	3.3	30
1995	139,177	37,815	4,608	42,422	3.3	30
2000	144,261	39,251	5,285	44,536	3.2	31
2005	148,453	40,801	6,032	46,832	3.2	32
2010	151,428	43,943	6,880	50,824	3.0	34
2015	152,614	49,654	7,351	57,005	2.7	37
2020	152,286	56,765	7,589	64,354	2.4	42
2025	151,648	63,320	7,970	71,290	2.1	47
2030	151,494	68,323	7,914	76,236	2.0	50
2035	151,830	71,078	7,799	78,877	1.9	52
2040	152,017	71,688	7,833	79,521	1.9	52
2045	151,895	72,033	8,091	80,124	1.9	53
2050	151,614	72,895	8,218	81,113	1.9	53
2055	151,478	73,982	8,211	82,193	1.8	54
2060	151,566	74,773	8,152	82,925	1.8	55
2065	151,668	75,232	8,177	83,409	1.8	55

Note: "—" indicates not available; "OASI" indicates Old-Age and Survivors' Insurance; "DI" indicates Disability Insurance. Projections (1990-2065) are the so-called Alternative II-B projections. See source for further reference.
[a] Workers who pay OASDI taxes at some time during the year.
[b] Beneficiaries with monthly benefits in current-payment status as of June 30.
[c] Preliminary.

Source: U.S. Congress, House, House Committee on Ways and Means, "1988 Annual Report of the Board of Trustees of the Federal Old-Age and Survivors' Insurance and Disability Insurance Trust Funds," 100th Cong., 2d sess., May 5, 1988, 79-80.

Figure 12-2 Social Security Receipts, Spending, and Reserve Estimates, 1988-2045

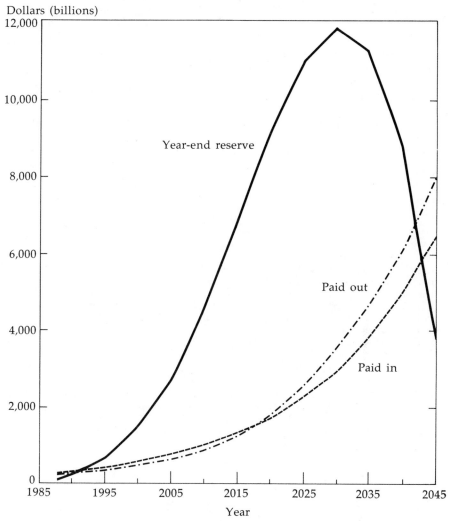

Source: U.S. Congress, House, House Committee on Ways and Means, "1988 Annual Report of The Board of Trustees of the Federal Old-Age and Survivors Insurance and Disability Insurance Trust Funds," 100th Cong., 2d sess., May 5, 1988, 141-142.

Table 12-9 Recipients of Social Insurance Programs, 1985

Program	Number of recipients (thousands)	Percentage of population
Nonmeans-tested		
Social Security (OASDI)	36,740.0	15.4
Medicare (hospital insurance)[a]	30,590.0	12.8
Veterans programs	4,015.0[b]	1.7
Railroad retirement	964.2	0.4
State unemployment insurance	2,287.0	1.0
State temporary disability	—	—
Means-tested		
Medicaid	21,808.0	9.1
Supplemental Security Income[c]	4,200.0	1.8
Aid to Families with Dependent Children[d]	10,855.0	4.5
Food stamps[e]	19,910.0	8.3
General assistance[d]	1,326.0	0.6

Note: "—" indicates not available. "Means-tested" refers to the requirement of demonstration of financial need based on income and assets. People may receive benefits from more than one program. In 1985, 16 percent of U.S. households received one or more means-tested benefits; in addition to the programs listed above, these include free or reduced-price school lunches and publicly owned or subsidized housing.
[a] Number of enrollees on July 1.
[b] Data on retirement veterans programs not available.
[c] Number of persons receiving payments in December 1985.
[d] Average monthly number of recipients.
[e] Average number of persons participating during year.

Sources: U.S. Department of Health and Human Services, Social Security Administration, *Social Security Bulletin, Annual Statistical Supplement, 1987* (Washington, D.C.: U.S. Government Printing Office, 1988), 238, 252, 257, 274, 294, 296, 301; *Statistical Abstract of the U.S., 1988,* 7; U.S. Bureau of the Census, Current Population Reports, "Receipt of Selected Noncash Benefits: 1985" (Washington, D.C.: U.S. Government Printing Office, 1987), Series P-60, no. 155, 2.

Table 12-10 Aid to Families with Dependent Children versus the Poverty Line, 1960-1985

Year	Average monthly benefit per family	Yearly benefit	Average poverty threshold
1960	$105.75	$1,269.00	$3,022
1961	110.97	1,331.64	3,054
1962	116.30	1,395.60	3,089
1963	120.19	1,442.28	3,128
1964	126.88	1,522.56	3,169
1965	133.20	1,598.40	3,223
1966	142.83	1,713.96	3,317
1967	155.19	1,862.28	3,410
1968	168.41	2,020.92	3,553
1969	174.89	2,098.68	3,743
1970	183.13	2,197.56	3,968
1971	187.16	2,245.92	4,137
1972	188.87	2,266.44	4,275
1973	190.91	2,290.92	4,540
1974	204.27	2,451.24	5,038
1975	219.44	2,633.28	5,500
1976	236.10	2,833.20	5,815
1977	246.27	2,955.24	6,191
1978	253.89	3,046.68	6,662
1979	262.86	3,154.32	7,412
1980	280.03	3,360.36	8,414
1981	282.04	3,384.48	9,287
1982	303.02	3,636.24	9,862
1983	312.84	3,754.08	10,178
1984	325.46	3,905.52	10,609
1985	342.15	4,105.80	10,989

Note: Poverty threshold is for a family of four.

Sources: U.S. Department of Health and Human Services, Social Security Administration, *Social Security Bulletin, Annual Statistical Supplement, 1987,* 294; U.S. Bureau of the Census, *Current Population Reports,* "Poverty in the United States: 1985," Series P-60, no. 158 (Washington, D.C.: U.S. Government Printing Office, 1987), 162.

Table 12-11 Years of School Completed by Age and Race, 1940-1987

Age/year	Median school years completed by all persons	Median school years completed by black persons
25 years and over		
1940	8.6	5.7
1950	9.3	6.8
1960	10.6	8.0
1970	12.1	9.8
1980	12.5	12.0
1987	12.7	12.4
25-29 years		
1940	10.3	7.0
1950	12.0	8.6
1960	12.3	9.9
1970	12.6	12.1
1980	12.9	12.6
1987	12.8	12.7

Source: Statistical Abstract of the U.S., 1989, 130.

Table 12-12   School Desegregation by Region, 1968-1986

Region/year	Percentage of black students in schools with more than half minority students	Percentage of Hispanic students in schools with more than half minority students	Percentage of white students in schools 90-100 percent white
South			
1968	80.9	69.6	70.6
1972	55.3	69.9	38.0
1976	54.9	70.9	34.6
1980	57.1	76.0	35.0
1984	56.9	75.4	—
1986	58.0	75.2	—
Change 1968 to 1986[a]	−12.9	+5.6	−35.6
Border			
1968	71.6	—	80.0
1972	67.2	—	75.9
1976	60.1	—	64.8
1980	59.2	—	64.1
1984	62.5	—	—
1986	59.3	29.9	—
Change 1968 to 1986[a]	−12.3	—	−15.9
Northeast			
1968	66.8	74.8	83.0
1972	69.9	74.4	82.9
1976	72.5	74.9	81.4
1980	79.9	76.3	80.2
1984	73.1	77.5	—
1986	72.8	78.2	—
Change 1968 to 1986[a]	+6.0	+3.4	−2.8
Midwest			
1968	77.3	31.8	89.4
1972	75.3	34.4	87.5
1976	70.3	39.3	84.7
1980	69.5	46.6	81.2
1984	70.7	53.9	—
1986	69.8	54.3	—
Change 1968 to 1986[a]	−7.5	+22.5	−8.2

(Table continues)

Table 12-12   *(Continued)*

Region/year	Percentage of black students in schools with more than half minority students	Percentage of Hispanic students in schools with more than half minority students	Percentage of white students in schools 90-100 percent white
West			
1968	72.2	42.4	63.0
1972	68.1	44.7	56.0
1976	67.4	52.7	49.9
1980	66.8	63.5	43.3
1984	66.9	68.4	—
1986	68.2	69.9	—
Change 1968 to 1986[a]	−4.0	+27.5	−19.7
Total			
1968	76.6	54.8	78.4
1972	63.6	56.6	68.9
1976	62.4	60.8	64.9
1980	62.9	68.1	61.2
1984	63.5	70.6	—
1986	63.3	71.5	—
Change 1968 to 1986[a]	−13.3	+16.7	−17.2

Note: "−" indicates not available. For composition of regions, see Appendix Table A-4.
[a] To 1980 for whites.

Sources: 1968-1980: Gary Orfield, testimony before the House Subcommittee on Civil and Constitutional Rights, *Civil Rights Implications of the Education Block Grant Program,* September 9, 1982, 67-72; 1984-1986: Gary Orfield, Franklin Monfort, Melissa Aaron, "Status of School Desegregation 1968-1986" (Alexandria, Va.: National School Boards Association, 1989), 5, 7.

Table 12-13 Public Opinion of Whites on School Integration,
1942-1985 (percent)

| Date | Blacks and whites should attend | | |
	Same schools	Separate schools	Don't know
June 1942	30	66	4
April 1956	49	47	4
June 1956	49	49	2
September 1956	48	49	3
May 1963	63	32	5
December 1963	65	29	6
June 1964	62	32	5
October 1964	64	34	2
June 1965	67	30	3
October 1965	68	28	4
April 1970	74	24	3
March 1972	85	14	2
November 1972	80	15	5
March 1976	83	15	3
March 1977	85	14	2
March 1980	86	12	2
March 1982	88	9	2
March 1984	90	8	2
March 1985	92	7	1

Note: Questions: "Do you think white students and (Negro/black) students should go to the same schools or to separate schools?" (October 1964): "Do you think white children and Negro children should go to the same schools or to separate but equal schools?" Questions asked of whites only.

Sources: 1942-1970, November 1972: National Opinion Research Center; March 1972, 1976-1985: General Social Survey, National Opinion Research Center, University of Chicago.

Table 12-14 Public Opinion on School Integration by Racial
Composition of School, 1958-1988 (percent)

	Object to own children attending school with		
Date	A few blacks	Half blacks	More than half blacks
September 1958	25	53	70
February 1959	20	47	71
May 1963	25	52	75
April 1965	16	42	67
June 1965	20	44	68
May 1966	11	41	67
July 1969	11	38	66
March 1970	8	32	66
April 1970	10	34	63
March 1972	6	25	55
August 1973	9	36	67
March 1974	4	33	67
March 1975	6	38	66
September 1975	7	35	62
March 1977	7	26	64
March 1978	4	24	61
July 1978	7	36	67
December 1980	6	28	62
March 1982	4	21	54
March 1983	3	25	65
March 1985	4	22	60
March 1986	4	24	64
March 1988	3	21	52

Note: Question: "Would you, yourself, have any objection to sending your children to a school where a few of the children are (Negroes/blacks)?" If no: "Where half of the children are (Negroes/blacks)?" If no: "Where more than half of the children are (Negroes/blacks)?" Those saying "don't know" were assumed to have expressed some objection. Question asked of whites with school-age children only.

Sources: 1958-1970, 1973, September 1975, 1978, 1980: Gallup surveys; other years: General Social Survey.

Table 12-15 Black Elected Officials by Category of Office,
1970-1988

Year	Federal	State	Substate/ regional	County	Municipal	Judicial, law en- forcement	Education	Total
1970	10	169	—	92	623	213	362	1,469
1971	14	202	—	120	785	274	465	1,860
1972	14	210	—	176	932	263	669	2,264
1973	16	240	—	211	1,053	334	767	2,621
1974	17	239	—	242	1,360	340	793	2,991
1975	18	281	—	305	1,573	387	939	3,503
1976	18	281	30	355	1,889	412	994	3,979
1977	17	299	33	381	2,083	447	1,051	4,311
1978	17	299	26	410	2,159	454	1,138	4,503
1979	17	313	25	398	2,224	486	1,144	4,607
1980	17	323	25	451	2,356	526	1,214	4,912
1981	18	341	30	449	2,384	549	1,267	5,038
1982	18	336	35	465	2,477	563	1,266	5,160
1983	21	379	29	496	2,697	607	1,377	5,606
1984[a]	21	389	30	518	2,735	636	1,371	5,700
1985	20	396	32	611	2,898	661	1,438	6,056
1986	20	400	31	681	3,112	676	1,504	6,424
1987	23	417	23	724	3,219	728	1,547	6,681
1988	23	413	22	742	3,341	738	1,550	6,829

Note: "—" indicates not available.
[a] The 1984 figures reflect blacks who took office during the seven-month period between July 1, 1983 and January 30, 1984.

Source: Joint Center for Political Studies, *Black Elected Officials: A National Roster* (Washington, D.C.: Joint Center for Political Studies, 1989), 8.

Table 12-16 Black Elected Officials and Black Voting-Age Population (VAP) by State, 1987

State	Number of black elected officials	Total number of elected officials	Percentage of black elected officials	Percentage black VAP	Ratio of percentages: black elected officials to black VAP
Alabama	448	4,160	10.8	22.9	0.470
Alaska	3	1,365	0.2	3.3	0.067
Arizona	15	2,412	0.6	3.1	0.201
Arkansas	319	10,692	3.0	13.6	0.219
California	293	18,135	1.6	7.5	0.215
Colorado	15	7,801	0.0	3.4	0.001
Connecticut	68	7,920	0.9	6.2	0.138
Delaware	21	999	2.1	14.7	0.143
District of Columbia	251	370	67.8	66.6	1.019
Florida	179	4,902	3.7	10.8	0.338
Georgia	445	6,672	6.7	24.9	0.268
Hawaii	1	176	0.6	2.1	0.271
Idaho	0	4,183	-	-	a
Illinois	434	40,422	1.1	13.6	0.079
Indiana	69	11,029	0.6	7.1	0.088
Iowa	9	17,730	0.0	1.2	0.000
Kansas	29	17,070	0.0	4.9	0.000
Kentucky	74	7,013	1.1	6.7	0.157
Louisiana	505	4,720	10.7	26.6	0.402
Maine	3	5,885	-	-	a
Maryland	119	2,172	5.5	22.5	0.244
Massachusetts	36	11,605	0.0	3.7	0.001
Michigan	316	19,403	1.6	12.3	0.132
Minnesota	12	19,153	0.0	1.2	0.001
Mississippi	548	5,278	10.4	30.8	0.337
Missouri	164	17,802	0.9	9.5	0.097
Montana	0	4,335	-	-	a
Nebraska	5	15,747	0.0	2.7	0.000
Nevada	10	1,145	0.9	5.5	0.159
New Hampshire	1	5,991	-	-	a
New Jersey	198	9,431	2.1	11.7	0.179
New Mexico	6	2,052	0.0	1.7	0.002
New York	250	24,112	1.0	13.1	0.079
North Carolina	353	5,308	6.7	20.7	0.321
North Dakota	0	18,045	-	-	a
Ohio	214	19,913	1.1	9.6	0.112
Oklahoma	117	9,018	1.3	6.1	0.213

(Table continues)

Table 12-16   *(Continued)*

State	Number of black elected officials	Total number of elected officials	Percentage of black elected officials	Percentage black VAP	Ratio of percentages: black elected officials to black VAP
Oregon	10	7,880	0.0	1.2	0.001
Pennsylvania	140	28,928	0.5	8.2	0.059
Rhode Island	11	1,107	1.0	2.4	0.414
South Carolina	340	3,233	10.5	27.7	0.380
South Dakota	3	9,191	-	-	a
Tennessee	143	7,256	2.0	14.4	0.137
Texas	282	24,757	1.1	11.0	0.104
Utah	1	2,363	-	-	a
Vermont	1	7,323	-	-	a
Virginia	123	3,053	4.0	17.9	0.225
Washington	19	7,467	0.0	2.5	0.001
West Virginia	20	2,899	0.7	3.0	0.230
Wisconsin	20	18,973	0.0	3.4	0.000
Wyoming	3	2,174	-	-	a
Total	6,646	490,770	1.4	10.8	0.125

Note: "-" indicates less than 0.5 percent. Data are as of January.
[a] Ratios not calculated when black voting-age population is below 0.5 percent.

Source: Joint Center for Political Studies, *Black Elected Officials* (1987), 11-12.

Table 12-17 Blacks, Hispanics, and Women as a Percentage of State Legislators and State Voting-Age Population (VAP)

State	Total number of legislators	Black legislators				Hispanic legislators				Women legislators			
		Number	Percentage	Percentage VAP	Ratio[a]	Number	Percentage	Percentage VAP	Ratio[a]	Number	Percentage	Percentage VAP	Ratio[a]
Alabama	140	24	17.1	23.2	.739	0	0.0	0.5	.000	8	5.7	53.0	.108
Alaska	60	1	1.7	3.3	.505	0	0.0	2.2	.000	12	20.0	47.2	.424
Arizona	90	3	3.3	2.4	1.389	10	11.1	14.5	.766	21	23.3	51.4	.454
Arkansas	135	5	3.7	13.6	.272	0	0.0	0.6	.000	9	6.7	52.8	.126
California	120	8	6.7	7.5	.889	7	5.8	21.6	.270	17	14.2	50.9	.278
Colorado	100	4	4.0	3.6	1.111	9	9.0	10.6	.849	28	28.0	50.6	.553
Connecticut	187	10	5.3	7.1	.753	1	0.5	3.9	.137	40	21.4	52.6	.407
Delaware	62	3	4.8	16.4	.295	0	0.0	1.5	.000	10	16.1	52.7	.306
Florida	160	12	7.5	11.8	.636	9	5.6	9.4	.598	33	20.6	52.8	.391
Georgia	236	28	11.9	24.4	.486	0	0.0	0.9	.000	26	11.0	52.7	.209
Hawaii	76	0	0.0	1.8	.000	0	0.0	6.3	.000	16	21.1	49.4	.426
Idaho	126	0	0.0	0.5	.000	0	0.0	4.0	.000	27	21.4	50.5	.424
Illinois	177	21	11.9	14.2	.836	3	1.7	6.6	.257	32	18.1	52.4	.345
Indiana	150	8	5.3	7.5	.711	1	0.7	1.4	.476	19	12.7	52.4	.242
Iowa	150	1	0.7	1.6	.417	0	0.0	0.9	.000	22	14.7	52.3	.280
Kansas	165	4	2.4	5.2	.466	2	1.2	2.8	.433	31	18.8	51.7	.363
Kentucky	138	2	1.4	6.9	.210	0	0.0	0.4	.000	8	5.8	52.1	.111
Louisiana	144	19	13.2	27.5	.480	1	0.7	2.3	.302	4	2.8	52.3	.053
Maine	186	0	0.0	0.3	.000	0	0.0	0.4	.000	53	28.5	52.4	.544
Maryland	188	27	14.4	23.9	.601	0	0.0	1.7	.000	39	20.7	52.4	.396
Massachusetts	200	7	3.5	4.2	.833	0	0.0	2.5	.000	37	18.5	53.4	.346
Michigan	148	16	10.8	13.2	.819	0	0.0	1.6	.000	22	14.9	52.2	.285
Minnesota	201	1	0.5	1.3	.383	0	0.0	0.8	.000	31	15.4	51.7	.298
Mississippi	174	20	11.5	31.4	.366	0	0.0	0.4	.000	10	5.7	52.9	.109
Missouri	197	15	7.6	9.7	.785	0	0.0	0.9	.000	31	15.7	52.9	.297
Montana	150	0	0.0	0.2	.000	1	0.7	1.2	.556	23	15.3	50.6	.303
Nebraska	49	1	2.0	3.0	.680	0	0.0	1.7	.000	9	18.4	51.9	.354
Nevada	63	3	4.8	5.9	.807	1	1.6	7.3	.217	10	15.9	49.3	.322

New Hampshire	424	1	0.2	0.6	.393	0	0.0	0.6	.000	138	32.5	51.6	.631
New Jersey	120	8	6.7	12.7	.525	1	0.8	7.3	.114	11	9.2	53.0	.173
New Mexico	112	0	0.0	1.6	.000	38	33.9	36.0	.942	11	9.8	51.3	.191
New York	211	20	9.5	14.5	.654	10	4.7	10.3	.460	22	10.4	53.6	.195
North Carolina	170	16	9.4	20.2	.466	0	0.0	0.6	.000	24	14.1	52.5	.269
North Dakota	159	0	0.0	0.5	.000	0	0.0	0.5	.000	20	12.6	49.8	.253
Ohio	132	13	9.8	10.0	.985	0	0.0	0.9	.000	15	11.4	52.7	.216
Oklahoma	149	5	3.4	6.0	.559	0	0.0	0.9	.000	13	8.7	51.9	.168
Oregon	90	3	3.3	1.4	2.381	1	1.1	2.1	.000	15	16.7	51.3	.325
Pennsylvania	253	18	7.1	8.6	.827	1	0.4	2.6	.427	17	6.7	53.2	.126
Rhode Island	150	6	4.0	3.2	1.250	1	0.7	1.2	.329	24	16.0	53.2	.301
South Carolina	170	20	11.8	27.3	.431	0	0.0	2.2	.303	13	7.6	52.2	.146
South Dakota	105	0	0.0	0.4	.000	0	0.0	0.6	.000	21	20.0	51.3	.390
Tennessee	132	13	9.8	14.7	.670	0	0.0	0.5	.000	12	9.1	52.8	.172
Texas	181	15	8.3	11.2	.740	25	13.8	21.1	.655	17	9.4	51.2	.183
Utah	104	0	0.0	0.7	.000	0	0.0	4.2	.000	8	7.7	51.0	.151
Vermont	180	1	0.6	0.3	1.852	0	0.0	0.7	.000	46	25.6	52.1	.491
Virginia	140	9	6.4	17.8	.361	0	0.0	1.6	.000	14	10.0	51.6	.194
Washington	147	3	2.0	2.3	.887	1	0.7	3.0	.227	37	25.2	50.5	.498
West Virginia	134	1	0.7	2.9	.257	0	0.0	0.4	.000	21	15.7	52.6	.298
Wisconsin	132	4	3.0	3.9	.777	0	0.0	1.3	.000	28	21.2	51.8	.410
Wyoming	94	1	1.1	0.7	1.520	0	0.0	4.9	.000	21	22.3	48.3	.463
United States	7,461	400	5.4	11.2	.479	123	1.6	7.1	.232	1,176	15.8	52.2	.302

Note: Hispanics may be of any race.

[a] The ratio between the percentage minority of state legislators and the percentage minority of the state population. Ratios calculated before rounding.

Sources: Number of legislators and women legislators: Center for the American Woman and Politics (CAWP), National Information Bank on Women in Public Office (NIB), Eagleton Institute of Politics, Rutgers University, "Women in State Legislatures 1988," August 2, 1988; black legislators: Joint Center for Political Studies, *Black Elected Officials: A National Roster,* 21–22; Hispanic legislators: *National Roster of Hispanic Elected Officials 1988* (Washington, D.C.: National Association of Latino Elected and Appointed Officials Education Fund, no date), 1–102; composition of voting-age population: Current Population Reports, "Projections of the Population of Voting Age for States: November 1988" (Washington, D.C.: U.S. Government Printing Office, 1988), Series P-25, no. 1019, 8–9.

Table 12-18 State and Local Government Employment and Salary by Sex, Race, and Hispanic Origin, 1973-1986 (thousands)

| | Employment | | | | | | | Median annual salary | | | | | | |
| | | | | | Minority | | | | | | | Minority | | |
Year	Total	Male	Female	White[a]	Total[b]	Black[a]	Hispanic	Total	Male	Female	White[a]	Total[b]	Black[a]	Hispanic
1973	3,809	2,486	1,322	3,115	693	523	125	$8.6	$9.6	$7.0	$8.8	$7.5	$7.4	$7.4
1975	3,899	2,436	1,464	3,102	797	602	147	9.8	11.3	8.2	10.2	8.8	8.6	8.9
1977	4,415	2,737	1,678	3,480	935	705	175	10.9	12.4	9.1	11.3	9.7	9.5	9.9
1978	4,447	2,711	1,736	3,481	966	723	181	11.7	13.3	9.7	12.0	10.4	10.1	10.7
1979	4,576	2,761	1,816	3,568	1,008	751	192	12.3	14.1	10.4	12.8	10.9	10.6	11.4
1980	3,987	2,350	1,637	3,146	842	619	163	13.3	15.2	11.4	13.8	11.8	11.5	12.3
1981	4,665	2,740	1,925	3,591	1,074	780	205	15.6	17.7	13.1	16.1	13.5	13.3	14.7
1983	4,492	2,674	1,818	3,423	1,069	768	219	18.0	20.1	15.3	18.5	15.9	15.6	17.3
1984	4,580	2,700	1,880	3,458	1,121	799	233	19.1	21.4	16.2	19.6	17.4	16.5	18.4
1985	4,742	2,789	1,952	3,563	1,179	835	248	—	22.3	17.3	20.6	18.4	17.5	19.2
1986	4,779	2,797	1,982	3,549	1,230	865	259	—	23.4	18.1	21.5	19.6	18.7	20.2

Note: "—" indicates not available. Full-time employment as of June 30, excludes school systems and educational institutions. Based on reports from state governments (44 in 1973, 48 in 1975, 47 in 1977, 45 in 1978, 48 in 1979, 42 in 1980, 49 in 1981, 47 in 1983, and 50 in 1984 through 1986) and a sample of county, municipal, township, and special district jurisdictions employing 15 or more nonelected, nonappointed full-time employees.

[a] Nonhispanic.

[b] Includes other minority groups, not shown separately.

Source: Statistical Abstract of the U.S., 1989, 294.

Table 12-19 Federal Employment by GS Salary Level, Race/Ethnic Group, and Sex, 1986

Government service (GS) salary level		Total number	Percentage black	Percentage Hispanic	Percentage female
GS-01	$ 9,619-12,036	5,590	39.1	11.8	75.8
GS-02	$10,816-13,611	18,255	33.8	8.3	73.6
GS-03	$11,802-15,339	83,960	28.1	6.7	76.7
GS-04	$13,248-17,226	174,989	25.0	5.8	77.0
GS-05	$14,822-19,268	209,664	22.0	5.4	72.4
GS-06	$16,521-21,480	98,840	22.8	4.7	76.0
GS-07	$18,358-23,866	149,669	18.2	5.3	59.2
GS-08	$20,333-26,435	33,172	21.3	3.6	57.1
GS-09	$22,458-29,199	168,498	12.8	5.2	44.8
GS-10	$24,732-32,148	31,249	12.6	5.3	45.8
GS-11	$27,172-35,326	199,363	10.4	4.1	35.1
GS-12	$32,567-42,341	190,882	8.5	3.1	23.0
GS-13	$38,727-50,346	122,816	6.2	2.4	15.2
GS-14	$45,763-59,488	66,642	5.1	1.9	11.4
GS-15	$53,830-69,976	39,107	3.6	2.1	9.8
Total, all pay plans		2,083,985	16.3	5.0	41.3
Total, GS and equivalent		1,592,696	15.9	4.5	49.3

Sources: Office of Personnel Management, *Federal Civilian Workforce Statistics, Affirmative Employment Statistics* (Washington, D.C.: U.S. Government Printing Office, September 30, 1986), 32, 38; Office of Personnel Management, *Federal Civilian Workforce Statistics, Pay Structure of the Federal Civil Service* (Washington, D.C.: U.S. Government Printing Office, March 31, 1987), 53.

Table 12-20 Crime Rates, 1960-1987

Year	Violent crime					Property crime				Total
	Murder	Forcible rape	Robbery	Aggravated assault	Total	Burglary	Larceny theft	Vehicle theft	Total	
1960	5.1	9.6	60	86	161	509	1,035	183	1,729	1,887
1965	5.1	12.1	72	111	200	663	1,329	257	2,249	2,249
1968	6.9	15.9	132	144	298	932	1,747	393	3,072	3,370
1969	7.3	18.5	148	155	329	984	1,931	436	3,351	3,680
1970	7.9	18.7	172	165	364	1,085	2,079	457	3,621	3,985
1971	8.6	20.5	188	179	396	1,164	2,146	460	3,769	4,165
1972	9.0	22.5	181	189	401	1,141	1,994	426	3,560	3,961
1973	9.4	24.5	183	201	417	1,223	2,072	443	3,737	4,154
1974	9.8	26.2	209	216	461	1,438	2,490	462	4,389	4,850
1975	9.6	26.3	218	227	482	1,526	2,805	469	4,800	5,282
1976	8.8	26.6	199	233	468	1,448	2,921	450	4,820	5,287
1977	8.8	29.4	191	247	476	1,420	2,730	452	4,602	5,078
1978	9.0	31.0	196	262	498	1,435	2,747	461	4,643	5,140
1979	9.7	34.7	218	286	549	1,512	2,999	506	5,017	5,566
1980	10.2	36.8	251	299	597	1,684	3,167	502	5,353	5,950
1981	9.8	36.0	259	290	594	1,650	3,140	475	5,264	5,858
1982	9.1	34.0	239	289	571	1,489	3,085	459	5,033	5,604
1983	8.3	33.7	217	279	538	1,338	2,869	431	4,637	5,175
1984	7.9	35.7	205	290	539	1,264	2,791	437	4,492	5,031
1985	7.9	36.7	209	303	556	1,287	2,901	462	4,651	5,207
1986	8.6	37.9	225	346	618	1,345	3,010	508	4,863	5,480
1987	8.3	37.4	213	351	610	1,330	3,081	529	4,940	5,550

Note: Figures are rates per 100,000 inhabitants. For definitions of crimes, see the source.

Source: Statistical Abstract of the U.S., 1976, 153, 1987, 155, 1989, 166.

Table 12-21   Number of Federal and State Prisoners and Cost per Inmate per Year, 1950-1987

Year	Number of inmates		Cost per inmate per year	
	Federal	State	Federal	State[a]
1950	17,134	149,031	—	—
1960	23,218	189,735	—	—
1965	21,040	189,855	—	—
1970	20,038	176,403	—	—
1975	24,131	216,462	—	—
1980	19,025	285,667	$13,505	$10,354
1981	21,311	322,972	14,758	13,572
1982	21,360	363,713	14,508	15,829
1983	23,836	381,665	20,826	16,245
1984	24,805	404,245	16,858	17,324
1985	29,215	436,021	14,520	14,591
1986[b]	36,531	485,954	13,162	15,220
1987[b]	39,523	517,733	14,071	15,892

Note: "—" indicates not available. Excludes state institutions in Alaska prior to 1970 and those in Hawaii for 1950. Figures through 1985 include persons in the physical custody of state and federal institutions at year-end. Represents inmates sentenced to maximum term of more than one year.
[a] Average for all states.
[b] Represents prisoners under the jurisdiction of state and federal correctional authorities.

Sources: 1950-1985: U.S. Department of Justice, Bureau of Justice Statistics, *Historical Statistics on Prisoners in State and Federal Institutions, Year-End 1925-86* (Washington, D.C.: U.S. Government Printing Office, 1988), 8-13; 1986-1987: U.S. Department of Justice, Bureau of Justice Statistics Bulletin, *Prisoners in 1987* (Washington, D.C.: U.S. Government Printing Office, 1988), 2; costs: Criminal Justice Institute, *The Corrections Yearbook* (South Salem, N.Y.: Criminal Justice Institute), annual volumes, 1981-1988.

Table 12-22 Public Opinion on the Courts, 1965-1988

Date	Too harsh	About right	Not harsh enough	Don't know
April 1965	2	34	48	16
August 1965	2	27	60	12
February 1968	2	19	63	16
January 1969	2	13	74	10
March 1972	7	16	66	11
December 1972	4	13	74	8
March 1973	5	13	73	9
March 1974[a]	5	6	60	29
March 1974	6	10	78	7
March 1975	4	10	79	7
March 1976	3	10	81	6
March 1977	3	8	83	6
March 1978	3	7	85	5
March 1980	3	8	83	6
January 1981	3	13	77	7
March 1982[a]	4	5	76	14
March 1982	3	8	86	4
March 1983	4	6	85	4
March 1984	3	11	82	4
March 1985	3	9	84	3
March 1986	3	8	85	4
March 1987	3	12	79	6
March 1988	4	10	82	5

Note: Question: "In general, do you think the courts in this area deal too harshly or not harshly enough with criminals?"

[a] In 1974 and 1982 half of the General Social Survey sample was asked the question as noted above and half the sample was asked the same question but with the phrase "or don't you have enough information about the courts to say" added at the end. The "don't know" column for these rows includes those saying "not enough information."

Sources: 1965-1969, December 1972: Gallup survey; 1981: *Los Angeles Times* survey (copyright © 1981, *Los Angeles Times,* reprinted by permission); others: General Social Survey.

Questions

1. In 1950 black family income was 54.3 percent of white family income (Table 12-1). Had the gap narrowed significantly by 1987?

2. In the 1970s and 1980s, when the proportion of whites and blacks below the poverty level was stable or rose very slightly, the proportion of those of Hispanic origin below the poverty level increased by over six percentage points (Table 12-2). State two hypotheses that might explain this result.

3. Which group is poorer, as measured by the percentage below the poverty line—the young or the elderly (Table 12-3)? If white income is so much higher than black income (Table 12-1), how can it be that nearly two-thirds of the poor people are white (Table 12-3)?

4. State and local social welfare expenditures (as a percentage of total outlays) have been relatively steady since 1960 (Table 12-4). What is there about state and local expenditures that kept them steady when total expenditures were increasing rapidly? (Hint: look at Table 12-5.)

5. If you add the expenditures under each category (for a given row), the amount exceeds the "total" column (Table 12-5). Similarly, if you add the percentages in a row of the next to last panel they total more than 100 percent. Why? (Hint: read carefully the explanatory material of the table—the heading, labels, footnotes.)

6. Did private or public social welfare expenditures have the greater absolute increase between 1972 and 1985 (Table 12-6)? What were those increases? Which had the greater percentage increase between 1972 and 1985? What were those percentages?

7. Why are pension and health spending likely to rise substantially in the late twentieth century and into the twenty-first century (Table 12-7)? (Hint: see Table 12-8.) What can be done to keep these costs down?

8. Apart from the early increases due to the expansion of Social Security to more types of workers, in what twenty-year period will the ratio of beneficiaries to covered workers increase the most (Table 12-8)? Why?

9. What are some of the assumptions that must go into projections of the sort shown in Table 12-8 and Figure 12-2? Which of these assumptions do you think is the weakest? Why?

10. On the basis of the percentages in the body of Table 12-9, what is the minimum proportion of the population that could be covered by one or more means-tested programs? The maximum proportion? How many in fact are covered by one or more means-tested benefits?

11. Have AFDC benefits increased or decreased since 1960 in relation to the poverty threshold (Table 12-10)? Calculate yearly benefit as a percentage of the poverty threshold for each year for 1960 to 1985. Now find the average percentage for Republican versus Democratic administrations (see Table 8-11 for administrations by year).

12. Combining information in Table 3-1 and Table 12-11, explain why the difference between black and white turnout rates is declining.

13. In what region, in 1968, was the greatest percentage of black students attending schools with more than half minority students (Table 12-12)? In 1984? In each of these years, which region had the smallest percentage of black students in minority-dominated schools? Which region, in 1980, had the fewest white students in almost totally white schools? Basing your answer on these data, which region currently appears to have the most segregated schools? The least segregated?

14. What conclusion would you draw about current attitudes on school integration from Table 12-13? Would you modify these conclusions in light of Table 12-14?

15. The District of Columbia is the "state" with the highest ratio of black elected officials to voting age population (Table 12-16). Why is it so high by comparison with the fifty states? Aside from D.C., Alabama has the largest ratio of elected officials to voting age population. Does this mean that Alabama elects a larger percentage of black officials than any other state? If not, what does it mean?

16. Many of the ratios in Table 12-16 don't seem quite correct. For example, for Alabama:

$$10.8/22.9 = .472$$

and for Arkansas:

$$3.0/13.6 = .221$$

Why don't these values match those in the table?

17. Which region (using the Census Bureau definition given in Table A-1 in the Appendix) has the lowest ratio of female legislators to population (Table 12-17)? There is less variation among states in the ratios for women (.053 to .631) than for blacks (.000 to 2.381) or for Hispanics (.000 to .942). Why?

18. Women in state and local government earned less than men in 1973 (Table 12-18). Thirteen years later, how much of the gap had they made up? What about blacks versus whites? How might the employment figures on the left side of the table help explain what you found for females' and blacks' earnings ratios? Insofar as the pattern at the federal level mirrors the state and local situation, how might Table 12-19 help explain the gap in earnings ratios?

19. Which category, violent crimes or property crimes, increased at a faster rate between 1960 and 1987 (Table 12-20)? What were these rates? Could changes in willingness to report crime affect data such as in Table 12-20? Why?

20. A comparison of endpoints—the first and last entries of a table or figure—sometimes masks part of the story. In Table 12-21, what is revealed about the change in the number of federal and state inmates if one looks at the years between 1950 and 1987?

21. There are at least two kinds of opinion change occurring in Table 12-22. Describe them.

13

Economic Policy

Economic policy makers labor under the burden of an overabundance of numbers. Statistics recording various aspects of the economy's performance appear regularly—often monthly. These statistics are important, not simply because of the conditions they report, but for the way they filter into economic calculations: expectations and reactions to indicators of past performance are critical determinants of how the economy performs in the future. Moreover, there is a direct link to politics because the public's perceptions of economic performance help shape choices in the voting booth: properly or not, presidents often get blamed when the economy turns down, and (less often) praised when it recovers. President Ronald Reagan's public approval ratings plummeted as an economic downturn continued through 1982 (Figure 8-2). The subsequent economic recovery played a substantial role in shaping the mood of the voters to secure Reagan's 1984 reelection in a landslide.

When one turns to even simple economic matters, fundamental issues and terms arise that distinguish the discourse from that in other areas of politics. One is the overall size of the economy, usually measured by the gross national product, or GNP (Table 13-1). Knowing what the GNP is and what it means are important to even a minimal understanding of economic statistics and policy. Without some sense of the size of the economy, it is impossible to make informed judgments about economic matters. For example, a trillion dollar national debt is unquestionably large, but many argue that it is not overburdening because it in fact represents the same proportion of the total economy as numerically smaller deficits did in earlier years (Figure 13-2).

A second key concept is that of constant dollars, which is explained in the introduction to Chapter 11, in connection with defense spending. A few additional points are appropriate here. Note that the basis for many constant dollar calculations is the Consumer Price Index, or CPI (Table 13-2). One can see from this index that a marketbasket of goods that cost $100 in 1982-1984 would have cost $29.60 in 1960. Unfortunately, while 1982-1984 is the base period in Table 13-2, other tabulations, such as those in Table 13-1, use a different base. This makes it more difficult to compare the data. However, the concept of a constant dollar is unchanged by which year is used as the base. (However, the CPI is not always used as the basis for such adjustments, and here it is not possible to move precisely from the figures in Table 13-2 to those in 13-1.)

During Ronald Reagan's and George Bush's presidencies, economic news has been dominated by the deficit. The growth in the federal deficit (Table 13-6) helped focus public attention on government spending and taxing, as politicians and economists alike tried to assess ways of reducing the gap between income and expenditures. Economic growth could provide the basis for greater tax revenues to balance the budget and reduce the deficit ("Grow our way out," as Reagan insisted). But as the national debt has continued to mount in relation to GNP (Figure 13-2), the political and economic demands for reduction of the debt have constrained government spending and compelled consideration of additional revenue sources. Tax increases are one means of reducing the federal deficit: Table 13-7 displays the revenue loss to the federal government from selected tax breaks, some of which have already been curtailed to raise revenue.

Cutting spending is another means of deficit reduction. Although federal budget outlays by function (Table 13-4) may give the impression of vast sums and a variety of programs suitable for cuts, Table 13-5 shows that barely a quarter of federal budget outlays can be changed by presidential decision. An increasing proportion of the federal budget has become relatively uncontrollable from the president's standpoint. Reducing spending in the relatively uncontrollable category would require that Congress rewrite laws affecting payments to which beneficiaries are entitled on the basis of past commitments. Programs that fall under this heading, such as Social Security, are referred to as entitlement programs.

It should come as no surprise to the reader that public opinion data are relevant to economic policy or that such data must be interpreted with care. A plurality of the public who claim knowledge about the issue favor a constitutional amendment requiring a balanced federal budget (Table 13-8). In some respects this tells us very little; a majority of the public is not in favor of spending cuts or tax increases, but at the same time it is in favor of balancing the budget. Despite these contradictory sentiments, feelings expressed in polls are closely watched by politicians. Questions about who has what sort of opinion as well as changes in opinions over time are important to the determination of future policies.

Unemployment and inflation are two other noteworthy features of the economic landscape that merit inclusion when considering politics. The large-scale entry of women into the labor force since World War II (Table 13-9), the fluctuations in the annual unemployment rate since 1929 (Table 13-10), and the relatively high unemployment rates among black teenagers (Table 13-11) document critical economic trends with political ramifications.

Because economic issues are an important aspect of political policy making and because economic conditions affect voter choices, economic data rank among the most vital of vital statistics on American politics.

Table 13-1 Gross National Product, 1929-1988 (billions)

Year	Current dollars	Annual percentage change	Constant (1982) dollars	Annual percentage change
1929	$103.9		$709.6	
1930	91.1	−12.3	642.8	−9.4
1931	76.4	−16.2	588.1	−8.5
1932	58.5	−23.4	509.2	−13.4
1933	56.0	−4.2	498.5	−2.1
1934	65.6	17.0	536.7	7.7
1935	72.8	11.0	580.2	8.1
1936	83.1	14.1	662.2	14.1
1937	91.3	9.8	695.3	5.0
1938	85.4	−6.5	664.2	−4.5
1939	91.3	7.0	716.6	7.9
1940	100.4	10.0	772.9	7.8
1941	125.5	25.0	909.4	17.7
1942	159.0	26.6	1,080.3	18.8
1943	192.7	21.2	1,276.2	18.1
1944	211.4	9.7	1,380.6	8.2
1945	213.4	0.9	1,354.8	−1.9
1946	212.4	−0.5	1,096.9	−19.0
1947	235.2	10.8	1,066.7	−2.8
1948	261.6	11.2	1,108.7	3.9
1949	260.4	−0.5	1,109.0	0.0
1950	288.3	10.7	1,203.7	8.5
1951	333.4	15.7	1,328.2	10.3
1952	351.6	5.5	1,380.0	3.9
1953	371.6	5.7	1,435.3	4.0
1954	372.5	0.2	1,416.2	−1.3
1955	405.9	9.0	1,494.9	5.6
1956	428.2	5.5	1,525.6	2.1
1957	451.0	5.3	1,551.1	1.7
1958	456.8	1.3	1,539.2	−0.8
1959	495.8	8.5	1,629.1	5.8
1960	515.3	3.9	1,665.3	2.2
1961	533.8	3.6	1,708.7	2.6
1962	574.6	7.6	1,799.4	5.3
1963	606.9	5.6	1,873.3	4.1
1964	649.8	7.1	1,973.3	5.3
1965	705.1	8.5	2,087.6	5.8
1966	772.0	9.5	2,208.3	5.8
1967	816.4	5.8	2,271.4	2.9
1968	892.7	9.3	2,365.6	4.1

(Table continues)

Table 13-1 *(Continued)*

Year	Current dollars	Annual percentage change	Constant (1982) dollars	Annual percentage change
1969	$963.9	8.0	$2,423.3	2.4
1970	1,015.5	5.4	2,416.2	−0.3
1971	1,102.7	8.6	2,484.8	2.8
1972	1,212.8	10.0	2,608.5	5.0
1973	1,359.3	12.1	2,744.1	5.2
1974	1,472.8	8.3	2,729.3	−0.5
1975	1,598.4	8.5	2,695.0	−1.3
1976	1,782.8	11.5	2,826.7	4.9
1977	1,990.5	11.7	2,958.6	4.7
1978	2,249.7	13.0	3,115.2	5.3
1979	2,508.2	11.5	3,192.4	2.5
1980	2,732.0	8.9	3,187.1	−0.2
1981	3,052.6	11.7	3,248.8	1.9
1982	3,166.0	3.7	3,166.0	−2.5
1983	3,405.7	7.6	3,279.1	3.6
1984	3,772.2	10.8	3,501.4	6.8
1985	4,014.9	6.4	3,618.7	3.4
1986	4,240.3	5.6	3,721.7	2.8
1987	4,526.7	6.8	3,847.0	3.4
1988	4,864.3	7.5	3,996.1	3.9

Sources: 1929-1987: U.S. Department of Commerce, *Survey of Current Business* (Washington, D.C.: U.S. Government Printing Office, September 1988), 57, 59; 1988: U.S. Department of Commerce, *News*, "Gross National Product: Fourth Quarter 1988 (Final)," press release, March 23, 1989, 7-8.

Table 13-2 Consumer Price Index, 1950-1988

Year	All items	Food	Shelter	Fuel, oil, and other household fuel commodities	Gas and electricity	Apparel and upkeep	Transportation Private[a]	Transportation Public	Medical care	All commodities	All services
1950	24.1	25.4	—	11.3	19.2	40.3	24.5	13.4	15.1	29.0	16.9
1951	26.0	28.2	—	11.8	19.3	43.9	25.6	14.8	15.9	31.6	17.8
1952	26.5	28.7	—	12.1	19.5	43.5	27.3	15.8	16.7	32.0	18.6
1953	26.7	28.3	22.0	12.6	19.9	43.1	27.8	16.8	17.3	31.9	19.4
1954	26.9	28.2	22.5	12.6	20.2	43.1	27.1	18.0	17.8	31.6	20.0
1955	26.8	27.8	22.7	12.7	20.7	42.9	26.7	18.5	18.2	31.3	20.4
1956	27.2	28.0	23.1	13.3	20.9	43.7	27.1	19.2	18.9	31.6	20.9
1957	28.1	28.9	24.0	14.0	21.1	44.5	28.6	19.9	19.7	32.6	21.8
1958	28.9	30.2	24.5	13.7	21.9	44.6	29.5	20.9	20.6	33.3	22.6
1959	29.1	29.7	24.7	13.9	22.4	45.0	30.8	21.5	21.5	33.3	23.3
1960	29.6	30.0	25.2	13.8	23.3	45.7	30.6	22.2	22.3	33.6	24.1
1961	29.9	30.4	25.4	14.1	23.5	46.1	30.8	23.2	22.9	33.8	24.5
1962	30.2	30.6	25.8	14.2	23.5	46.3	31.4	24.0	23.5	34.1	25.0
1963	30.6	31.1	26.1	14.4	23.5	46.9	31.6	24.3	24.1	34.4	25.5
1964	31.0	31.5	26.5	14.4	23.5	47.3	32.0	24.7	24.6	34.8	26.0
1965	31.5	32.2	27.0	14.6	23.5	47.8	32.5	25.2	25.2	35.2	26.6
1966	32.4	33.8	27.8	15.0	23.6	49.0	32.9	26.1	26.3	36.1	27.6
1967	33.4	34.1	28.8	15.5	23.7	51.0	33.8	27.4	38.2	36.8	28.8
1968	34.8	35.3	30.1	16.0	23.9	53.7	34.8	28.7	29.9	38.1	30.3
1969	36.7	37.1	32.6	16.3	24.3	56.8	36.0	30.9	31.9	39.9	32.4
1970	38.8	39.2	35.5	17.0	25.4	59.2	37.5	35.2	34.0	41.7	35.0

(Table continues)

383

Table 13-2 *(Continued)* 384

Year	All items	Food	Shelter	Fuel, oil, and other household fuel commodities	Gas and electricity	Apparel and upkeep	Transportation Private[a]	Transportation Public	Medical care	All commodities	All services
1971	40.5	40.4	37.0	18.2	27.1	61.1	39.4	37.8	36.1	43.2	37.0
1972	41.8	42.1	38.7	18.3	28.5	62.3	39.7	39.3	37.3	44.5	38.4
1973	44.4	48.2	40.5	21.1	29.9	64.6	41.0	39.7	38.8	47.8	40.1
1974	49.3	55.1	44.4	33.2	34.5	69.4	46.2	40.6	42.4	53.5	43.8
1975	53.8	59.8	48.8	36.4	40.1	72.5	50.6	43.5	47.5	58.2	48.0
1976	56.9	61.6	51.5	38.8	44.7	75.2	55.6	47.8	52.0	60.7	52.0
1977	60.6	65.6	54.9	43.9	50.5	78.6	59.7	50.0	57.0	64.2	56.0
1978	65.2	72.0	60.5	46.2	55.0	81.4	62.5	51.5	61.8	68.8	60.8
1979	72.6	79.9	68.9	62.4	61.0	84.9	71.7	54.9	67.5	76.6	67.5
1980	82.4	86.8	81.0	86.1	71.4	90.9	84.2	69.0	74.9	86.0	77.9
1981	90.9	93.6	90.5	104.6	81.9	95.3	93.8	85.6	82.9	93.2	88.1
1982	96.5	97.4	96.9	103.4	93.2	97.8	97.1	94.9	92.5	97.0	96.0
1983	99.6	99.4	99.1	97.2	101.5	100.2	99.3	99.5	100.6	99.8	99.4
1984	103.9	103.2	104.0	99.4	105.4	102.1	103.6	105.7	106.8	103.2	104.6
1985	107.6	105.6	109.8	95.9	107.1	105.0	106.2	110.5	113.5	105.4	109.9
1986	109.6	109.0	115.8	77.6	105.7	105.9	101.2	117.0	122.0	104.4	115.4
1987	113.6	113.5	121.3	77.9	103.8	110.6	104.2	121.1	130.1	107.7	120.2
1988	118.3	118.2	127.1	78.1	104.6	115.4	107.6	123.3	138.6	111.5	125.7

Note: "—" indicates not available. 1982-1984 equals 100. Data beginning in 1978 are for all urban consumers; earlier data are for all urban wage earners and clerical workers. Data beginning 1983 incorporate a rental equivalence measure for homeowners' costs and therefore are not strictly comparable with earlier figures.

[a] Includes direct pricing of new trucks and motorcycles beginning September 1982.

Sources: 1950-1987: U.S. President, *Economic Report of the President* (Washington, D.C.: U.S. Government Printing Office, 1989), 373-376; 1988: Department of Labor, Bureau of Labor Statistics.

Table 13-3 Federal Budget: Total, Defense, and Nondefense
Expenditures, 1940-1994 (billions)

Year	Current dollars			Constant (1982) dollars		
	National defense	Non-defense	Total	National defense	Non-defense	Total
1940	$1.7	$7.8	$9.5	$15.1	$68.1	$83.2
1941	6.4	7.2	13.7	51.2	61.3	112.6
1942	25.7	9.5	35.1	174.7	85.9	260.5
1943	66.7	11.9	78.6	414.8	115.2	530.1
1944	79.1	12.2	91.3	522.1	116.0	638.0
1945	83.0	9.7	92.7	591.3	77.6	668.9
1946	42.7	12.6	55.2	339.8	75.4	415.3
1947	12.8	21.7	34.5	89.9	122.9	212.8
1948	9.1	20.7	29.8	55.8	102.4	158.2
1949	13.2	25.7	38.8	77.4	125.0	202.5
1950	13.7	28.8	42.6	83.9	136.5	220.5
1951	23.6	21.9	45.5	150.3	100.4	250.6
1952	46.1	21.6	67.9	258.9	90.5	349.3
1953	52.8	23.3	76.1	271.5	95.8	367.5
1954	49.3	21.6	70.9	250.0	81.0	330.9
1955	42.7	25.7	68.4	211.0	100.1	311.1
1956	42.5	28.1	70.6	198.5	107.6	306.2
1957	45.4	31.1	76.6	203.5	115.3	318.8
1958	46.8	35.6	82.4	198.3	124.4	322.8
1959	49.0	43.1	92.1	196.0	150.9	346.9
1960	48.1	44.1	92.2	192.1	148.4	340.4
1961	49.6	48.1	97.7	195.2	159.4	354.6
1962	52.3	54.5	106.8	202.2	181.5	383.7
1963	53.4	57.9	111.3	197.1	187.6	384.6
1964	54.8	63.8	118.5	198.8	204.1	402.9
1965	50.6	67.6	118.2	181.4	213.2	394.6
1966	58.1	76.4	134.5	197.9	233.3	431.2
1967	71.4	86.0	157.5	235.1	253.5	488.4
1968	81.9	96.2	178.1	254.8	270.7	525.5
1969	82.5	101.1	183.6	243.4	267.0	510.4
1970	81.7	114.0	195.6	225.6	283.7	509.4
1971	78.9	131.3	210.2	202.7	306.7	509.4
1972	79.2	151.5	230.7	190.9	336.7	527.6
1973	76.7	169.0	245.7	175.1	352.4	527.5
1974	79.3	190.0	269.4	163.3	365.3	528.7
1975	86.5	245.8	332.3	159.8	426.2	586.0
1976	89.6	282.2	371.8	153.6	456.2	609.8
TQ[a]	22.3	73.7	96.0	37.1	115.3	152.4
1977	97.2	312.0	409.2	154.3	468.3	622.6

(Table continues)

Table 13-3 *(Continued)*

Year	Current dollars			Constant (1982) dollars		
	National defense	Non-defense	Total	National defense	Non-defense	Total
1978	$104.5	$354.2	$458.7	$155.0	$497.1	$652.2
1979	116.3	387.1	503.5	159.1	501.0	660.2
1980	134.0	456.9	590.9	164.0	535.1	699.1
1981	157.5	520.7	678.2	171.4	555.2	726.5
1982	185.3	560.4	745.7	185.3	560.4	745.7
1983	209.9	598.4	808.3	201.3	573.7	775.0
1984	227.4	624.4	851.8	211.3	576.8	788.1
1985	252.7	693.6	946.3	230.0	619.7	849.6
1986	273.4	716.9	990.3	243.7	623.8	867.5
1987	282.0	721.8	1,003.8	250.3	607.4	857.8
1988	290.4	773.7	1,064.0	252.9	626.3	879.2
1989 est.	298.3	838.8	1,137.0	250.0	652.4	902.4
1990 est.	303.0	848.9	1,151.8	244.6	636.5	881.2
1991 est.	314.4	892.9	1,207.3	245.6	647.1	892.7
1992 est.	326.4	918.0	1,244.4	248.3	646.6	894.9
1993 est.	339.9	939.1	1,279.0	253.0	646.7	899.7
1994 est.	354.3	957.3	1,311.6	259.4	647.0	906.3

[a] Transitional quarter when fiscal year start was shifted from July 1 to October 1.

Source: Office of Management and Budget, *Budget of the United States Government, Fiscal Year 1990, Historical Tables* (Washington, D.C.: U.S. Government Printing Office, 1989), Table 6-1, 122-131.

Table 13-4 Federal Budget Outlays by Function, 1940-1994 (billions)

Function	1940	1950	1960	1970	1975	1980	1984	1985	1986	1987	1988	1990 est.	1994 est.
National defense	$1.7	$13.7	$48.1	$81.7	$86.5	$134.0	$227.4	$252.7	$273.4	$282.0	$290.4	$303.0	$354.3
Human resources	4.1	14.2	26.2	75.3	173.2	313.4	432.0	471.8	481.6	502.2	533.4	600.0	748.5
Income security	1.5	4.1	7.4	15.6	50.2	86.5	112.7	128.2	119.8	123.3	129.3	136.8	160.9
Health	0.1	0.3	0.8	5.9	12.9	23.2	30.4	33.5	35.9	40.0	44.5	52.2	71.1
Veterans' benefits and services	0.6	8.8	5.4	8.7	16.6	21.2	25.6	26.3	26.4	26.8	29.4	29.9	32.0
Education, training, employment[a]	2.0	0.2	1.0	8.6	16.0	31.8	27.6	29.3	30.6	29.7	31.9	39.5	38.0
Social Security and Medicare	0.0	0.8	11.6	36.5	77.5	150.6	235.8	254.4	268.9	282.5	298.2	341.6	446.5
Other nondefense	3.7	14.6	17.9	38.6	72.6	143.6	192.3	221.7	235.3	219.6	240.3	248.8	208.7
Commerce and housing credit	0.6	1.0	1.6	2.1	9.9	9.4	6.9	4.2	4.9	6.2	18.8	8.3	5.9
Transportation	0.4	1.0	4.1	7.0	10.9	21.3	23.7	25.8	28.1	26.2	27.3	28.3	28.3
Natural resources and environment	1.0	1.3	1.6	3.1	7.3	13.9	12.6	13.4	13.6	13.4	14.6	14.4	14.4
Energy	0.1	0.3	0.5	1.0	2.9	10.2	7.1	5.7	4.7	4.1	2.3	2.3	3.1
Community, regional development	0.3	0.0	0.2	2.4	4.3	11.3	7.7	7.7	7.2	5.1	5.3	6.4	4.7
Agriculture	0.4	2.0	2.6	5.2	3.0	8.8	13.6	25.6	31.4	26.6	17.2	15.9	8.7
Net interest	0.9	4.8	6.9	14.4	23.2	52.5	111.1	129.4	136.0	138.6	151.7	170.1	132.3
International affairs	0.1	4.7	3.0	4.3	7.1	12.7	15.9	16.2	14.2	11.6	10.5	17.3	17.4
General science, space, technology	0.0	0.1	0.6	4.5	4.0	5.8	8.3	8.6	9.0	9.2	10.8	14.9	20.1
General government	0.3	1.0	1.2	2.3	10.4	13.0	11.8	11.6	12.5	7.6	9.5	10.0	9.5
Administration of justice	0.1	0.2	0.4	1.0	3.0	4.6	5.7	6.3	6.6	7.5	9.2	10.6	11.4
Undistributed offsetting receipts	−0.3	−1.8	−4.8	−8.6	−13.6	−19.9	−32.0	−32.8	−33.0	−36.5	−37.0	−42.0	−45.9
Total outlays	9.5	42.6	92.2	195.6	332.3	590.9	851.8	946.3	990.3	1,003.8	1,064.0	1,151.8	1,311.6

Note: For 1940-1975, ending June 30. Beginning 1980, ending September 30.
[a] Includes social services.

Source: Office of Management and Budget, *Budget of the U.S. Government, Fiscal Year 1990, Historical Tables*, Table 3-1, 39-45; percentages calculated by the editors.

Figure 13-1 Federal Outlays as a Percentage of GNP, 1869-1988

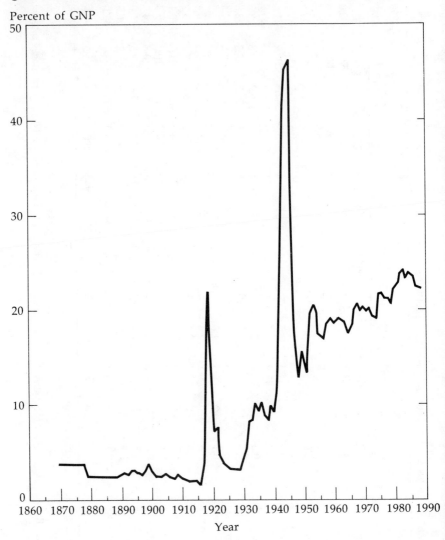

Percent of GNP

Year

Note: Averaged by decade for 1869-1888. 1971-1988 data are based on fiscal rather than calendar year GNP.

Source: 1869-1946: U.S. Bureau of the Census, *Historical Statistics of the U.S.* (Washington, D.C.: U.S. Government Printing Office, 1975), 224, 1114; 1947-1988: Office of Management and Budget, *Budget of the U.S. Government, Fiscal Year 1990, Historical Tables*, Table 15-3, 361-362.

Table 13-5 Executive Controllability of Federal Budget Outlays, 1970-1990

Outlays	1970	1975	1980	1981	1985	1986	1987	1988	1989 est.	1990 est.
Relatively uncontrollable outlays (billions)	$120.3	$222.2	$413.8	$476.4	$689.4	$746.0	$769.3	$807.4	$865.1	$902.9
Open-ended programs and fixed costs[a]	78.3	168.9	310.7	367.8	527.3	564.7	584.0	620.6	668.2	690.9
Payments for individuals[a]	60.1	139.5	246.6	287.6	380.6	402.6	421.7	448.0	481.5	516.5
Social Security and railroad retirement	30.7	67.3	120.0	141.2	189.9	199.9	208.6	220.3	233.7	248.1
Medical care	9.4	20.6	47.2	57.2	91.0	97.8	105.9	114.7	128.7	145.1
Federal employees' retirement and insurance[b]	8.7	18.4	34.7	40.5	49.8	52.9	55.2	59.3	60.9	65.7
Food and nutrition assistance	—	1.6	3.5	3.5	3.7	3.8	4.1	4.3	4.7	5.0
Public assistance and related programs	6.4	12.2	17.5	19.3	22.2	24.5	25.7	28.8	31.2	30.8
Unemployment assistance	3.1	12.8	16.8	18.2	16.2	16.3	15.7	13.8	14.3	14.8
Net interest	14.4	23.2	52.5	68.7	129.4	136.0	138.6	151.7	165.7	169.9
Farm price supports[c]	3.8	0.6	2.8	4.0	17.7	25.8	22.4	12.2	13.9	11.8
Prior-year contracts and obligations[d]	41.9	53.3	103.2	108.6	162.2	181.3	185.3	186.8	196.9	212.0
Relatively controllable outlays (billions)	83.8	113.2	178.7	198.7	284.0	272.6	265.1	290.1	306.3	282.3
National defense	57.6	64.2	97.4	115.9	160.5	165.4	169.1	174.8	181.9	189.7
Civilian programs	26.3	49.1	81.3	82.8	123.5	107.1	96.0	115.3	124.4	92.6
Undistributed employer share, employee retirement (billions)	−8.4	−11.2	−15.8	−17.9	−27.2	−28.3	−30.6	−33.4	−34.3	−33.4
Total outlays	195.6	332.3	590.9	678.2	946.3	990.3	1,003.8	1,064.0	1,137.0	1,151.8
Relatively uncontrollable outlays as a percentage of total outlays	61.5%	66.9%	70.0%	70.2%	72.9%	75.3%	76.6%	75.9%	76.1%	78.4%

(Notes follow)

Table 13-5 (*Continued*)

Note: "—" indicates not available.
[a] Includes other outlays not shown separately.
[b] Includes items previously classified in the veterans' benefits grouping.
[c] Prices from Commodity Credit Corporation.
[d] Excludes prior-year contracts and obligations for items under open-ended programs and fixed costs.

Sources: 1970-1981: U.S. Bureau of the Census, *Statistical Abstract of the U.S., 1987* (Washington, D.C.: U.S. Government Printing Office, 1986), 296; 1985-1990: Office of Management and Budget, *Budget of the U.S. Government, Fiscal Year 1990, Historical Tables,* Table 8-1, 154-155.

Table 13-6   The National Debt, 1940-1994

Year	Debt held by the public (millions)	As a percentage of GNP
1940	$42,772	44.6
1941	48,223	42.7
1942	67,753	47.6
1943	127,766	72.7
1944	184,796	91.5
1945	235,182	110.7
1946	241,861	113.6
1947	224,339	100.3
1948	216,270	87.3
1949	214,322	81.2
1950	219,023	82.1
1951	214,326	68.0
1952	214,758	62.7
1953	218,383	59.7
1954	224,499	60.8
1955	226,616	58.6
1956	222,156	53.1
1957	219,320	49.8
1958	226,336	50.3
1959	234,701	48.7
1960	236,840	46.7
1961	238,357	46.0
1962	248,010	44.5
1963	253,978	43.2
1964	256,849	40.8
1965	260,778	38.8
1966	263,714	35.7
1967	266,626	33.6
1968	289,545	34.1
1969	278,108	29.9
1970	283,198	28.6
1971	303,037	28.7
1972	322,377	28.0
1973	340,910	26.6
1974	343,699	24.3
1975	394,700	25.9
1976	477,404	28.1
TQ[a]	495,509	27.6
1977	549,103	28.4
1978	607,125	28.0
1979	639,761	26.1

(Table continues)

Table 13-6 *(Continued)*

Year	Debt held by the public (millions)	As a percentage of GNP
1980	$709,291	26.6
1981	784,791	26.3
1982	919,238	29.3
1983	1,131,049	34.0
1984	1,299,951	35.3
1985	1,499,362	37.9
1986	1,736,163	41.5
1987	1,888,134	42.6
1988	2,050,196	42.9
1989 est.	2,193,818	42.9
1990 est.	2,285,014	41.7
1991 est.	2,351,234	40.2
1992 est.	2,382,881	38.4
1993 est.	2,379,896	36.3
1994 est.	2,345,980	34.1

[a] Transitional quarter when fiscal year start was shifted from July 1 to October 1.

Source: Office of Management and Budget, *Budget of the U.S. Government, Fiscal Year 1990, Historical Tables,* Table 7-1, 144-145.

Figure 13-2 The National Debt as a Percentage of GNP, 1940-1994

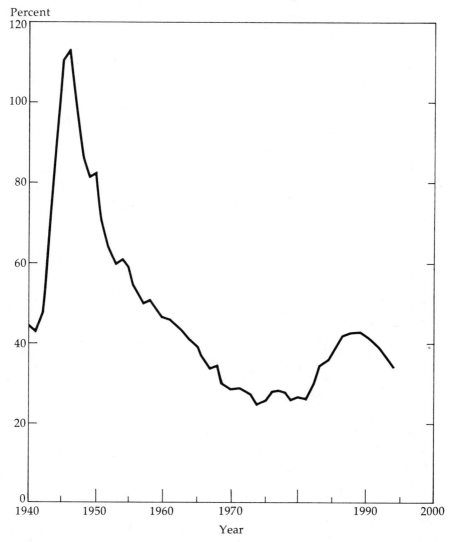

Note: 1989-1994 percentages are estimates. Figures reflect debt held by the public and do not include debt held by federal government accounts.

Source: Budget of the U.S. Government, Fiscal Year 1990, Historical Tables, Table 7-1, 144-145.

Table 13-7 Revenue Loss Estimates for Selected Tax Expenditures, 1980-1988 (millions)

Type of tax expenditure	1980	1985	1988
Commerce and housing credit			
Exclusion of interest on life insurance savings	$3,490	$2,175	$5,410
Deductibility of interest on consumer credit	4,745	15,530	6,530
Deductibility of mortgage interest on owner-occupied homes	15,615	24,785	33,675
Deductibility of property tax on owner-occupied homes	7,310	9,315	10,100
Deferral of capital gains on home sales	1,010	1,775	3,700
Exclusion of capital gains on home sales for persons age 55 and over	535	830	2,860
Investment credit, other than ESOP's, rehabilitation of structures, energy property, and reforestation expenditures	18,250	24,445	9,195
Accelerated depreciation of machinery and equipment[a]	—	20,145	21,920
Education, training, employment, and social services			
Deductibility of charitable contributions (education)	1,090	1,345	1,520
Credit for child and dependent care expenses	885	2,700	3,920
Deductibility of charitable contributions, other than education and health	6,270	10,175	10,460
Health			
Exclusion of employer contributions for medical insurance premiums and medical care	12,075	21,095	24,690
Deductibility of medical expenses	3,150	3,620	1,960
Exclusion of interest on state and local debt for private nonprofit health facilities	425	1,405	2,230
Deductibility of charitable contributions (health)	1,370	1,615	1,375
Social Security and Medicare			
Exclusion of Social Security benefits			
Disability insurance benefits	690	1,170	1,095
OASI benefits for retired workers	6,890	12,955	13,470
Benefits for dependents and survivors	1,015	3,755	2,850

Income security			
Exclusion of workmen's compensation benefits	2,200	2,225	2,660
Net exclusion of pension contributions and earnings			
Employer plans	19,785	48,525	41,765
Individual Retirement Accounts	—	12,695	9,080
Keoghs	1,925	1,960	1,520
Veterans benefits and services			
Exclusion of veterans disability compensation	1,065	1,695	1,470
General purpose fiscal assistance			
Deductibility of nonbusiness state and local taxes other than on owner-occupied homes	14,690	21,455	17,250

Note: "—" indicates not available. Fiscal year basis. Tax expenditures are defined as revenue losses attributable to provisions of the federal tax laws which allow a special exclusion, exemption, or deduction from gross income or which provide a special credit, a preferential rate of tax, or a deferral of liability. The Internal Revenue Service collected slightly under $500 billion in 1987 through individual and corporate income taxes.
[a] Pre-1983 budget method.

Source: U.S. Office of Management and Budget, *Special Analyses, Budget of the U.S. Government,* annual.

Table 13-8   Public Opinion on the Budget-Balancing Amendment, Cross-Section, 1985 (percent)

| | Heard/read about amendment | | | | |
	Yes	No	Favor	Oppose	No opinion
Sex					
Male	64	36	55	28	17
Female	51	49	44	26	30
Race/ethnicity					
White	59	41	50	26	24
Nonwhite	45	55	44	33	23
Black	48	52	44	35	21
Education					
Less than high school	44	56	39	28	33
High school	45	55	47	28	25
College	78	22	59	27	14
Income					
Under $10,000	46	54	38	27	35
$10,000-14,999	45	55	36	29	35
$15,000-24,999	57	43	51	31	18
$25,000 and over	67	33	59	25	16
Political affiliation					
Democrat	54	46	44	36	20
Independent	60	40	51	25	24
Republican	60	40	55	22	23
National	57	43	49	27	24

Note: Question: "Have you heard or read about a proposal for a constitutional amendment that would require the federal government to balance the national budget each year? Under the proposed amendment, any federal budget passed by Congress would have projected tax revenues that are equal to projected government spending unless a three-fifths majority of Congress voted not to do so. Would you favor or oppose this amendment to the Constitution?"

Source: The Gallup Report (September 1985), 10-11.

Table 13-9 Civilian Labor Force Participation Rate Overall and by Sex and Race, 1948-1988 (percent)

Year	Total	Male	Female	White	Black and other nonwhite
1948	58.8	86.6	32.7	—	—
1949	58.9	86.4	33.1	—	—
1950	59.2	86.4	33.9	—	—
1951	59.2	86.3	34.6	—	—
1952	59.0	86.3	34.7	—	—
1953	58.9	86.0	34.4	—	—
1954	58.8	85.5	34.6	58.2	64.0
1955	59.3	85.4	35.7	58.7	64.2
1956	60.0	85.5	36.9	59.4	64.9
1957	59.6	84.8	36.9	59.1	64.4
1958	59.5	84.2	37.1	58.9	64.8
1959	59.3	83.7	37.1	58.7	64.3
1960	59.4	83.3	37.7	58.8	64.5
1961	59.3	82.9	38.1	58.8	64.1
1962	58.8	82.0	37.9	58.3	63.2
1963	58.7	81.4	38.3	58.2	63.0
1964	58.7	81.0	38.7	58.2	63.1
1965	58.9	80.7	39.3	58.4	62.9
1966	59.2	80.4	40.3	58.7	63.0
1967	59.6	80.4	41.1	59.2	62.8
1968	59.6	80.1	41.6	59.3	62.2
1969	60.1	79.8	42.7	59.9	62.1
1970	60.4	79.7	43.3	60.2	61.8
1971	60.2	79.1	43.4	60.1	60.9
1972	60.4	78.9	43.9	60.4	60.2
1973	60.8	78.8	44.7	60.8	60.5
1974	61.3	78.7	45.7	61.4	60.3
1975	61.2	77.9	46.3	61.5	59.6
1976	61.6	77.5	47.3	61.8	59.8
1977	62.3	77.7	48.4	62.5	60.4
1978	63.2	77.9	50.0	63.3	62.2
1979	63.7	77.8	50.9	63.9	62.2
1980	63.8	77.4	51.5	64.1	61.7
1981	63.9	77.0	52.1	64.3	61.3
1982	64.0	76.6	52.6	64.3	61.6
1983	64.0	76.4	52.9	64.3	62.1
1984	64.4	76.4	53.6	64.6	62.6
1985	64.8	76.3	54.5	65.0	63.3
1986	65.3	76.3	55.3	65.5	63.7
1987	65.6	76.2	56.0	65.8	64.3
1988	65.9	76.2	56.6	66.2	64.0

Note: "—" indicates not available. Figures are for persons sixteen years of age and over. The participation rate is the percentage of adults considered to be in the labor force. It is roughly those persons who are working, temporarily laid off, or looking for work. For details, see *Statistical Abstract of the U.S., 1987,* 372.

Sources: U.S. President, *Economic Report of the President* (1989), 349; U.S. Department of Labor, Bureau of Labor Statistics, *Employment and Earnings, January 1989, 1988 Annual Averages* (Washington, D.C.: U.S. Government Printing Office, 1989), 158-159, 161, 163.

Table 13-10   Unemployment Rate Overall, 1929-1988, and by Sex and Race, 1948-1988 (percent)

Year	Civilian workers	Male	Female	White	Nonwhite
1929	3.2	—	—	—	—
1933	24.9	—	—	—	—
1939	17.2	—	—	—	—
1940	14.6	—	—	—	—
1941	9.9	—	—	—	—
1942	4.7	—	—	—	—
1943	1.9	—	—	—	—
1944	1.2	—	—	—	—
1945	1.9	—	—	—	—
1946	3.9	—	—	—	—
1947	3.9	—	—	—	—
1948	3.8	3.6	4.1	3.5	5.9
1949	5.9	5.9	6.0	5.6	8.9
1950	5.3	5.1	5.7	4.9	9.0
1951	3.3	2.8	4.4	3.1	5.3
1952	3.0	2.8	3.6	2.8	5.4
1953	2.9	2.8	3.3	2.7	4.5
1954	5.5	5.3	6.0	5.0	9.9
1955	4.4	4.2	4.9	3.9	8.7
1956	4.1	3.8	4.8	3.6	8.3
1957	4.3	4.1	4.7	3.8	7.9
1958	6.8	6.8	6.8	6.1	12.6
1959	5.5	5.2	5.9	4.8	10.7
1960	5.5	5.4	5.9	5.0	10.2
1961	6.7	6.4	7.2	6.0	12.4
1962	5.5	5.2	6.2	4.9	10.9
1963	5.7	5.2	6.5	5.0	10.8
1964	5.2	4.6	6.2	4.6	9.6
1965	4.5	4.0	5.5	4.1	8.1
1966	3.8	3.2	4.8	3.4	7.3
1967	3.8	3.1	5.2	3.4	7.4
1968	3.6	2.9	4.8	3.2	6.7
1969	3.5	2.8	4.7	3.1	6.4
1970	4.9	4.4	5.9	4.5	8.2
1971	5.9	5.3	6.9	5.4	9.9
1972	5.6	5.0	6.6	5.1	10.0
1973	4.9	4.2	6.0	4.3	9.0
1974	5.6	4.9	6.7	5.0	9.9
1975	8.5	7.9	9.3	7.8	13.8
1976	7.7	7.1	8.6	7.0	13.1
1977	7.1	6.3	8.2	6.2	13.1
1978	6.1	5.3	7.2	5.2	11.9
1979	5.8	5.1	6.8	5.1	11.3

(Table continues)

Table 13-10   *(Continued)*

Year	Civilian workers	Male	Female	White	Nonwhite
1980	7.1	6.9	7.4	6.3	13.1
1981	7.6	7.4	7.9	6.7	14.2
1982	9.7	9.9	9.4	8.6	17.3
1983	9.6	9.9	9.2	8.4	17.8
1984	7.5	7.4	7.6	6.5	14.4
1985	7.2	7.0	7.4	6.2	13.7
1986	7.0	6.9	7.1	6.0	13.1
1987	6.2	6.2	6.2	5.3	11.6
1988	5.5	5.5	5.6	4.7	11.7

Note: "—" indicates not available. 1929-1947 figures are for persons fourteen years of age and over. 1948-1988 figures are for persons sixteen years of age and over.

Sources: 1981-1987: U.S. President, *Economic Report of the President* (1988), 344, 352; 1988: U.S. Department of Labor, Bureau of Labor Statistics, *Employment and Earnings, January 1989, 1988 Annual Averages,* 158-159, 161-162.

Table 13-11 Unemployment by Race, Sex, and Age, 1972-1988 (percent)

| | White | | | | Black | | | |
| | Male | | Female | | Male | | Female | |
Year	16-19	20 and over	16-19	20 and over	16-19	20 and over	16-19	20 and over
1972	14.2	3.6	14.2	4.9	31.7	7.0	40.5	9.0
1973	12.3	3.0	13.0	4.3	27.8	6.0	36.1	8.6
1974	13.5	3.5	14.5	5.1	33.1	7.4	37.4	8.8
1975	18.3	6.2	17.4	7.5	38.1	12.5	41.0	12.2
1976	17.3	5.4	16.4	6.8	37.5	11.4	41.6	11.7
1977	15.0	4.7	15.9	6.2	39.2	10.7	43.4	12.3
1978	13.5	3.7	14.4	5.2	36.7	9.3	40.8	11.2
1979	13.9	3.6	14.0	5.0	34.2	9.3	39.1	10.9
1980	16.2	5.3	14.8	5.6	37.5	12.4	39.8	11.9
1981	17.9	5.6	16.6	5.9	40.7	13.5	42.2	13.4
1982	21.7	7.8	19.0	7.3	48.9	17.8	47.1	15.4
1983	20.2	7.9	18.3	6.9	48.8	18.1	48.2	16.5
1984	16.8	5.7	15.2	5.8	42.7	14.3	42.6	13.5
1985	16.5	5.4	14.8	5.7	41.0	13.2	39.2	13.1
1986	16.3	5.3	14.9	5.4	39.3	12.9	39.2	12.4
1987	15.5	4.8	13.4	4.6	34.4	11.1	34.9	11.6
1988	13.9	4.1	12.3	4.1	32.7	10.1	32.0	10.4

Sources: U.S. President, *Economic Report of the President* (1989): 353; 1988: U.S. Department of Labor, Bureau of Labor Statistics, *Employment and Earnings, January 1989, 1988 Annual Averages,* 161-162, 164.

Questions

1. How can it happen, as it did in 1945, 1954, and other years, that the gross national product increases in current dollars but declines in constant dollars (Table 13-1)? What accounts for the greatest increase in GNP when measured in constant dollars? The biggest decrease in current GNP? In GNP in constant dollars? Do the biggest increases and decreases in current GNP coincide with the biggest increases and decreases in GNP in constant dollars? Why or why not?

2. Which component of the Consumer Price Index increased the most between 1967 and 1981 (Table 13-2)? What has happened to this component since 1981? Has inflation for all items been negative in any year since 1950?

3. Employee A got a job in 1967 for $8,000 per year. Twelve years later employee B got the same kind of job with an annual salary of $16,000. Using Table 13-2 and the numbers for "all items" in those years, decide whether starting salaries had increased or decreased in constant terms? If a basket of food cost $20.00 in 1960, what would the same food cost in 1988?

4. Ronald Reagan made the charge in 1980 that an increase in defense spending was overdue because spending had been reduced under President Jimmy Carter. Was Reagan correct (Table 13-3)? Did President Reagan increase military spending? Which increased more under Carter (1977-1980), defense spending or nondefense spending? Under Reagan (1981-1988)?

5. Excepting the combined categories (human resources and other nondefense), of the relatively large categories of expenditures (say, more than 3 percent of total outlays in 1960), only three categories were a larger percentage of the budget in 1988 than in 1960 (Table 13-4). What were they? In which category was the increase greatest? In constant dollars (using the CPI for "all items" from Table 13-2), did outlays for agriculture increase between 1960 and 1988?

6. What does it mean to say that Social Security, medical care, farm price supports, and so forth are relatively uncontrollable outlays (Table 13-5)? Table 13-5 indicates why it is increasingly difficult to reduce the federal budget deficit. What is that reason?

7. What milestone in the size of the national debt was passed in 1983 (Table 13-6)? Some people argue that the national debt is not a big problem despite its tremendous size. On what basis could one possibly make that argument (Table 13-6 and Figure 13-2)?

8. Based on the list in Table 13-7, do you personally benefit from any exclusions, exemptions, or deductions? Do your parents? How? (There is no single right and wrong answer.) There is at least one benefit that students certainly benefit from indirectly, more or less depending on whether they attend a public or a private school. What is this benefit?

9. Assuming that the proportions who favor, oppose, and have no opinion are the same for those who have heard or read about the budget-balancing amendment and those who have not, what proportion of the sample heard or read about the amendment and favored it (Table 13-8)? Is this assumption likely to be correct? Why or why not? Is there any evidence in the rest of the table that supports your reasoning?

10. Among the groups shown in Tables 13-10 and 13-11, which had the highest unemployment rate through 1981? Since 1982?

11. For all sets of teenagers, the absolute percentage point decline in unemployment between 1982 and 1988 exceeded the decline among those aged twenty and over (Table 13-11). Why? (Hint: the same factor explains why it was easier for students today to get into their chosen college than for those who graduated just a few years ago.)

Appendix

Table A-1 Regions as Defined by the U.S. Census Bureau

Northeast	Midwest	South	West
New England	East north central	South Atlantic	Mountain
Connecticut	Illinois	Delaware	Arizona
New Hampshire	Indiana	District of	Colorado
Maine	Michigan	Columbia	Idaho
Massachusetts	Ohio	Florida	Montana
Rhode Island	Wisconsin	Georgia	Nevada
Vermont	West north central	Maryland	New Mexico
Middle Atlantic	Iowa	North Carolina	Utah
New Jersey	Kansas	South Carolina	Wyoming
New York	Minnesota	Virginia	Pacific
Pennsylvania	Missouri	West Virginia	Alaska
	Nebraska	East south central	California
	North Dakota	Alabama	Hawaii
	South Dakota	Kentucky	Oregon
		Mississippi	Washington
		Tennessee	
		West south central	
		Arkansas	
		Louisiana	
		Oklahoma	
		Texas	

Source: U.S. Bureau of the Census, *Statistical Abstract of the U.S., 1987* (Washington, D.C.: U.S. Government Printing Office, 1986), Figure I.

Table A-2 Regions as Defined by the Gallup Poll and Congressional Quarterly

East	Midwest	South	West
Connecticut	Illinois	Alabama	Alaska
Delaware	Indiana	Arkansas	Arizona
District of Columbia	Iowa	Florida	California
Maine	Kansas	Georgia	Colorado
Maryland	Michigan	Kentucky	Hawaii
Massachusetts	Minnesota	Louisiana	Idaho
New Hampshire	Missouri	Mississippi	Montana
New Jersey	Nebraska	North Carolina	Nevada
New York	North Dakota	Oklahoma	New Mexico
Pennsylvania	Ohio	South Carolina	Oregon
Rhode Island	South Dakota	Tennessee	Utah
Vermont	Wisconsin	Texas	Washington
West Virginia		Virginia	Wyoming

Source: The Gallup Report (November 1984), 30; Congressional Quarterly Weekly Report (1988), 112.

Table A-3 Regions for Partisan Competition Table (Table 4-3)

New England	Middle Atlantic	Midwest	Plains
Connecticut	Delaware	Illinois	Iowa
Maine	New Jersey	Indiana	Kansas
Massachusetts	New York	Michigan	Minnesota
New Hampshire	Pennsylvania	Ohio	Nebraska
Rhode Island		Wisconsin	North Dakota
Vermont			South Dakota

South	Border	Rocky Mountain	Pacific Coast
Alabama	District of Columbia	Arizona	Alaska
Arkansas	Kentucky	Colorado	California
Florida	Maryland	Idaho	Hawaii
Georgia	Missouri	Montana	Oregon
Louisiana	Oklahoma	Nevada	Washington
Mississippi	West Virginia	New Mexico	
North Carolina		Utah	
South Carolina		Wyoming	
Tennessee			
Texas			
Virginia			

Table A-4 Regions for School Desegregation Table (Table 12-12)

South	Border	Northeast	Midwest	West	Excluded
Alabama	Delaware	Connecticut	Illinois	Arizona	Alaska
Arkansas	District of	Maine	Indiana	California	Hawaii
Florida	Columbia	Massachusetts	Iowa	Colorado	
Georgia	Kentucky	New	Kansas	Idaho	
Louisiana	Maryland	Hampshire	Michigan	Montana	
Mississippi	Missouri	New Jersey	Minnesota	Nevada	
North	Oklahoma	New York	Nebraska	New Mexico	
Carolina	West Virginia	Pennsylvania	North	Oregon	
South		Rhode Island	Dakota	Utah	
Carolina		Vermont	Ohio	Washington	
Tennessee			South	Wyoming	
Texas			Dakota		
Virginia			Wisconsin		

Source: Gary Orfield, testimony before the House Subcommittee on Civil and Constitutional Rights, *Civil Rights Implications of the Education Block Grant Program,* September 9, 1982, 67-72.

Guide to References
for Political Statistics

General

Alonso, William, and Paul Starr, eds., *The Politics of Numbers*. New York: Russell Sage, 1987.
Excellent analysis of issues relating to the collection and publication of statistics, especially the U.S. census.

Austin, Erik W., and Jerome M. Clubb. *Political Facts of the United States Since 1789*. New York: Columbia University Press, 1986.
Convenient one-volume compilation of otherwise all-too-often elusive data on politics in the nation; one strength is the long time series.

Congressional Information Service. *American Statistics Index: A Comprehensive Guide and Index to the Statistical Publications of the U.S. Government*. Washington, D.C.: Congressional Information Service, 1973-. Annual, with monthly supplements.
Definitive guide, multiply indexed, to statistics "of probable research significance" in government publications; 1974 "Annual and Retrospective Edition" includes not only items in print but also significant items published over the preceding decade.

Congressional Information Service. *Statistical Reference Index: A Selective Guide to American Statistical Publications from Sources Other than the U.S. Government*. Washington, D.C. Congressional Information Service, 1980-. Annual, with bimonthly supplements.
A complement to *American Statistics Index*, indexes statistics from private and public sources other than the U.S. federal government.

Congressional Quarterly Weekly Report. Washington, D.C.: Congressional Quarterly, 1945-. Weekly.
Newsweekly covering political developments in Congress, the presidency, the Supreme Court, and national politics; individual voting records on all

roll-call votes in the House and Senate; texts of presidential press conferences and major statements.

National Journal. Washington, D.C.: National Journal, Inc., 1969-. Weekly.
Newsweekly about government; reviews recent actions and features analyses of policy and political issues.

U.S. Bureau of the Census. *Historical Statistics of the U.S., Colonial Times to 1970.* Bicentennial edition. Washington, D.C.: U.S. Government Printing Office, 1975.
Invaluable, broad-ranging collection of over 12,000 time series covering the nation's history; often the series can be updated by the annual *Statistical Abstract of the U.S.* (see below).

U.S. Bureau of the Census. *Statistical Abstract of the U.S.* Washington, D.C.: U.S. Government Printing Office, 1879-. Annual.
Strong, indispensable collection of nationally significant statistics from public and private sources on economics, politics, and society; generally worth checking first; also a useful guide to sources for additional statistics; indicates which time series update those in *Historical Statistics* (see above).

The Constitution

Balinski, Michel, and H. P. Young. *Fair Representation.* New Haven, Conn.: Yale University Press, 1982.
Analysis of statistical methods of apportionment of representatives among the states.

Congressional Research Service. *The Constitution of the United States: Analysis and Interpretation.* Washington, D.C.: U.S. Government Printing Office, 1987. 99th Cong., 1st sess., S.Doc. 99-16. Supplement issued 100th Cong., 1st sess., S.Doc. 100-9.
Not statistics laden, but the essential document with commentary and annotations of cases decided by the Supreme Court; handy tables on proposed constitutional amendments pending and unratified, laws (congressional, state, or local) held unconstitutional by the Supreme Court, and Supreme Court decisions overruled by subsequent decisions; U.S. law requires a new edition every ten years with biennial supplements between editions to keep this work current.

Dixon, Robert G., Jr. *Democratic Representation: Reapportionment in Law and Politics.* New York: Oxford University Press, 1968.
A comprehensive early account of districting theory and practice, with a strong statistical base.

U.S. Congress. House. *Constitution, Jefferson's Manual, and Rules of the House of Representatives of the United States.* Washington, D.C.: U.S. Government Printing Office. Biennial.
Handy reference for the Constitution containing complete notes of all ratifications; indexed.

The Mass Media

Adams, William C. "As New Hampshire Goes..." In *Media and Momentum*, Gary R. Orren and Nelson W. Polsby, eds. Chatham, N.J.: Chatham House, 1987.
Media coverage of the 1984 presidential nomination.

ADI Book. Beltsville, Md.: Arbitron Television. Annual.
Reports of television usage, including demographic and market analyses.

Broadcasting Publications. *Broadcasting Cablecasting Yearbook.* Washington, D.C.: Broadcasting Publications, 1982-. Annual. Continues *Broadcasting Cable Yearbook*, which combined *Broadcasting Yearbook* (1968-1979) and *Broadcasting Cable Sourcebook* (1973-1979).
International directory of radio, television, and cable industries as well as related fields; presents some statistical overviews.

Editor & Publisher—The Fourth Estate. New York: Editor & Publisher Co., 1884-. Weekly.
Weekly periodical covering the media.

Lichter, Robert, Daniel Amundson, and Richard Noyes. *The Video Campaign.* Washington, D.C.: American Enterprise Institute for Public Policy Research, 1988.
Detailed content analyses of national television news coverage of the 1988 presidential primaries.

Magazine Index. Belmont, Calif.: Information Access Co., 1977-.
Indexes a long list of magazines, including a number of political news magazines.

Multimedia Audiences: Television Audiences. New York: Mediamark Research, Inc., 1979-. Semiannual.
Detailed reports of demographic and marketing segments of media audiences.

National Newspaper Index. Belmont, Calif.: Information Access Co., 1977-.
Indexes major national newspapers. The current list includes the *New York Times, Wall Street Journal, Christian Science Monitor, Los Angeles Times,* and the *Washington Post.* The *New York Times* has its own longstanding index.

Newsbank. New Canaan, Conn.: NewsBank, 1971-.
Microfiche collection of indexed newspaper articles from hundreds of American newspapers, covering 1970 to the present; includes newspapers from every state.

Nielsen Television Index. Northbrook, Ill.: A. C. Nielsen, 1955. Annual.
Overall and market section reports on television viewing and network program audiences.

Public Affairs Video Archives Catalogue. West Lafayette, Ind.: Public Affairs Video Archives, Purdue University, 1988-.

Archives of C-SPAN programming. Partial coverage 1987-September 1988, complete coverage since October 1988.

Robinson, Michael J., and Margaret A. Sheehan. *Over the Wire and on TV: CBS and UPI in Campaign 1980.* New York: Russell Sage, 1983.
Analytical volume that contains content analyses of television stories and wire service reports of the 1980 presidential campaign.

Sterling, Christopher H. *Electronic Media: A Guide to Trends in Broadcasting and Newer Technologies: 1920-1983.* New York: Praeger, 1984.
Data on growth, ownership, economics, employment and training, contents, audience and regulation of radio, television, and cable; strong on trends and time series.

Television Digest. *Cable and Station Coverage Atlas, 1986.* Washington, D.C.: Television Digest, 1986.
Data on television stations and the growing reach of cable systems.

Television Digest. *Television and Cable Factbook.* Washington, D.C.: Television Digest, 1946-. Annual.
Data on cable, television, and related industries; published in two volumes: "Stations" and "Cable and Services."

Television News Index and Abstracts. Nashville, Tenn.: Vanderbilt Television News Archives, Vanderbilt University, 1972-. Monthly.
Archives of nightly network news.

Elections and Campaigns

Alexander, Herbert E., and Brian A. Haggerty. *Financing the 1984 Election.* Lexington, Mass.: Lexington Books, 1987.
Detailed statistical coverage of fund-raising and spending in all phases of the presidential campaign; continues a series of books by Alexander on financing presidential campaigns since 1960.

Bartley, Numan V., and Hugh D. Graham. *Southern Elections: County and Precinct Data, 1950-1972.* Baton Rouge, La.: Louisiana State University Press, 1978.
Gubernatorial and senatorial contests, meaningful primaries, and referenda in eleven southern states; some socioeconomic and geographic analysis of the pattern of the votes.

Congressional Quarterly. *Congressional Quarterly's Guide to U.S. Elections.* 2d ed. Washington, D.C.: Congressional Quarterly, 1985.
Superb collection of vote returns for presidential, gubernatorial, and House elections since 1824, electoral college votes since 1789, senatorial elections since 1913, presidential primaries since 1912, and primaries for governor and senator since 1956 (in southern states since 1919); general and candidate indexes; biographies of presidential and vice-presidential candidates; lists of governors and senators since 1789; discussions of and

data on political parties and presidential nominating conventions throughout the nation's history.

Federal Election Commission. *Annual Report.* Washington, D.C.: U.S. Government Printing Office, 1976-.
Cumulative figures since the mid-1970s on contributions and spending in federal election campaigns; also information on political action committee (PAC) growth and activities.

Federal Election Commission. *Reports on Financial Activity.* Washington, D.C.: U.S. Government Printing Office, 1980-.
Multi-volume work reporting revenues and spending in congressional and presidential campaigns by candidates, party, and nonparty political committees (PACs); reports typically cover a two-year campaign cycle (for example, 1987-1988).

Glashan, Roy R. *American Governors and Gubernatorial Elections, 1775-1978.* Westport, Conn.: Meckler, 1979.
Details about state governors (such as birthdates, party affiliations, principal occupations, terms of office) and election data.

Heard, Alexander E. *The Costs of Democracy.* Chapel Hill, N.C.: University of North Carolina Press, 1960.
A classic work, published in 1960 when hard data on campaign contributions and spending were hard to secure.

Kallenbach, Joseph E., and Jessamine S. Kallenbach. *American State Governors, 1776-1976.* Dobbs Ferry, N.Y.: Oceana Publications, 1977-1982.
Election results and biographical data on governors.

Mullaney, Marie. *American Governors and Gubernatorial Elections, 1978-1987: A Statistical Compilation.* Westport, Conn.: Meckler, 1988.
Details about state governors (such as birth dates, party affiliations, principal occupations, terms of office) and election data.

Republican National Committee. *The (Year) Republican Almanac: State Political Profiles.* Washington, D.C.: Republican National Committee, 1973-. Biennial.
In its most recent edition, a voluminous statistical report of political, especially election, data about each state of the nation.

Runyon, John H., Jennefer Verdini, and Sally S. Runyan, eds. *Source Book of American Presidential Campaign and Election Statistics, 1948-1968.* New York: Frederick Ungar, 1971.
Information on presidential campaign staffs, candidate itineraries, media exposure, campaign costs, and public opinion polls.

Scammon, Richard M., and Alice V. McGillivray, eds. *America at the Polls: A Handbook of American Presidential Election Statistics, 1968-1984.* Washington, D.C.: Congressional Quarterly, Elections Research Center, 1988.

Two volumes span 1920-1984, providing popular votes (state and county) for president as well as state presidential primary results.

Scammon, Richard M., and Alice V. McGillivray, eds. *America Votes: A Handbook of Contemporary American Election Statistics.* Washington, D.C.: Congressional Quarterly, Elections Research Center, 1956-. Biennial.

Convenient compilation of vote totals and statistics by state for general elections and primaries for president, governor, senator, principally since 1945 (comparable district-level data for members of Congress); county-level totals and statistics for most recent general election for president, governor, and senator; state maps with county and congressional districts boundaries.

U.S. Bureau of the Census. Current Population Reports. Population Characteristics, series P-20. *Voting and Registration in the Election of November (Year).* Washington, D.C.: U.S. Government Printing Office, 1964-. Biennial.

Survey results on voter registration and turnout in presidential and midterm general elections for the nation and regions (and sometimes states and metropolitan areas) for various groups.

U.S. Congress. Secretary of the U.S. Senate. *Nomination and Election of the President and Vice President of the United States Including the Manner of Selecting Delegates to National Political Conventions.* Washington, D.C.: U.S. Government Printing Office, 1984.

Account of variations among the states in laws and rules concerning presidential elections and convention delegate selection procedures.

Political Parties

Bain, Richard C., and Judith H. Parris. *Convention Decisions and Voting Records.* 2d ed. Washington, D.C.: Brookings, 1973.

Data on convention actions through 1972.

Congressional Quarterly. *National Party Conventions, 1831-1984.* 4th ed. Washington, D.C.: Congressional Quarterly, 1987.

Summarizes each convention, giving results of ballots, nominees, and profiles of the parties.

Cotter, Cornelius P., James L. Gibson, John F. Bibby, and Robert J. Huckshorn. *Party Organizations in American Politics.* New York: Praeger, 1984.

Contains information on the characteristics of state parties and assessments of their organizational strength as of the late 1970s. Also rates states on support for and regulation of political parties.

David, Paul T. *Party Strength in the United States 1872-1970.* Charlottesville, Va.: University Press of America, 1972. Updated for 1972 in

Journal of Politics 36 (1972): 785-796; for 1974 in *Journal of Politics* 38 (1974): 416-425; for 1976 in *Journal of Politics* 40 (1976): 770-780.
Measures of party competition in the states covering several offices and an admirably lengthy historical span.

Miller, Warren E., and M. Kent Jennings. *Parties in Transition.* New York: Russell Sage, 1986.
Descriptions and analyses of delegates to the 1972-1980 Republican and Democratic national conventions.

Schapsmeier, Edward L., and Frederick H. Schapsmeier. *Political Parties and Civic Action Groups.* Westport, Conn.: Greenwood Press, 1981.
Brief descriptions of political organizations, current and past. Includes political parties, civics organizations, and all types of special interest groups.

Public Opinion

Astin, Alexander W. *The American Freshman Twenty Year Trends, 1966-1985.* Los Angeles: Higher Education Research Institute, University of California, Los Angeles, 1987; *National Norms for Fall, 1986-.* Annual.
Reports of national surveys of college freshmen, including attitudes toward jobs, subject interests, liberalism/conservatism.

Converse, Philip E., Jean D. Dotson, Wendy J. Hoag, and William H. McGee III. *American Social Attitudes Data Sourcebook 1947-1978.* Cambridge, Mass.: Harvard University Press, 1980.
Compendium of national polling data from the Survey Research Center at the University of Michigan, ranging across major social issues.

The Gallup Poll: Public Opinion 1935-71, 3 vols. New York: Random House, 1972. Wilmington, Del.: Scholarly Resources, Inc., 1972-. Annual. Years 1972-1977 contained in 2 vols.
Poll data from thousands of Gallup surveys since 1935 on then-current topics, presented chronologically.

The Gallup Report: Political, Social and Economic Trends. Princeton, N.J.: American Institute of Public Opinion, 1965-. Monthly. Previously titled Gallup Opinion Index and The Gallup Political Report.
Monthly compilation of recent Gallup public opinion data on political and social issues, often presented with historical trends.

Miller, Warren E., Arthur H. Miller, and Edward J. Schneider. *American National Election Studies Data Sourcebook, 1952-1978.* Cambridge, Mass.: Harvard University Press, 1980.
Compendium of national polling data from the National Election Studies covering presidential and congressional election years.

Niemi, Richard G., John E. Mueller, and Tom W. Smith. *Trends in Public Opinion.* Westport, Conn.: Greenwood Press, 1989.
> Public opinion polls on numerous political and other topics; based primarily on the General Social Survey. Provides time series, often quite long, of identically-worded questions.

Opinion Research Service. *American Public Opinion Index.* Louisville, Ky.: Opinion Research Service, 1981-. Annual.
> Indexes scientifically drawn samples of national, state, and local universes.

Public Opinion. Washington, D.C.: American Enterprise Institute for Public Policy Research, 1978-. Bimonthly.
> Analysis of public opinion about current issues and trends; regular "Opinion Roundup" section presents poll data from several sources on selected topics.

Public Opinion Quarterly. Chicago: University of Chicago Press, 1937-. Quarterly.
> Analysis of the mechanics and findings of survey research; regular thematic presentation of poll results.

Interest Groups

Cigler, Allan J., and Burdett A. Loomis. *Interest Group Politics.* 2d ed. Washington, D.C.: CQ Press, 1986.
> Examines interest groups in the policy-making process—a rapidly changing field.

Close, Arthur C., and John P. Gregg. *Washington Representatives.* Washington, D.C.: Columbia Books, 1977-. Annual.
> Lists Washington representatives of major corporations, unions, and national associations as well as registered foreign agents and the organizations represented by an individual or an office in Washington.

Congressional Quarterly. *The Washington Lobby.* 5th ed. Washington, D.C.: Congressional Quarterly, 1987.
> Lobbying developments in strategies and techniques, highlighting political action committees (PACs); explores federal laws, regulations, and court cases that govern lobbyists as well as interest group ratings of members of Congress.

Koek, Karin E., Susan B. Martin, and Annette Novallo, eds. *Encyclopedia of Associations.* Detroit, Mich.: Gale Research, Inc., 1960-. Annual.
> Guide to over 23,000 organizations, both national and international, spanning various sectors of society.

Interstate Bureau of Regulations. *State Political Action Legislation and Regulations: Index and Directory of Organizations.* Westport, Conn.: Quorum Books, 1984.
> Information on regulation of political action committees in the states.

Malbin, Michael J. *Parties, Interest Groups, and Campaign Finance Laws.* Washington, D.C.: American Enterprise Institute for Public Policy Research, 1980.
  Early (1980) collection pulling together analyses in an increasingly investigated area.

Troy, Leo, and Neil Sheflin. *U.S. Union Sourcebook.* West Orange, N.J.: Industrial Relations Data and Information Services, 1985.
  Excellent source of statistical information on membership in American and Canadian unions; long historical coverage.

Weinberger, Marvin I., and David U. Greevy. *The PAC Directory: A Complete Guide to Political Action Committees.* Cambridge, Mass.: Ballinger, 1982.
  Useful, though now dated, assemblage of information on political action committees in the political process.

Congress

Barone, Michael, and Grant Ujifusa. *The Almanac of American Politics.* Washington, D.C.: National Journal, 1972-. Biennial.
  Data-rich political analyses of each state, congressional district, representative, senator, and governor; current composition of committees; state maps with congressional district and county boundaries.

Congressional Quarterly. *American Leaders 1789-1987.* Washington, D.C.: Congressional Quarterly, 1987.
  Material on more than 11,000 members of Congress: age, religion, occupations, women, blacks, turnover, and shifts between chambers; data on congressional sessions, party composition, and leadership. Also includes biographical summaries of presidents, vice presidents, Supreme Court justices, and governors.

Congressional Quarterly. *Congress and the Nation.* Washington, D.C.: Congressional Quarterly, 1965-. Quadrennial. Years 1945-1964 contained in 1 vol.
  Akin to *Congressional Quarterly Almanac* (see below), but each volume now covers a presidential term.

Congressional Quarterly. *Congressional Districts in the 1980s.* Washington, D.C.: Congressional Quarterly, 1983.
  Profiles of each congressional district containing statistics on election returns, economic makeup, and demographics.

Congressional Quarterly. *Congressional Quarterly Almanac.* Washington, D.C.: Congressional Quarterly, 1945-. Annual.
  Each volume now covers legislation for a single session of Congress, appendices contain particularly useful data on Congress and politics.

Congressional Quarterly. *Congressional Roll Call.* Washington, D.C.: Congressional Quarterly, 1974-. Annual.
Annual compilation of every roll-call vote by every member of Congress and summary voting measures (ideology, party unity, presidential support, and voting participation).

Congressional Quarterly. *Guide to Congress.* 3d ed. Washington, D.C.: Congressional Quarterly, 1982.
Massive, rich accounting of how Congress works and how it developed. Check here first for data covering all but the most recent years.

Congressional Quarterly. *Politics in America.* Washington, D.C.: Congressional Quarterly, 1981-. Biennial.
Data-rich political analyses of each state, congressional district, representative, and senator; current composition of committees; state maps with congressional district and county boundaries.

(Year) Congressional Staff Directory. Mt. Vernon, Va.: Congressional Staff Directory, Ltd., 1959-. Biannual.
Names, addresses, phone numbers, and numerous biographies of senators' and representatives' personal staffs and the staffs of congressional committees and subcommittees.

Ornstein, Norman J., Thomas E. Mann, and Michael J. Malbin, eds. *Vital Statistics on Congress.* Washington, D.C.: Congressional Quarterly, 1980-. Biennial.
Data on characteristics of members, elections, campaign finance, committees, staff, expenses, workload, budgeting, and voting alignments; most data series stretch back to World War II, some longer.

Parsons, Stanley B., William W. Beach, Dan Hermann, and Michael J. Dubin. *United States Congressional Districts and Data,* 2 vols. Westport, Conn.: Greenwood Press, 1978, 1986.
Demographic and geographic data about American congressional districts. Currently two volumes available, covering 1789-1883.

U.S. Bureau of the Census. *Congressional District Atlas.* Washington, D.C.: U.S. Government Printing Office, 1960-. Frequency varies.
Detailed maps of congressional districts.

U.S. Bureau of the Census. *Congressional District Data Book.* Washington, D.C.: U.S. Government Printing Office, 1961-. Frequency varies.
Census data by congressional district with maps.

U.S. Congress. Joint Committee on Printing. *Official Congressional Directory.* Washington, D.C.: U.S. Government Printing Office, 1865-. Biennial (in recent years).
Biographical data on current members, statistics on the sessions of Congress, useful reference source on committees and subcommittees, foreign representatives and consular offices in the United States, press representatives, and state delegations.

U.S. Congress. Senate. *Biographical Directory of the American Congress, 1774-1989.* Washington, D.C.: U.S. Government Printing Office, 1989. 100th Cong., 2d sess., S.Doc. 100-34.
Biographies of U.S. senators and representatives to January 3, 1989.

The Presidency and the Executive Branch

Congressional Quarterly. *Federal Regulatory Directory.* Washington, D.C.: Congressional Quarterly, 1979-. Frequency varies.
Descriptions and data provide extensive profiles of the major and minor regulatory agencies—over 100 in all.

Congressional Quarterly. *Guide to the Presidency.* Washington, D.C.: Congressional Quarterly, 1989.
Detailed coverage of numerous aspects of presidents and administrations. Focus on the institution complements CQ's volumes on elections.

Congressional Quarterly. *Presidential Elections Since 1789.* 4th ed. Washington, D.C.: Congressional Quarterly, 1987.
Facts and figures on presidential elections; electoral college vote since 1789; primary returns since 1912; major-party candidate vote shares state-by-state; minor candidate vote totals; recent turnout and party support trends.

Congressional Quarterly. *Washington Information Directory.* Washington, D.C.: Congressional Quarterly, 1975-. Annual.
Names, addresses, phone numbers, and heads of thousands of federal government and private, nonprofit agencies in and about Washington, D.C.

DeGregorio, William A. *The Complete Book of U.S. Presidents.* New York: Dembner, 1984.
Biographies of presidents and cabinet members.

(Year) Federal Staff Directory. Mt. Vernon, Va.: Congressional Staff Directory, Ltd., 1982-. Biannual.
Names, addresses, phone numbers, and numerous biographies of key executives and assistants in the executive branch of the federal government.

Kane, Joseph Nathan. *Facts about the Presidents: A Compilation of Biographical and Historical Information.* 5th ed. New York: H. H. Wilson, 1985.
Chapter on each president and comparative statistics on all presidents.

King, Gary, and Lyn Ragsdale. *The Elusive Executive: Discovering Statistical Patterns in the Presidency.* Washington, D.C.: CQ Press, 1988.
A statistical evaluation of the presidency in its various aspects, focusing on postwar presidencies with some longer time series.

U.S. Government Organization Manual. Washington, D.C.: U.S. Government Printing Office, 1935-. Annual.
Official federal government handbook detailing the organization, activities, and current officials in legislative, judicial, and executive governmental units.

Weekly Compilation of Presidential Documents. Washington, D.C.: U.S. Government Printing Office.
Highly useful collection of presidential activities; includes texts of proclamations, executive orders, speeches, and other presidential communications; supplements include acts gaining presidential approval, nominations submitted for Senate confirmation, and a list of White House press releases; indexed.

The Judiciary

The American Bench. Sacramento, Calif.: Reginald Bishop Forster & Associates, 1977-. Biennial.
Comprehensive listing of all judges in the United States, along with brief biographies of approximately 18,000 judges.

Congressional Quarterly. *Guide to the U.S. Supreme Court.* 2d ed. Washington, D.C.: Congressional Quarterly, 1989.
Solid, broad coverage of the Supreme Court and the development of the law; an excellent source that also refers readers to additional references.

The Corrections Yearbook. South Salem, N.Y.: Criminal Justice Institute, 1980-. Annual.
Inmate populations, budgets, facilities, staff, and other data for jails with average daily populations of 200 or more.

Curran, Barbara A., et al. *The Lawyer Statistical Report: A Statistical Profile of the U.S. Legal Profession in the 1980s.* Chicago: American Bar Foundation, 1985. *U.S. Legal Profession in 1985* (Supplement to Statistical Report), 1987.
A statistical profile of a changing profession, by age, gender, and place of employment; also profiles 1980 lawyer populations within states, metropolitan, and nonmetropolitan areas.

Director of the Administrative Office of the United States Courts. *Annual Report.* Washington, D.C.: U.S. Government Printing Office, 1940-. Annual.
Numerous statistics about the kind, timing, and disposition of cases in the federal courts and about numbers and workloads of federal judges.

Dornette, W. Stuart, and Robert R. Cross. *Federal Judiciary Almanac.* New York: Wiley, 1986.
Data on various aspects of the federal judiciary.

Friedman, Leon, and Fred L. Israel, eds. *The Justices of the United States Supreme Court*, 5 vols. New York: Chelsea House, 1978.
    Biography on each justice including several typical opinions; tables showing acts of Congress held unconstitutional, decisions overruled by subsequent decisions, and summary biographical data.

Judges of the United States. Washington, D.C.: U.S. Government Printing Office, 1978.
    Biographies of all federal judges through 1978.

(Year) Judicial Staff Directory. Mt. Vernon, Va.: Congressional Staff Directory, Ltd., 1986-. Annual.
    Personnel listings for federal courts, maps of court jurisdictions, biographies of judges and staffs.

State Court Caseload Statistics: Annual Report 1987. Williamsburg, Va.: Conference of State Court Administrators and the National Center for State Courts, 1989. Annual.
    Data on judicial workload in the state courts.

Widman, Iris J., and Mark J. Handler, comps. *Federal Judges and Justices: A Current Listing of Nominations, Confirmations, Elevations, Resignations, Retirements.* Littleton, Colo.: Rothman, 1987.
    Useful compendium with revealing subtitle.

Federalism

Alexander, Herbert E., and Mike Eberts. *Public Financing of State Elections: A Data Book and Election Guide to Public Funding of Political Parties and Candidates in Twenty States.* Los Angeles: Citizens' Research Foundation, 1986.
    Important compendium for understanding and comparing state regulation of campaign finances.

Beyle, Thad, ed. *State Government.* Washington, D.C.: Congressional Quarterly, 1985-. Annual.
    Analysis of recent developments in state governments; reprints articles from a diverse set of state publications.

The Book of the States. Lexington, Ky.: Council of State Governments, 1935-. Biennial.
    Definitive reference to the current data on state government activities across the board.

Campaign Finance, Ethics and Lobby Law Blue Book. Lexington, Ky.: Council on Governmental Ethics Laws, Council of State Governments, 1988.
    Information about ethics laws, campaign finance reports and limits,

personal disclosure requirements, and lobby laws in the states and in the Canadian provinces.

Campaign Finance Law 88. Washington, D.C.: D. T. Skelton Service Associates, Inc., Federal Election Commission's National Clearinghouse of Election Administration, 1988.
Rules and regulations for campaign financing in the states and nation.

The County Year Book. Washington, D.C.: National Association of Counties and International City Management Association, 1975-. Annual.
Surveys issues and trends in county government and administration; a reliable source of data on county government.

Holli, Melvin G., and Peter Jones, eds. *Biographical Dictionary of American Mayors, 1820-1980*. Westport, Conn.: Greenwood Press, 1981.
Covers 679 mayors in over a dozen cities; contains lists categorizing mayors by characteristics such as party, religion, and ethnicity.

Hornor, Edith R., ed. *Almanac of the 50 States: Basic Data Profiles with Comparative Tables, 1988 Edition*. Palo Alto, Calif.: Information Publications, 1988.
State-level summaries of data on government and elections, state expenditures, federal aid, population characteristics, crime, and so forth.

International City Management Association. *The Municipal Year Book*. New York: International City Management Association, 1934-. Annual.
Reliable source for urban data and developments.

Marlin, John Tepper, and James S. Avery. *The Book of American City Rankings*. New York: Facts on File, 1983.
Nearly 300 thematic tables with data on the 100 largest U.S. cities.

National Directory of State Agencies. Bethesda, Md.: National Standards Association, 1976-. Annual since 1986.
Names of agency heads, addresses, and phone numbers of state agencies.

The New Book of American Rankings. New York: Facts on File, 1984.
State rankings and statistics on over 300 items. Some of the material is now dated.

Significant Features of Fiscal Federalism. Washington, D.C.: U.S. Advisory Commission on Intergovernmental Relations, 1976-. Annual.
Convenient compilation of comparative state data on revenues, expenditures, and related matters; tables and figures present comparisons across states as well as state-by-state in-depth treatment.

State Administrative Officials Classified by Functions. Lexington, Ky.: Council of State Governments, 1977-. Biennial.
Lists state administrative officials by function; before 1977 issued as a supplement to *The Book of the States*.

State Elective Officials and the Legislatures. Lexington, Ky.: Council of State Governments, 1977-. Biennial.
Lists state elected officials and legislators; before 1977 issued as a supplement to *The Book of the States.*

State Information Book. Rockville, Md.: Infax, 1973-. Biennial.
Some statistics, but emphasizes names, addresses, phone numbers, and heads of departments and agencies, plus county seats and phone numbers.

State Legislative Sourcebook. Topeka, Kan.: Government Research Service, 1986-. Annual.
Tells how to find detailed information about state legislative activity, including offices, addresses, phone numbers, and price lists.

State Policy Data Book. McConnellsburg, Pa.: Brizius & Foster, 1984-. Annual.
State-by-state rankings, with relevant percentages, averages, or other entries, on hundreds of items, including demographics, economics, health, education, etc.

State statistical abstracts.
A list of state statistical abstracts (or near equivalents) can be found in the *Statistical Abstract of the U.S., 1989,* 883-887. They are of widely varying quality.

Tax Foundation. *Facts and Figures on Government Finance.* Englewood Cliffs, N.J.: Prentice Hall, 1941-. Annual.
Data on government revenues, spending and debt at the federal, state, and local levels.

The Transformation in American Politics: Implications for Federalism. Washington, D.C.: U.S. Advisory Commission on Intergovernmental Relations, 1986.
Wide-ranging treatment (much broader than the subtitle implies) of major recent trends in American politics with emphasis on relevant data.

U.S. Bureau of the Census. *Census of Governments.* Washington, D.C.: U.S. Government Printing Office, 1972-. Frequency varies.
Numbers and characteristics of governments, including special district governments dealing with subjects such as schools, parks and recreation, and sewage.

U.S. Bureau of the Census. *City Government Finances; Government Finances; State Government Finances.* Washington, D.C.: U.S. Government Printing Office, 1909-; 1965-; 1916-. Annual.
These three series summarize government finances at city and state levels; great detail for states and the larger cities.

U.S. Bureau of the Census. *County and City Data Book.* Washington, D.C.: U.S. Government Printing Office, 1952-. Frequency varies.
Demographic, economic, health, agricultural, and other information about counties, cities, and towns. Presidential voting by county.

U.S. Bureau of the Census. *State and Metropolitan Area Data Book.* Washington, D.C.: U.S. Government Printing Office, 1979-. Frequency varies.
Demographic, economic, health, education, and other data about states and metropolitan statistical areas.

Foreign and Military Policy

Cochran, Thomas B., William A. Arkin, and Milton M. Hoenig. *Nuclear Weapons Databook.* Cambridge, Mass.: Ballinger, 1987.
Descriptions, specifications, and deployments of American and Soviet nuclear weapons systems.

Joint Chiefs of Staff. *Military Posture for Fiscal Year (Year).* Washington, D.C.: U.S. Government Printing Office. Annual.
Brief review of all aspects of military preparedness of the U.S. and of the world military environment.

The Military Balance. London: International Institute of Strategic Studies, 1959-. Annual.
Statistical analysis of military forces and defense spending; figures given for countries and regional organizations such as NATO (North Atlantic Treaty Organization).

U.S. Arms Control and Disarmament Agency. *World Military Expenditures and Arms Transfers.* Washington, D.C.: U.S. Government Printing Office, 1965-. Annual (title varies).
Annual statistical accounts of military spending and the arms race.

World Armaments and Disarmament: SIPRI Yearbook. Stockholm: Almqvist & Wiksell, New York: Oxford University Press, 1970-. Annual.
Overview of the arms race and efforts to promote disarmament; detailed data on world military spending.

Social Policy

Black Elected Officials: A National Roster. Washington, D.C.: Joint Center for Political Studies, 1971-. Annual.
Lists black elected officials by office and address with summary tabulations on the historical trends and comparative state figures.

Bogue, Donald J. *The Population of the United States: Historical Trends and Future Projections.* New York: Free Press, 1985.
Extensive description of nation's population characteristics, focusing on the years since 1960; topics include poverty, income, housing, educational attainment, ethnicity, migration, and so forth.

Center for the American Woman and Politics, National Information Bank on Women in Public Office, Eagleton Institute of Politics, Rutgers University.

Various reports provide data on women in public office, electoral turnout of women, and so forth. Both historical and contemporary information.

National Center for Health Statistics. *Monthly Vital Statistics Report.* Hyattsville, Md.: U.S. Department of Health and Human Services. 1952-.
Statistical reports and analyses of various aspects of health.

National Roster of Hispanic Elected Officials, (Year). Washington, D.C.: National Association of Latino Elected and Appointed Officials Education Fund, no date. Annual.
Lists Hispanic elected officials by office and state.

The State of Black America. New York: National Urban League, 1976-. Annual.
Yearly review assessing the conditions of blacks in the nation.

U.S. Department of Education. Center for Statistics. *Digest of Education Statistics.* Washington, D.C.: U.S. Government Printing Office, 1962-. Annual.
Current data on school enrollments, teachers, retention rates, educational attainment, finances, achievement, schools and school districts, federal education programs, and so forth.

U.S. Department of Education. Office of Educational Research and Improvement. *The Condition of Education: A Statistical Report.* Washington, D.C.: U.S. Government Printing Office, 1975-.
Data survey reviewing trends in elementary, secondary, and higher education; data portray student characteristics and performance as well as fiscal, material, and human resources deployed in education.

U.S. Department of Energy. Energy Information Administration. *Annual Energy Review.* Washington, D.C.: U.S. Government Printing Office, 1977-.
Data on energy supply and disposition, exploration, and reserves.

U.S. Department of Justice. Bureau of Criminal Justice Statistics. *Sourcebook of Criminal Justice Statistics.* Washington, D.C.: U.S. Government Printing Office, 1974-. Annual.
Brings together nationwide statistical data on the criminal justice system, public opinion, illegal activities, persons arrested, judicial proceedings, and persons under correctional supervision.

U.S. Department of Justice. Federal Bureau of Investigation. *Uniform Crime Reports for the United States.* Washington, D.C.: U.S. Government Printing Office, 1930-. Annual.
Variety of charts and tables on types and frequencies of crimes, persons arrested, and law enforcement personnel; several forty-year trends.

Economic Policy

(Year) Historical Chart Book, Washington, D.C.: Board of Governors of the Federal Reserve System, 1965. Annual.
Long-range financial and business data, mostly from series maintained by the Federal Reserve Board.

Hoel, Arline Alchian, Kenneth W. Clarkson, and Roger LeRoy Miller. *Economics Sourcebook of Government Statistics.* Lexington, Mass.: Lexington Books, 1983.
Ranges across inflation, general business conditions, interest rates, employment and earnings, international finance and trade, and the budget; critical discussions of over fifty major statistical series produced by the federal government in these areas; also refers to primary and secondary sources containing the series.

Office of Management and Budget. *Budget of the United States Government.* Washington, D.C.: U.S. Government Printing Office. Annual.
Multi-volume annual presentation of data on federal revenues and expenditures; while the details of the federal budget documents may be numbing to the uninitiated, even the novice can find two volumes particularly useful: *Historical Tables* and *The Budget in Brief,* both of which are designed for the general public.

O'Hara, Frederick M., and Robert Sicignano. *Handbook of United States Economic and Financial Indicators.* Westport, Conn.: Greenwood Press, 1985.
Defines a couple of hundred economic indicators culled from over fifty sources; provides information on publication schedules and historical trends.

U.S. Bureau of Labor Statistics. *Employment and Earnings.* Washington, D.C.: U.S. Government Printing Office, 1961-. Annual
Various statistics on the nation's nonfarm work force, including lengthy time series with data beginning in 1909.

U.S. Bureau of Labor Statistics. *Handbook of Labor Statistics.* Washington, D.C.: U.S. Government Printing Office, 1927-. Frequency varies.
Collection of data concerning employment, unemployment, earnings, school enrollment and educational attainment, productivity, prices, strikes, and so forth.

U.S. Bureau of Labor Statistics. *Monthly Labor Review.* Washington, D.C.: U.S. Government Printing Office, 1915-.
Covers most Bureau of Labor Statistics series, giving data concerning employment, hours, pay, strikes, prices and inflation, and so forth.

U.S. Council of Economic Advisers. *Economic Indicators.* Washington, D.C.: U.S. Government Printing Office, 1948-. Monthly.
Data on total output, income, and spending; employment, unemployment,

and wages; production and business activity; prices, currency, credit, and security markets; and federal finance.

U.S. Department of Agriculture. *Agricultural Statistics.* Washington, D.C.: U.S. Government Printing Office, 1937-. Annual.
   Vast array of agricultural data, including politically relevant displays, such as farm economic trends, price-support programs, and agricultural imports and exports.

U.S. Department of Commerce. *Survey of Current Business.* Washington, D.C.: U.S. Government Printing Office, 1921-. Monthly.
   Monthly publication with data on U.S. income and trade developments.

U.S. President. *The Economic Report of the President.* Washington, D.C.: U.S. Government Printing Office, 1947-. Annual.
   Reviews the national economic situation; presents a substantial appendix with long time series of critical economic data.

World Bank. *World Development Report.* New York: Oxford University Press, 1978-. Annual.
   Analysis of and data on worldwide capital and economic indicators, with an emphasis on development.

Miscellaneous

Some politically relevant information is found in general purpose almanacs. Such information is usually very limited, but these sources have the advantage of being very readily available.

Information Please Almanac: Atlas and Yearbook. Boston: Houghton Mifflin, 1947-. Annual.

Reader's Digest Almanac. Pleasantville, N.Y.: Reader's Digest, 1966-. Annual.

The World Almanac and Book of Facts. New York: Pharos Books, 1868-. Annual since 1886.

Index

Vice presidents, 234-236
Video cassette recorders
  percentage of households with, 48
Vietnam War
  forces and casualties, 326
  most important problem, 152
  public opinion, 327
  see also Military conflicts
Voter registration
  by population characteristic, 80-81
  provisions by state, 35-37

Voter turnout, 78-81
Voting Rights Act, 41

War
  casualties, cost, draftees, personnel,
    325
  party better able to avoid war, 153
Welfare
  see Social welfare; Social welfare
    spending